Better Homes and Gardens®

Slow Cooker

Recipes for 2, 4 or More

Better Homes and Gardens®
Slow Cooker Recipes for 2, 4 or More
Editor: Tricia Laning
Contributing Project Editor: Spectrum Communication
   Services, Inc.
Contributing Writer: Cynthia Pearson
Graphic Designer: Chad Jewell
Copy Chief: Doug Kouma
Copy Editor: Kevin Cox
Publishing Operations Manager: Karen Schirm
Edit and Design Production Coordinator:
   Mary Lee Gavin
Editorial Assistant: Sheri Cord
Book Production Managers: Marjorie J. Schenkelberg,
   Mark Weaver
Contributing Copy Editor: Joyce Gemperlein
Contributing Proofreaders: Karen Grossman,
   Abbie Hansen, Donna Segal
Contributing Indexer: Elizabeth T. Parsons
Test Kitchen Director: Lynn Blanchard
Test Kitchen Culinary Specialists: Marilyn Cornelius,
   Juliana Hale, Maryellyn Krantz, Jill Moberly,
   Colleen Weeden, Lori Wilson
Test Kitchen Nutrition Specialists: Elizabeth Burt,
   R.D., L.D.; Laura Marzen, R.D., L.D.

Meredith® Books
Editorial Director: John Riha
Managing Editor: Kathleen Armentrout
Deputy Editor: Jennifer Darling
Brand Manager: Janell Pittman
Group Editor: Jan Miller
Senior Associate Design Director: Mick Schnepf

Director, Marketing and Publicity: Amy Nichols
Executive Director, Sales: Ken Zagor
Director, Operations: George A. Susral
Director, Production: Douglas M. Johnston
Business Director: Janice Croat

Vice President and General Manager, SIM: Jeff Myers

Better Homes and Gardens® Magazine
Editor in Chief: Gayle Goodson Butler
Deputy Editor, Food and Entertaining:
   Nancy Hopkins

Meredith Publishing Group
President: Jack Griffin
Executive Vice President: Doug Olson

Meredith Corporation
Chairman of the Board: William T. Kerr
President and Chief Executive Officer:
   Stephen M. Lacy

In Memoriam: E. T. Meredith III (1933–2003)

Copyright © 2008 by Meredith Corporation,
Des Moines, Iowa.
First Edition.
All rights reserved.
Printed in China.
Library of Congress Control Number:
      978-0-696-23928-1
ISBN: 2008922146

All of us at Meredith® Books are dedicated
to providing you with the information and
ideas you need to create delicious foods. We
welcome your comments and suggestions.
Write to us at: Meredith Books, Cookbook
Editorial Department, 1716 Locust St.,
Des Moines, IA 50309-3023.

Our seal assures you that every recipe in
Slow Cooker Recipes for 2, 4 or More has
been tested in the Better Homes and Gardens®
Test Kitchen. This means that each recipe
is practical and reliable and meets our high
standards of taste appeal. We guarantee your
satisfaction with this book for as long
as you own it.

Table of Contents

Slow Cooking: The Basics

You're on the go—no time to cook—but you know the pleasures of scrumptious, nutritious food. And a good meal is so restorative and such a pleasure. Your tastes are eclectic too. When full-flavored dishes and globally inspired fare are served in cafes and your favorite restaurants, you crave them at home too. But how do you get them?

First, you need a slow cooker. The only other items you may need are a cutting board and knife and measuring cups for prep work. Following a recipe that suits your fancy, put a few choice ingredients in the cooker and set the lid on top. Let the slow cooker go to work, using its low, moist heat to coax a symphony of flavors from the food while you work, play, or pursue your passion.

Second, you need *Slow Cooker Recipes for 2, 4 or More* as your guide.

If you've ever felt limited by slow-cookbooks' predominance of large-yield recipes or stew-type, same-brown-hue concoctions, take heart. If you're new to slow cooking, you're meeting the slow-cook method at its best.

Slow cooking has grown up, traveled the world, and come home more sophisticated, producing a broader variety of fresh flavors, cuisines, shapes, and textures to ever emerge from a slow cooker. Within these pages you'll find more than 350 recipes, featuring the best of American regional fare along with globally inspired dishes representing Asian, African, Greek, Italian, and Mediterranean cuisine. Plating your slow-cooked meal is a feast for your eyes too: Meats and poultry, for example, are whole, bone-in, cubed, shredded, layered, or wrapped. The recipes don't begin and end with main-dish fare, either. With this book's help, you can put your slow cooker to work on appetizers and snacks, side dishes, and delicious desserts—Sweet Spiced Nuts, Chai, Maple-Ginger Sweet Potatoes, and Orange Pudding Caramel Cake to name a few.

And if you're cooking for two tonight, 10 tomorrow, you won't be left on your own to muddle through down or upsizing a recipe yield. *Slow Cooker Recipes for 2, 4 or More*

offers mouthwatering dishes perfectly sized to the situation.

Here's what you'll find inside:

Favorites for 2 or 3
Making dinners for two or three has never been simpler or more enticing. You'll find more than 50 recipes designed primarily for 1½- or 2-quart cookers. But more importantly, they deliver stew, poultry, meat-based, and meatless dishes that reflect contemporary tastes. How about Sweet and Smoky Chicken, Herbed-Port Pot Roast, Saucy Lamb and Vegetables, Chipotle Country-Style Ribs, or Thai-Style Vegetable Rice? Of course, you'll find small-size versions of beloved favorites too, including soups, chilies, and stews.

Fix-and-Forget Meals for 4 to 6
Who's around the table tonight? You never know until it's time to eat, and you love it that way. Family, a friend or two, there's always room for someone else. There are more than 155 soups; dishes featuring chicken, turkey, beef, lamb, pork, or sausage; meatless choices; tempting sides; and homey desserts that make four to six servings. And if you have a smaller-than-expected table group, you have leftovers.

Big-Batch Recipes for a Crowd
Everyone's coming to your house . . . after the game or performance. But that's OK—slow-cooked recipes simmer while you're out and are ready to enjoy when you walk in the door with the gang. This section is your go-to for 75 offerings that include party starters and sippers, savory entrées for sit-down affairs, chilies and soups for a crowd, side dishes, sweets, and potluck fare.

Double-Duty Dinners
This awesome back-of-the-book section deserves up-front attention. Each recipe comes with a companion next-day recipe. Recipe one is today's slow-cooked meal . . . but before sitting down to devour it, set aside a portion as the base for

tomorrow's recipe. Honey Curry Chicken tonight becomes Asian Chicken Salad tomorrow. Fire-Roasted Tomato and Italian Sausage Grinders on Monday becomes Sausage-Stuffed Manicotti on Tuesday. Friday's Sage-Scented Pork Chops becomes Saturday's Pork and Potato Gratin with Gruyère Cheese. With more than 35 recipe combos—more than 70 recipes altogether—this twofer chapter is one you'll look forward to and rely upon.

30-Minute Prep & Go
Who's got time to dally? You won't spend more than a half hour prepping any recipe in *Slow Cooker Recipes for 2, 4 or More*.

5 Ingredient Recipe
Look for this icon next to delicious recipes built on five or fewer choice ingredients.

Winter, spring, summer, fall . . . active living isn't seasonal and neither is your cooker. Every season creates a new appetite. Make Kickin' Hot Chili in the fall, Cranberry Pork Roast in the winter, Chicken with Figs and Blue Cheese or Lemon Pesto New Potatoes for spring, and Cuban Pork Sandwiches for a summer deck picnic. Regardless of the season, *Slow Cooker Recipes for 2, 4 or More* makes simple work of producing what you want to eat.

Tips for Successful Slow Cooking

Get Fresh with Herbs
Though most slow-cooker recipes call for dried herbs for seasoning, fresh herbs offer many delights, from the simple sensory pleasure of handling them to enjoying their magic in a cooked dish. Here's how to use them in slow-cooker recipes successfully:
* Measure three times as much fresh herbs as dried. Example: If a recipe calls for 1 teaspoon dried basil, substitute 1 tablespoon snipped fresh basil.
* Stir most fresh herbs into the pot near the end of cooking. For example, if a soup calls for several hours of slow cooking, stir in the fresh-snipped herbs just before serving.

Go Low-Fat
Good news: Very little fat is needed to flavor slow-cooker dishes. So skip it, opting for lean meat cuts such as those listed below. Trim all visible fat from meats or poultry and remove the skin from poultry before adding it to the cooker. When cooking is complete, move the solid cooked food to a serving dish and let the liquid stand for a minute or two, then use a metal spoon to skim off fat.

Beef:
Brisket
Chuck short ribs
Roasts
   Chuck pot
   Rump
Crosscut shanks
Steaks
   Chuck
   Flank
   Round
   Sirloin
Stew meat

Chicken & Turkey:
Breasts
Drumsticks
Thighs

Pork:
Loin chops
Ribs
   Country-style
   Loin back
Roasts
   Shoulder
   Sirloin
Smoked pork hocks

Roots Go on the Bottom
Hours of slow, moist heat coaxes incredible flavor and sweetness from root veggies such as potatoes, carrots, parsnips, beets, and rutabagas, making them a perfect match for stew meats and roasts. Cook them evenly by keeping them submerged: These veggies generally go in the cooker first, followed by meat and liquid.

Lid Lifting = Cooking Time Adjustment
Savory aroma wafting through the kitchen has tempted many to lift the lid of a cooker for a closer scent. Resist! Lost low heat isn't quickly regained. If stirring or adding an ingredient requires lid lifting, get the cover back on ASAP. And if you lift the lid without the recipe telling you to do so, extend the cooking time by about 30 minutes.

Leftovers: Fridge or Freeze for Later
Meal's over? If you're one who loves leftovers right away, slip what remains into sealed containers and tuck them into the fridge to enjoy tomorrow or the next day. If you prefer leftovers later, spoon them into freezer-safe containers right away, label, and date. They'll keep in your freezer for up to six months. Thaw your frozen treasure overnight in the fridge (this can take up to 24 hours), empty the contents into a saucepan or microwave-safe dish, and heat thoroughly.

Your Cooker Is Your Kitchen Help

Think of your cooker as your kitchen staff, toiling over a hot element following your direction while you're at work or play.

If you're new to slow cooking, start by getting a cooker sized for your most common serving size. Or go for one of the newer three-in-one cookers featuring a single heating element designed to use its 2-, 4-, and 6-quart liner pots—you choose which to use in each instance.

As you get comfy with the concept, you'll likely want to increase your staff, so to speak, especially if you enjoy serving several dishes at once for a crowd. And with suggested retail prices for cookers ranging from $10 for the little ones to $80 for the most fully featured, capacious models, having a selection of cookers at the ready is both affordable and smart.

Most of today's cookers feature removable liners that are easy to wash and are dishwasher safe, with glass lids and two heat settings. Some of the larger versions have a third keep-it-warm setting. You'll find cookers in round and oval shapes, especially on midsize to larger models. Ovals do well with bone-in meat cuts and whole poultry.

Basic models perform well, but as an enthusiast you might enjoy the following bells-and-whistles features:

- Lid-securing mechanism and larger handle (for safe toting)
- Insulated carrying case
- Candle-function warming base (for tabletop serving, fondues)
- Sectioning (for cooking multiple dishes)
- Digital, programmable functioning
- Meat thermometer probe

The Right Size Matters
Slow cookers deliver the best results—tasty fare cooked to perfection within the recipe-specified time—when the pot's at least half full but no more than two-thirds full. The slow cooker that's most practical for you depends on the size of your family. Although you should use the size cooker indicated in each recipe, refer to the general guidelines in the chart below to help you select the right cooker.

Cooker Size & Function

You're Cooking for How Many?	Use This Size Cooker	In Order To
1	1½-quart	Cook two meals at once. (Freeze leftovers or reheat for tomorrow's meal.)
2	1½- or 2-quart	Fix dinner for two with no leftovers.
	3½-quart	Cook a 2- to 2½-pound roast. (Freeze leftovers or use during the next four days for main-dish salads or sandwiches.)
3 or 4	3½- to 4½-quart	Prepare comfort food favorites such as soups, stews, chilies, or meat-and-veggie dishes.
5 to 7	4½- or 5-quart	Make meals for family and friends with some luscious leftovers to enjoy.
8 or more	1½-quart	Warm party buffet dips, sauces, or fondue.
	3½-quart	Warm party appetizers.
	6- to 8-quart	Simmer party beverages or prepare party food or potluck fare for a crowd.

Favorites for 2 or 3

In the 1800s early Virginia settlers made this hearty stew with squirrel meat. This updated version features chicken and ham that simmers all day in a slow cooker.

Brunswick-Style Stew

❦

MAKES 2 SERVINGS

Prep: 15 minutes
Cook: Low 8 to 10 hours,
High 4 to 5 hours,
plus 45 minutes (high)

1	medium onion, cut into thin wedges
1	pound meaty chicken pieces (breast halves, thighs, and drumsticks), skinned
¾	cup diced cooked ham
½	teaspoon dry mustard
½	teaspoon dried thyme, crushed
⅛	teaspoon black pepper
¾	cup chicken broth
1	medium tomato, chopped (½ cup)
2	teaspoons Worcestershire sauce
⅛	teaspoon bottled hot pepper sauce
2	cloves garlic, minced
½	cup frozen baby lima beans
½	cup frozen whole kernel corn

1. Place onion in a 1½- or 2-quart slow cooker. Place chicken and ham on top of onion. Sprinkle with dry mustard, thyme, and black pepper. Add broth, tomato, Worcestershire sauce, hot pepper sauce, and garlic.

2. Cover and cook on low-heat setting for 8 to 10 hours or on high-heat setting for 4 to 5 hours. If no heat setting is available, cook for 7½ to 8 hours.

3. If desired, remove chicken from cooker. When cool enough to handle, remove chicken from bones; discard bones. Cut chicken into bite-size pieces.

4. If using low-heat setting, turn to high-heat setting (or if no heat setting is available, continue cooking). Return chicken pieces to cooker. Stir in frozen lima beans and frozen corn. Cover and cook for 45 minutes more.

Nutrition Facts per serving: 415 cal., 13 g total fat (4 g sat. fat), 122 mg chol., 1,187 mg sodium, 31 g carbo., 6 g fiber, 46 g pro.

This satisfying cassoulet features white beans with meaty chicken pieces and smoked Polish sausage slow cooked so all flavors meld. The saucy liquid made with tomato juice and herbs adds a hearty depth.

Chicken Cassoulet

MAKES 2 SERVINGS

Prep: 25 minutes
Stand: 1 hour
Cook: Low 9 to 10 hours,
High 4½ to 5 hours

½	cup dried navy beans
¼	cup chopped carrot
¼	cup chopped celery
¼	cup chopped onion
1¼	to 1½ pounds meaty chicken pieces (breast halves, thighs, and drumsticks), skinned
4	ounces cooked smoked Polish sausage, halved lengthwise and cut into 1-inch pieces
½	cup tomato juice
2	teaspoons Worcestershire sauce
½	teaspoon instant beef or chicken bouillon granules
¼	teaspoon dried basil, crushed
¼	teaspoon dried oregano, crushed
¼	teaspoon paprika

1. Rinse beans. In a medium saucepan combine beans and enough water to cover beans by 2 inches. Bring to boiling; reduce heat. Simmer, uncovered, for 10 minutes. Remove from heat. Cover and let stand for 1 hour. Drain and rinse beans. Set aside.

2. In a 2-quart slow cooker combine carrot, celery, and onion. Place chicken on top of vegetables. Add beans and sausage. In a small bowl combine tomato juice, Worcestershire sauce, bouillon granules, basil, oregano, and paprika. Pour over mixture in cooker.

3. Cover and cook on low-heat setting for 9 to 10 hours or on high-heat setting for 4½ to 5 hours. If no heat setting is available, cook for 8½ to 9 hours.

Nutrition Facts per serving: 608 cal., 24 g total fat (8 g sat. fat), 155 mg chol., 1,107 mg sodium, 42 g carbo., 9 g fiber, 55 g pro.

In this distinctive soup the enticing flavors let you sample the spectrum of Latino cooking. The color of fork-tender chicken contrasts nicely with the red sweet pepper pieces, cilantro, and corn, making it a multihued soup.

Mexican Chicken Soup

MAKES 2 SERVINGS

Prep: 25 minutes
Cook: Low 5 to 6 hours,
High 2½ to 3 hours

Nonstick cooking spray
6   ounces skinless, boneless chicken thighs), cut into 1-inch pieces
4   ounces skinless, boneless chicken breast halves, cut into 1-inch pieces
1¼ cups reduced-sodium chicken broth
1   medium red or green sweet pepper, coarsely chopped (¾ cup)
½   cup frozen whole kernel corn
¼   cup chopped onion
1   small fresh jalapeño chile pepper, seeded and finely chopped (see tip, right)
½   teaspoon ground cumin
⅛   teaspoon salt
⅛   teaspoon black pepper
1   clove garlic, minced
1   tablespoon snipped fresh cilantro
2   tablespoons shredded Monterey Jack cheese or Monterey Jack cheese with jalapeño peppers

1. Lightly coat a medium skillet with nonstick cooking spray; heat skillet over medium-high heat. Cook chicken in hot skillet until brown. Drain off fat. Transfer chicken to a 1½-quart slow cooker.

2. Stir in broth, sweet pepper, frozen corn, onion, chile pepper, cumin, salt, black pepper, and garlic.

3. Cover and cook on low-heat setting for 5 to 6 hours or on high-heat setting for 2½ to 3 hours. If no heat setting is available, cook for 4 to 5 hours.

4. Before serving, stir in cilantro. Sprinkle individual servings with cheese.

Nutrition Facts per serving: 271 cal., 7 g total fat (3 g sat. fat), 107 mg chol., 634 mg sodium, 16 g carbo., 3 g fiber, 36 g pro.

Test Kitchen Tip: Because chile peppers contain oils that can burn your skin and eyes, avoid direct contact with them as much as possible. When working with chile peppers, wear plastic or rubber gloves. If your bare hands do touch the peppers, wash your hands and nails well with soap and warm water.

Chicken, hominy, and tomatoes with green chile peppers star in this Southwestern-style favorite. (Photo on page 267.)

Crock Posole

MAKES 2 SERVINGS

Prep: 20 minutes
Cook: Low 5 to 6 hours,
High 2½ to 3 hours

1	15.5-ounce can golden hominy, drained
1	10-ounce can diced tomatoes and green chile peppers, undrained
¾	cup reduced-sodium chicken broth
1	small onion, finely chopped (⅓ cup)
½	teaspoon dried oregano, crushed
¼	teaspoon salt
¼	teaspoon ground cumin
	Dash bottled hot pepper sauce
1	clove garlic, minced
8	ounces skinless, boneless chicken thighs, cut into 1-inch pieces
	Dairy sour cream (optional)
	Snipped fresh cilantro (optional)

1. In a 1½- or 2-quart slow cooker combine drained hominy, undrained tomatoes and chile peppers, broth, onion, oregano, salt, cumin, hot pepper sauce, and garlic. Stir in chicken.

2. Cover and cook on low-heat setting for 5 to 6 hours or on high-heat setting for 2½ to 3 hours. If no heat setting is available, cook for 4½ to 5 hours.

3. If desired, serve with sour cream and snipped fresh cilantro.

Nutrition Facts per serving: 343 cal., 6 g total fat (1 g sat. fat), 94 mg chol., 1,452 mg sodium, 41 g carbo., 8 g fiber, 29 g pro.

Soups and stews don't always have to feed the masses. This heartwarming recipe was made for two. When the temperatures plunge, cozy up and enjoy a steaming bowl of chunky beef stew.

Beef Stew for Two

MAKES 2 SERVINGS

Prep: 20 minutes
Cook: Low 11 to 12 hours,
High 5½ to 6 hours

8	ounces boneless beef chuck roast
1	cup tomato juice
½	cup chopped red or yellow potato
1	medium carrot, chopped (½ cup)
1	stalk celery, chopped (½ cup)
½	cup frozen cut green beans
½	cup chicken broth
2	teaspoons quick-cooking tapioca
½	teaspoon dried thyme, crushed
⅛	teaspoon salt
⅛	teaspoon black pepper
1	clove garlic, minced

1. Trim fat from meat. Cut meat into 1-inch pieces. Transfer meat to a 1½-quart slow cooker. Stir in tomato juice, potato, carrot, celery, frozen green beans, broth, tapioca, thyme, salt, pepper, and garlic.

2. Cover and cook on low-heat setting for 11 to 12 hours or on high-heat setting for 5½ to 6 hours. If no heat setting is available, cook for 9 to 10 hours.

Nutrition Facts per serving: 235 cal., 4 g total fat (1 g sat. fat), 68 mg chol., 836 mg sodium, 21 g carbo., 3 g fiber, 27 g pro.

Ground beef or lamb are wonderful with the vegetables in this recipe. Pick the one that suits your taste. Fresh mint and feta cheese infuse Mediterranean flavors.

Mediterranean Soup

MAKES 2 SERVINGS

Prep: 20 minutes
Cook: Low 4 to 5 hours,
High 2 to 2½ hours

6	ounces lean ground beef or ground lamb
¼	cup chopped onion
1¼	cups reduced-sodium chicken broth
¾	cup coarsely chopped zucchini
1	medium tomato, coarsely chopped (½ cup)
2	teaspoons lemon juice
⅛	teaspoon black pepper
1	clove garlic, minced
1	tablespoon snipped fresh mint
2	tablespoons crumbled feta cheese

1. In a medium skillet cook ground meat and onion until meat is brown and onion is tender. Drain off fat.

2. Transfer meat mixture to a 1½-quart slow cooker. Stir in broth, zucchini, tomato, lemon juice, pepper, and garlic.

3. Cover and cook on low-heat setting for 4 to 5 hours or on high-heat setting for 2 to 2½ hours. If no heat setting is available, cook for 3 to 4 hours.

4. Before serving, stir in mint. Sprinkle individual servings with cheese.

Nutrition Facts per serving: 201 cal., 10 g total fat (5 g sat. fat), 62 mg chol., 498 mg sodium, 8 g carbo., 2 g fiber, 19 g pro.

A flavorful mix of spices teams up with dried apricots and dates to provide an exotic spicy-sweet taste. Serve the stew with couscous, a tiny semolina grain that's a staple of North African cuisine.

Moroccan Lamb and Fruit Stew

MAKES 2 SERVINGS

Prep: 25 minutes
Cook: Low 7 to 9 hours,
High 3½ to 4½ hours,
plus 30 minutes (high)

1	pound boneless leg of lamb or beef bottom round roast
½	teaspoon crushed red pepper
¼	teaspoon salt
¼	teaspoon ground ginger
¼	teaspoon ground cinnamon
¼	teaspoon ground turmeric
1	tablespoon olive oil or cooking oil
1	large onion, chopped (1 cup)
2	cloves garlic, minced
1	cup beef broth
1	tablespoon cold water
2	teaspoons cornstarch
½	cup dried apricots, halved
½	cup pitted whole dates, halved
1	cup hot cooked couscous or rice
2	tablespoons slivered almonds, toasted (see tip, page 29)

1. Trim fat from meat. Cut meat into 1- to 1½-inch pieces. Transfer meat to a medium bowl. In a small bowl combine crushed red pepper, salt, ginger, cinnamon, and turmeric. Sprinkle mixture over meat; toss gently to coat.

2. In a large skillet brown meat in hot oil over medium heat. Drain off fat. Transfer meat to a 1½- or 2-quart slow cooker. Stir in onion and garlic. Pour broth over mixture in cooker.

3. Cover and cook on low-heat setting for 7 to 9 hours or on high-heat setting for 3½ to 4½ hours. If no heat setting is available, cook for 6½ to 7 hours. Skim off fat.

4. If using low-heat setting, turn to high-heat setting (or if no heat setting is available, continue cooking). In a small bowl combine water and cornstarch; stir into mixture in cooker. Stir in dried apricots and dates. Cover and cook about 30 minutes more or until mixture is slightly thickened and bubbly.

5. Serve stew over hot cooked couscous. Sprinkle with almonds.

Nutrition Facts per serving: 714 cal., 18 g total fat (4 g sat. fat), 143 mg chol., 886 mg sodium, 85 g carbo., 10 g fiber, 55 g pro.

Cola, root vegetables, and simple seasonings simmer together to form a full-flavored broth that gives an appealing flavor spin to old-fashioned pork stew.

Cola and Pork Stew

MAKES 2 SERVINGS

Prep: 15 minutes
Cook: Low 10 to 12 hours, High 5 to 6 hours

¾	to 1 pound boneless pork shoulder roast
8	ounces red potatoes or turnips, peeled and cut into 1-inch pieces
1	cup packaged peeled baby carrots
¾	cup cola (do not use diet cola)
1	tablespoon dried minced onion
2	teaspoons instant beef bouillon granules
½	teaspoon onion powder
¼	teaspoon seasoned salt

1. Trim fat from meat. Cut meat into 1-inch pieces. Transfer meat to a 1½- or 2-quart slow cooker. Add potato and carrots.

2. In a small bowl combine cola, dried onion, bouillon granules, onion powder, and seasoned salt. Pour over mixture in cooker.

3. Cover and cook on low-heat setting for 10 to 12 hours or on high-heat setting for 5 to 6 hours. If no heat setting is available, cook for 9½ to 10 hours.

Nutrition Facts per serving: 373 cal., 10 g total fat (4 g sat. fat), 110 mg chol., 1,256 mg sodium, 32 g carbo., 3 g fiber, 36 g pro.

Brown lentils actually are yellowish green outside and creamy yellow inside. Look for them with the dried beans at the supermarket. If you can't find them, substitute yellow lentils— they cook in about the same time. (Photo on page 137.)

Lentil and Ham Soup

MAKES 2 SERVINGS

Prep: 20 minutes
Cook: Low 7 to 8 hours,
High 3½ to 4 hours

1	cup reduced-sodium chicken broth
1	cup water
1	stalk celery, chopped (½ cup)
1	medium carrot, thinly sliced (½ cup)
⅓	cup brown lentils, rinsed and drained
⅓	cup diced cooked ham
½	of a small onion, cut into thin wedges
½	teaspoon dried thyme, crushed
1	cup shredded fresh spinach
1	tablespoon finely shredded Parmesan cheese

1. In a 1½-quart slow cooker combine broth, water, celery, carrot, lentils, ham, onion, and thyme.

2. Cover and cook on low-heat setting for 7 to 8 hours or on high-heat setting for 3½ to 4 hours. If no heat setting is available, cook for 5½ to 6 hours.

3. Before serving, top with spinach and sprinkle with Parmesan cheese.

Nutrition Facts per serving: 193 cal., 3 g total fat (1 g sat. fat), 15 mg chol., 795 mg sodium, 25 g carbo., 12 g fiber, 17 g pro.

Fresh ginger, jerk seasoning, lime, and garlic turn simple white fish and humble sweet potatoes into a tropical delight. The result is wonderful.

Caribbean Fish Stew

MAKES 2 SERVINGS

Prep: 20 minutes
Cook: Low 6 to 8 hours,
High 3 to 4 hours,
plus 15 minutes (high)

2	to 3 medium sweet potatoes (1 pound), peeled and coarsely chopped
1	medium tomato, coarsely chopped (½ cup)
1	small red sweet pepper, coarsely chopped (½ cup)
1	small onion, chopped (⅓ cup)
¼	teaspoon finely shredded lime peel
2	teaspoons lime juice
1	teaspoon grated fresh ginger
½	teaspoon Jamaican jerk seasoning
1	clove garlic, minced
1	14-ounce can chicken broth
8	ounces fresh or frozen firm-fleshed white fish
1	tablespoon snipped fresh cilantro

1. In a 1½- or 2-quart slow cooker combine sweet potato, tomato, sweet pepper, onion, lime peel, lime juice, ginger, jerk seasoning, and garlic. Pour broth over mixture in cooker.

2. Cover and cook on low-heat setting for 6 to 8 hours or on high-heat setting for 3 to 4 hours. If no heat setting is available, cook for 5½ to 6 hours.

3. Meanwhile, thaw fish, if frozen. Rinse fish; pat dry with paper towels. Cut fish into 1-inch pieces. Cover and chill until needed.

4. If using low-heat setting, turn to high-heat setting (or if no heat setting is available, continue cooking). Stir in fish. Cover and cook about 15 minutes more or until fish flakes easily when tested with a fork.

5. Sprinkle individual servings with cilantro.

Nutrition Facts per serving: 287 cal., 2 g total fat (0 g sat. fat), 51 mg chol., 1,028 mg sodium, 43 g carbo., 7 g fiber, 27 g pro.

Garbanzo beans are also known as chickpeas.
Look for them in the Mexican foods section of your
grocery store or next to the canned beans.

Eggplant and Tomato Stew with Garbanzo Beans

❋

MAKES 2 SERVINGS

Prep: 20 minutes
Cook: Low 10 to 11 hours,
High 5 to 5½ hours

1	15-ounce can garbanzo beans (chickpeas), rinsed and drained
1	cup peeled and cubed eggplant
¾	cup chopped tomato
1	medium carrot, sliced (½ cup)
1	stalk celery, sliced (½ cup)
1	small onion, chopped (⅓ cup)
1	cup vegetable broth
3	tablespoons Italian-style tomato paste
½	teaspoon dried Italian seasoning, crushed
⅛	to ¼ teaspoon crushed red pepper
⅛	teaspoon salt
2	cloves garlic, minced
1	bay leaf

1. In a 1½- or 2-quart slow cooker combine drained beans, eggplant, tomato, carrot, celery, and onion.

2. In a medium bowl combine broth, tomato paste, Italian seasoning, crushed red pepper, salt, garlic, and bay leaf. Pour over vegetables in cooker.

3. Cover and cook on low-heat setting for 10 to 11 hours or on high-heat setting for 5 to 5½ hours. If no heat setting is available, cook for 9½ to 10 hours. Remove bay leaf.

Nutrition Facts per serving: 342 cal., 3 g total fat (0 g sat. fat), 0 mg chol., 1,512 mg sodium, 67 g carbo., 14 g fiber, 15 g pro.

Turn an ordinary cheese chowder into a standout meal. Use black beans and add these delicious components: yellow sweet pepper, jalapeño chile, a can of enchilada sauce, and a generous stir-in of shredded Mexican-blend cheeses.

Cheese Enchilada Chowder

MAKES 3 SERVINGS

Prep: 20 minutes
Cook: Low 6 to 8 hours,
High 3 to 4 hours

1   15-ounce can black beans, rinsed and drained

½   cup frozen whole kernel corn

¼   cup chopped onion

¼   cup chopped yellow, green, or red sweet pepper

1   small fresh jalapeño chile pepper, seeded if desired and finely chopped (see tip, page 10)

1   10.75-ounce can condensed cream of chicken soup

1   10-ounce can enchilada sauce

¾   cup milk

1   cup shredded Mexican-blend cheeses

1   medium tomato, chopped (½ cup)

     Dairy sour cream (optional)

     Purchased guacamole (optional)

     Tortilla chips, coarsely broken (optional)

1. In a 1½- or 2-quart slow cooker combine drained beans, frozen corn, onion, sweet pepper, and jalapeño pepper. In a large bowl stir together soup and enchilada sauce. Gradually stir in milk until smooth. Pour over mixture in cooker.

2. Cover and cook on low-heat setting for 6 to 8 hours or on high-heat setting for 3 to 4 hours. If no heat setting is available, cook for 4½ to 5 hours.

3. Stir in cheese and tomato. If desired, top individual servings with sour cream, guacamole, and tortilla chips.

Nutrition Facts per serving: 429 cal., 22 g total fat (11 g sat. fat), 46 mg chol., 2,257 mg sodium, 44 g carbo., 9 g fiber, 21 g pro.

Serve this white chili in bread bowls if your supermarket bakery sells them, or spoon it over corn bread squares.

Chicken Chili

MAKES 2 SERVINGS

Prep: 20 minutes
Cook: Low 5 to 6 hours,
High 2½ to 3 hours

	Nonstick cooking spray
8	ounces skinless, boneless chicken breast halves, cut into 1-inch pieces
1	15-ounce can cannellini beans (white kidney beans) or Great Northern beans, rinsed and drained
1¼	cups reduced-sodium chicken broth
⅓	cup chopped green sweet pepper
¼	cup chopped onion
½	of a small fresh jalapeño chile pepper, seeded and finely chopped (see tip, page 10)
¼	teaspoon ground cumin
¼	teaspoon dried oregano, crushed
⅛	teaspoon white pepper
1	clove garlic, minced
¼	cup shredded Monterey Jack cheese (optional)

1. Lightly coat a medium skillet with nonstick cooking spray; heat skillet over medium-high heat. Cook chicken in hot skillet until brown. Drain off fat. Transfer chicken to a 1½-quart slow cooker.

2. Stir in drained beans, broth, sweet pepper, onion, chile pepper, cumin, oregano, white pepper, and garlic.

3. Cover and cook on low-heat setting for 5 to 6 hours or on high-heat setting for 2½ to 3 hours. If no heat setting is available, cook for 4 to 5 hours.

4. If desired, sprinkle individual servings with cheese.

Nutrition Facts per serving: 275 cal., 2 g total fat (0 g sat. fat), 66 mg chol., 750 mg sodium, 33 g carbo., 11 g fiber, 40 g pro.

Unwind after a busy day with a quiet meal built around this dynamite bowl of red with cheesy tortilla wedges on the side. Set it all out on a big tray for a fireside dinner. (Photo on page 272.)

Fireside Chili for Two

MAKES 2 SERVINGS

Prep: 20 minutes
Cook: Low 6 to 8 hours,
High 3 to 4 hours

8	ounces boneless beef top round steak or pork shoulder roast*
1	15-ounce can chili beans in chili gravy, undrained
½	of a 14.5-ounce can (¾ cup) stewed tomatoes, undrained and cut up
1	small green, red, or yellow sweet pepper, chopped (½ cup)
1	small onion, chopped (⅓ cup)
¼	cup beef broth
1	to 2 teaspoons finely chopped canned chipotle pepper in adobo sauce (see tip, page 10)
¼	teaspoon garlic salt
¼	teaspoon ground cumin
¼	teaspoon dried oregano, crushed
1	recipe Fried Cheese Tortilla
	Fresh rosemary sprigs (optional)
	Dairy sour cream, shredded Mexican-blend cheeses, and/or chopped avocado (optional)

1. Trim fat from meat. Cut meat into ½-inch pieces. Transfer meat to a 1½-quart slow cooker. Stir in undrained chili beans in chili gravy, undrained tomatoes, sweet pepper, onion, broth, chipotle pepper, garlic salt, cumin, and oregano.

2. Cover and cook on low-heat setting for 6 to 8 hours or on high-heat setting for 3 to 4 hours. If no heat setting is available, cook for 5 to 6 hours.

3. Serve chili with Fried Cheese Tortilla. Garnish each with a fresh rosemary sprig. If desired, top individual servings with sour cream, cheese, and/or avocado.

Fried Cheese Tortilla: Lightly brush one 8-inch flour tortilla with cooking oil. Heat a large nonstick skillet or griddle over medium heat. Add tortilla; cook about 1 minute or until bottom is golden and crisp. Turn tortilla over; sprinkle with 1 tablespoon shredded Mexican-blend cheeses. Cook about 1 minute more or until bottom is golden and crisp and cheese is melted. Cut into wedges.

Nutrition Facts per serving: 485 cal., 11 g total fat (2 g sat. fat), 67 mg chol., 1,139 mg sodium, 55 g carbo., 14 g fiber, 41 g pro.

*Note: If desired, substitute 8 ounces lean ground beef or ground pork for the beef steak or pork roast. In a medium skillet cook ground meat until brown. Drain off fat before using.

Eager taste testers will flock to the kitchen when they catch the aroma of this mildly spiced meatless chili. Tangy sour cream spooned on top adds a nice finishing touch.

Vegetable Chili

MAKES 2 SERVINGS

Prep: 20 minutes
Cook: Low 6 to 8 hours,
High 3 to 4 hours

1	15-ounce can black beans, rinsed and drained
1½	cups tomato juice
1	cup frozen whole kernel corn
¾	cup coarsely chopped zucchini or yellow summer squash
⅓	cup coarsely chopped red or yellow sweet pepper
¼	cup chopped onion
1	teaspoon chili powder
¼	teaspoon dried oregano, crushed
⅛	teaspoon salt
1	clove garlic, minced
2	tablespoons dairy sour cream

1. In a 1½-quart slow cooker combine drained beans, tomato juice, frozen corn, zucchini, sweet pepper, onion, chili powder, oregano, salt, and garlic.

2. Cover and cook on low-heat setting for 6 to 8 hours or on high-heat setting for 3 to 4 hours. If no heat setting is available, cook for 5 to 6 hours.

3. Top individual servings with sour cream.

Nutrition Facts per serving: 291 cal., 4 g total fat (2 g sat. fat), 5 mg chol., 1,188 mg sodium, 60 g carbo., 14 g fiber, 19 g pro.

Wondering what to do with the extra chipotle peppers?
Pack them in a freezer container, covering them with the sauce
from the can. Seal, label, and freeze the chiles for up to two
months. Thaw them in the refrigerator when you need them.

Sweet and Smoky Chicken

MAKES 2 SERVINGS

Prep: 15 minutes
Cook: Low 6 to 7 hours,
High 3 to 3½ hours

4	chicken thighs (1 to 1½ pounds total), skinned
⅛	teaspoon salt
⅛	teaspoon black pepper
½	cup chicken broth
¼	cup seedless red raspberry jam
¼	cup snipped dried apricots
½	to 1 canned chipotle pepper in adobo sauce, chopped (see tip, page 10), plus 1 teaspoon adobo sauce
2	teaspoons quick-cooking tapioca, crushed

1. Place chicken in a 1½- or 2-quart slow cooker. Sprinkle chicken with salt and black pepper. For sauce, in a small bowl stir together broth, jam, dried apricots, chipotle pepper and adobo sauce, and tapioca. Pour over chicken in cooker.

2. Cover and cook on low-heat setting for 6 to 7 hours or on high-heat setting for 3 to 3½ hours. If no heat setting is available, cook for 5½ to 6 hours.

3. Transfer the chicken to a serving platter. Spoon sauce over chicken.

Nutrition Facts per serving: 341 cal., 6 g total fat (1 g sat. fat), 115 mg chol., 1,051 mg sodium, 42 g carbo., 2 g fiber, 28 g pro.

Serve this superb dish with a salad of torn mixed greens, shredded carrots, and sliced fresh mushrooms; drizzle with dried tomato vinaigrette. It's simple enough for weeknight dining but outstanding enough for a special occasion.

Creamy Lemon Chicken

MAKES 2 SERVINGS

Prep: 15 minutes
Cook: Low 4 to 5 hours,
High 2 to 2½ hours

1	9-ounce package frozen cut green beans
½	of a small onion, cut into very thin wedges
2	chicken breast halves (with bone) (about 1 pound total), skinned
⅛	teaspoon black pepper
1	clove garlic, minced
¼	cup chicken broth
2	ounces cream cheese, cubed
½	teaspoon finely shredded lemon peel

1. In a 1½-quart slow cooker combine frozen green beans and onion. Add chicken. Sprinkle chicken with pepper and garlic. Pour broth over mixture in cooker.

2. Cover and cook on low-heat setting for 4 to 5 hours or on high-heat setting for 2 to 2½ hours. If no heat setting is available, cook for 3½ to 4 hours.

3. Using a slotted spoon, transfer chicken and vegetables to dinner plates; cover with foil to keep warm.

4. For sauce, in a small bowl beat cream cheese and lemon peel with an electric mixer on low speed until smooth. Slowly add cooking liquid, beating on low speed until combined. Spoon sauce over chicken and vegetables.

Nutrition Facts per serving: 314 cal., 12 g total fat (7 g sat. fat), 117 mg chol., 285 mg sodium, 13 g carbo., 4 g fiber, 39 g pro.

This delightful dish redefines convenience. It may be simple, but there is nothing plain about its very appealing flavor. If you like chicken bold and tongue-tingling, use medium or hot chunky salsa instead of mild.

Salsa Chicken

MAKES 2 SERVINGS

Prep: 10 minutes
Cook: Low 5 to 6 hours,
High 2½ to 3 hours

¼ cup bottled mild chunky salsa

1 tablespoon quick-cooking tapioca

1 tablespoon jalapeño chile pepper jelly

1 tablespoon lime juice or lemon juice

¼ teaspoon salt

4 chicken thighs (1 to 1½ pounds total), skinned

1. In a 1½-quart slow cooker combine salsa, tapioca, jelly, lime juice, and salt. Place chicken on top of mixture in cooker.

2. Cover and cook on low-heat setting for 5 to 6 hours or on high-heat setting for 2½ to 3 hours. If no heat setting is available, cook for 4 to 5 hours. Stir before serving.

Nutrition Facts per serving: 213 cal., 5 g total fat (1 g sat. fat), 114 mg chol., 458 mg sodium, 13 g carbo., 0 g fiber, 28 g pro.

Some recipes are set in stone; this recipe leaves room to play. Try sliced mushrooms instead of quartered, change the pasta to rotini or penne, or instead of the dried herb, stir in a tablespoon of fresh marjoram or thyme just before serving.

Chicken Marsala

MAKES 2 SERVINGS

Prep: 20 minutes
Cook: Low 5 to 6 hours,
High 2½ to 3 hours

1½	cups fresh mushrooms, quartered
4	chicken thighs (1 to 1½ pounds total), skinned
¼	teaspoon salt
¼	teaspoon dried marjoram or thyme, crushed
⅛	teaspoon black pepper
1	clove garlic, minced
¼	cup dry Marsala or dry sherry
3	ounces dried linguine or fettuccine
1	tablespoon cold water
2	teaspoons cornstarch

1. Place mushrooms in a 1½-quart slow cooker. Add chicken. Sprinkle chicken with salt, marjoram, pepper, and garlic. Pour Marsala over mixture in cooker.

2. Cover and cook on low-heat setting for 5 to 6 hours or on high-heat setting for 2½ to 3 hours. If no heat setting is available, cook for 4 to 5 hours.

3. Before serving, cook pasta according to package directions; drain. Divide pasta between shallow bowls. Using a slotted spoon, spoon chicken on top of pasta. Cover chicken and pasta with foil to keep warm.

4. For sauce, pour cooking liquid into a small saucepan. In a small bowl stir together water and cornstarch; stir into cooking liquid. Cook and stir over medium heat until thickened and bubbly. Cook and stir for 2 minutes more. Spoon sauce over chicken and pasta.

Nutrition Facts per serving: 395 cal., 7 g total fat (2 g sat. fat), 114 mg chol., 392 mg sodium, 39 g carbo., 2 g fiber, 35 g pro.

Orange marmalade and teriyaki sauce blend into a sweet sauce for this Asian-style chicken. Use orange sections or slices to garnish the dish. For variety and to pack in extra nutrition, serve with hot cooked brown rice. (Photo on page 141.)

Teriyaki Chicken with Orange Sauce

MAKES 2 SERVINGS

Prep: 15 minutes
Cook: Low 4 to 5 hours,
High 2 to 2½ hours

½	of a 16-ounce package frozen (yellow, green, and red) pepper and onion stir-fry vegetables
1	tablespoon quick-cooking tapioca
8	ounces skinless, boneless chicken thighs, cut into 1-inch pieces
⅓	cup chicken broth
2	tablespoons orange marmalade
1	tablespoon bottled teriyaki sauce
½	teaspoon dry mustard
¼	teaspoon ground ginger
1	cup hot cooked rice

1. Place frozen vegetables in a 1½- or 2-quart slow cooker. Stir in tapioca. Place chicken on top of vegetable mixture.

2. In a small bowl stir together broth, marmalade, teriyaki sauce, dry mustard, and ginger. Pour over mixture in cooker.

3. Cover and cook on low-heat setting for 4 to 5 hours or on high-heat setting for 2 to 2½ hours. If no heat setting is available, cook for 3½ to 4 hours. Serve chicken mixture with hot cooked rice.

Nutrition Facts per serving: 348 cal., 5 g total fat (1 g sat. fat), 95 mg chol., 622 mg sodium, 47 g carbo., 2 g fiber, 27 g pro.

Italian seasoning is a mix of herbs and spices. If you don't have it on hand, substitute dried basil, oregano, or a mixture of the two. For a colorful variation, try spinach or red pepper fettuccine. (Photo on page 135.)

Italian Chicken and Pasta

MAKES 2 SERVINGS

Prep: 15 minutes
Cook: Low 5 to 6 hours,
High 2½ to 3 hours

1 cup frozen cut Italian or regular green beans

½ cup fresh mushrooms, quartered

1 small onion, cut into ¼-inch-thick slices

8 ounces skinless, boneless chicken thighs, cut into 1-inch pieces

1 8-ounce can tomato sauce

½ teaspoon dried Italian seasoning, crushed

1 roma tomato, chopped

1 cup hot cooked noodles

Finely shredded Parmesan cheese (optional)

1. In a 1½-quart slow cooker combine frozen beans, mushrooms, and onion. Add chicken. In a small bowl combine tomato sauce and Italian seasoning. Pour over mixture in cooker.

2. Cover and cook on low-heat setting for 5 to 6 hours or on high-heat setting for 2½ to 3 hours. If no heat setting is available, cook for 4 to 5 hours. Stir in tomato.

3. Serve chicken mixture over hot cooked noodles. If desired, sprinkle with Parmesan cheese.

Nutrition Facts per serving: 318 cal., 7 g total fat (2 g sat. fat), 117 mg chol., 614 mg sodium, 33 g carbo., 4 g fiber, 30 g pro.

Many turkey breast tenderloins are larger than 8 ounces.
Trim the tenderloin down, and wrap the remaining turkey to
store in the freezer for another meal.

Hoisin-Sauced Turkey Tenderloin

MAKES 2 SERVINGS

Prep: 20 minutes
Cook: Low 3 to 4 hours,
High 1½ to 2 hours

½	of a medium red sweet pepper, cut into thin bite-size strips
½	of a small onion, cut into thin wedges
8	ounces turkey breast tenderloin, halved crosswise
⅛	teaspoon salt
⅛	teaspoon black pepper
1	clove garlic, minced
2	tablespoons orange juice
2	tablespoons bottled hoisin sauce
¾	cup uncooked instant brown rice
2	tablespoons sliced green onion (1)
1	tablespoon chopped almonds, toasted (see tip, right)

1. In a 1½-quart slow cooker combine sweet pepper and onion. Add turkey. Sprinkle turkey with salt, black pepper, and garlic. In a small bowl combine orange juice and hoisin sauce. Pour over mixture in cooker.

2. Cover and cook on low-heat setting for 3 to 4 hours or on high-heat setting for 1½ to 2 hours. If no heat setting is available, cook for 2 to 3 hours.

3. Before serving, cook rice according to package directions. Serve turkey mixture with hot cooked rice. Sprinkle with green onion and almonds.

Nutrition Facts per serving: 325 cal., 5 g total fat (1 g sat. fat), 68 mg chol., 408 mg sodium, 37 g carbo., 4 g fiber, 32 g pro.

Test Kitchen Tip: For a richer, fuller flavor, toast nuts, coconut, or sesame seeds by placing them in a single layer in a shallow baking pan. Bake in a 350°F oven for 5 to 10 minutes or until golden brown. Watch carefully and stir once or twice to keep them from burning.

This slow cooker version of mu shu differs from the classic because it features chicken, not pork, and is served in tortillas instead of thin pancakes. The result is delicious enough to impress even the most adamant Chinese-takeout fanatic.

Mu Shu-Style Chicken

MAKES 2 SERVINGS

Prep: 20 minutes
Cook: Low 6 to 7 hours,
High 3 to 3½ hours

1¼	to 1½ pounds meaty chicken pieces (breast halves, thighs, and drumsticks), skinned
⅛	teaspoon salt
⅛	teaspoon black pepper
¼	cup water
2	tablespoons soy sauce
1	teaspoon toasted sesame oil
½	teaspoon ground ginger
4	7- to 8-inch flour tortillas
¼	cup bottled plum sauce
1	cup packaged shredded broccoli (broccoli slaw mix) or packaged shredded cabbage with carrot (coleslaw mix)

1. Place chicken in a 1½- or 2-quart slow cooker. Sprinkle chicken with salt and pepper. In a small bowl stir together water, soy sauce, sesame oil, and ginger. Pour over chicken in cooker.

2. Cover and cook on low-heat setting for 6 to 7 hours or on high-heat setting for 3 to 3½ hours. If no heat setting is available, cook for 5½ to 6 hours.

3. Remove chicken from cooker, reserving cooking liquid. When cool enough to handle, remove chicken from bones; discard bones. Shred chicken by pulling two forks through it in opposite directions. Return chicken to cooker; stir to combine with cooking liquid.

4. To serve, spread each tortilla with 1 tablespoon of the plum sauce. Using a slotted spoon, spoon shredded chicken onto tortillas just below the centers. Top with broccoli slaw mix. Fold bottom edge of each tortilla up and over filling. Fold in opposite sides; roll up from bottom.

Nutrition Facts per serving: 532 cal., 16 g total fat (4 g sat. fat), 115 mg chol., 1,722 mg sodium, 50 g carbo., 3 g fiber, 43 g pro.

Sesame sauce accented with ginger and broccoli slaw mix make a tantalizing fusion of flavor. This combo is also great with chicken thighs.

Sesame-Ginger Turkey Wraps

MAKES 2 SERVINGS

Prep: 20 minutes
Cook: Low 6 to 7 hours,
High 3 to 3½ hours
Stand: 5 minutes

	Nonstick cooking spray
1½	pounds turkey thighs, skinned
½	cup bottled sesame-ginger stir-fry or grilling sauce
2	tablespoons water
2	cups packaged shredded broccoli (broccoli slaw mix)
4	8- to 10-inch flour tortillas, warmed (see tip, page 118)
⅓	cup sliced green onion (3)

1. Lightly coat the inside of a 1½- or 2-quart slow cooker with nonstick cooking spray. Place turkey in the prepared cooker. In a small bowl stir together stir-fry sauce and water. Pour over turkey in cooker.

2. Cover and cook on low-heat setting for 6 to 7 hours or on high-heat setting for 3 to 3½ hours. If no heat setting is available, cook for 5½ to 6 hours.

3. Using a slotted spoon, remove turkey from cooker, reserving cooking liquid. When cool enough to handle, remove turkey from bones; discard bones. Shred turkey by pulling two forks through it in opposite directions. Return turkey to cooker.

4. Stir in broccoli slaw mix. Let stand, covered, for 5 minutes. Using the slotted spoon, remove turkey mixture from cooker.

5. Spoon turkey mixture onto warm tortillas. Top with green onion. If desired, drizzle with some of the cooking liquid. Roll up tortillas.

Nutrition Facts per serving: 685 cal., 19 g total fat (4 g sat. fat), 198 mg chol., 1,835 mg sodium, 69 g carbo., 2 g fiber, 56 g pro.

Pick your salsa—mild, medium, or hot—to make this black bean and smoked turkey sausage mélange mild or tongue-tingling. Serve with corn bread or muffins. (Photo on page 139.)

Mexican-Style Sausage and Beans

❧

MAKES 2 SERVINGS

Prep: 20 minutes
Cook: Low 5½ to 6½ hours,
High 2½ to 3 hours

1   15-ounce can black beans or cannellini beans (white kidney beans), rinsed and drained

8   ounces cooked smoked turkey sausage, sliced

½   cup frozen whole kernel corn

1   small green sweet pepper, chopped (½ cup)

1   medium onion, chopped (½ cup)

½   cup bottled salsa

¼   teaspoon ground cumin

2   cloves garlic, minced

Dairy sour cream (optional)

Shredded cheddar cheese (optional)

1. In a 1½- or 2-quart slow cooker combine drained beans, turkey sausage, frozen corn, sweet pepper, onion, salsa, cumin, and garlic.

2. Cover and cook on low-heat setting for 5½ to 6½ hours or on high-heat setting for 2½ to 3 hours. If no heat setting is available, cook for 5 to 5½ hours.

3. If desired, top individual servings with sour cream and cheese.

Nutrition Facts per serving: 379 cal., 11 g total fat (4 g sat. fat), 60 mg chol., 2,245 mg sodium, 53 g carbo., 15 g fiber, 29 g pro.

Port is the star flavor here. No need to buy expensive port, which is aged for several years. The less expensive ruby port is sufficient. This seasoned gravy also is tasty over polenta or mashed potatoes.

Herbed-Port Pot Roast

MAKES 2 SERVINGS

Prep: 20 minutes
Cook: Low 6½ to 7½ hours, High 3½ to 4 hours

1	1¼-pound boneless beef chuck pot roast
½	cup tomato sauce
¼	cup chopped onion
¼	cup port or apple juice
4	teaspoons quick-cooking tapioca
1½	teaspoons Worcestershire sauce
½	teaspoon dried thyme, crushed
½	teaspoon dried oregano, crushed
¼	teaspoon salt
1	clove garlic, minced
1½	cups hot cooked noodles

1. Trim fat from meat. If necessary, cut meat to fit into a 1½- or 2-quart slow cooker. Place meat in cooker.

2. In a small bowl combine tomato sauce, onion, port, tapioca, Worcestershire sauce, thyme, oregano, salt, and garlic. Pour over meat in cooker.

3. Cover and cook on low-heat setting for 6½ to 7½ hours or on high-heat setting for 3½ to 4 hours. If no heat setting is available, cook for 5½ to 6 hours. Transfer meat to a serving platter, reserving cooking liquid.

4. Skim fat from cooking liquid. Serve meat with cooking liquid and hot cooked noodles.

Nutrition Facts per serving: 706 cal., 22 g total fat (8 g sat. fat), 205 mg chol., 850 mg sodium, 48 g carbo., 3 g fiber, 67 g pro.

Looking for a slow-cooked pot roast that serves just two?
This fiery chuck roast seasoned with chipotle is a
delicious possibility.

Cranberry-Chipotle Beef

❧

MAKES 2 SERVINGS

Prep: 10 minutes
Cook: Low 6 to 8 hours,
High 3 to 4 hours

12	ounces boneless beef chuck pot roast
1	small onion, cut into thin wedges
⅛	teaspoon salt
⅛	teaspoon black pepper
1	clove garlic, minced
½	of a 16-ounce can (about ¾ cup) whole cranberry sauce
½	to 1 teaspoon finely chopped canned chipotle pepper in adobo sauce (see tip, page 10)
1	cup uncooked instant brown rice

1. Trim fat from meat. If necessary, cut meat to fit into a 1½-quart slow cooker. Set aside.

2. Place onion in the cooker. Add meat. Sprinkle meat with salt, black pepper, and garlic. In a small bowl combine cranberry sauce and chipotle pepper. Pour over mixture in cooker.

3. Cover and cook on low-heat setting for 6 to 8 hours or on high-heat setting for 3 to 4 hours. If no heat setting is available, cook for 4½ to 5½ hours.

4. Before serving, cook rice according to package directions. Serve meat and onion mixture with hot cooked rice.

Nutrition Facts per serving: 506 cal., 7 g total fat (2 g sat. fat), 101 mg chol., 296 mg sodium, 71 g carbo., 4 g fiber, 40 g pro.

Soothing mashed potatoes and sour cream provide the perfect counterpoint to these tomatoey beef strips that get their devilish kick from horseradish mustard. (Photo on page 136.)

Deviled Steak Strips

MAKES 2 OR 3 SERVINGS

Prep: 15 minutes
Cook: Low 6 to 8 hours, High 3 to 4 hours

12	ounces boneless beef round steak, cut ¾ inch thick
1	8-ounce can tomato sauce
1	medium onion, chopped (½ cup)
1	4.5-ounce jar (drained weight) sliced mushrooms, drained
¼	cup water
1	tablespoon quick-cooking tapioca, crushed
1	tablespoon horseradish mustard
1	teaspoon instant beef bouillon granules
⅛	teaspoon black pepper
1	to 1½ cups hot mashed potatoes
	Dairy sour cream (optional)
	Snipped fresh chives (optional)

1. Trim fat from meat. Thinly slice meat across the grain into bite-size strips. Set aside.

2. In a 1½-quart slow cooker combine tomato sauce, onion, drained mushrooms, water, tapioca, horseradish mustard, bouillon granules, and pepper. Stir in meat.

3. Cover and cook on low-heat setting for 6 to 8 hours or on high-heat setting for 3 to 4 hours. If no heat setting is available, cook for 5 to 6 hours.

4. Serve meat mixture over hot mashed potatoes. If desired, top with sour cream and chives.

Nutrition Facts per serving: 407 cal., 9 g total fat (3 g sat. fat), 83 mg chol., 1,627 mg sodium, 36 g carbo., 5 g fiber, 43 g pro.

Slow simmering in teriyaki sauce and garlic lends a delightful
Asian accent to this colorful blend of beef and vegetables.

Pepper Steak

MAKES 2 SERVINGS

Prep: 20 minutes
Cook: Low 5 to 6 hours,
High 2½ to 3 hours

8	ounces boneless beef top round steak, cut ¾ inch thick
1	tablespoon cooking oil
2	tablespoons bottled teriyaki sauce
2	cloves garlic, minced
1	medium onion, thinly sliced (½ cup)
1	small green sweet pepper, thinly sliced (½ cup)
1	large tomato, chopped (1 cup)
1	cup hot cooked orzo pasta or rice

1. Trim fat from meat. Thinly slice meat across the grain into bite-size strips. In a large skillet brown meat in hot oil over medium-high heat. Drain off fat. Set aside.

2. In a 1½-quart slow cooker combine teriyaki sauce and garlic. Stir in meat, onion, and sweet pepper.

3. Cover and cook on low-heat setting for 5 to 6 hours or on high-heat setting for 2½ to 3 hours. If no heat setting is available, cook for 4 to 5 hours. Stir in tomato.

4. Serve meat mixture over hot cooked pasta.

Nutrition Facts per serving: 350 cal., 10 g total fat (2 g sat. fat), 49 mg chol., 682 mg sodium, 33 g carbo., 4 g fiber, 33 g pro.

Rich, tangy feta cheese and the aromatic seasoning blend give this dish a flavor reminiscent of the cooking of the Greek isles.

Greek Beef and Orzo

MAKES 2 SERVINGS

Prep: 15 minutes
Cook: Low 8 to 9 hours,
High 4 to 4½ hours,
plus 30 minutes (high)

	Nonstick cooking spray
12	ounces beef stew meat
1	medium onion, cut into thin wedges
¼	teaspoon salt
⅛	teaspoon black pepper
1	cup beef broth
3	tablespoons tomato paste
¾	teaspoon Greek seasoning
1	small zucchini or yellow summer squash, halved lengthwise and sliced (1 cup)
⅓	cup dried orzo pasta
	Crumbled feta cheese

1. Lightly coat the inside of a 1½- or 2-quart slow cooker with nonstick cooking spray; set aside. Trim fat from meat. Cut meat into 1-inch pieces. Set aside.

2. Place onion in the prepared cooker. Add meat. Sprinkle meat with salt and pepper. In a small bowl combine broth, tomato paste, and Greek seasoning. Pour over mixture in cooker.

3. Cover and cook on low-heat setting for 8 to 9 hours or on high-heat setting for 4 to 4½ hours. If no heat setting is available, cook for 7½ to 8 hours.

4. If using low-heat setting, turn to high-heat setting (or if no heat setting is available, continue cooking). Stir in zucchini and pasta. Cover and cook for 30 minutes more. Sprinkle individual servings with feta cheese.

Nutrition Facts per serving: 472 cal., 16 g total fat (7 g sat. fat), 96 mg chol., 1,231 mg sodium, 33 g carbo., 4 g fiber, 47 g pro.

This hearty, satisfying main dish features beef pieces seasoned with lots of Hungarian paprika, garlic, and thyme. Imported Hungarian paprika is lighter in color than other paprikas but more pungent and full of flavor.

Hungarian Goulash

MAKES 2 SERVINGS

Prep: 20 minutes
Cook: Low 10 to 12 hours,
High 5 to 6 hours

12	ounces beef stew meat
1	medium tomato, chopped (½ cup)
½	of a 6-ounce can (⅓ cup) tomato paste
1	tablespoon quick-cooking tapioca
2	teaspoons Hungarian paprika or regular paprika
½	teaspoon salt
¼	teaspoon dried thyme, crushed
¼	teaspoon black pepper
2	cloves garlic, minced
¾	cup chopped onion
1	small green sweet pepper, coarsely chopped (½ cup)
½	cup dairy sour cream
1½	cups hot cooked noodles

1. Trim fat from meat. Cut meat into 1-inch pieces. Set aside.

2. In a 1½- or 2-quart slow cooker stir together tomato, tomato paste, tapioca, paprika, salt, thyme, black pepper, and garlic. Add meat, onion, and sweet pepper to mixture in cooker.

3. Cover and cook on low-heat setting for 10 to 12 hours or on high-heat setting for 5 to 6 hours. If no heat setting is available, cook for 9½ to 10 hours.

4. In a small bowl combine sour cream and about ⅓ cup of the hot mixture from cooker. Stir into the mixture in cooker until combined. Serve over hot cooked noodles.

Nutrition Facts per serving: 619 cal., 21 g total fat (9 g sat. fat), 157 mg chol., 769 mg sodium, 60 g carbo., 8 g fiber, 51 g pro.

The slow cooker produces unbelievably tender meat for this south-of-the-border favorite. Set the table with tortillas, a platter of seasoned shredded meat, and small bowls of sour cream, guacamole, or diced tomatoes.

Beef Fajitas

MAKES 2 SERVINGS

Prep: 20 minutes
Cook: Low 4 to 5 hours,
High 2 to 2½ hours

8	ounces boneless beef round steak, cut ¾ inch thick
⅛	teaspoon salt
⅛	teaspoon ground cumin
⅛	teaspoon ground coriander
⅛	teaspoon black pepper
1	small onion, cut into thin wedges
½	of a small green or red sweet pepper, cut into thin bite-size strips
¼	cup beef broth
2	8- to 10-inch whole wheat or plain flour tortillas, warmed (see tip, page 118)
¼	cup shredded carrot
¼	cup shredded lettuce

1. Trim fat from meat. Sprinkle one side of meat with salt, cumin, coriander, and black pepper; rub in with your fingers. Cut meat across the grain into thin bite-size strips. Set aside.

2. In a 1½-quart slow cooker combine onion and sweet pepper. Add meat. Pour broth over mixture in cooker.

3. Cover and cook on low-heat setting for 4 to 5 hours or on high-heat setting for 2 to 2½ hours. If no heat setting is available, cook for 3½ to 4 hours.

4. Using a slotted spoon, spoon meat mixture onto warm tortillas. If desired, drizzle with enough of the cooking liquid to moisten. Top with carrot and lettuce. Roll up tortillas.

Nutrition Facts per serving: 342 cal., 10 g total fat (3 g sat. fat), 65 mg chol., 709 mg sodium, 32 g carbo., 4 g fiber, 31 g pro.

Incorporate slow cooking into a weeknight supper starring these sandwiches. Serve fresh vegetables with a savory dip to complete the easy meal. (Photo on page 138.)

Peppery Beef Sandwiches

MAKES 2 SANDWICHES

Prep: 15 minutes
Cook: Low 10 to 12 hours,
High 5 to 6 hours,
plus 30 minutes (high)

1¼ to 1½ pounds boneless beef chuck pot roast or beef chuck steak

1 medium onion, chopped (½ cup)

2 tablespoons Worcestershire sauce

1 teaspoon instant beef bouillon granules

½ teaspoon dried oregano, crushed

¼ teaspoon dried basil, crushed

¼ teaspoon dried thyme, crushed

1 clove garlic, minced

¼ cup chopped pepperoncini (Italian pickled peppers) or other pickled peppers

2 hoagie buns or kaiser rolls, split and toasted

2 1-ounce slices Swiss cheese

1. Trim fat from meat. Cut meat into 1-inch pieces. Transfer meat to a 1½- or 2-quart slow cooker. Stir in onion, Worcestershire sauce, bouillon granules, oregano, basil, thyme, and garlic.

2. Cover and cook on low-heat setting for 10 to 12 hours or on high-heat setting for 5 to 6 hours. If no heat setting is available, cook for 9½ to 10 hours.

3. If using low-heat setting, turn to high-heat setting (or if no heat setting is available, continue cooking). Stir to break up meat. Stir in pepperoncini. Cover and cook for 30 minutes more.

4. Preheat broiler. Using a slotted spoon, spoon meat mixture onto bottoms of buns. Top with cheese. Place sandwiches on a baking sheet. Broil 4 to 5 inches from the heat about 1 minute or until cheese is melted. Add tops of buns.

Nutrition Facts per serving: 992 cal., 36 g total fat (15 g sat. fat), 196 mg chol., 1,752 mg sodium, 85 g carbo., 5 g fiber, 80 g pro.

For a simple yet sophisticated taste, try this rich sauce studded with mushrooms and served over spaghetti or fettuccine. To get the best flavor from your pasta, cook it only until al dente, which means it is still slightly firm and a little chewy.

Beefy Pasta Sauce

MAKES 2 SERVINGS

Prep: 20 minutes
Cook: Low 4 to 5 hours,
High 2 to 2½ hours

8	ounces lean ground beef
¼	cup chopped onion
1	clove garlic, minced
2	medium tomatoes, chopped (1 cup)
1	4.5-ounce jar (drained weight) sliced mushrooms, drained
¼	cup tomato paste
½	teaspoon dried Italian seasoning, crushed
¼	teaspoon salt
⅛	teaspoon black pepper
3	ounces dried spaghetti or fettuccine
1	tablespoon finely shredded Parmesan cheese

1. In a medium skillet cook ground beef, onion, and garlic until meat is brown and onion is tender. Drain off fat. Set aside.

2. In a 1½-quart slow cooker combine tomato, drained mushrooms, tomato paste, Italian seasoning, salt, and pepper. Stir in meat mixture.

3. Cover and cook on low-heat setting for 4 to 5 hours or on high-heat setting for 2 to 2½ hours. If no heat setting is available, cook for 3 to 4 hours.

4. Before serving, cook pasta according to package directions; drain. Serve meat sauce over hot cooked pasta. Sprinkle with Parmesan cheese.

Nutrition Facts per serving: 430 cal., 13 g total fat (5 g sat. fat), 73 mg chol., 643 mg sodium, 48 g carbo., 5 g fiber, 31 g pro.

If ease and simplicity are first on your list when selecting the perfect meal for two, this slow-cooker dish may be just what you're looking for. With only 20 minutes of prep time, it contains everything in one pot—meat, potatoes, and vegetables.

Saucy Lamb and Vegetables

❀

MAKES 2 SERVINGS

Prep: 20 minutes
Cook: Low 10 to 12 hours, High 5 to 6 hours

1	1¼- to 1½-pound boneless lamb shoulder roast
5	or 6 tiny new potatoes or 2 medium red potatoes (8 ounces)
⅔	cup packaged peeled baby carrots
1	small onion, cut into wedges
2	teaspoons honey
½	teaspoon ground ginger
¼	teaspoon salt
¼	teaspoon ground cinnamon
⅛	teaspoon ground allspice
⅛	teaspoon cayenne pepper
⅔	cup beef broth
¼	cup cold water
2	tablespoons all-purpose flour
½	teaspoon finely shredded orange peel

1. Trim fat from meat. If necessary, cut meat to fit into a 1½- or 2-quart slow cooker. Set aside.

2. Remove a narrow strip of peel from the center of each new potato, or peel (if desired) and quarter each medium potato. In the cooker combine potatoes, carrots, and onion. Drizzle with honey and sprinkle with ginger, salt, cinnamon, allspice, and cayenne pepper. Add meat. Pour broth over mixture in cooker.

3. Cover and cook on low-heat setting for 10 to 12 hours or on high-heat setting for 5 to 6 hours. If no heat setting is available, cook for 9½ to 10 hours.

4. Using a slotted spoon, transfer meat and vegetables to a serving platter; cover with foil to keep warm.

5. For gravy, pour cooking liquid into a glass measuring cup; skim off fat. Measure ½ cup liquid. In a small saucepan combine water, flour, and orange peel; stir in the ½ cup liquid. Cook and stir over medium heat until thickened and bubbly. Cook and stir for 1 minute more. Serve meat and vegetables with gravy.

Nutrition Facts per serving: 551 cal., 15 g total fat (5 g sat. fat), 181 mg chol., 821 mg sodium, 40 g carbo., 5 g fiber, 60 g pro.

A pleasing combination of plum jam, soy sauce, rice vinegar, and fresh ginger gives these chops an exotic taste of the Orient. The flavorful dish makes a choice selection for a welcome-home dinner.

Plum-Sauced Pork Chops

MAKES 2 SERVINGS

Prep: 15 minutes
Cook: Low 4 to 5 hours,
High 2 to 2½ hours

2	pork rib chops (with bone), cut ¾ inch thick
2	teaspoons cooking oil
1	cup packaged peeled baby carrots, halved lengthwise
½	of a small onion, cut into thin wedges
½	teaspoon dry mustard
½	teaspoon grated fresh ginger
⅛	teaspoon salt
⅛	teaspoon black pepper
¼	cup plum jam or apricot preserves
1	tablespoon soy sauce
1	tablespoon rice vinegar
½	cup uncooked instant brown rice

1. Trim fat from chops. In a medium skillet brown chops on both sides in hot oil over medium heat. Drain off fat. Set aside.

2. In a 1½-quart slow cooker combine carrot and onion. Add chops. Sprinkle chops with dry mustard, ginger, salt, and pepper. In a small bowl combine jam, soy sauce, and vinegar. Pour over mixture in cooker.

3. Cover and cook on low-heat setting for 4 to 5 hours or on high-heat setting for 2 to 2½ hours. If no heat setting is available, cook for 3½ to 4 hours.

4. Before serving, cook rice according to package directions. Serve chops and vegetable mixture with hot cooked rice.

Nutrition Facts per serving: 508 cal., 11 g total fat (2 g sat. fat), 53 mg chol., 772 mg sodium, 72 g carbo., 5 g fiber, 27 g pro.

In late summer when the corn is its sweetest, these meaty chops are the season's best. Control the heat level of this zesty dish by choosing mild, medium, or hot salsa. (Photo on page 140.)

Southwest Pork Chops

MAKES 2 SERVINGS

Prep: 15 minutes
Cook: Low 4½ to 5 hours,
High 2 to 2¼ hours,
plus 30 minutes (high)

2   boneless pork loin chops, cut ½ to ¾ inch thick

1   15-ounce can chili beans in chili gravy, undrained

½   cup bottled salsa

½   cup fresh or frozen whole kernel corn*

Hot cooked brown rice (optional)

Snipped fresh cilantro (optional)

1. Trim fat from chops. Place one of the chops in a 1½- or 2-quart slow cooker. In a medium bowl combine undrained chili beans in chili gravy and salsa. Pour about half of the bean mixture over chop in cooker. Add the remaining chop and the remaining bean mixture.

2. Cover and cook on low-heat setting for 4½ to 5 hours or on high-heat setting for 2 to 2¼ hours. If no heat setting is available, cook for 4 to 4½ hours.

3. If using low-heat setting, turn to high-heat setting (or if no heat setting is available, continue cooking). Stir in fresh or frozen corn. Cover and cook for 30 minutes more.

4. If desired, serve chops and bean mixture with hot cooked brown rice and sprinkle with cilantro.

Nutrition Facts per serving: 563 cal., 14 g total fat (4 g sat. fat), 124 mg chol., 1,032 mg sodium, 46 g carbo., 14 g fiber, 63 g pro.

*Note: For fresh corn, cut off the kernels from 1 medium ear of fresh corn to make about ½ cup whole kernel corn.

Apple juice and sage team up for a full-flavored sauce to coat chops and butternut squash. Steam green beans or asparagus to serve alongside. If you have one large chop that weighs 10 to 12 ounces, cut it into two pieces before browning.

Pork Chops with Winter Squash

MAKES 2 SERVINGS

Prep: 25 minutes
Cook: Low 5 to 5½ hours, High 2 to 2½ hours

1	or 2 boneless pork sirloin chops, cut ¾ to 1 inch thick (10 to 12 ounces total)
	Nonstick cooking spray
½	of a small onion, cut into thin wedges
½	of a small butternut squash, peeled, seeded, and cut into 1- to 1½-inch pieces (1½ cups)
¼	teaspoon salt
⅛	teaspoon ground sage or ¼ teaspoon dried sage, crushed
⅛	teaspoon black pepper
⅓	cup apple juice or apple cider

1. Trim fat from chops. Lightly coat a medium skillet with nonstick cooking spray; heat skillet over medium heat. Cook chops and onion in hot skillet until chops are brown, turning chops once and stirring onion occasionally. Drain off fat.

2. Transfer onion to a 1½-quart slow cooker. Stir in squash. Add chops. Sprinkle chops with salt, sage, and pepper. Pour apple juice over mixture in cooker.

3. Cover and cook on low-heat setting for 5 to 5½ hours or on high-heat setting for 2 to 2½ hours. If no heat setting is available, cook for 4 to 4½ hours.

Nutrition Facts per serving: 263 cal., 8 g total fat (3 g sat. fat), 89 mg chol., 369 mg sodium, 16 g carbo., 2 g fiber, 31 g pro.

Easier than stir-fry, this Chinese-inspired meal is destined to become a mainstay in your repertoire of fuss-free weeknight dinners. Soy sauce, oyster sauce, and fresh ginger give the pork and vegetables an irresistible flavor.

Pineapple-Ginger Pork

MAKES 2 SERVINGS

Prep: 20 minutes
Cook: Low 6 to 8 hours,
High 3 to 4 hours,
plus 10 minutes (high)

12	ounces boneless pork shoulder roast
1	tablespoon cooking oil
⅓	cup chicken broth
2	tablespoons quick-cooking tapioca
2	tablespoons reduced-sodium soy sauce
1	tablespoon oyster sauce (optional)
½	teaspoon grated fresh ginger
1	8-ounce can pineapple chunks (juice pack), undrained
2	medium carrots, cut into ½-inch pieces
1	small onion, cut into 1-inch pieces
1	8-ounce can sliced water chestnuts, drained
¾	cup fresh snow pea pods, halved diagonally
1½	cups hot cooked rice
	Cashews (optional)

1. Trim fat from meat. Cut meat into 1-inch pieces. In a large skillet brown meat, half at a time, in hot oil over medium heat. Drain off fat. Set aside.

2. In a 1½- or 2-quart slow cooker combine broth, tapioca, soy sauce, oyster sauce (if desired), and ginger. Drain pineapple, reserving juice. Cover and chill pineapple until needed. Stir pineapple juice into broth mixture. Stir in carrot, onion, and drained water chestnuts. Add meat to mixture in cooker.

3. Cover and cook on low-heat setting for 6 to 8 hours or on high-heat setting for 3 to 4 hours. If no heat setting is available, cook for 4½ to 5 hours.

4. If using low-heat setting, turn to high-heat setting (or if no heat setting is available, continue cooking). Stir in pineapple and pea pods. Cover and cook for 10 to 15 minutes more or until pea pods are crisp-tender.

5. Serve meat mixture over hot cooked rice. If desired, sprinkle with cashews.

Nutrition Facts per serving: 770 cal., 23 g total fat (5 g sat. fat), 110 mg chol., 870 mg sodium, 104 g carbo., 4 g fiber, 43 g pro.

Very little work is needed to get a pork shoulder roast seasoned and ready for the slow cooker. A creamy lime dressing provides a cooling complement to gutsy jerk-seasoned pork.

Jerk Pork Wraps with Lime Mayo

MAKES 2 SERVINGS

Prep: 25 minutes
Cook: Low 8 to 10 hours, High 4 to 5 hours

1	pound boneless pork shoulder roast
1	tablespoon Jamaican jerk seasoning
¼	teaspoon dried thyme, crushed
½	cup water
2	teaspoons lime juice
4	8-inch flour tortillas
4	lettuce leaves (optional)
½	cup chopped mango or pineapple
¼	cup chopped red or green sweet pepper
1	recipe Lime Mayo

1. Trim fat from meat. Sprinkle jerk seasoning and thyme evenly over meat; rub in with your fingers. Place meat in a 1½- or 2-quart slow cooker. Pour water around meat in cooker.

2. Cover and cook on low-heat setting for 8 to 10 hours or on high-heat setting for 4 to 5 hours. If no heat setting is available, cook for 7½ to 8 hours.

3. Remove meat from cooker; discard cooking liquid. Shred meat by pulling two forks through it in opposite directions. Transfer meat to a medium bowl. Drizzle lime juice over meat; toss to combine.

4. If desired, line tortillas with lettuce leaves. Spoon meat mixture onto tortillas just below the centers. Add mango and sweet pepper. Top with Lime Mayo. Fold the bottom edge of each tortilla up and over filling. Fold in opposite sides; roll up from the bottom.

Lime Mayo: In a small bowl stir together ¼ cup light or regular mayonnaise, 2 tablespoons finely chopped red onion, ¼ teaspoon finely shredded lime peel, 2 teaspoons lime juice, and 1 clove garlic, minced. Cover and chill until ready to serve.

Nutrition Facts per serving: 632 cal., 29 g total fat (8 g sat. fat), 158 mg chol., 1,082 mg sodium, 42 g carbo., 2 g fiber, 50 g pro.

So few ingredients, so very much tender meat and kicky flavor. What's not to love? Pork ribs cook with a generous amount of chipotle chiles and barbecue sauce.

Chipotle Country-Style Ribs

MAKES 2 SERVINGS

Prep: 15 minutes
Cook: Low 10 to 12 hours,
High 5 to 6 hours

1 pound boneless pork
country-style ribs

1 cup bottled barbecue
sauce

2 canned chipotle peppers
in adobo sauce, finely
chopped (see tip, page 10)

1. Place ribs in a 1½- or 2-quart slow cooker. In a medium bowl combine barbecue sauce and chipotle pepper. Pour half of the sauce over ribs in cooker. Cover and chill the remaining sauce until ready to serve.

2. Cover and cook on low-heat setting for 10 to 12 hours or on high-heat setting for 5 to 6 hours. If no heat setting is available, cook for 9½ to 10 hours.

3. Transfer ribs to a serving platter. Reheat the reserved sauce and serve with ribs.

Nutrition Facts per serving: 394 cal., 11 g total fat (4 g sat. fat), 81 mg chol., 1,554 mg sodium, 46 g carbo., 1 g fiber, 24 g pro.

The simple pleasure of eating ribs so tender that they fall apart starts with a premixed seasoning blend, barbecue sauce, and honey mustard. (Photo on page 132.)

5 Ingredient Recipe

Honey-Mustard Barbecue Pork Ribs

MAKES 2 SERVINGS

Prep: 15 minutes
Cook: Low 8 to 10 hours, High 4 to 5 hours

1¾ pounds pork country-style ribs
½ cup bottled barbecue sauce
½ cup honey mustard
1 teaspoon desired flavor grilling seasoning blend

1. Place ribs in a 1½- or 2-quart slow cooker. In a small bowl stir together barbecue sauce, honey mustard, and seasoning blend. Pour over ribs in cooker.

2. Cover and cook on low-heat setting for 8 to 10 hours or on high-heat setting for 4 to 5 hours. If no heat setting is available, cook for 7½ to 8 hours.

3. Transfer ribs to a serving platter. Strain sauce into a bowl; skim off fat. Drizzle some of the sauce over ribs; pass the remaining sauce.

Nutrition Facts per serving: 503 cal., 19 g total fat (6 g sat. fat), 142 mg chol., 1,548 mg sodium, 35 g carbo., 0 g fiber, 43 g pro.

This no-fuss sauce picks up its traditional old-world flavor from Italian sausage, garlic, and herb-seasoned tomatoes. To make the cheese shards, use a vegetable peeler or cheese shaver to cut pieces from a block of Parmesan.

Penne Sauce Italiano

MAKES 2 SERVINGS

Prep: 20 minutes
Cook: Low 8 to 9 hours,
High 4 to 4½ hours

6	ounces bulk Italian sausage and/or lean ground beef
1	clove garlic, minced
1	14.5-ounce can diced tomatoes with basil, garlic, and oregano, undrained
1	8-ounce can no-salt-added tomato sauce
¼	cup chopped green sweet pepper
1	tablespoon quick-cooking tapioca
⅛	teaspoon crushed red pepper (optional)
1	cup hot cooked penne pasta or spaghetti
	Shaved or finely shredded Parmesan cheese (optional)

1. In a medium skillet cook sausage and/or ground beef and garlic until meat is brown. Drain off fat. Set aside.

2. In a 1½-quart slow cooker combine undrained tomatoes, tomato sauce, sweet pepper, tapioca, and, if desired, crushed red pepper. Stir in meat mixture.

3. Cover and cook on low-heat setting for 8 to 9 hours or on high-heat setting for 4 to 4½ hours. If no heat setting is available, cook for 7 to 8 hours.

4. Serve meat sauce over hot cooked pasta. If desired, sprinkle with Parmesan cheese.

Nutrition Facts per serving: 525 cal., 27 g total fat (10 g sat. fat), 65 mg chol., 1,550 mg sodium, 50 g carbo., 3 g fiber, 20 g pro.

Some good crusty bread and a selection of your favorite mustards are perfect sides for this robust, German-style meal.

Potato, Kraut, and Sausage Supper

MAKES 2 SERVINGS

Prep: 20 minutes
Cook: Low 5 to 6 hours,
High 2½ to 3 hours,
plus 30 minutes (high)

12	ounces cooked smoked Polish sausage, cut into 2-inch pieces
1½	cups refrigerated diced potatoes with onions
1	small green sweet pepper, chopped (½ cup)
1	medium carrot, chopped (½ cup)
⅓	cup apple juice or apple cider
2	teaspoons cider vinegar
¼	teaspoon caraway seeds
⅛	teaspoon salt
⅛	teaspoon black pepper
1	cup sauerkraut, drained
1	tablespoon snipped fresh parsley

1. In a 1½- or 2-quart slow cooker combine sausage, potatoes, sweet pepper, carrot, apple juice, vinegar, caraway seeds, salt, and black pepper.

2. Cover and cook on low-heat setting for 5 to 6 hours or on high-heat setting for 2½ to 3 hours. If no heat setting is available, cook for 3 to 3½ hours.

3. If using low-heat setting, turn to high-heat setting (or if no heat setting is available, continue cooking). Stir in sauerkraut. Cover and cook for 30 minutes more.

4. To serve, transfer sausage mixture to a serving dish. Sprinkle with parsley.

Nutrition Facts per serving: 641 cal., 41 g total fat (15 g sat. fat), 119 mg chol., 2,768 mg sodium, 41 g carbo., 7 g fiber, 27 g pro.

Curry is an Indian or Far Eastern dish that features foods seasoned with curry powder—a blend of up to 20 ground spices, herbs, and seeds.

Vegetable Curry

MAKES 2 OR 3 SERVINGS

Prep: 20 minutes
Cook: Low 7 to 9 hours,
High 3½ to 4½ hours
Stand: 5 minutes

1	15-ounce can garbanzo beans (chickpeas), rinsed and drained
¾	cup sliced carrot
¾	cup cubed red or round white potato
4	ounces fresh green beans, trimmed and cut into 1-inch pieces
1	small onion, coarsely chopped (⅓ cup)
1	tablespoon quick-cooking tapioca
1	teaspoon curry powder
½	teaspoon ground coriander
¼	teaspoon salt
⅛	to ¼ teaspoon crushed red pepper
⅛	teaspoon ground cinnamon
2	cloves garlic, minced
¾	cup vegetable broth
1	medium tomato, chopped (½ cup)
1	cup hot cooked white or brown rice

1. In a 1½- or 2-quart slow cooker combine drained garbanzo beans, carrot, potato, green beans, onion, tapioca, curry powder, coriander, salt, crushed red pepper, cinnamon, and garlic. Pour broth over mixture in cooker.

2. Cover and cook on low-heat setting for 7 to 9 hours or on high-heat setting for 3½ to 4½ hours. If no heat setting is available, cook for 5 to 5½ hours.

3. Stir in tomato. Let stand, covered, for 5 minutes. Serve vegetable mixture with hot cooked rice.

Nutrition Facts per serving: 487 cal., 3 g total fat (0 g sat. fat), 0 mg chol., 1,324 mg sodium, 100 g carbo., 16 g fiber, 18 g pro.

For a little crunch, sprinkle crumbled tortilla chips on top of each serving of these creamy beans.

Cheesy Green Chiles and Beans

❧

MAKES 2 OR 3 SERVINGS

Prep: 15 minutes
Cook: Low 6 to 8 hours,
High 3 to 4 hours

1	15-ounce can pinto beans, rinsed and drained
1	14.5-ounce can diced tomatoes, undrained
½	cup bottled salsa
1	4-ounce can diced green chile peppers, undrained
½	teaspoon ground cumin
½	teaspoon dried oregano, crushed
1	3-ounce package cream cheese, cubed
1	cup hot cooked rice
¼	cup shredded Colby Jack cheese

1. In a 1½- or 2-quart slow cooker stir together drained beans, undrained tomatoes, salsa, undrained chile peppers, cumin, and oregano.

2. Cover and cook on low-heat setting for 6 to 8 hours or on high-heat setting for 3 to 4 hours. If no heat setting is available, cook for 5½ to 6 hours. Add cream cheese, stirring until melted.

3. Serve bean mixture over hot cooked rice. Sprinkle with cheese.

Nutrition Facts per serving: 554 cal., 21 g total fat (13 g sat. fat), 59 mg chol., 1,865 mg sodium, 71 g carbo., 16 g fiber, 22 g pro.

To ease preparations at the end of the day, cut up the zucchini in the morning. In the evening just add to the potatoes and carrots that have been cooking all day.

Potatoes and Tofu over Brown Rice

❧

MAKES 2 OR 3 SERVINGS

Prep: 25 minutes
Cook: Low 8 to 10 hours,
High 4 to 5 hours,
plus 30 minutes (high)

1   cup chopped red potato

2   medium carrots, cut into
     ¼-inch-thick slices (1 cup)

⅔   cup vegetable broth

1   small red onion, cut into
     thin wedges

1   tablespoon quick-cooking
     tapioca

1   teaspoon curry powder

½   teaspoon grated fresh
     ginger

¼   teaspoon salt

6   ounces extra-firm tofu
     (fresh bean curd), drained
     and cut into ¾-inch pieces

1   small zucchini, halved
     lengthwise and sliced
     ¼ inch thick (1 cup)

½   cup frozen peas

2   tablespoons golden raisins

1   to 1½ cups hot cooked
     brown rice

     Bottled chutney (optional)

1. In a 1½-quart slow cooker combine potato, carrot, broth, red onion, tapioca, curry powder, ginger, and salt; stir well to distribute tapioca.

2. Cover and cook on low-heat setting for 8 to 10 hours or on high-heat setting for 4 to 5 hours. If no heat setting is available, cook for 7½ to 8 hours.

3. If using low-heat setting, turn to high-heat setting (or if no heat setting is available, continue cooking). Gently stir in tofu, zucchini, frozen peas, and raisins. Cover and cook for 30 minutes more.

4. Serve vegetable mixture over hot cooked brown rice. If desired, serve with chutney.

Nutrition Facts per serving: 351 cal., 3 g total fat (1 g sat. fat), 0 mg chol., 759 mg sodium, 68 g carbo., 9 g fiber, 14 g pro.

This signature dish of Cuba and the Caribbean has soared in popularity stateside. It's just spicy enough to satisfy the timid palate, is low in fat, and is extra easy to prepare in the slow cooker.

Black Beans and Rice

MAKES 2 SERVINGS

Prep: 20 minutes
Stand: 1 hour
Cook: High 4 to 5 hours, plus 15 minutes (high)

¾	cup dried black beans
1¾	cups water
3	medium onions, chopped (1½ cups)
⅓	cup chopped red or yellow sweet pepper
1	small fresh jalapeño chile pepper, seeded and finely chopped (see tip, page 10)
1	teaspoon salt
1	teaspoon ground cumin
¼	teaspoon black pepper
3	cloves garlic, minced
1	bay leaf
1	cup uncooked instant brown rice
	Chopped tomato, snipped fresh cilantro, jalapeño chile pepper slices, and/or lime wedges (optional)

1. Rinse beans. In a medium saucepan combine beans and enough water to cover beans by 2 inches. Bring to boiling; reduce heat. Simmer, uncovered, for 10 minutes. Remove from heat. Cover and let stand for 1 hour. Drain and rinse beans. Transfer beans to a 1½- or 2-quart slow cooker.

2. Stir in the 1¾ cups water, the onion, sweet pepper, the finely chopped jalapeño pepper, the salt, cumin, black pepper, garlic, and bay leaf.

3. Cover and cook on high-heat setting (do not use low-heat setting) for 4 to 5 hours. If no heat setting is available, cook for 7½ to 8 hours. Remove bay leaf.

4. Stir in brown rice. Cover and cook for 15 to 30 minutes more or until rice is tender and liquid is absorbed.

5. If desired, serve with tomato, cilantro, jalapeño pepper slices, and/or lime wedges.

Nutrition Facts per serving: 648 cal., 3 g total fat (0 g sat. fat), 0 mg chol., 1,222 mg sodium, 131 g carbo., 18 g fiber, 25 g pro.

Coconut milk made from pressed coconuts is available in specialty stores and many supermarkets. (Photo on page 133.)

Thai-Style Vegetable Rice

MAKES 2 SERVINGS

Prep: 20 minutes
Cook: Low 4½ to 5 hours,
High 2 to 2½ hours,
plus 10 minutes (high)

1¼	cups chicken broth
1	cup frozen shelled sweet soybeans (edamame)
1	small sweet potato, peeled and cut into 1-inch pieces (1 cup)
1	medium carrot, thinly sliced (½ cup)
½	teaspoon curry powder
¼	teaspoon ground cumin
⅛	teaspoon ground ginger
1	clove garlic, minced
1	cup uncooked instant brown rice
¼	cup unsweetened coconut milk
1	tablespoon snipped fresh cilantro
2	tablespoons chopped cashews

1. In a 1½-quart slow cooker combine broth, frozen soybeans, sweet potato, carrot, curry powder, cumin, ginger, and garlic.

2. Cover and cook on low-heat setting for 4½ to 5 hours or on high-heat setting for 2 to 2½ hours. If no heat setting is available, cook for 4 to 4½ hours.

3. If using low-heat setting, turn to high-heat setting (or if no heat setting is available, continue cooking). Stir in brown rice. Cover and cook for 10 to 15 minutes more or until rice is tender and most of the liquid is absorbed. Stir in coconut milk and cilantro.

4. Sprinkle individual servings with cashews.

Nutrition Facts per serving: 402 cal., 15 g total fat (7 g sat. fat), 2 mg chol., 674 mg sodium, 55 g carbo., 12 g fiber, 15 g pro.

Spoon the satisfying mixture into warm flour tortillas if you like. Top with salsa and roll up tortillas. Or spoon it into hollowed tomatoes for a quick and easy salad.

Vegetable-Barley Medley

MAKES 2 SERVINGS

Prep: 20 minutes
Cook: Low 7 to 8 hours,
High 3½ to 4 hours,
plus 30 minutes (high)

1	15-ounce can black beans, rinsed and drained
½	cup regular barley
½	cup frozen whole kernel corn
1	medium onion, chopped (½ cup)
⅓	cup chopped green sweet pepper
¼	cup thinly sliced carrot
½	teaspoon dried basil, crushed, or ¼ teaspoon dried oregano, crushed
¼	teaspoon salt
⅛	teaspoon black pepper
1	clove garlic, minced
¾	cup vegetable broth
1	small zucchini, halved lengthwise and thinly sliced (1 cup)
1	medium tomato, coarsely chopped (½ cup)
2	teaspoons lemon juice

1. In a 1½- or 2-quart slow cooker combine drained beans, barley, frozen corn, onion, sweet pepper, carrot, basil, salt, black pepper, and garlic. Stir in broth.

2. Cover and cook on low-heat setting for 7 to 8 hours or on high-heat setting for 3½ to 4 hours. If no heat setting is available, cook for 6½ to 7 hours.

3. If using low-heat setting, turn to high-heat setting (or if no heat setting is available, continue cooking). Stir in zucchini, tomato, and lemon juice. Cover and cook for 30 minutes more.

Nutrition Facts per serving: 394 cal., 1 g total fat (0 g sat. fat), 0 mg chol., 1,476 mg sodium, 91 g carbo., 22 g fiber, 19 g pro.

Peeling the eggplant is strictly a personal choice—
it's just fine to leave the peel on.

Ratatouille with Toasted Pita Chips

MAKES 2 SERVINGS

Prep: 20 minutes
Cook: Low 4½ to 5 hours,
High 2 to 2½ hours

¼	of a medium eggplant, peeled if desired and cubed (1½ cups)
½	cup coarsely chopped yellow summer squash or zucchini
1	medium tomato, coarsely chopped (½ cup)
½	of an 8-ounce can (½ cup) tomato sauce
⅓	cup coarsely chopped red or green sweet pepper
¼	cup finely chopped onion
¼	teaspoon salt
⅛	teaspoon black pepper
1	clove garlic, minced
1	large pita bread round
1	teaspoon olive oil
3	tablespoons finely shredded Parmesan cheese
¼	teaspoon dried thyme, crushed
1	tablespoon snipped fresh basil

1. In a 1½-quart slow cooker combine eggplant, squash, tomato, tomato sauce, sweet pepper, onion, salt, black pepper, and garlic.

2. Cover and cook on low-heat setting for 4½ to 5 hours or on high-heat setting for 2 to 2½ hours. If no heat setting is available, cook for 4 to 4½ hours.

3. Meanwhile, for pita chips, preheat oven to 350°F. Cut pita round in half horizontally; cut each circle into 6 wedges. Place wedges in a single layer on a baking sheet. Brush with oil. Sprinkle with 1 tablespoon of the cheese and the thyme. Bake for 12 to 15 minutes or until chips are crisp and golden.

4. Before serving, stir basil into ratatouille. Serve in shallow bowls with baked pita chips. Sprinkle with the remaining 2 tablespoons cheese.

Nutrition Facts per serving: 192 cal., 5 g total fat (2 g sat. fat), 5 mg chol., 882 mg sodium, 30 g carbo., 5 g fiber, 9 g pro.

Fix-and-Forget Meals for 4 to 6

The tender chicken in this distinctive, tangy soup contrasts well with the crisp tortilla strips. The flavors offer a hint of Latino cooking.

Mexican Chicken-Lime Soup

MAKES 6 SERVINGS

Prep: 20 minutes
Cook: Low 5 to 6 hours, High 2½ to 3 hours

1	14.5-ounce can diced tomatoes, undrained
1	medium green sweet pepper, chopped (¾ cup)
1	medium onion, chopped (½ cup)
1	teaspoon finely shredded lime peel
3	tablespoons lime juice
1	tablespoon snipped fresh oregano or 1 teaspoon dried oregano, crushed
2	cloves garlic, minced
3	14-ounce cans chicken broth
1¼	to 1½ pounds skinless, boneless chicken breast halves
6	6-inch corn tortillas (optional)
	Nonstick cooking spray (optional)
	Thin lime slices (optional)

1. In a 3½- to 5-quart slow cooker combine undrained tomatoes, sweet pepper, onion, lime peel, lime juice, dried oregano (if using), and garlic. Add broth. Stir chicken into mixture in cooker.

2. Cover and cook on low-heat setting for 5 to 6 hours or on high-heat setting for 2½ to 3 hours.

3. Using a slotted spoon, transfer chicken to a cutting board. Shred chicken by pulling two forks through it in opposite directions. Return chicken to cooker; stir to combine with cooking liquid. Stir in fresh oregano (if using).

4. Meanwhile, if desired, preheat oven to 350°F. Cut tortillas in half. Cut crosswise into ½-inch-wide strips. Lightly coat tortilla strips with nonstick cooking spray. Arrange strips in a single layer on a baking sheet. Bake about 10 minutes or until lightly browned and crisp.

5. To serve, divide chicken mixture among soup bowls. If desired, top with tortilla strips and garnish with lime slices.

Nutrition Facts per serving: 150 cal., 2 g total fat (0 g sat. fat), 57 mg chol., 959 mg sodium, 8 g carbo., 1 g fiber, 23 g pro.

It's the coconut milk and curry powder that give this splendid soup exotic flair. Top with chopped peanuts and toasted coconut and serve it with wedges of pita bread—perfect for mopping up the last few drops.

Creamy Curry Soup

MAKES 6 SERVINGS

Prep: 20 minutes
Cook: Low 4 to 5 hours,
High 2 to 2½ hours,
plus 15 minutes (low)

1	10.75-ounce can condensed cream of chicken or cream of celery soup
1	cup water
2	teaspoons curry powder
1¼	pounds skinless, boneless chicken thighs or breasts, cut into ¾-inch pieces
2	large carrots, sliced (2 cups)
1	14-ounce can unsweetened coconut milk
1	medium red sweet pepper, cut into thin bite-size strips
½	cup sliced green onion (4)
	Chopped peanuts (optional)
	Toasted coconut (optional) (see tip, page 29)

1. In a 3½- to 4½-quart slow cooker combine soup and water. Stir in curry powder. Stir in chicken and carrot.

2. Cover and cook on low-heat setting for 4 to 5 hours or on high-heat setting for 2 to 2½ hours.

3. If using high-heat setting, turn to low-heat setting. Stir in coconut milk, sweet pepper, and green onion. Cover and cook for 15 minutes more.

4. If desired, sprinkle individual servings with peanuts and/or toasted coconut.

Nutrition Facts per serving: 309 cal., 19 g total fat (12 g sat. fat), 80 mg chol., 479 mg sodium, 13 g carbo., 2 g fiber, 22 g pro.

This new spin on chicken noodle soup boasts the popular flavors of Asian cuisine: rice vinegar, soy sauce, and grated fresh ginger. Look for rice vermicelli noodles in the ethnic foods aisle of the supermarket.

Soy-Ginger Soup with Chicken

MAKES 5 SERVINGS

Prep: 20 minutes
Cook: Low 4 to 6 hours,
High 2 to 3 hours,
plus 10 minutes (high)

1	pound skinless, boneless chicken thighs, cut into 1-inch pieces
1	tablespoon cooking oil
3	14-ounce cans reduced-sodium chicken broth
2	medium carrots, cut into thin bite-size strips
1	cup water
2	tablespoons rice vinegar
1	tablespoon reduced-sodium soy sauce
2	to 3 teaspoons grated fresh ginger or ½ to ¾ teaspoon ground ginger
¼	teaspoon black pepper
2	ounces dried rice vermicelli noodles* or medium noodles
1	6-ounce package frozen pea pods, thawed and, if desired, halved diagonally
	Reduced-sodium soy sauce (optional)

1. In a large skillet cook chicken, half at a time, in hot oil over medium heat until brown. Drain off fat. Transfer chicken to a 3½- or 4-quart slow cooker. Stir in broth, carrot, water, rice vinegar, the 1 tablespoon soy sauce, the ginger, and pepper.

2. Cover and cook on low-heat setting for 4 to 6 hours or on high-heat setting for 2 to 3 hours.

3. If using low-heat setting, turn to high-heat setting. Stir in noodles and pea pods. Cover and cook for 10 to 15 minutes more or until noodles are tender. If desired, pass additional soy sauce.

Nutrition Facts per serving: 221 cal., 6 g total fat (1 g sat. fat), 72 mg chol., 805 mg sodium, 16 g carbo., 2 g fiber, 23 g pro.

*Note: For easier eating, cut or break the uncooked rice vermicelli noodles into 2-inch pieces.

For a weeknight supper or weekend party, try a fresh new twist on chicken and rice. This saffron-flavored dish is sure to get rave reviews.

Chicken-Saffron Rice Soup

MAKES 4 TO 6 SERVINGS

Prep: 15 minutes
Cook: Low 4 to 5 hours,
High 2 to 2½ hours,
plus 15 minutes (high)

1   pound skinless, boneless chicken breast halves, cut into 1-inch pieces

1   14.5-ounce can diced tomatoes, undrained

1   14-ounce can reduced-sodium chicken broth

1   14-ounce can artichoke hearts, drained and quartered

1   medium onion, chopped (½ cup)

½   cup bottled roasted red sweet peppers, drained and cut into strips

1   clove garlic, minced

½   cup frozen peas

1   5-ounce package saffron-flavored yellow rice mix

2   tablespoons slivered almonds, toasted (see tip, page 29)

1. Place chicken in a 3½- or 4-quart slow cooker. Stir in undrained tomatoes, broth, artichokes, onion, roasted red pepper, and garlic.

2. Cover and cook on low-heat setting for 4 to 5 hours or on high-heat setting for 2 to 2½ hours. If using low-heat setting, turn to high-heat setting. Stir in frozen peas. Cover and cook for 15 minutes more.

3. Meanwhile, prepare rice mix according to package directions.

4. To serve, divide chicken mixture among soup bowls. Mound the cooked rice in the center of each bowl. Sprinkle with almonds.

Nutrition Facts per serving: 415 cal., 10 g total fat (1 g sat. fat), 66 mg chol., 1,315 mg sodium, 44 g carbo., 9 g fiber, 35 g pro.

Loaded with tender, chunky chicken and potatoes, this stew takes a Mediterranean turn with the addition of tomatoes and olives. Can you taste the sun?

Spanish Chicken Stew

MAKES 4 SERVINGS

Prep: 20 minutes
Cook: Low 10 to 11 hours,
High 5 to 5½ hours,
plus 15 minutes (high)

1¼	pounds skinless, boneless chicken thighs, cut into 1½-inch pieces
1	14.5-ounce can diced tomatoes, undrained
12	ounces red potatoes, cut into ½-inch-thick wedges
1	cup chicken broth
1	medium red sweet pepper, cut into thin strips
1	medium onion, thinly sliced (½ cup)
½	teaspoon dried thyme, crushed
¼	teaspoon salt
¼	teaspoon black pepper
2	cloves garlic, minced
⅓	cup pimiento-stuffed green olives, cut up

1. In a 3½- or 4-quart slow cooker combine chicken, undrained tomatoes, potato, broth, sweet pepper, onion, thyme, salt, black pepper, and garlic.

2. Cover and cook on low-heat setting for 10 to 11 hours or on high-heat setting for 5 to 5½ hours.

3. If using low-heat setting, turn to high-heat setting. Stir in olives. Cover and cook for 15 minutes more.

Nutrition Facts per serving: 286 cal., 31 g total fat (2 g sat. fat), 118 mg chol., 856 mg sodium, 24 g carbo., 4 g fiber, 31 g pro.

Test Kitchen Tip: Potatoes with a firm, waxy texture, such as the red ones in Spanish Chicken Stew, are best for slow-cooked meals because they hold their shape well during long hours of cooking. Some varieties, such as russets, fall apart into mushy pieces. Other potato varieties that work well in the slow cooker are yellow, round white, and tiny new potatoes.

Never mind traditional pairings. Beef soup mix and red wine combine with chicken thighs for a succulent stew that's oh-so-satisfying on a cold night.

Coq au Vin Stew

MAKES 4 SERVINGS

Prep: 20 minutes
Cook: Low 5 to 6 hours,
High 2½ to 3 hours

Nonstick cooking spray
3 pounds chicken thighs, skinned
1 envelope (½ of a 2.2-ounce package) beef soup mix
2 cups fresh button or wild mushrooms, quartered
1½ cups frozen small whole onions
½ cup dry red wine

1. Lightly coat a large skillet with nonstick cooking spray; heat skillet over medium heat. Cook chicken, several pieces at a time, on all sides in hot skillet until brown. Drain off fat. Transfer chicken to a 3½- or 4-quart slow cooker.

2. Sprinkle chicken with soup mix. Add mushrooms and frozen onions. Pour wine over mixture in cooker.

3. Cover and cook on low-heat setting for 5 to 6 hours or on high-heat setting for 2½ to 3 hours.

Nutrition Facts per serving: 305 cal., 8 g total fat (2 g sat. fat), 161 mg chol., 759 mg sodium, 12 g carbo., 2 g fiber, 41 g pro.

This nutrient-packed soup couldn't be easier. A 12-ounce package of edamame, which are immature green soybeans, punches up the fiber, protein, vitamins, and minerals in this chicken chowder.

Chicken Edamame Chowder

MAKES 6 SERVINGS

Prep: 20 minutes
Cook: Low 7 to 8 hours,
High 3½ to 4 hours,
plus 20 minutes (high)

1   pound skinless, boneless chicken breast halves

1   tablespoon cooking oil

1   12-ounce package frozen shelled sweet soybeans (edamame)

1   large green sweet pepper, coarsely chopped

1   large onion, chopped (1 cup)

2   fresh jalapeño chile peppers, seeded and finely chopped (see tip, page 10)

2   teaspoons ground cumin

2   teaspoons ground coriander

2   14-ounce cans chicken broth

1   8-ounce carton dairy sour cream

3   tablespoons all-purpose flour

2   medium zucchini, halved lengthwise and thinly sliced (2½ cups)

    Shredded Monterey Jack cheese (optional)

1. Cut chicken into 1-inch pieces. In a large skillet cook chicken in hot oil over medium-high heat until brown. Drain off fat. Transfer chicken to a 3½- or 4-quart slow cooker. Stir in frozen soybeans, sweet pepper, onion, jalapeño pepper, cumin, coriander, ½ teaspoon salt, and ¼ teaspoon black pepper. Pour broth over mixture in cooker; stir to combine.

2. Cover and cook on low-heat setting for 7 to 8 hours or on high-heat setting for 3½ to 4 hours.

3. If using low-heat setting, turn to high-heat setting. In a small bowl combine sour cream and flour; stir into chicken mixture in cooker. Stir in zucchini.

4. Cover and cook for 20 to 30 minutes more or until mixture is thickened and zucchini is crisp-tender. If desired, top individual servings with cheese.

Nutrition Facts per serving: 314 cal., 14 g total fat (6 g sat. fat), 62 mg chol., 806 mg sodium, 17 g carbo., 8 g fiber, 28 g pro.

Using prepared items such as frozen potatoes, canned corn, and canned soup saves on the prep time for this recipe.

Sausage-Corn Chowder

MAKES 6 SERVINGS

Prep: 15 minutes
Cook: Low 8 to 10 hours,
High 4 to 5 hours

12	ounces cooked smoked turkey sausage, halved lengthwise and cut into ½-inch pieces
3	cups frozen diced hash brown potatoes with onions and peppers
2	medium carrots, coarsely chopped (1 cup)
2½	cups water
1	14.75-ounce can no-salt-added cream-style corn
1	10.75-ounce can condensed golden mushroom soup
½	cup bottled roasted red sweet peppers, drained and cut into strips
1	teaspoon dried thyme, crushed

1. In a 3½- to 5-quart slow cooker combine sausage, frozen potatoes, and carrot. In a large bowl combine water, corn, soup, roasted red pepper, and thyme. Add to mixture in cooker; stir to combine.

2. Cover and cook on low-heat setting for 8 to 10 hours or on high-heat setting for 4 to 5 hours.

Nutrition Facts per serving: 258 cal., 7 g total fat (2 g sat. fat), 40 mg chol., 893 mg sodium, 37 g carbo., 4 g fiber, 13 g pro.

Nutritious and delicious ground turkey stands in for ground beef in this colorful, veggie-filled family pleaser.

Hearty Turkey-Vegetable Stew

✦

MAKES 4 OR 5 SERVINGS

Prep: 20 minutes
Cook: Low 5 to 6 hours,
High 2½ to 3 hours

1	pound uncooked ground turkey or chicken
2	stalks celery, sliced (1 cup)
1	medium carrot, thinly sliced (½ cup)
1	medium onion, chopped (½ cup)
3	cups tomato juice
2	cups frozen French-cut green beans
2	cups sliced fresh mushrooms
1	large tomato, chopped (1 cup)
1½	teaspoons dried Italian seasoning, crushed
1½	teaspoons Worcestershire sauce
1	teaspoon garlic salt
½	teaspoon sugar
¼	teaspoon black pepper

1. In a large skillet cook ground turkey, celery, carrot, and onion until meat is brown. Drain off fat. Transfer turkey mixture to a 3½- or 4-quart slow cooker.

2. Stir in tomato juice, frozen green beans, mushrooms, tomato, Italian seasoning, Worcestershire sauce, garlic salt, sugar, and pepper.

3. Cover and cook on low-heat setting for 5 to 6 hours or on high-heat setting for 2½ to 3 hours.

Nutrition Facts per serving: 277 cal., 12 g total fat (3 g sat. fat), 93 mg chol., 1,041 mg sodium, 19 g carbo., 3 g fiber, 26 g pro.

Choose from numerous varieties of cooked smoked turkey at your supermarket deli. Also check out the selection of turkey sausage at the meat counter.

Split Pea and Smoked Turkey Soup

MAKES 4 SERVINGS

Prep: 15 minutes
Cook: Low 10 to 12 hours,
High 5 to 6 hours

2½ cups dried green split peas, rinsed and drained

2 cups chopped cooked smoked turkey or sliced cooked smoked turkey sausage

3 medium carrots, coarsely chopped (1½ cups)

1 large yellow or green sweet pepper, coarsely chopped (1 cup)

1 medium onion, chopped (½ cup)

1 teaspoon dried basil, crushed

1 teaspoon dried oregano, crushed

2 cloves garlic, minced

3 14-ounce cans chicken broth

1. In a 3½- or 4-quart slow cooker combine split peas, smoked turkey, carrot, sweet pepper, onion, basil, oregano, and garlic. Pour broth over mixture in cooker.

2. Cover and cook on low-heat setting for 10 to 12 hours or on high-heat setting for 5 to 6 hours. Stir before serving.

Nutrition Facts per serving: 551 cal., 5 g total fat (1 g sat. fat), 22 mg chol., 2,258 mg sodium, 86 g carbo., 33 g fiber, 45 g pro.

For a cozy dinner with friends, accompany this thick, rich stew
with a full-bodied red wine and crusty bread.

Provençal Beef Stew

MAKES 6 SERVINGS

Prep: 20 minutes
Cook: Low 10 to 12 hours,
High 5 to 6 hours

1½	pounds boneless beef chuck roast
8	or 9 tiny new potatoes (12 ounces)
1	pound small carrots with tops, peeled and trimmed, or one 16-ounce package peeled baby carrots
1	medium onion, cut into wedges
½	cup pitted ripe olives or kalamata olives
1	tablespoon quick-cooking tapioca
1	cup beef broth
1	teaspoon dried herbes de Provence, crushed
¼	teaspoon salt
¼	teaspoon cracked black pepper
4	to 6 cloves garlic, minced
¼	cup dry red wine
	Snipped fresh parsley (optional)
	Capers (optional)

1. Trim fat from meat. Cut meat into 2-inch pieces; set aside. Peel a strip from the center of each potato. In a 3½- or 4-quart slow cooker combine potatoes, carrots, onion, and olives. Sprinkle with tapioca. Add meat.

2. In a small bowl combine broth, herbes de Provence, salt, pepper, and garlic. Pour over mixture in cooker.

3. Cover and cook on low-heat setting for 10 to 12 hours or on high-heat setting for 5 to 6 hours, stirring in wine during the last 30 minutes of cooking.

4. If desired, sprinkle individual servings with parsley and capers.

Nutrition Facts per serving: 232 cal., 5 g total fat (1 g sat. fat), 53 mg chol., 460 mg sodium, 22 g carbo., 3 g fiber, 21 g pro.

Tender, juicy beef takes on an Asian dimension with the addition of bottled sweet-and-sour sauce. The "sweet" in the sauce comes from sugar. Vinegar contributes the "sour."

5 Ingredient Recipe

Sweet-and-Sour Beef Stew

MAKES 6 SERVINGS

Prep: 15 minutes
Cook: Low 10 to 11 hours,
High 5 to 5½ hours

1½ pounds beef stew meat

1 16-ounce package frozen stew vegetables

2 11-ounce cans condensed beefy mushroom soup

½ cup bottled sweet-and-sour sauce

½ cup water

⅛ to ¼ teaspoon cayenne pepper

1. Trim fat from meat. Cut meat into ¾- to 1-inch pieces. Transfer meat to a 3½- or 4-quart slow cooker. Add frozen vegetables. Stir in soup, sweet-and-sour sauce, water, and cayenne pepper.

2. Cover and cook on low-heat setting for 10 to 11 hours or on high-heat setting for 5 to 5½ hours.

Nutrition Facts per serving: 291 cal., 9 g total fat (3 g sat. fat), 62 mg chol., 1,019 mg sodium, 19 g carbo., 2 g fiber, 30 g pro.

Gremolata is a fragrant garnish made with fresh parsley, lemon peel, and minced garlic. It typically tops osso buco, a classic Italian veal shank dish. (Photo on page 258.)

Mediterranean Beef Ragoût

MAKES 6 SERVINGS

Prep: 25 minutes
Cook: Low 7 to 9 hours,
High 3½ to 4½ hours,
plus 30 minutes (high)

1½	pounds beef stew meat
1	tablespoon olive oil
3	medium carrots, cut into ½-inch pieces
2	medium onions, cut into wedges
1	14.5-ounce can diced tomatoes, undrained
1¼	cups beef broth
1½	teaspoons dried thyme, crushed
¼	teaspoon salt
¼	teaspoon black pepper
2	cloves garlic, minced
6	ounces fresh green beans, trimmed and cut into 2-inch pieces (1¾ cups)
1	medium zucchini, halved lengthwise and sliced (1¼ cups)
	Hot cooked couscous or brown rice (optional)
1	recipe Gremolata

1. Trim fat from meat. Cut meat into 1-inch pieces. In a large skillet brown meat, half at a time, in hot oil over medium heat. Drain off fat. Transfer meat to a 3½- or 4-quart slow cooker. Add carrot and onion.

2. In a medium bowl combine undrained tomatoes, broth, thyme, salt, pepper, and garlic. Pour over mixture in cooker.

3. Cover and cook on low-heat setting for 7 to 9 hours or on high-heat setting for 3½ to 4½ hours.

4. If using low-heat setting, turn to high-heat setting. Stir in green beans and zucchini. Cover and cook for 30 minutes more.

5. If desired, serve meat mixture with hot cooked couscous. Top with Gremolata.

Gremolata: In a small bowl combine ¼ cup snipped fresh parsley, 1 tablespoon finely shredded lemon peel, and 2 cloves garlic, minced.

Nutrition Facts per serving: 263 cal., 11 g total fat (3 g sat. fat), 55 mg chol., 516 mg sodium, 14 g carbo., 4 g fiber, 28 g pro.

If you like Southwestern fare, you'll love this plucky stew seasoned with canned chipotle chile peppers packed in tomatoey adobo sauce. Chipotle chiles are smoked jalapeño chiles.

New Mexico Beef Stew

MAKES 6 SERVINGS

Prep: 30 minutes
Cook: Low 8 to 10 hours,
High 4 to 5 hours

1½	pounds boneless beef chuck roast
2	cups fresh corn kernels or one 10-ounce package frozen whole kernel corn, thawed
2	cups chopped peeled celery root or 2 stalks celery, sliced (1 cup)
1	15-ounce can garbanzo beans (chickpeas), rinsed and drained
1	large onion, chopped (1 cup)
2	to 3 canned chipotle peppers in adobo sauce, chopped (see tip, page 10)
3	cloves garlic, minced
1	teaspoon salt
½	teaspoon dried thyme, crushed
½	teaspoon black pepper
1	28-ounce can diced tomatoes, undrained

1. Trim fat from meat. Cut meat into ¾-inch pieces. Set aside.

2. In a 4- to 5½-quart slow cooker combine corn, celery root, drained garbanzo beans, onion, chipotle pepper, and garlic. Add meat. Sprinkle meat with salt, thyme, and black pepper. Pour undrained tomatoes over mixture in cooker.

3. Cover and cook on low-heat setting for 8 to 10 hours or on high-heat setting for 4 to 5 hours. Stir before serving.

Nutrition Facts per serving: 471 cal., 21 g total fat (6 g sat. fat), 73 mg chol., 962 mg sodium, 42 g carbo., 8 g fiber, 30 g pro.

Only five ingredients—frozen meatballs, stewed tomatoes, white beans, basil pesto, and Parmesan cheese—make up this wholesome, filling, and appealing stew. Round out the meal with thick slices of Italian bread.

Pesto Meatball Stew

MAKES 6 SERVINGS

Prep: 10 minutes
Cook: Low 5 to 7 hours,
High 2½ to 3½ hours

1   16-ounce package (32) frozen cooked Italian-style meatballs, thawed

2   14.5-ounce cans Italian-style stewed tomatoes, undrained

1   15- or 19-ounce can cannellini beans (white kidney beans), rinsed and drained

½   cup water

¼   cup refrigerated basil pesto

½   cup finely shredded Parmesan cheese

1. In a 3½- or 4-quart slow cooker combine meatballs, undrained tomatoes, drained beans, water, and pesto.

2. Cover and cook on low-heat setting for 5 to 7 hours or on high-heat setting for 2½ to 3½ hours.

3. Sprinkle individual servings with Parmesan cheese.

Nutrition Facts per serving: 408 cal., 27 g total fat (10 g sat. fat), 34 mg chol., 1,201 mg sodium, 24 g carbo., 6 g fiber, 17 g pro.

With this easy chowder, you can enjoy corned beef and cabbage any time you're in the mood for an Irish classic—not just on Saint Patrick's Day. Pair it with a cold mug of stout beer.

St. Paddy's Day Chowder

MAKES 6 SERVINGS

Prep: 20 minutes
Cook: Low 10 to 11 hours,
High 5 to 5½ hours
Stand: 5 minutes

2   cups water
1   10.75-ounce can reduced-fat and reduced-sodium cream of celery soup
2½ to 3 pounds corned beef round or brisket
2   large red or yellow potatoes, cut into 1-inch pieces
2   medium carrots, cut into ½-inch pieces
2   cups packaged shredded cabbage with carrot (coleslaw mix)
½   cup dairy sour cream
2   tablespoons Dijon-style mustard

1. In a 4- to 5-quart slow cooker combine water and soup; set aside.

2. Discard spice packet from meat, if present, or save for another use. Trim fat from the outside of meat; cut meat into ¾-inch pieces. Add meat, potato, and carrot to cooker.

3. Cover and cook on low-heat setting for 10 to 11 hours or on high-heat setting for 5 to 5½ hours. Turn off cooker. Stir in cabbage. Let stand, covered, for 5 minutes.

4. In a small bowl combine sour cream and mustard. Top individual servings with sour cream mixture.

Nutrition Facts per serving: 461 cal., 27 g total fat (9 g sat. fat), 104 mg chol., 1,596 mg sodium, 22 g carbo., 2 g fiber, 32 g pro.

Barley is great for a slow-cooker stew because it retains its shape and chewy texture during the long cooking. Use regular rather than quick-cooking barley for this mouthwatering dish.

Lamb and Barley Stew with Mint

❧

MAKES 4 TO 6 SERVINGS

Prep: 20 minutes
Cook: Low 8 to 10 hours,
High 4 to 5 hours

1½	pounds lamb stew meat
2½	cups reduced-sodium chicken broth
1	14.5-ounce can diced tomatoes, undrained
½	cup regular barley
1	medium onion, chopped (½ cup)
¼	cup dry white wine (optional)
2	tablespoons snipped fresh dill or 1½ teaspoons dried dill
½	teaspoon salt
¼	teaspoon black pepper
4	cloves garlic, minced
½	cup bottled roasted red sweet peppers, drained and thinly sliced
¼	cup snipped fresh mint

1. Trim fat from meat. Cut meat into 1-inch pieces. Place meat in a 3½- or 4-quart slow cooker. Stir in broth, undrained tomatoes, barley, onion, wine (if desired), dried dill (if using), salt, black pepper, and garlic.

2. Cover and cook on low-heat setting for 8 to 10 hours or on high-heat setting for 4 to 5 hours.

3. Stir in fresh dill (if using), roasted red pepper, and mint.

Nutrition Facts per serving: 337 cal., 6 g total fat (2 g sat. fat), 107 mg chol., 956 mg sodium, 28 g carbo., 6 g fiber, 41 g pro.

Cinnamon, garlic, chili powder, oregano, and fresh cilantro blend delightfully in this hearty meal. Look for poblano peppers in the supermarket produce section or at farmers' markets. They have a long, irregular sweet-pepper shape.

Pork, Potato, and Chile Stew

MAKES 6 SERVINGS

Prep: 30 minutes
Cook: Low 8 to 10 hours,
High 4 to 5 hours

1½	pounds boneless pork shoulder roast
1	tablespoon cooking oil
10	to 12 tiny new potatoes (1 pound), quartered
1	large onion, chopped (1 cup)
2	fresh poblano chile peppers, seeded and cut into 1-inch pieces (see tip, page 10)
1	fresh jalapeño chile pepper, seeded and finely chopped (see tip, page 10)
4	cloves garlic, minced
2	inches stick cinnamon
3	cups chicken broth
1	14.5-ounce can diced tomatoes, undrained
1	tablespoon chili powder
1	teaspoon dried oregano, crushed
¼	teaspoon black pepper
¼	cup snipped fresh cilantro or parsley
	Dairy sour cream (optional)

1. Trim fat from meat. Cut meat into 1-inch pieces. In a large skillet brown meat in hot oil over medium-high heat. Drain off fat. Set meat aside.

2. In a 3½- or 4-quart slow cooker combine potato, onion, poblano pepper, jalapeño pepper, garlic, and cinnamon. Add meat. Stir in broth, undrained tomatoes, chili powder, oregano, and black pepper.

3. Cover and cook on low-heat setting for 8 to 10 hours or on high-heat setting for 4 to 5 hours. Remove cinnamon.

4. Before serving, stir in cilantro. If desired, top individual servings with sour cream.

Nutrition Facts per serving: 290 cal., 10 g total fat (3 g sat. fat), 75 mg chol., 731 mg sodium, 24 g carbo., 4 g fiber, 26 g pro.

If you haven't thought of using parsnips, it's time to give this sweet, aromatic root vegetable a try. Buy small to medium parsnips that are firm with fairly smooth skin and few rootlets.

Harvest Stew

MAKES 4 SERVINGS

Prep: 25 minutes
Cook: Low 7 to 8 hours,
High 3½ to 4 hours

1	pound boneless pork shoulder roast
2	medium sweet potatoes, peeled and cut into ½-inch pieces
2	medium parsnips, peeled and cut into ½-inch pieces
2	small apples, cored and sliced ¼ inch thick
1	medium onion, chopped (½ cup)
¾	teaspoon dried thyme, crushed
½	teaspoon salt
½	teaspoon dried rosemary, crushed
¼	teaspoon black pepper
1	cup chicken broth or beef broth
1	cup apple cider or apple juice

1. Trim fat from meat. Cut meat into 1-inch pieces; set aside.

2. In a 3½- or 4-quart slow cooker combine sweet potato, parsnip, apple, and onion. Add meat. Sprinkle with thyme, salt, rosemary, and pepper. Pour broth and apple cider over mixture in cooker.

3. Cover and cook on low-heat setting for 7 to 8 hours or on high-heat setting for 3½ to 4 hours.

Nutrition Facts per serving: 336 cal., 8 g total fat (3 g sat. fat), 76 mg chol., 660 mg sodium, 40 g carbo., 7 g fiber, 25 g pro.

The intriguing rub adds spicy flavor as well as just-right heat to this delectable stew.

Spicy Pork and Onion Stew with Beer

MAKES 6 SERVINGS

Prep: 30 minutes
Cook: Low 7 to 8 hours,
High 3½ to 4 hours

1¼ pounds lean boneless pork
1 recipe Spice Rub
   Nonstick cooking spray
1 14-ounce can beef, chicken, or vegetable broth
1 12-ounce can light beer
2 cups frozen small whole onions
1 medium sweet potato (6 to 8 ounces), peeled and cut into chunks
2 medium carrots, coarsely chopped (1 cup)
2 stalks celery, cut into ½-inch-thick slices (1 cup)
1 small turnip or rutabaga, peeled and cut into bite-size pieces
2 tablespoons packed brown sugar
1 15.5-ounce can hominy, rinsed and drained
2 tablespoons snipped fresh cilantro
4 teaspoons lemon juice

1. Trim fat from meat. Cut meat into 1-inch pieces. Place Spice Rub in a plastic bag. Add meat, a few pieces at a time, shaking to coat.

2. Lightly coat a large nonstick skillet with nonstick cooking spray; heat skillet over medium heat. Brown meat, half at a time, in hot skillet. Drain off fat. Transfer meat to a 3½- to 5-quart slow cooker. Stir in broth, beer, frozen onions, sweet potato, carrot, celery, turnip, and brown sugar.

3. Cover and cook on low-heat setting for 7 to 8 hours or on high-heat setting for 3½ to 4 hours. Stir in hominy, cilantro, and lemon juice.

Spice Rub: In a small bowl combine 1 teaspoon ground cumin; ¾ teaspoon salt; ¾ teaspoon dried oregano, crushed; ½ teaspoon ground ginger; ¼ teaspoon cayenne pepper; ¼ teaspoon dried thyme, crushed; ¼ teaspoon ground allspice; and 2 cloves garlic, minced.

Nutrition Facts per serving: 273 cal., 6 g total fat (2 g sat. fat), 52 mg chol., 738 mg sodium, 26 g carbo., 4 g fiber, 24 g pro.

Satay is an Indonesian specialty of spicy marinated meat that's skewered, then broiled or grilled. Bring its lively flavors home with this easy stew.

Pork Satay Stew

MAKES 6 SERVINGS

Prep: 15 minutes
Cook: Low 7 to 8 hours,
High 3½ to 4 hours

1½ pounds boneless pork shoulder roast

2 medium red and/or green sweet peppers, cut into 1-inch pieces

1 large red onion, cut into wedges

1 cup bottled thick and chunky salsa

½ cup creamy peanut butter

1 tablespoon reduced-sodium soy sauce

1 tablespoon lime juice

1½ teaspoons grated fresh ginger

½ teaspoon ground coriander

¾ cup half-and-half or light cream

3 cups hot cooked white or brown rice

⅓ cup chopped dry-roasted peanuts

¼ cup sliced green onion (2)

1. Trim fat from meat. Cut meat into 1-inch pieces. In a 3½-quart slow cooker combine meat, sweet pepper, red onion, salsa, peanut butter, soy sauce, lime juice, ginger, and coriander.

2. Cover and cook on low-heat setting for 7 to 8 hours or on high-heat setting for 3½ to 4 hours. Stir in half-and-half.

3. Serve meat mixture over hot cooked rice. Sprinkle with peanuts and green onion.

Nutrition Facts per serving: 502 cal., 25 g total fat (7 g sat. fat), 84 mg chol., 462 mg sodium, 36 g carbo., 3 g fiber, 34 g pro.

*Two kinds of meat, pork roast and Italian sausage, make this
robust stew extra flavorful. Sop up the wine-flavored gravy
with crusty Italian bread.*

Italian Pork and Bean Stew

MAKES 6 SERVINGS

Prep: 35 minutes
Stand: 1 hour
Cook: Low 8 to 9 hours,
High 4 to 4½ hours,
plus 15 minutes (high)

2	cups dried Great Northern beans
1	pound boneless pork shoulder roast
8	ounces bulk Italian sausage
3	medium carrots, cut into ½-inch pieces
3	medium onions, coarsely chopped (1½ cups)
3	cloves garlic, minced
3	cups water
1	teaspoon instant beef bouillon granules
½	teaspoon dried thyme, crushed
½	teaspoon dried oregano, crushed
½	of a 6-ounce can (⅓ cup) tomato paste
¼	cup dry red wine
¼	cup snipped fresh parsley

1. Rinse beans. In a large saucepan combine beans and enough water to cover beans by 2 inches. Bring to boiling; reduce heat. Simmer, uncovered, for 10 minutes. Remove from heat. Cover and let stand for 1 hour. Drain and rinse beans. Transfer beans to a 4- to 5-quart slow cooker.

2. Trim fat from pork roast. Cut pork roast into ¾-inch pieces; set aside. In a large skillet cook sausage until brown. Using a slotted spoon, transfer sausage to cooker. In the same skillet cook pork pieces, half at a time, until brown. Drain off fat. Transfer pork pieces to cooker. Add carrot, onion, and garlic. Stir in the 3 cups water, the bouillon granules, thyme, and oregano.

3. Cover and cook on low-heat setting for 8 to 9 hours or on high-heat setting for 4 to 4½ hours.

4. If using low-heat setting, turn to high-heat setting. In a small bowl combine tomato paste and wine; stir into mixture in cooker. Stir in parsley. Cover and cook for 15 minutes more.

Nutrition Facts per serving: 473 cal., 13 g total fat (5 g sat. fat), 73 mg chol., 566 mg sodium, 49 g carbo., 15 g fiber, 37 g pro.

Think twice before substituting regular milk or cream for evaporated milk. They do not behave the same. Evaporated milk gives an extra creamy richness to foods and will not break down or curdle during long, slow cooking.

Swiss, Ham, and Broccoli Chowder

MAKES 6 SERVINGS

Prep: 15 minutes
Cook: Low 6 to 7 hours,
High 3 to 3½ hours,
plus 30 minutes (high)

2	10.75-ounce cans condensed cream of celery soup
1	12-ounce can evaporated milk
½	cup water
1	18- or 20-ounce package refrigerated diced potatoes or 3 cups frozen diced hash brown potatoes with onions and peppers, thawed
2	cups diced cooked ham
2	stalks celery, finely chopped (1 cup)
2	cups chopped fresh broccoli or frozen chopped broccoli, thawed
8	ounces process Swiss cheese slices, torn into small pieces

1. In a 3½- or 4-quart slow cooker combine soup, evaporated milk, and water. Stir in potatoes, ham, and celery.

2. Cover and cook on low-heat setting for 6 to 7 hours or on high-heat setting for 3 to 3½ hours.

3. If using low-heat setting, turn to high-heat setting. Stir in broccoli and cheese. Cover and cook for 30 minutes more.

Nutrition Facts per serving: 460 cal., 24 g total fat (13 g sat. fat), 78 mg chol., 2,148 mg sodium, 34 g carbo., 4 g fiber, 24 g pro.

Commonly used in Italian cuisine, the complex taste of balsamic vinegar boosts the flavor of this herbed medley of beans and vegetables.

Summertime Vegetable Stew

MAKES 4 SERVINGS

Prep: 25 minutes
Cook: Low 8 to 10 hours,
High 4 to 5 hours

1	small eggplant (8 ounces)
1	large zucchini, quartered lengthwise and cut into ½-inch pieces
1	large yellow summer squash, quartered lengthwise and cut into ½-inch pieces
1	15- or 19-ounce can cannellini beans (white kidney beans), rinsed and drained
1	large tomato, chopped (1 cup)
1	tablespoon snipped fresh basil or 1 teaspoon dried basil, crushed
¼	teaspoon dried rosemary or thyme, crushed
¼	teaspoon black pepper
4	cloves garlic, minced
1½	cups tomato juice
1	tablespoon balsamic vinegar
2	tablespoons finely shredded Romano cheese
	Seasoned croutons (optional)

1. If desired, peel eggplant. Cut eggplant into ¾-inch pieces (you should have about 3 cups). Place eggplant in a 3½- or 4-quart slow cooker.

2. Stir in zucchini, yellow squash, drained beans, tomato, dried basil (if using), rosemary, pepper, and garlic. Pour tomato juice over mixture in cooker.

3. Cover and cook on low-heat setting for 8 to 10 hours or on high-heat setting for 4 to 5 hours. Stir in fresh basil (if using) and balsamic vinegar.

4. Sprinkle individual servings with Romano cheese and, if desired, croutons.

Nutrition Facts per serving: 163 cal., 1 g total fat (1 g sat. fat), 3 mg chol., 566 mg sodium, 33 g carbo., 10 g fiber, 12 g pro.

Fire-roasted diced tomatoes give a smoky flavor to this simmered mélange of fresh vegetables and cannellini beans. Aromatic oregano adds even more depth to the stew.

Roasted Tomato and Vegetable Stew

❦

MAKES 6 SERVINGS

Prep: 20 minutes
Cook: Low 7 to 8 hours,
High 3½ to 4 hours,
plus 30 minutes (high)

3	14-ounce cans reduced-sodium chicken broth
2	cups peeled, seeded, and cut up butternut squash (about 1 pound)
1	15- or 19-ounce can cannellini beans (white kidney beans), rinsed and drained
1	14.5-ounce can fire-roasted or regular diced tomatoes, undrained
1	medium onion, chopped (½ cup)
1	stalk celery, sliced (½ cup)
1	medium carrot, chopped (½ cup)
1	tablespoon snipped fresh oregano or 1 teaspoon dried oregano, crushed
2	cloves garlic, minced
1	small zucchini, halved lengthwise and sliced (1 cup)
1	cup small broccoli and/or cauliflower florets
	Finely shredded Parmesan cheese (optional)

1. In a 3½- or 4-quart slow cooker combine broth, squash, drained beans, undrained tomatoes, onion, celery, carrot, dried oregano (if using), and garlic.

2. Cover and cook on low-heat setting for 7 to 8 hours or on high-heat setting for 3½ to 4 hours.

3. If using low-heat setting, turn to high-heat setting. Stir in zucchini, broccoli, ¼ teaspoon salt, and ¼ teaspoon pepper. Cover and cook for 30 minutes more. Stir in fresh oregano (if using).

4. If desired, sprinkle individual servings with Parmesan cheese.

Nutrition Facts per serving: 102 cal., 0 g total fat (0 g sat. fat), 0 mg chol., 852 mg sodium, 21 g carbo., 5 g fiber, 8 g pro.

This spunky corn chowder uses the "three sisters" of Native American cooking: corn, beans, and squash. You'll find this Eastern Woodlands combination appealing and flavorful.

Corn and Chile Chowder

MAKES 6 SERVINGS

Prep: 20 minutes
Cook: Low 8 to 9 hours,
High 4 to 4½ hours,
plus 30 minutes (high)

3	large red potatoes (1¼ pounds), peeled, if desired, and cut into ½-inch pieces
1½	cups frozen whole kernel corn
1	cup frozen baby lima beans
1	medium onion, chopped (½ cup)
1	small red sweet pepper, chopped (½ cup)
½	cup chopped fresh Anaheim or poblano chile pepper (see tip, page 10) or green sweet pepper
1	4-ounce can diced green chile peppers, drained
½	teaspoon salt
3	cloves garlic, minced
2	14-ounce cans vegetable broth or chicken broth
1	14.75-ounce can cream-style corn, undrained
1	small zucchini, halved lengthwise and sliced (1 cup)
1	cup whipping cream

1. In a 4- to 6-quart slow cooker combine potato, frozen corn, frozen lima beans, onion, sweet pepper, Anaheim pepper, drained green chile peppers, salt, and garlic. Pour broth over mixture in cooker.

2. Cover and cook on low-heat setting for 8 to 9 hours or on high-heat setting for 4 to 4½ hours.

3. If using low-heat setting, turn to high-heat setting. Stir in undrained cream-style corn and zucchini. Cover and cook for 30 minutes more. Stir in cream.

Nutrition Facts per serving: 383 cal., 17 g total fat (9 g sat. fat), 55 mg chol., 1,073 mg sodium, 54 g carbo., 6 g fiber, 10 g pro.

Convenience products such as canned vegetable broth, beans, and bottled garlic make preparation extra speedy and easy as can be. Fresh spinach with its slightly bitter taste adds a lively flavor to this weeknight dinner dish.

Savory Bean and Spinach Soup

MAKES 6 SERVINGS

Prep: 15 minutes
Cook: Low 5 to 7 hours,
High 2½ to 3½ hours

2	14-ounce cans vegetable broth
1	15-ounce can tomato puree
1	15-ounce can small white beans or Great Northern beans, rinsed and drained
1¾	cups water
2	small onions, finely chopped (⅔ cup)
½	cup uncooked converted rice (do not substitute long grain rice)
1½	teaspoons dried basil, crushed
¼	teaspoon black pepper
2	cloves garlic, minced
8	cups coarsely chopped fresh spinach
2	tablespoons finely shredded Parmesan cheese

1. In a 3½- or 4-quart slow cooker combine broth, tomato puree, drained beans, water, onion, converted rice, basil, pepper, and garlic.

2. Cover and cook on low-heat setting for 5 to 7 hours or on high-heat setting for 2½ to 3½ hours.

3. Before serving, stir in spinach. Sprinkle individual servings with Parmesan cheese.

Nutrition Facts per serving: 157 cal., 1 g total fat (0 g sat. fat), 1 mg chol., 724 mg sodium, 32 g carbo., 5 g fiber, 8 g pro.

Test Kitchen Tip: Converted or parboiled rice is treated in a steam-pressure process before milling to make the cooked rice extra fluffy without sacrificing nutrients. Because converted rice takes a little longer to cook than regular rice, it's ideal for dishes made in a slow cooker. The rice stands up to long hours of cooking and holds its shape well.

Be a dinnertime hero with a long-simmered soup that will win applause. Serve this one-dish meal with crusty whole grain bread for a tantalizing supper.

Barley Vegetable Soup

MAKES 6 SERVINGS

Prep: 20 minutes
Cook: Low 8 to 10 hours, High 4 to 5 hours

1	15-ounce can red beans, rinsed and drained
1	14.5-ounce can stewed tomatoes, undrained
1	10-ounce package frozen whole kernel corn
2	cups sliced fresh mushrooms
1	large onion, chopped (1 cup)
½	cup regular barley
1	medium carrot, coarsely chopped (½ cup)
1	stalk celery, coarsely chopped (½ cup)
2	teaspoons dried Italian seasoning, crushed
¼	teaspoon black pepper
3	cloves garlic, minced
5	cups vegetable broth

1. In a 3½- to 5-quart slow cooker combine drained beans, undrained tomatoes, frozen corn, mushrooms, onion, barley, carrot, celery, Italian seasoning, pepper, and garlic. Pour broth over mixture in cooker.

2. Cover and cook on low-heat setting for 8 to 10 hours or on high-heat setting for 4 to 5 hours.

Nutrition Facts per serving: 228 cal., 2 g total fat (0 g sat. fat), 0 mg chol., 1,211 mg sodium, 47 g carbo., 8 g fiber, 9 g pro.

*Sip a spoonful of this meatless meal in a bowl and enjoy
the pleasantly spicy taste of fresh ginger, curry powder,
and jalapeño chile pepper. (Photo on page 133.)*

Curried Lentil Soup

MAKES 4 TO 6 SERVINGS

Prep: 20 minutes
Cook: Low 8 to 10 hours,
High 4 to 5 hours

2   to 3 medium sweet
    potatoes (1 pound), peeled
    and coarsely chopped

1   cup brown or yellow lentils,
    rinsed and drained

1   medium onion, chopped
    (½ cup)

1   fresh jalapeño chile pepper,
    seeded and finely chopped
    (see tip, page 10)

3   cloves garlic, minced

3   14-ounce cans vegetable
    broth

1   14.5-ounce can diced
    tomatoes, undrained

1   tablespoon curry powder

1   teaspoon grated fresh
    ginger

    Plain yogurt or dairy sour
    cream (optional)

    Small fresh chile peppers
    and/or crushed red pepper
    (optional)

1. In a 4- to 5-quart slow cooker combine sweet potato, lentils, onion, jalapeño pepper, and garlic. Stir in broth, undrained tomatoes, curry powder, and ginger.

2. Cover and cook on low-heat setting for 8 to 10 hours or on high-heat setting for 4 to 5 hours.

3. If desired, top individual servings with yogurt and garnish with small chile peppers and/or crushed red pepper.

Nutrition Facts per serving: 316 cal., 2 g total fat (0 g sat. fat), 0 mg chol., 1,425 mg sodium, 60 g carbo., 18 g fiber, 18 g pro.

Chunks of cod or white fish get a flavor boost in this creamy, zesty chowder. Serve it with a basket of blue corn tortilla chips and cold Mexican beer. It's one of those dishes that proves conclusively that fabulous food doesn't have to be complicated.

5 Ingredient Recipe

Mexican-Style Fish Chowder

MAKES 6 SERVINGS

Prep: 15 minutes
Cook: Low 3 to 4 hours,
High 1½ to 2 hours,
plus 1 hour (high)

Nonstick cooking spray
2   10.75-ounce cans condensed cream of celery soup
1   16-ounce package frozen whole kernel corn
1½   cups milk
1   pound fresh or frozen cod or other white-fleshed fish fillets
2   14.5-ounce cans Mexican-style stewed tomatoes, undrained

1. Lightly coat the inside of a 3½- or 4-quart slow cooker with nonstick cooking spray. In the prepared cooker combine soup, frozen corn, and milk.

2. Cover and cook on low-heat setting for 3 to 4 hours or on high-heat setting for 1½ to 2 hours.

3. Meanwhile, thaw fish, if frozen. Rinse fish; pat dry with paper towels.

4. If using low-heat setting, turn to high-heat setting. Stir corn mixture in cooker. Place fish on top of corn mixture. Cover and cook for 1 hour more. Stir in undrained tomatoes.

Nutrition Facts per serving: 293 cal., 8 g total fat (3 g sat. fat), 39 mg chol., 1,296 mg sodium, 36 g carbo., 2 g fiber, 21 g pro.

Cioppino may sound like a classic from the Old Country, but it was actually created in San Francisco. It's an aromatic dish of fish and seafood in a tomato-sparked stew. Delicious!

Cioppino

MAKES 6 SERVINGS

Prep: 25 minutes
Cook: Low 4 to 5 hours,
High 2 to 2½ hours,
plus 15 minutes (high)

1   pound fresh or frozen cod fillets or halibut steaks

8   ounces fresh or frozen peeled and deveined shrimp

1   28-ounce can fire-roasted or regular crushed tomatoes

1¾ cups water

1   medium yellow or green sweet pepper, chopped (¾ cup)

1   medium onion, finely chopped (½ cup)

½   cup dry white wine

2   teaspoons dried Italian seasoning, crushed

¼   teaspoon salt

4   cloves garlic, minced

1   10-ounce can whole baby clams, drained

 · Lemon wedges

    Snipped fresh basil

1. Thaw fish and shrimp, if frozen. Rinse fish and shrimp; pat dry with paper towels. Cut fish into bite-size pieces. Cover and chill fish and shrimp until needed.

2. In a 3½- or 4-quart slow cooker combine tomatoes, water, sweet pepper, onion, wine, Italian seasoning, salt, and garlic.

3. Cover and cook on low-heat setting for 4 to 5 hours or on high-heat setting for 2 to 2½ hours.

4. If using low-heat setting, turn to high-heat setting. Add fish and shrimp to cooker. Cover and cook about 15 minutes more or until shrimp are opaque. Stir in drained clams.

5. Garnish individual servings with lemon wedges and basil.

Nutrition Facts per serving: 213 cal., 2 g total fat (0 g sat. fat), 112 mg chol., 610 mg sodium, 13 g carbo., 1 g fiber, 31 g pro.

Create a slow-cooker chili that has a perfect spooning consistency by slightly mashing the beans. For tasty toppers to complete the dish, offer lush avocado slices and tangy sour cream.

Fix-and-Forget White Chili

❖

MAKES 6 SERVINGS

Prep: 15 minutes
Cook: Low 7 to 8 hours,
High 3½ to 4 hours

12	ounces skinless, boneless chicken breast halves, cut into ½-inch pieces
1	tablespoon cooking oil
3	15-ounce cans Great Northern beans or navy beans, rinsed and drained
2½	cups chicken broth
2	4-ounce cans diced green chile peppers, undrained
1	medium onion, chopped (½ cup)
1½	teaspoons cumin seeds
¼	to 1 teaspoon cayenne pepper
¼	teaspoon salt
3	cloves garlic, minced
	Dairy sour cream (optional)
	Avocado slices (optional)

1. In a large skillet cook chicken in hot oil over medium heat until brown. Drain off fat. Set chicken aside.

2. Place drained beans in a 3½- or 4-quart slow cooker; mash slightly with a potato masher. Add chicken to cooker. Stir in broth, undrained chile peppers, onion, cumin seeds, cayenne pepper, salt, and garlic.

3. Cover and cook on low-heat setting for 7 to 8 hours or on high-heat setting for 3½ to 4 hours.

4. If desired, top individual servings with sour cream and avocado slices.

Nutrition Facts per serving: 377 cal., 5 g total fat (1 g sat. fat), 33 mg chol., 724 mg sodium, 52 g carbo., 12 g fiber, 32 g pro.

When your schedule calls for quick prep, this is your go-to recipe. Big on flavor, it looks like chili but tastes like a taco.

Taco Chili

MAKES 5 SERVINGS

Prep: 15 minutes
Cook: Low 4 to 6 hours, High 2 to 3 hours

1   pound lean ground beef
1   28-ounce can diced tomatoes in sauce
1   15.5-ounce can hominy or one 15.25-ounce can whole kernel corn, undrained
1   15-ounce can chili beans in chili gravy, undrained
1   1.25-ounce envelope taco seasoning mix
     Dairy sour cream (optional)
     Shredded cheddar cheese (optional)

1. In a large skillet cook ground beef until meat is brown. Drain off fat. Transfer meat to a 3½- or 4-quart slow cooker.

2. Stir in tomatoes, undrained hominy, undrained chili beans in chili gravy, and taco seasoning mix.

3. Cover and cook on low-heat setting for 4 to 6 hours or on high-heat setting for 2 to 3 hours. If desired, top individual servings with sour cream and cheese.

Nutrition Facts per serving: 477 cal., 18 g total fat (6 g sat. fat), 71 mg chol., 1,998 mg sodium, 49 g carbo., 12 g fiber, 35 g pro.

Dumplings made from a corn muffin mix and embellished with cheddar cheese, green onions, and sour cream provide the finishing touch for this chili that is simmered all day.

Family-Style Chili and Dumplings

MAKES 6 SERVINGS

Prep: 25 minutes
Cook: Low 8 to 10 hours, High 4 to 5 hours, plus 20 minutes (high)

1	pound boneless beef round steak or pork shoulder roast*
1	15-ounce can chili beans in chili gravy, undrained
1	15-ounce can kidney beans or pinto beans, rinsed and drained
1	14.5-ounce can Mexican-style stewed tomatoes, undrained and cut up
1	large green, red, or yellow sweet pepper, chopped
1	large onion, chopped (1 cup)
1	cup beef broth
1	to 2 teaspoons chopped canned chipotle pepper in adobo sauce (see tip, page 10) or ¼ to ½ teaspoon crushed red pepper
1	teaspoon ground cumin
¾	teaspoon garlic salt
½	teaspoon dried oregano, crushed
1	recipe Corn Bread Dumplings
	Shredded cheddar cheese

1. Trim fat from meat. Cut meat into ½-inch pieces. In a 3½- or 4-quart slow cooker combine meat, undrained chili beans in chili gravy, drained kidney beans, undrained tomatoes, sweet pepper, onion, broth, chipotle pepper, cumin, garlic salt, and oregano.

2. Cover and cook on low-heat setting for 8 to 10 hours or on high-heat setting for 4 to 5 hours.

3. If using low-heat setting, turn to high-heat setting. If you have an oval cooker, drop all of the Corn Bread Dumplings batter onto the bubbling meat mixture. (If you have a round cooker, preheat oven to 400°F. Drop half of the batter onto the bubbling mixture. Spoon the remaining batter into two or three greased muffin cups. Bake for 15 to 18 minutes or until a toothpick inserted in the centers comes out clean.)

4. Cover cooker and cook for 20 to 25 minutes more or until a toothpick inserted into dumplings comes out clean. Top individual servings with cheese.

Corn Bread Dumplings: In a large bowl combine one 8.5-ounce package corn muffin mix, ½ cup shredded cheddar or Monterey Jack cheese, and ¼ cup sliced green onion (2). In a small bowl combine 1 slightly beaten egg and ¼ cup dairy sour cream; stir into cheese mixture.

Nutrition Facts per serving: 529 cal., 17 g total fat (6 g sat. fat), 101 mg chol., 1,256 mg sodium, 61 g carbo., 9 g fiber, 35 g pro.

*Note: If desired, substitute 1 pound lean ground beef or ground pork for the beef steak or pork shoulder. In a large skillet cook ground beef or pork until brown. Drain off fat before using.

Cumin, chili powder, cinnamon, and a can of your favorite brew spike pork and beef in a richly seasoned tomato base. The meaty blend treats the palate to a satisfying meal.

Southwest Two-Meat and Beer Chili

MAKES 6 SERVINGS

Prep: 20 minutes
Cook: Low 8 to 10 hours,
High 4 to 5 hours

12	ounces lean boneless pork
12	ounces boneless beef sirloin steak, cut 1 inch thick
¼	cup all-purpose flour
1	tablespoon cooking oil
2	14.5-ounce cans diced tomatoes with basil, garlic, and oregano, undrained
1	15-ounce can red kidney beans, rinsed and drained
1	12-ounce can beer
1	8-ounce can tomato sauce
1	medium onion, chopped (½ cup)
2	tablespoons chili powder
1	teaspoon ground cumin
¼	teaspoon ground cinnamon

1. Trim fat from meat. Cut meat into 1-inch pieces. Place flour in a plastic bag. Add meat, a few pieces at a time, shaking to coat.

2. In a large skillet brown meat, half at a time, in hot oil over medium heat. Drain off fat. Transfer meat to a 4- to 5-quart slow cooker.

3. Stir in undrained tomatoes, drained beans, beer, tomato sauce, onion, chili powder, cumin, and cinnamon.

4. Cover and cook on low-heat setting for 8 to 10 hours or on high-heat setting for 4 to 5 hours.

Nutrition Facts per serving: 339 cal., 8 g total fat (2 g sat. fat), 71 mg chol., 1,105 mg sodium, 34 g carbo., 6 g fiber, 32 g pro.

When chicken seasoned with chili powder cooks with pickled jalapeño peppers, the resulting juices are the fired-up base for a tantalizing sauce embellished with cream cheese and bacon. Sprinkle the bacon on just before serving so it stays crisp.

Jalapeño and Bacon Chicken Breasts

❧

MAKES 6 SERVINGS

Prep: 15 minutes
Cook: Low 5 to 6 hours,
High 2½ to 3 hours,
plus 15 minutes (high)

6	chicken breast halves (with bone) (about 3 pounds total), skinned
1	tablespoon chili powder
½	cup reduced-sodium chicken broth
2	tablespoons lemon juice
⅓	cup bottled sliced pickled jalapeño chile peppers, drained
1	tablespoon cornstarch
1	tablespoon cold water
1	8-ounce package cream cheese, softened and cut into cubes
2	slices bacon or turkey bacon, crisp-cooked, drained, and crumbled (optional)

1. Sprinkle chicken with chili powder. Place chicken, bone sides down, in a 4½- to 6-quart slow cooker. Pour broth and lemon juice around chicken in cooker. Top with jalapeño pepper slices.

2. Cover and cook on low-heat setting for 5 to 6 hours or on high-heat setting for 2½ to 3 hours.

3. Transfer chicken and jalapeño pepper slices to a serving platter, reserving cooking liquid. Cover chicken with foil to keep warm.

4. If using low-heat setting, turn to high-heat setting. For sauce, in a small bowl combine cornstarch and water; stir into liquid in cooker. Whisk in cream cheese until combined. Cover and cook about 15 minutes more or until thickened.

5. If desired, sprinkle chicken with crumbled bacon. Serve chicken with sauce.

Nutrition Facts per serving: 363 cal., 16 g total fat (9 g sat. fat), 155 mg chol., 451 mg sodium, 5 g carbo., 1 g fiber, 49 g pro.

This dish contains the best ingredients of the Mediterranean—olives, capers, garlic, red wine, fresh basil, and tomatoes. Served with mixed salad greens and chunks of warm crusty bread, it's a memorable Greek meal from your own kitchen.

Greek Chicken with Olives

MAKES 4 SERVINGS

Prep: 15 minutes
Cook: Low 6 to 7 hours,
High 3 to 3½ hours

3	large tomatoes, coarsely chopped (3 cups)
1	large onion, halved lengthwise and thinly sliced
¼	cup Greek olives or ripe olives, pitted and sliced
¼	cup dry red wine or reduced-sodium chicken broth
1	tablespoon quick-cooking tapioca, crushed
1	tablespoon capers, drained
¼	teaspoon salt
⅛	teaspoon black pepper
2	cloves garlic, minced
4	skinless, boneless chicken breast halves (about 1¼ pounds total)
¼	cup snipped fresh basil
2	cups hot cooked couscous

1. In a 3½- or 4-quart slow cooker combine tomato, onion, olives, wine, tapioca, capers, salt, pepper, and garlic. Add chicken, spooning some of the tomato mixture over chicken.

2. Cover and cook on low-heat setting for 6 to 7 hours or on high-heat setting for 3 to 3½ hours.

3. Before serving, stir in basil. Serve chicken and tomato mixture over hot cooked couscous.

Nutrition Facts per serving: 326 cal., 4 g total fat (1 g sat. fat), 82 mg chol., 373 mg sodium, 32 g carbo., 4 g fiber, 38 g pro.

This combo of chicken and fruit gets its kick from a mix of curry powder, cayenne pepper, and mango chutney. Chutneys vary in flavor, so try a few different kinds to find the one you like best.

Chicken in Mango Cream Sauce

MAKES 6 SERVINGS

Prep: 15 minutes
Cook: Low 6 to 7 hours, High 3 to 3½ hours

	Nonstick cooking spray
2	teaspoons curry powder
1	teaspoon garlic salt
⅛	to ¼ teaspoon cayenne pepper
6	skinless, boneless chicken breast halves (about 2 pounds total)
3	medium Granny Smith apples, cored and sliced
½	cup golden raisins
1	8- or 9-ounce jar mango chutney
¼	cup apple juice
1	8-ounce tub cream cheese spread
	Hot cooked whole wheat couscous (optional)

1. Lightly coat the inside of a 4- to 5-quart slow cooker with nonstick cooking spray; set aside. In a small bowl combine curry powder, garlic salt, and cayenne pepper; sprinkle over chicken. Place chicken in the prepared cooker. Add apple and raisins. Top with chutney and apple juice.

2. Cover and cook on low-heat setting for 6 to 7 hours or on high-heat setting for 3 to 3½ hours. Using a slotted spoon, transfer chicken and apple to a serving platter, reserving cooking liquid.

3. For sauce, whisk cream cheese spread into cooking liquid until sauce is smooth. Serve sauce over chicken, apple, and, if desired, hot cooked whole wheat couscous.

Nutrition Facts per serving: 464 cal., 16 g total fat (9 g sat. fat), 129 mg chol., 603 mg sodium, 40 g carbo., 3 g fiber, 39 g pro.

Here's a mild Asian-style chicken recipe that gets its irresistible flavor from a lively mix of plum sauce, ground ginger, and dry mustard.

Ginger-Plum Chicken

MAKES 6 SERVINGS

Prep: 20 minutes
Cook: Low 5 to 6 hours,
High 2½ to 3 hours

1½	cups packaged julienned carrots
4	medium leeks, thinly sliced (1⅓ cups), or 1 large onion, chopped (1 cup)
6	skinless, boneless chicken breast halves (about 2 pounds total)
¾	cup bottled plum sauce
2	tablespoons quick-cooking tapioca, crushed
½	teaspoon ground ginger
½	teaspoon dry mustard
	Hot cooked long grain or wild rice (optional)
1	recipe Peanut Topper or sesame seeds, toasted (see tip, page 29)

1. In a 3½- or 4-quart slow cooker combine carrots and leek. Add chicken. In a small bowl combine plum sauce, tapioca, ginger, and dry mustard. Spoon evenly over chicken in cooker.

2. Cover and cook on low-heat setting for 5 to 6 hours or on high-heat setting for 2½ to 3 hours.

3. If desired, serve chicken mixture over hot cooked rice. Sprinkle with Peanut Topper.

Peanut Topper: In a small bowl combine ¼ cup chopped honey-roasted peanuts, ¼ cup thinly sliced green onion, and 2 tablespoons finely shredded fresh basil.

Nutrition Facts per serving: 301 cal., 5 g total fat (1 g sat. fat), 88 mg chol., 309 mg sodium, 26 g carbo., 2 g fiber, 38 g pro.

It's amazing how well so many international favorites can be adapted to the slow cooker. This tasty takeout classic is yet another case in point!

Cashew Chicken

MAKES 6 SERVINGS

Prep: 15 minutes
Cook: Low 6 to 8 hours,
High 3 to 4 hours

1	10.75-ounce can condensed golden mushroom soup
2	tablespoons soy sauce
½	teaspoon ground ginger
1½	pounds chicken breast tenderloins
2	stalks celery, sliced (1 cup)
2	medium carrots, shredded (1 cup)
1	cup sliced fresh mushrooms or one 4.5-ounce jar (drained weight) sliced mushrooms, drained
1	8-ounce can sliced water chestnuts, drained
½	cup cashews
	Hot cooked brown rice (optional)

1. In a 3½- or 4-quart slow cooker combine soup, soy sauce, and ginger. Stir in chicken, celery, carrot, mushrooms, and drained water chestnuts.

2. Cover and cook on low-heat setting for 6 to 8 hours or on high-heat setting for 3 to 4 hours.

3. Stir cashews into chicken mixture. If desired, serve over hot cooked brown rice.

Nutrition Facts per serving: 251 cal., 9 g total fat (2 g sat. fat), 67 mg chol., 847 mg sodium, 15 g carbo., 2 g fiber, 31 g pro.

A few simple ingredients—garlic, thyme, orange juice, and a
splash of balsamic vinegar—result in a big flavor payoff for
these moist, fork-tender chicken breasts.

Chicken with Thyme and Garlic Sauce

MAKES 6 SERVINGS

Prep: 20 minutes
Cook: Low 6 to 7 hours,
High 3 to 3½ hours

3	to 4 pounds chicken breast halves (with bone), skinned
1½	teaspoons dried thyme, crushed
½	teaspoon salt
3	cloves garlic, minced
¼	cup orange juice
1	tablespoon balsamic vinegar

1. Place chicken in a 3½- or 4-quart slow cooker. Sprinkle chicken with thyme, salt, and garlic. Pour orange juice and balsamic vinegar over chicken in cooker.

2. Cover and cook on low-heat setting for 6 to 7 hours or on high-heat setting for 3 to 3½ hours. Using a slotted spoon, transfer chicken to a serving platter, reserving cooking liquid. Cover chicken with foil to keep warm.

3. For sauce, strain cooking liquid into a small saucepan; skim off fat. Bring to boiling; reduce heat. Boil gently, uncovered, for 5 to 6 minutes or until reduced to about 1 cup. Spoon some of the sauce over chicken; pass the remaining sauce.

Nutrition Facts per serving: 158 cal., 2 g total fat (1 g sat. fat), 72 mg chol., 263 mg sodium, 3 g carbo., 0 g fiber, 29 g pro.

Don't skimp on the six cloves of garlic. Gentle simmering in the slow cooker transforms their feisty flavor from pungent and harsh to mellow and smooth. Start cooking the brown rice the moment you walk in the door or use microwavable brown rice.

Rosemary Chicken and Artichokes

MAKES 6 SERVINGS

Prep: 15 minutes
Cook: Low 5 to 6 hours,
High 2½ to 3 hours,
plus 30 minutes (high)

1	medium onion, chopped (½ cup)
⅓	cup reduced-sodium chicken broth
1	tablespoon quick-cooking tapioca
2	to 3 teaspoons finely shredded lemon peel
2	teaspoons snipped fresh rosemary or 1 teaspoon dried rosemary, crushed
¾	teaspoon black pepper
6	cloves garlic, minced
2½	to 3 pounds chicken thighs, skinned
½	teaspoon salt
1	8- or 9-ounce package frozen artichoke hearts, thawed
1	medium red sweet pepper, cut into strips
	Hot cooked brown rice (optional)

1. In a 3½- or 4-quart slow cooker combine onion, broth, tapioca, 1 teaspoon of the lemon peel, the rosemary, ½ teaspoon of the black pepper, and the garlic. Add chicken. Sprinkle chicken with salt and the remaining ¼ teaspoon black pepper.

2. Cover and cook on low-heat setting for 5 to 6 hours or on high-heat setting for 2½ to 3 hours.

3. If using low-heat setting, turn to high-heat setting. Stir in artichokes and sweet pepper. Cover and cook for 30 minutes more.

4. If desired, serve chicken and artichoke mixture with hot cooked brown rice. Sprinkle with the remaining 1 to 2 teaspoons lemon peel.

Nutrition Facts per serving: 168 cal., 4 g total fat (1 g sat. fat), 89 mg chol., 328 mg sodium, 8 g carbo., 3 g fiber, 23 g pro.

A little gourmet, a little down-home. Chicken with lots of garlic experiences a comfort food revival with a can of condensed soup. Fine angel hair pasta is the right texture for soaking up the creamy cheese- and herb-flavored sauce.

Parmesan Chicken with Green Beans

MAKES 6 SERVINGS

Prep: 15 minutes
Cook: Low 4 to 5 hours,
High 2 to 2½ hours

1	16-ounce package frozen French-cut green beans, thawed
1	large onion, finely chopped (1 cup)
½	cup bottled roasted red sweet peppers, drained and chopped
6	skinless, boneless chicken breast halves (about 2 pounds total)
1	10.75-ounce can condensed cream of chicken with herbs soup
½	cup grated Parmesan cheese
½	teaspoon salt
¼	teaspoon black pepper
8	large cloves garlic, thinly sliced
3	cups hot cooked angel hair pasta

1. In a 4- to 5-quart slow cooker combine green beans, onion, and roasted red pepper. Arrange chicken on top of vegetables. In a medium bowl combine soup, ¼ cup of the Parmesan cheese, the salt, black pepper, and garlic. Pour over mixture in cooker.

2. Cover and cook on low-heat setting for 4 to 5 hours or on high-heat setting for 2 to 2½ hours.

3. Serve chicken mixture over hot cooked pasta. Sprinkle with the remaining ¼ cup Parmesan cheese.

Nutrition Facts per serving: 384 cal., 6 g total fat (2 g sat. fat), 98 mg chol., 776 mg sodium, 36 g carbo., 5 g fiber, 45 g pro.

Try this easy, healthful, and delicious recipe if you love the pleasant sweetness and tang of pineapple. Add a crisp lettuce salad and rolls, and dinner is complete.

Tangy Pineapple Chicken

MAKES 6 SERVINGS

Prep: 30 minutes
Cook: Low 5 to 6 hours,
High 2½ to 3 hours

2	pounds skinless, boneless chicken thighs, cut into 1-inch-wide strips
1	tablespoon cooking oil
1	20-ounce can pineapple tidbits (juice pack), drained
1	large red sweet pepper, chopped (1 cup)
½	cup bottled barbecue sauce
¼	cup bottled clear Italian salad dressing
2	teaspoons dried oregano, crushed

1. In a large skillet cook chicken, half at a time, in hot oil over medium heat until brown. Drain off fat. Transfer chicken to a 3½- or 4-quart slow cooker. Add drained pineapple and sweet pepper.

2. In a small bowl combine barbecue sauce, salad dressing, and oregano. Pour over mixture in cooker.

3. Cover and cook on low-heat setting for 5 to 6 hours or on high-heat setting for 2½ to 3 hours.

Nutrition Facts per serving: 314 cal., 12 g total fat (2 g sat. fat), 121 mg chol., 436 mg sodium, 20 g carbo., 2 g fiber, 31 g pro.

Adding yellow and red sweet pepper strips near the end of cooking lends plenty of color and a crisp-tender texture to the cooked chicken and mushrooms.

Chicken with Peppers and Mushrooms

❧

MAKES 6 SERVINGS

Prep: 25 minutes
Cook: Low 4 to 5 hours,
High 2 to 2½ hours,
plus 15 minutes (high)

8	ounces fresh mushrooms, quartered
2	shallots, sliced
2½	pounds chicken thighs, skinned
¼	cup chicken broth
¼	cup dry white wine
1	teaspoon dried basil, crushed
½	teaspoon salt
¼	teaspoon black pepper
2	tablespoons cornstarch
2	tablespoons cold water
1	medium yellow sweet pepper, cut into 1-inch-wide strips
1	medium red sweet pepper, cut into 1-inch-wide strips
2	medum roma tomatoes, chopped (⅔ cup)
⅓	cup finely shredded Parmesan cheese

1. In a 3½- or 4-quart slow cooker combine mushrooms and shallot. Add chicken. In a small bowl combine broth, wine, basil, salt, and black pepper. Pour over mixture in cooker.

2. Cover and cook on low-heat setting for 4 to 5 hours or on high-heat setting for 2 to 2½ hours. Transfer chicken and vegetables to a serving platter, reserving cooking liquid. Cover chicken and vegetables with foil to keep warm.

3. If using low-heat setting, turn to high-heat setting. For sauce, in a small bowl combine cornstarch and water. Stir into liquid in cooker. Stir in sweet pepper strips. Cover and cook about 15 minutes more or until thickened.

4. To serve, spoon sauce over chicken and vegetables. Sprinkle with tomato and Parmesan cheese.

Nutrition Facts per serving: 175 cal., 6 g total fat (2 g sat. fat), 70 mg chol., 377 mg sodium, 9 g carbo., 1 g fiber, 21 g pro.

Here's a mild sweet-sour chicken made with mango chutney and chili sauce. Brown rice has a slightly nutty flavor and pleasantly chewy texture. Served as a bed for the chicken, it soaks up every drop of goodness.

Ginger Chicken

MAKES 6 SERVINGS

Prep: 20 minutes
Cook: Low 5 to 6 hours,
High 2½ to 3 hours

½ cup mango chutney or orange marmalade

¼ cup bottled chili sauce

2 tablespoons quick-cooking tapioca

1½ teaspoons grated fresh ginger or ½ teaspoon ground ginger

12 chicken thighs (about 4 pounds total), skinned

Hot cooked brown rice (optional)

Sliced green onion (optional)

1. Cut up any large pieces of fruit in the chutney. In a 4- to 5-quart slow cooker combine chutney, chili sauce, tapioca, and ginger. Add chicken, turning to coat.

2. Cover and cook on low-heat setting for 5 to 6 hours or on high-heat setting for 2½ to 3 hours.

3. If desired, serve chicken and chutney mixture over hot cooked brown rice and sprinkle with green onion.

Nutrition Facts per serving: 264 cal., 7 g total fat (2 g sat. fat), 143 mg chol., 494 mg sodium, 16 g carbo., 1 g fiber, 34 g pro.

The slow cooker is often the domain of stick-to-your-ribs comfort food, but it can produce light, contemporary dishes as well. Figs, balsamic vinegar, and polenta are trendsetting ingredients today's chefs love using in a bistro-style entrée.

Chicken with Figs and Blue Cheese

❖

MAKES 6 SERVINGS

Prep: 20 minutes
Cook: Low 5 to 6 hours,
High 2½ to 3 hours

1	9-ounce package dried mission figs, stems removed
1	large onion, thinly sliced
2½	pounds skinless, boneless chicken thighs
1	cup chicken broth
¼	cup balsamic vinegar
1	tablespoon finely shredded orange peel
1	teaspoon salt
½	teaspoon black pepper
¼	teaspoon ground ginger
1	16-ounce tube refrigerated cooked polenta
⅔	cup crumbled blue cheese

1. Coarsely chop the figs. In a 4- to 5-quart slow cooker combine figs and onion. Add chicken. In a small bowl stir together broth, balsamic vinegar, orange peel, salt, pepper, and ginger. Pour over mixture in cooker.

2. Cover and cook on low-heat setting for 5 to 6 hours or on high-heat setting for 2½ to 3 hours.

3. Before serving, prepare polenta according to package directions for polenta mush.

4. Using tongs, remove chicken from cooker. Transfer fig mixture to a serving bowl. If necessary, skim off fat. Serve chicken and fig mixture with polenta mush. Sprinkle with blue cheese.

Nutrition Facts per serving: 481 cal., 12 g total fat (5 g sat. fat), 162 mg chol., 1,174 mg sodium, 47 g carbo., 7 g fiber, 45 g pro.

Chicken and hearty vegetables simmer in a delicate wine-flavored sauce. Choose dark meat for this dish and use a dry white wine such as a Chardonnay or pinot grigio for the aromatic herbed sauce.

Chicken in Wine Sauce

MAKES 6 SERVINGS

Prep: 30 minutes
Cook: Low 8 to 9 hours,
High 4 to 4½ hours

4	medium red potatoes (1⅓ pounds), quartered
4	medium carrots, cut into ½-inch pieces
2	stalks celery, cut into 1-inch pieces
1	small onion, sliced
3	pounds chicken thighs and/or drumsticks, skinned
1	tablespoon snipped fresh parsley
½	teaspoon salt
½	teaspoon dried rosemary, crushed
½	teaspoon dried thyme, crushed
¼	teaspoon black pepper
1	clove garlic, minced
1	cup chicken broth
½	cup dry white wine
3	tablespoons butter or margarine
3	tablespoons all-purpose flour

1. In a 5- to 6-quart slow cooker combine potato, carrot, celery, and onion. Place chicken on top of vegetables. Sprinkle chicken with parsley, salt, rosemary, thyme, pepper, and garlic. Pour broth and wine over mixture in cooker.

2. Cover and cook on low-heat setting for 8 to 9 hours or on high-heat setting for 4 to 4½ hours. Using a slotted spoon, transfer chicken and vegetables to a serving platter, reserving cooking liquid. Cover chicken and vegetables with foil to keep warm.

3. For sauce, skim fat from cooking liquid; strain liquid. In a large saucepan melt butter over medium heat. Stir in flour; cook and stir for 1 minute. Add cooking liquid. Cook and stir until thickened and bubbly. Cook and stir for 2 minutes more. Serve chicken and vegetables with sauce.

Nutrition Facts per serving: 328 cal., 11 g total fat (5 g sat. fat), 124 mg chol., 544 mg sodium, 24 g carbo., 3 g fiber, 29 g pro.

Already creamy Alfredo sauce joins forces with cream cheese to boost this luscious dish into a flavor category all its own. Save time by buying skinned chicken thighs.

Basil-Cream Chicken Thighs

MAKES 6 SERVINGS

Prep: 20 minutes
Cook: Low 5 to 6 hours,
High 2½ to 3 hours

2½   pounds chicken thighs, skinned
¼   teaspoon black pepper
2   10-ounce containers refrigerated light Alfredo pasta sauce
¼   cup water
2   teaspoons dried basil, crushed
1   16-ounce package frozen broccoli, cauliflower, and carrots
1   3-ounce package cream cheese, cubed
    Hot cooked whole wheat pasta (optional)

1. Place chicken in a 3½- or 4-quart slow cooker. Sprinkle chicken with pepper. In a small bowl combine Alfredo sauce, water, and basil. Pour over chicken in cooker. Top with frozen vegetables.

2. Cover and cook on low-heat setting for 5 to 6 hours or on high-heat setting for 2½ to 3 hours. Using a slotted spoon, transfer chicken and vegetables to a serving platter, reserving cooking liquid.

3. For sauce, whisk cream cheese into cooking liquid until sauce is smooth. Serve sauce over chicken and vegetables. If desired, serve with hot cooked pasta.

Nutrition Facts per serving: 332 cal., 17 g total fat (10 g sat. fat), 138 mg chol., 757 mg sodium, 12 g carbo., 2 g fiber, 31 g pro.

You can make this family-pleasing chicken any time of year because the pears are dried.

Fennel and Pear Chicken Thighs

MAKES 6 SERVINGS

Prep: 15 minutes
Cook: Low 7 to 8 hours,
High 3½ to 4 hours

1	medium fennel bulb, trimmed and sliced (1¼ cups)
2	4.5-ounce jars (drained weight) sliced mushrooms, drained
½	cup coarsely snipped dried pears
2	tablespoons quick-cooking tapioca, crushed
¾	teaspoon salt
½	teaspoon dried thyme, crushed
½	teaspoon cracked black pepper
2½	pounds skinless, boneless chicken thighs
1	cup pear nectar or apple juice
3	cups hot cooked couscous or rice
	Snipped fennel tops (optional)

1. In a 3½- or 4-quart slow cooker combine sliced fennel, drained mushrooms, and dried pears. Sprinkle with tapioca, salt, thyme, and pepper. Add chicken. Pour pear nectar over mixture in cooker.

2. Cover and cook on low-heat setting for 7 to 8 hours or on high-heat setting for 3½ to 4 hours.

3. Serve chicken mixture over hot cooked couscous. If desired, sprinkle with snipped fennel tops.

Nutrition Facts per serving: 407 cal., 7 g total fat (2 g sat. fat), 157 mg chol., 657 mg sodium, 41 g carbo., 4 g fiber, 42 g pro.

Similar to the Italian classic, this meal-in-a-pot is brimming with onions, mushrooms, and tomatoes. Serve with plenty of pasta to support the chunky sauce. (Photo on page 266.)

Cacciatore-Style Chicken

MAKES 6 SERVINGS

Prep: 25 minutes
Cook: Low 7 to 8 hours,
High 3 to 3½ hours,
plus 15 minutes (high)

2	cups fresh mushrooms
2	medium onions, cut into wedges
2	stalks celery, sliced (1 cup)
2	medium carrots, chopped
4	cloves garlic, minced
3	tablespoons quick-cooking tapioca, crushed
1	teaspoon sugar
1	teaspoon dried oregano, crushed
2	bay leaves
12	chicken drumsticks (about 3 pounds total), skinned
½	cup chicken broth
¼	cup dry white wine or chicken broth
1	14.5-ounce can diced tomatoes, undrained
1	medium green or red sweet pepper, cut into strips
⅓	to ½ cup tomato paste
3	cups hot cooked pasta
	Fresh oregano sprigs (optional)

1. Cut mushrooms into halves or quarters. In a 5- to 6-quart slow cooker combine mushrooms, onion, celery, carrot, and garlic. Sprinkle with tapioca, sugar, the 1 teaspoon dried oregano, bay leaves, ½ teaspoon salt, and ¼ teaspoon black pepper. Add chicken. Pour broth and wine over mixture in cooker.

2. Cover and cook on low-heat setting for 7 to 8 hours or on high-heat setting for 3 to 3½ hours.

3. If using low-heat setting, turn to high-heat setting. Stir in undrained tomatoes, sweet pepper, and tomato paste. Cover and cook for 15 minutes more. Remove bay leaves.

4. Serve chicken and tomato mixture over hot cooked pasta. If desired, garnish with fresh oregano sprigs.

Nutrition Facts per serving: 452 cal., 8 g total fat (2 g sat. fat), 157 mg chol., 627 mg sodium, 42 g carbo., 5 g fiber, 50 g pro.

The herb-lemon dry rub adds color to the chicken pieces, and the feta cheese and snipped fresh parsley make a pretty garnish for this Mediterranean-inspired chicken dish. It's lovely with a spinach salad and wedges of warm pita bread.

Feta-Topped Chicken

MAKES 6 SERVINGS

Prep: 15 minutes
Cook: Low 5 to 6 hours,
High 2½ to 3 hours

1   teaspoon finely shredded lemon peel
1   teaspoon dried basil, crushed
1   teaspoon dried rosemary, crushed
½   teaspoon salt
¼   teaspoon black pepper
2   cloves garlic, minced
3½ to 4 pounds meaty chicken pieces (breast halves, thighs, and drumsticks), skinned
½   cup reduced-sodium chicken broth
½   cup crumbled feta cheese
2   tablespoons snipped fresh Italian (flat-leaf) parsley

1. In a small bowl combine lemon peel, basil, rosemary, salt, pepper, and garlic. Sprinkle lemon mixture evenly over chicken; rub in with your fingers. Place chicken in a 4- to 5-quart slow cooker. Pour broth around chicken in cooker.

2. Cover and cook on low-heat setting for 5 to 6 hours or on high-heat setting for 2½ to 3 hours.

3. Using a slotted spoon, transfer chicken to a serving platter; discard cooking liquid. Sprinkle chicken with cheese and parsley.

Nutrition Facts per serving: 179 cal., 6 g total fat (2 g sat. fat), 97 mg chol., 425 mg sodium, 1 g carbo., 0 g fiber, 29 g pro.

Earthy portobello mushrooms, garlic, chicken, rosemary, and white wine—these are simple secrets to this fabulous dish. Top it off with a sophisticated yet easy sauce: a luscious combo of tangy sour cream and coarse-grain mustard.

Chicken and Portobellos with Mustard Cream

❧

MAKES 6 SERVINGS

Prep: 15 minutes
Cook: Low 5 to 6 hours,
High 2½ to 3 hours

3	fresh portobello mushroom caps, sliced
2	cloves garlic, minced
3½	to 4 pounds meaty chicken pieces (breast halves, thighs, and drumsticks), skinned
2	teaspoons dried rosemary, crushed
½	teaspoon salt
¼	teaspoon black pepper
¼	cup reduced-sodium chicken broth
¼	cup dry white wine
½	cup light dairy sour cream
1	tablespoon coarse-grain Dijon-style mustard

1. In a 4- to 5-quart slow cooker combine mushrooms and garlic. Add chicken. Sprinkle chicken with rosemary, salt, and pepper. Pour broth and wine over mixture in cooker.

2. Cover and cook on low-heat setting for 5 to 6 hours or on high-heat setting for 2½ to 3 hours.

3. Using a slotted spoon, transfer chicken and mushrooms to a serving platter; discard cooking liquid.

4. For mustard cream, in a small bowl combine sour cream and mustard. Serve chicken and mushrooms with mustard cream.

Nutrition Facts per serving: 207 cal., 7 g total fat (2 g sat. fat), 96 mg chol., 392 mg sodium, 4 g carbo., 1 g fiber, 31 g pro.

Lemon and lime juice combine with savory chicken broth and seep into the chicken pieces to make this tantalizing dish ultra tasty and tender. Chili powder adds plenty of spicy flavor.

Lemon-Lime Chili Chicken

MAKES 6 SERVINGS

Prep: 15 minutes
Cook: Low 5 to 6 hours,
High 2½ to 3 hours

2	tablespoons chili powder
1	teaspoon salt
½	teaspoon black pepper
3	to 3½ pounds meaty chicken pieces (breast halves, thighs, and drumsticks), skinned
1	medium zucchini or yellow summer squash, halved lengthwise and cut into 1-inch pieces
1	medium onion, cut into wedges
¼	cup reduced-sodium chicken broth
¼	cup lime juice
¼	cup lemon juice
2	cloves garlic, minced

1. In a small bowl combine chili powder, salt, and pepper. Sprinkle spice mixture over chicken; rub in with your fingers. Place chicken in a 4- to 5-quart slow cooker. Add zucchini and onion. In a small bowl combine broth, lime juice, lemon juice, and garlic. Pour over mixture in cooker.

2. Cover and cook on low-heat setting for 5 to 6 hours or on high-heat setting for 2½ to 3 hours.

3. Using a slotted spoon, transfer chicken and vegetables to a serving platter. Discard cooking liquid.

Nutrition Facts per serving: 156 cal., 4 g total fat (1 g sat. fat), 76 mg chol., 525 mg sodium, 6 g carbo., 1 g fiber, 24 g pro.

Fresh mushrooms come in all shapes and sizes. Small whole button mushrooms make a great presentation when serving this meal, but if unavailable, use sliced button mushrooms or baby portobellos as a substitute.

Chicken and Mushrooms

MAKES 4 SERVINGS

Prep: 25 minutes
Cook: Low 8 to 9 hours,
High 4 to 4½ hours

- 2 cups small whole or sliced fresh mushrooms
- 1 14.5-ounce can diced tomatoes with basil, garlic, and oregano, undrained
- 1 medium red sweet pepper, cut into bite-size strips
- 1 medium onion, thinly sliced
- ¼ cup dry red wine or beef broth
- 2 tablespoons quick-cooking tapioca
- 2 tablespoons balsamic vinegar
- 3 cloves garlic, minced
- 2 to 2½ pounds meaty chicken pieces (breast halves, thighs, and drumsticks), skinned
- ¼ teaspoon salt
- ¼ teaspoon paprika
- ¼ teaspoon black pepper
- 2 cups hot cooked pasta

1. In a 5- to 6-quart slow cooker combine mushrooms, undrained tomatoes, sweet pepper, onion, wine, tapioca, balsamic vinegar, and garlic. Add chicken. Sprinkle chicken with salt, paprika, and black pepper.

2. Cover and cook on low-heat setting for 8 to 9 hours or on high-heat setting for 4 to 4½ hours.

3. Serve chicken and mushroom mixture over cooked pasta.

Nutrition Facts per serving: 421 cal., 8 g total fat (2 g sat. fat), 92 mg chol., 766 mg sodium, 45 g carbo., 4 g fiber, 38 g pro.

Calling all hearty appetites! To add to the flavor and appeal of this satisfying meal, serve with a side of nutritionally rich baked sweet potatoes. Snip fresh parsley to add a last-minute garnish.

Creamy Tarragon Turkey

❧

MAKES 6 SERVINGS

Prep: 15 minutes
Cook: Low 5 to 6 hours,
High 2½ to 3 hours,
plus 15 minutes (high)

2	medium fennel bulbs, trimmed and cut into thin wedges (2 cups)
1	large onion, cut into thin wedges
2¼	pounds turkey breast tenderloin
½	cup reduced-sodium chicken broth
1	tablespoon Dijon-style mustard
½	teaspoon dried tarragon, crushed
¼	teaspoon salt
¼	teaspoon black pepper
¼	cup half-and-half or light cream
4	teaspoons cornstarch
½	cup crumbled goat cheese (chèvre)
¼	cup snipped fresh parsley

1. In a 3½- or 4-quart slow cooker combine fennel and onion. Add turkey. In a small bowl combine broth, mustard, tarragon, salt, and pepper. Pour over mixture in cooker.

2. Cover and cook on low-heat setting for 5 to 6 hours or on high-heat setting for 2½ to 3 hours.

3. Using a slotted spoon, transfer turkey to a serving platter, reserving cooking liquid. Cover turkey with foil to keep warm.

4. If using low-heat setting, turn to high-heat setting. In a small bowl combine half-and-half and cornstarch. Stir into mixture in cooker. Cover and cook about 15 minutes more or until thickened.

5. To serve, cut turkey into serving-size pieces. Spoon the vegetable mixture over turkey. Sprinkle with cheese and parsley.

Nutrition Facts per serving: 258 cal., 4 g total fat (2 g sat. fat), 113 mg chol., 323 mg sodium, 7 g carbo., 1 g fiber, 45 g pro.

Rice and steamed Brussels sprouts make eye-catching, taste-tempting partners for this savory fruited chicken. For a change of pace, prepare your favorite rice pilaf mix and substitute it for the plain, hot cooked rice.

Cranberry Chicken

MAKES 6 SERVINGS

Prep: 15 minutes
Cook: Low 5 to 6 hours,
High 2½ to 3 hours

2½	to 3 pounds chicken thighs and/or drumsticks, skinned
1	16-ounce can whole cranberry sauce
2	tablespoons onion soup mix
2	tablespoons quick-cooking tapioca
3	cups hot cooked rice

1. Place chicken in a 3½- or 4-quart slow cooker. In a medium bowl combine cranberry sauce, dry soup mix, and tapioca. Pour over chicken in cooker.

2. Cover and cook on low-heat setting for 5 to 6 hours or on high-heat setting for 2½ to 3 hours. Serve chicken and sauce over hot cooked rice.

Nutrition Facts per serving: 357 cal., 4 g total fat (1 g sat. fat), 89 mg chol., 268 mg sodium, 55 g carbo., 1 g fiber, 23 g pro.

Water chestnuts and slivered almonds give this creamy chicken-and-vegetable medley plenty of crunch and taste appeal. The tapioca thickens the cooking liquid to make it perfect for serving over cooked rice.

Nutty Chicken

MAKES 6 SERVINGS

Prep: 20 minutes
Cook: Low 6 to 7 hours,
High 3 to 3½ hours

1	10.75-ounce can condensed golden mushroom soup
¼	cup reduced-sodium soy sauce
3	tablespoons quick-cooking tapioca, crushed
¼	to ½ teaspoon crushed red pepper
1½	pounds skinless, boneless chicken thighs, cut into ½-inch pieces
1	16-ounce package frozen French-cut green beans
3	stalks celery, thinly sliced (1½ cups)
1	8-ounce can sliced water chestnuts, drained
1	2-ounce jar sliced pimiento or ¼ cup bottled roasted red sweet peppers, drained and chopped
1	cup slivered almonds or broken walnuts, toasted (see tip, page 29), or cashew halves
3	cups hot cooked rice

1. In a 4- to 5-quart slow cooker combine soup, soy sauce, tapioca, and crushed red pepper. Stir in chicken, frozen green beans, celery, drained water chestnuts, and pimiento.

2. Cover and cook on low-heat setting for 6 to 7 hours or on high-heat setting for 3 to 3½ hours. Stir in nuts.

3. Serve chicken mixture over hot cooked rice.

Nutrition Facts per serving: 513 cal., 20 g total fat (3 g sat. fat), 93 mg chol., 862 mg sodium, 54 g carbo., 6 g fiber, 34 g pro.

*Rich hoisin sauce, a deep reddish-brown Chinese condiment,
and plums impart a sweet-and-spicy flavor to the chicken.
Look for hoisin sauce in the specialty food section of the
supermarket and in Asian markets.*

Plum-Sauced Chicken in Tortillas

MAKES 6 SERVINGS

Prep: 15 minutes
Cook: Low 4 to 5 hours,
High 2 to 2½ hours

1	30-ounce can whole unpitted purple plums, drained
1	cup hot-style vegetable juice
¼	cup bottled hoisin sauce
4½	teaspoons quick-cooking tapioca
2	teaspoons grated fresh ginger
½	teaspoon five-spice powder
¼	teaspoon salt
⅛	to ¼ teaspoon cayenne pepper
1¼	pounds skinless, boneless chicken thighs, cut into bite-size strips
6	7- to 8-inch flour tortillas, warmed (see tip, right)
2	cups packaged shredded broccoli (broccoli slaw mix) or shredded cabbage with carrot (coleslaw mix)

1. Remove pits from drained plums. Place plums in a blender or food processor. Cover and blend or process until smooth. Transfer plums to a 3½- or 4-quart slow cooker. Stir in vegetable juice, hoisin sauce, tapioca, ginger, five-spice powder, salt, and cayenne pepper. Stir in chicken.

2. Cover and cook on low-heat setting for 4 to 5 hours or on high-heat setting for 2 to 2½ hours. Using a slotted spoon, remove chicken from cooker, reserving cooking liquid.

3. Spoon about ⅓ cup of the chicken onto each warm tortilla just below the center. Drizzle with some of the reserved cooking liquid. Top each with ⅓ cup of the shredded broccoli. Roll up tortillas.

Nutrition Facts per serving: 331 cal., 4 g total fat (1 g sat. fat), 55 mg chol., 575 mg sodium, 47 g carbo., 3 g fiber, 26 g pro.

Test Kitchen Tip: When you want to warm flour tortillas, stack the tortillas between paper towels and heat them in the microwave oven on 100 percent power (high). For two to four tortillas, allow 20 to 30 seconds; for six or more tortillas, allow 30 to 45 seconds. Or warm them in the oven by wrapping the tortillas in foil and heating them in a 350°F oven for about 10 minutes.

French, Spanish, and African cuisines are the foundation of Creole cooking. With such wide and varied origins, it's no wonder this popular cooking style appeals to such a broad range of people.

Creole Chicken

MAKES 6 SERVINGS

Prep: 25 minutes
Cook: Low 5 to 6 hours,
High 2½ to 3 hours (high)
Stand: 10 minutes

1	pound skinless, boneless chicken thighs, cut into ¾-inch pieces
1	14.5-ounce can diced tomatoes, undrained
1	14-ounce can chicken broth
8	ounces cooked smoked Polish sausage, coarsely chopped
1	cup diced cooked ham
¾	cup chopped onion
1	6-ounce can tomato paste
½	cup water
1½	teaspoons Cajun seasoning
	Several dashes bottled hot pepper sauce
2	cups uncooked instant white or brown rice
1	large green sweet pepper, chopped (1 cup)
	Bottled hot pepper sauce (optional)

1. In a 3½- or 4-quart slow cooker combine chicken, undrained tomatoes, broth, sausage, ham, onion, tomato paste, water, Cajun seasoning, and the several dashes hot pepper sauce.

2. Cover and cook on low-heat setting for 5 to 6 hours or on high-heat setting for 2½ to 3 hours. Turn off cooker.

3. Stir in rice and sweet pepper. Let stand, covered, for 10 to 15 minutes or until rice is tender and most of the liquid is absorbed. If desired, serve with additional hot pepper sauce.

Nutrition Facts per serving: 439 cal., 18 g total fat (6 g sat. fat), 99 mg chol., 1,362 mg sodium, 41 g carbo., 2 g fiber, 28 g pro.

*A down-home favorite goes uptown! Here smoked salmon and
dill add a gourmet angle to creamed turkey and mushrooms. For
a colorful accompaniment, try a medley of steamed vegetables
and toss with your favorite salad dressing.*

Creamed Turkey and Smoked Salmon

MAKES 6 SERVINGS

Prep: 20 minutes
Cook: Low 3½ hours,
High 1½ hours,
plus 15 minutes (high)

2	pounds turkey breast tenderloin
8	ounces fresh mushrooms, quartered
⅓	cup water
1	teaspoon salt
½	teaspoon dried dill
¼	teaspoon black pepper
¾	cup half-and-half or light cream
2	tablespoons cornstarch
4	ounces smoked salmon (not lox-style), skinned and flaked
¼	cup sliced green onion (2)

1. Cut turkey into 1-inch pieces. In a 3½- or 4-quart slow cooker combine turkey and mushrooms. Stir in water, salt, dill, and pepper.

2. Cover and cook on low-heat setting for 3½ hours or on high-heat setting for 1½ hours.

3. If using low-heat setting, turn to high-heat setting. In a small bowl combine half-and-half and cornstarch. Stir into mixture in cooker. Cover and cook for 15 minutes more. Stir in salmon and green onion.

Nutrition Facts per serving: 254 cal., 7 g total fat (3 g sat. fat), 106 mg chol., 623 mg sodium, 5 g carbo., 1 g fiber, 41 g pro.

Many chain restaurants serve a version of an Asian Chicken Salad, but tonight drive past them knowing that a home-cooked version is waiting at home. The fresh-tasting recipe makes plenty, so it is ideal for a gathering. (Photo on page 269.)

Chinese Chicken Salad

MAKES 6 SERVINGS

Prep: 15 minutes
Cook: Low 5 to 6 hours,
High 2½ to 3 hours

2	pounds chicken thighs, skinned
	Black pepper
2	stalks celery, chopped (1 cup)
1	medium onion, chopped (½ cup)
2	cloves garlic, minced
½	cup bottled hoisin sauce
3	tablespoons reduced-sodium soy sauce
2	tablespoons grated fresh ginger
1	tablespoon dry sherry
2	teaspoons Asian chili sauce
1	teaspoon toasted sesame oil
¼	cup rice vinegar
8	cups shredded romaine lettuce
2	medium carrots, shredded (1 cup)
2	tablespoons snipped fresh cilantro
½	cup unsalted dry-roasted cashews (optional)

1. Sprinkle chicken with pepper. Place chicken in a 3- to 4-quart slow cooker. Add celery, onion, and garlic. In a small bowl combine hoisin sauce, soy sauce, ginger, sherry, chili sauce, and sesame oil. Stir into mixture in cooker.

2. Cover and cook on low-heat setting for 5 to 6 hours or on high-heat setting for 2½ to 3 hours.

3. Using a slotted spoon, transfer chicken to a cutting board, reserving ½ cup of the cooking liquid. When chicken is cool enough to handle, remove chicken from bones and discard bones. Shred chicken by pulling two forks through it in opposite directions.

4. For dressing, in a screw-top jar combine the reserved ½ cup cooking liquid and the rice vinegar. Cover and shake until combined; set aside.

5. In a large salad bowl combine chicken, lettuce, carrot, and cilantro. Before serving, top with cashews, if desired. Shake dressing and drizzle over salad. Toss to coat.

Nutrition Facts per serving: 191 cal., 5 g total fat (1 g sat. fat), 71 mg chol., 682 mg sodium, 14 g carbo., 3 g fiber, 20 g pro.

Ground turkey gets a Tex-Mex treatment with green salsa in this homey meal. Any leftovers can be used another day to make nachos.

Green Chile Taco Salad

MAKES 6 SERVINGS

Prep: 20 minutes
Cook: Low 6 to 8 hours,
High 3 to 3½ hours

1   pound uncooked ground turkey or chicken, or lean ground beef
1   16-ounce jar mild green salsa
1   15-ounce can Great Northern beans, rinsed and drained
1   large green sweet pepper, chopped (1 cup)
1   large onion, finely chopped (1 cup)
1   10-ounce package romaine salad mix
3   cups crushed tortilla chips
½   cup sliced green onion (4)
½   cup snipped fresh cilantro
    Chopped tomato (optional)

1. In a large skillet cook ground turkey until meat is brown. Drain off fat. Transfer turkey to a 3½- or 4-quart slow cooker. Stir in salsa, drained beans, sweet pepper, and onion.

2. Cover and cook on low-heat setting for 6 to 8 hours or on high-heat setting for 3 to 3½ hours.

3. To serve, divide romaine mix among salad plates. Top with turkey mixture. Sprinkle with tortilla chips, green onion, cilantro, and, if desired, tomato.

Nutrition Facts per serving: 375 cal., 13 g total fat (2 g sat. fat), 60 mg chol., 475 mg sodium, 44 g carbo., 9 g fiber, 22 g pro.

As an alternative, try a fragrant rice, such as jasmine or basmati, with this fork-tender beef and rich, slightly sweet brown gravy.

Jerk Beef Roast

MAKES 6 SERVINGS

Prep: 20 minutes
Cook: Low 8 to 10 hours,
High 4 to 5 hours

1	2- to 2½-pound boneless beef chuck pot roast
¾	cup water
¼	cup raisins
¼	cup bottled steak sauce
3	tablespoons balsamic vinegar
2	tablespoons sugar
2	tablespoons quick-cooking tapioca
1	teaspoon cracked black pepper
1	teaspoon Jamaican jerk seasoning
2	cloves garlic, minced
3	cups hot cooked brown rice

1. Trim fat from meat. If necessary, cut meat to fit into a 3½- or 4-quart slow cooker. Place meat in the cooker. In a small bowl combine water, raisins, steak sauce, balsamic vinegar, sugar, tapioca, pepper, jerk seasoning, and garlic. Pour over meat in cooker.

2. Cover and cook on low-heat setting for 8 to 10 hours or on high-heat setting for 4 to 5 hours.

3. Transfer meat to a serving platter, reserving cooking liquid. Skim fat from liquid. Serve meat and cooking liquid with hot cooked brown rice.

Nutrition Facts per serving: 359 cal., 7 g total fat (3 g sat. fat), 92 mg chol., 269 mg sodium, 39 g carbo., 1 g fiber, 33 g pro.

Serve this comforting dinner with plenty of crusty French bread to soak up the garlicky cooking juices flavored with thyme and wine.

French-Style Pot Roast

MAKES 6 SERVINGS

Prep: 20 minutes
Cook: Low 11 to 12 hours,
High 5½ to 6 hours

1	3-pound boneless beef chuck pot roast
6	medium carrots, cut into 2-inch pieces
1	large onion, sliced
1	4.5-ounce jar (drained weight) sliced mushrooms, drained
2	tablespoons quick-cooking tapioca
¾	cup dry red wine or beef broth
2	teaspoons instant beef bouillon granules
¼	teaspoon dried thyme, crushed
¼	teaspoon black pepper
4	cloves garlic, minced
1	14.5-ounce can cut Italian or regular green beans, drained

1. Trim fat from meat. If necessary, cut meat to fit into a 4½- to 6-quart slow cooker. Set aside.

2. In the cooker combine carrot, onion, and drained mushrooms. Sprinkle with tapioca. Place meat on top of vegetables. In a small bowl combine wine, bouillon granules, thyme, pepper, and garlic. Pour over mixture in cooker.

3. Cover and cook on low-heat setting for 11 to 12 hours or on high-heat setting for 5½ to 6 hours. Using a slotted spoon, transfer meat to a serving platter; cover with foil to keep warm.

4. Stir drained green beans into vegetable mixture. Using the slotted spoon, transfer vegetables to the serving platter. Skim fat from cooking liquid. Serve meat and vegetables with cooking liquid.

Nutrition Facts per serving: 375 cal., 9 g total fat (3 g sat. fat), 134 mg chol., 662 mg sodium, 17 g carbo., 4 g fiber, 50 g pro.

Pot roast heads for the untamed West when slow cooked with chili beans, corn, tomatoes, and spicy chipotle peppers in adobo sauce. Yellow corn bread makes a quick and tasty side.

Cowboy Beef

MAKES 6 SERVINGS

Prep: 10 minutes
Cook: Low 10 to 12 hours, High 5 to 6 hours

- 1 2- to 2½-pound boneless beef chuck pot roast
- 1 15-ounce can chili beans in chili gravy, undrained
- 1 11-ounce can whole kernel corn with sweet peppers, drained
- 1 10-ounce can diced tomatoes and green chile peppers, undrained
- 1 to 2 teaspoons finely chopped canned chipotle pepper in adobo sauce (see tip, page 10)

1. Trim fat from meat. If necessary, cut meat to fit into a 3½- or 4-quart slow cooker. Place meat in the cooker.

2. In a medium bowl combine undrained beans in chili gravy, drained corn, undrained tomatoes and chile peppers, and chipotle pepper. Pour over meat in cooker.

3. Cover and cook on low-heat setting for 10 to 12 hours or on high-heat setting for 5 to 6 hours.

4. Transfer meat to a cutting board. Slice meat; transfer to a shallow serving bowl. Using a slotted spoon, spoon bean mixture over meat. Drizzle with enough of the cooking liquid to moisten.

Nutrition Facts per serving: 307 cal., 7 g total fat (2 g sat. fat), 89 mg chol., 655 mg sodium, 23 g carbo., 5 g fiber, 37 g pro.

Unusual and delicious, this tender beef roast with veggies and a thick brown gravy gets a sweet kick from a can of cola.

Cola Pot Roast

MAKES 6 SERVINGS

Prep: 15 minutes
Cook: Low 7 to 8 hours,
High 3½ to 4 hours

1   2½- to 3-pound boneless beef chuck pot roast

     Nonstick cooking spray

2   16-ounce packages frozen stew vegetables

1   12-ounce can cola

1   envelope (½ of a 2-ounce package) onion soup mix

2   tablespoons quick-cooking tapioca

1. Trim fat from meat. If necessary, cut meat to fit into a 4½- or 5-quart slow cooker. Lightly coat a large skillet with nonstick cooking spray; heat skillet over medium heat. Brown meat on all sides in hot skillet. Drain off fat.

2. Transfer meat to the cooker. Add frozen vegetables. In a medium bowl combine cola, soup mix, and tapioca; pour over mixture in cooker.

3. Cover and cook on low-heat setting for 7 to 8 hours or on high-heat setting for 3½ to 4 hours.

Nutrition Facts per serving: 278 cal., 5 g total fat (2 g sat. fat), 75 mg chol., 582 mg sodium, 28 g carbo., 2 g fiber, 29 g pro.

Fresh green beans, black bean garlic sauce, and rice turn everyday pot roast into a Chinese feast. Look for the bold-flavored bean sauce in the Asian section of your supermarket or at a specialty market.

Black Bean Pot Roast

MAKES 6 SERVINGS

Prep: 30 minutes
Cook: Low 9 to 10 hours,
High 4½ to 5 hours,
plus 15 minutes (high)

1	2-pound boneless beef chuck pot roast
1½	cups water
¼	cup black bean garlic sauce
1	tablespoon sugar
1	teaspoon instant beef bouillon granules
12	ounces fresh green beans, trimmed and cut in 2-inch pieces (2½ cups)
½	of a medium onion, cut into thin strips
3	tablespoons cornstarch
3	tablespoons cold water
1	medium red sweet pepper, cut into thin strips
3	cups hot cooked rice

1. Trim fat from meat. If necessary, cut meat to fit into a 4- to 5-quart slow cooker. Set aside. In the cooker combine the 1½ cups water, the garlic sauce, sugar, and bouillon granules. Stir in green beans and onion. Place meat on top of mixture in cooker.

2. Cover and cook on low-heat setting for 9 to 10 hours or on high-heat setting for 4½ to 5 hours.

3. Transfer meat to a cutting board and vegetables to a serving platter, reserving cooking liquid. Slice meat and transfer to the serving platter; cover with foil to keep warm.

4. If using low-heat setting, turn to high-heat setting. For sauce, in a small bowl combine cornstarch and the 3 tablespoons water; stir into cooking liquid. Stir in sweet pepper. Cover and cook about 15 minutes more or until sauce is slightly thickened and sweet pepper is tender.

5. Serve meat and vegetables with sauce and hot cooked rice.

Nutrition Facts per serving: 358 cal., 7 g total fat (2 g sat. fat), 89 mg chol., 471 mg sodium, 36 g carbo., 3 g fiber, 37 g pro.

Cut precious minutes from dinner prep by using fresh pasta found in your grocer's refrigerator case. It takes about half the time to cook as dried pasta.

Italian-Style Round Steak

MAKES 6 SERVINGS

Prep: 20 minutes
Cook: Low 9 to 10 hours,
High 4½ to 5 hours

1½	pounds boneless beef round steak, cut ¾ inch thick
1	14.5-ounce can Italian-style stewed tomatoes, undrained
2	medium carrots, cut into ½-inch pieces
2	stalks celery, cut into ½-inch pieces
1	cup quartered fresh mushrooms
1	cup beef broth
½	cup sliced green onion (4)
½	cup dry red or white wine or beef broth
3	tablespoons quick-cooking tapioca
1	teaspoon dried Italian seasoning, crushed
½	teaspoon salt
¼	teaspoon black pepper
1	bay leaf
3	cups hot cooked noodles

1. Trim fat from meat. Cut meat into 1-inch pieces. Place meat in a 3½- or 4-quart slow cooker. Add undrained tomatoes, carrot, celery, mushrooms, broth, green onion, wine, tapioca, Italian seasoning, salt, pepper, and bay leaf.

2. Cover and cook on low-heat setting for 9 to 10 hours or on high-heat setting for 4½ to 5 hours. Remove bay leaf.

3. Serve meat mixture over hot cooked noodles.

Nutrition Facts per serving: 324 cal., 7 g total fat (2 g sat. fat), 83 mg chol., 552 mg sodium, 33 g carbo., 3 g fiber, 27 g pro.

Vegetable Stew with Parmesan Toast
(Recipe on page 293)

Smoky Barbecued Beef Brisket
(Recipe on page 156)

130

Chicken Tostadas
(Recipe on page 306)

Honey-Mustard Barbecue Pork Ribs
(Recipe on page 49)

Thai-Style Vegetable Rice
(Recipe on page 56)

Curried Lentil Soup
(Recipe on page 88)

Steak Sandwiches with Ratatouille
(Recipe on page 152)

Italian Chicken and Pasta
(Recipe on page 28)

Deviled Steak Strips
(Recipe on page 35)

Greek Sandwich Wraps
(Recipe on page 309)

Lentil and Ham Soup
(Recipe on page 16)

Peppery Beef Sandwiches
(Recipe on page 40)

Mexican-Style Sausage and Beans
(Recipe on page 32)

Southwest Pork Chops
(Recipe on page 44)

Fruit Compote with Ginger
(Recipe on page 322)

Teriyaki Chicken with Orange Sauce
(Recipe on page 27)

Acorn Squash with Orange-Cranberry Sauce
(Recipe on page 217)

Garlic and Artichoke Pasta
(Recipe on page 193)

Red Curry Chicken Wings
(Recipe on page 247)

This long-simmering entrée will fill your home with an enchanting fragrance. Strong-brewed coffee may sound like a bizarre ingredient in a meat dish, but it enriches the flavor of the full-bodied brown sauce.

Swiss Steak Café

MAKES 6 SERVINGS

Prep: 20 minutes
Cook: Low 8 to 10 hours,
High 4 to 5 hours,
plus 15 minutes (high)

2	pounds boneless beef round steak, cut ¾ inch thick
1	tablespoon cooking oil
3	medium onions, cut into wedges
1	cup strong-brewed coffee
2	tablespoons reduced-sodium soy sauce
½	teaspoon dried oregano, crushed
2	cloves garlic, minced
2	bay leaves
4	teaspoons cornstarch
4	teaspoons cold water

1. Trim fat from meat. Cut meat into 6 serving-size pieces. In a large skillet brown meat, half at a time, on both sides in hot oil over medium heat. Drain off fat. Set aside.

2. Place onion in a 3½- or 4-quart slow cooker. Add meat. In a small bowl combine coffee, soy sauce, oregano, garlic, and bay leaves. Pour over mixture in cooker.

3. Cover and cook on low-heat setting for 8 to 10 hours or on high-heat setting for 4 to 5 hours.

4. Using a slotted spoon, transfer meat and onion to a serving platter, reserving cooking liquid. Cover meat and onion with foil to keep warm.

5. If using low-heat setting, turn to high-heat setting. For sauce, in a small bowl combine cornstarch and water; stir into liquid in cooker. Cover and cook about 15 minutes more or until thickened. Remove bay leaves.

6. To serve, spoon some of the sauce over meat and onion; pass the remaining sauce.

Nutrition Facts per serving: 224 cal., 6 g total fat (1 g sat. fat), 85 mg chol., 387 mg sodium, 6 g carbo., 1 g fiber, 36 g pro.

Sassy and lively like the classic cocktail, this easy steak dinner is sensational served with torn greens and steamed yellow summer squash.

Bloody Mary Steak

MAKES 6 SERVINGS

Prep: 20 minutes
Cook: Low 8 to 9 hours,
High 4 to 4½ hours

2	pounds boneless beef round steak, cut ¾ inch thick
	Nonstick cooking spray
¾	cup hot-style tomato juice
¼	cup water
2	cloves garlic, minced
4	teaspoons cornstarch
2	tablespoons cold water
2	teaspoons prepared horseradish

1. Trim fat from meat. Cut meat into 6 serving-size pieces. Lightly coat a large skillet with nonstick cooking spray; heat skillet over medium-high heat. Brown meat on both sides in hot skillet. Drain off fat. Transfer meat to a 2½- to 3½-quart slow cooker. Add tomato juice, the ¼ cup water, and the garlic to meat in cooker.

2. Cover and cook on low-heat setting for 8 to 9 hours or on high-heat setting for 4 to 4½ hours.

3. Transfer meat to a cutting board, reserving cooking liquid. Slice meat. Transfer meat to a serving platter; cover with foil to keep warm.

4. For gravy, pour cooking liquid into a glass measuring cup; skim off fat. Measure 1½ cups liquid (add water, if necessary).

5. In a small saucepan combine cornstarch and the 2 tablespoons water; stir in the 1½ cups liquid. Cook and stir over medium heat until thickened and bubbly. Cook and stir for 2 minutes more. Stir in horseradish. Serve meat with gravy.

Nutrition Facts per serving: 196 cal., 4 g total fat (1 g sat. fat), 85 mg chol., 292 mg sodium, 3 g carbo., 0 g fiber, 35 g pro.

The addition of spicy bratwurst brings a new flavor dimension to slow-cooked beef round steak that simmers in an herbed tomato sauce. To complete the hearty meal, serve the meat mixture over noodles or heat-and-serve refrigerated spuds.

Beef and Brats

MAKES 4 SERVINGS

Prep: 20 minutes
Cook: Low 8 to 9 hours,
High 4 to 4½ hours

1¼	pounds boneless beef round steak, cut 1 inch thick
8	ounces uncooked bratwurst or other sausage, cut into ¾-inch-thick slices
1	tablespoon cooking oil
1	small onion, sliced and separated into rings
2	tablespoons quick-cooking tapioca
1	teaspoon dried thyme, crushed
¼	teaspoon salt
¼	teaspoon black pepper
1	14.5-ounce can diced tomatoes with basil, garlic, and oregano, undrained
2	cups hot cooked noodles

1. Trim fat from steak. Cut steak into 4 serving-size pieces. In a large skillet brown steak and bratwurst on all sides in hot oil over medium heat. Drain off fat. Set aside.

2. Place onion in a 3½- or 4-quart slow cooker. Sprinkle with tapioca, thyme, salt, and pepper. Add steak and bratwurst. Pour undrained tomatoes over mixture in cooker.

3. Cover and cook on low-heat setting for 8 to 9 hours or on high-heat setting for 4 to 4½ hours. Serve steak, bratwurst, and tomato mixture with hot cooked noodles.

Nutrition Facts per serving: 570 cal., 23 g total fat (9 g sat. fat), 145 mg chol., 1,261 mg sodium, 37 g carbo., 2 g fiber, 50 g pro.

These delicious steak rolls have an Italian flair from the addition of Parmesan cheese and pasta sauce. If you can't find tenderized beef round steak, ask your butcher to tenderize two pounds of boneless beef round steak and cut it into six pieces.

Italian Steak Rolls

MAKES 6 SERVINGS

Prep: 30 minutes
Cook: Low 8 to 10 hours,
High 4 to 5 hours

1   medum carrot, shredded
    (½ cup)
⅓   cup chopped zucchini
⅓   cup chopped red or green
    sweet pepper
¼   cup sliced green onion (2)
2   tablespoons grated
    Parmesan cheese
1   tablespoon snipped fresh
    parsley
¼   teaspoon black pepper
1   clove garlic, minced
6   tenderized beef round
    steaks (about 2 pounds
    total)
2   cups purchased meatless
    pasta sauce
    Hot cooked pasta
    (optional)

1. For filling, in a medium bowl combine carrot, zucchini, sweet pepper, green onion, Parmesan cheese, parsley, black pepper, and garlic. Spoon ¼ cup of the filling onto each steak. Roll up steak around the filling and tie each roll with 100-percent-cotton kitchen string or secure with wooden toothpicks.

2. Transfer steak rolls to a 3½- or 4-quart slow cooker. Pour pasta sauce over steak rolls in cooker.

3. Cover and cook on low-heat setting for 8 to 10 hours or on high-heat setting for 4 to 5 hours.

4. Remove string or toothpicks. If desired, serve steak rolls and sauce with hot cooked pasta.

Nutrition Facts per serving: 280 cal., 9 g total fat (3 g sat. fat), 89 mg chol., 524 mg sodium, 12 g carbo., 1 g fiber, 36 g pro.

Brimming with all the flavors and fixings of a traditional stir-fry, this easy beef and veggie combo is dressed with a soy-flavored sauce that begins with an envelope of brown gravy mix.

Ginger Beef with Broccoli

MAKES 6 SERVINGS

Prep: 20 minutes
Cook: Low 7 to 8 hours,
High 3½ to 4 hours,
plus 15 minutes (high)

1½	pounds boneless beef round steak, cut ¾ inch thick
6	medium carrots, cut into 1-inch pieces
2	medium onions, cut into wedges
2	tablespoons grated fresh ginger or 2 teaspoons ground ginger
2	cloves garlic, minced
½	cup water
2	tablespoons soy sauce
1	0.87-ounce envelope brown gravy mix
4	cups broccoli florets
3	cups hot cooked rice

1. Trim fat from meat. Thinly slice meat diagonally across the grain. In a 3½- or 4-quart slow cooker combine meat, carrot, onion, ginger, and garlic. In a small bowl combine water, soy sauce, and brown gravy mix. Pour over mixture in cooker.

2. Cover and cook on low-heat setting for 7 to 8 hours or on high-heat setting for 3½ to 4 hours.

3. If using low-heat setting, turn to high-heat setting. Stir in broccoli. Cover and cook about 15 minutes more or until broccoli is crisp-tender. Serve meat mixture over rice.

Nutrition Facts per serving: 338 cal., 7 g total fat (2 g sat. fat), 76 mg chol., 676 mg sodium, 37 g carbo., 5 g fiber, 31 g pro.

Test Kitchen Tip: If you plan to start a slow-cooked dish before you head out for the day, ease the last-minute rush by preparing the ingredients the night before. Chop vegetables and refrigerate them in separate containers. Assemble, cover, and chill liquid ingredients or sauces. Brown ground meat or poultry and bulk sausage ahead, making sure it is no longer pink. Then store it, tightly covered, in the refrigerator.

Add a flavor wallop to the herb-seasoned round steak with canned chipotle peppers in adobo sauce. The smoky, sweet, and almost chocolate-flavored pepper comes packed in a thick dark red paste made piquant with spices and vinegar.

Beef and Chipotle Burritos

MAKES 6 SERVINGS

Prep: 20 minutes
Cook: Low 8 to 10 hours,
High 4 to 5 hours

1½	pounds boneless beef round steak, cut ¾ inch thick
1	14.5-ounce can diced tomatoes, undrained
1	small onion, chopped (⅓ cup)
1	to 2 canned chipotle peppers in adobo sauce, chopped (see tip, page 10)
1	teaspoon dried oregano, crushed
¼	teaspoon ground cumin
1	clove garlic, minced
6	9- to 10-inch flour tortillas, warmed (see tip, page 118)
¾	cup shredded cheddar cheese
1	recipe Pico de Gallo Salsa or bottled picante sauce
	Shredded jicama or radishes (optional)
	Dairy sour cream (optional)

1. Trim fat from meat. If necessary, cut meat to fit into a 3½- or 4-quart slow cooker. Place meat in cooker. In a medium bowl combine undrained tomatoes, onion, chipotle pepper, oregano, cumin, and garlic; pour over meat in cooker.

2. Cover and cook on low-heat setting for 8 to 10 hours or on high-heat setting for 4 to 5 hours.

3. Using a slotted spoon, remove meat from cooker, reserving cooking liquid. Shred meat by pulling two forks through it in opposite directions. Transfer meat to a medium bowl. Drizzle with enough of the liquid to moisten.

4. Spoon meat onto warm tortillas just below the centers. Top with cheese, Pico de Gallo Salsa, and, if desired, jicama and sour cream. Roll up tortillas.

Pico de Gallo Salsa: In a small bowl combine 1 cup finely chopped tomatoes (2 medium); 2 tablespoons finely chopped onion; 2 tablespoons snipped fresh cilantro; 1 fresh serrano chile pepper, seeded and finely chopped (see tip, page 10); and dash sugar. Cover and chill until ready to serve.

Nutrition Facts per serving: 382 cal., 13 g total fat (5 g sat. fat), 69 mg chol., 663 mg sodium, 32 g carbo., 3 g fiber, 34 g pro.

Queso fresco (KAY-so FRESK-o) means "fresh cheese" in Spanish. It is in the refrigerated section of large supermarkets and Latino food stores.

Spicy Steak and Beans

MAKES 6 SERVINGS

Prep: 25 minutes
Cook: Low 7 to 9 hours,
High 3½ to 4½ hours,
plus 30 minutes (high)

1½	pounds beef flank steak
1	14.5-ounce can diced tomatoes and green chile peppers, undrained
1	medium onion, chopped (½ cup)
1½	to 2 teaspoons chili powder
1	teaspoon dried oregano, crushed
1	teaspoon ground cumin
¼	to ½ teaspoon black pepper
2	cloves garlic, minced
2	medium green, red, and/or yellow sweet peppers, cut into strips
1	15-ounce can pinto beans, rinsed and drained
3	cups hot cooked brown rice
¼	cup crumbled queso fresco or feta cheese (optional)

1. Trim fat from meat. Cut meat to fit into a 3½- or 4-quart slow cooker. Place meat in cooker. In a medium bowl combine undrained tomatoes, onion, chili powder, oregano, cumin, black pepper, and garlic. Pour over meat in cooker.

2. Cover and cook on low-heat setting for 7 to 9 hours or on high-heat setting for 3½ to 4½ hours.

3. If using low-heat setting, turn to high-heat setting. Stir in sweet pepper and pinto beans. Cover and cook for 30 minutes more. Transfer meat to a cutting board. Shred or thinly slice meat across the grain.

4. To serve, divide hot cooked brown rice among shallow bowls. Top with meat. Spoon bean mixture over meat. If desired, sprinkle with cheese.

Nutrition Facts per serving: 372 cal., 8 g total fat (3 g sat. fat), 48 mg chol., 604 mg sodium, 41 g carbo., 7 g fiber, 33 g pro.

Although ratatouille traditionally contains eggplant, this appealing artichoke version is served in bistro-style steak sandwiches. For extra color, use half of a medium yellow squash and half of a medium zucchini. (Photo on page 134.)

Steak Sandwiches with Ratatouille

MAKES 6 SERVINGS

Prep: 30 minutes
Cook: Low 7 to 9 hours,
High 3½ to 4½ hours,
plus 30 minutes (high)

1½	pounds beef flank steak
1	teaspoon dried Italian seasoning, crushed
1½	cups sliced fresh mushrooms
1	medium onion, finely chopped (½ cup)
2	cloves garlic, minced
1	14.5-ounce can diced tomatoes, undrained
2	tablespoons red wine vinegar
1	medium yellow summer squash or zucchini, halved lengthwise and sliced (1¼ cups)
1	cup red, yellow, and/or green sweet pepper strips
1	9- to 10-inch Italian flatbread (focaccia)
1	6-ounce jar quartered marinated artichoke hearts, drained
⅓	cup finely shredded Asiago or Parmesan cheese

1. Trim fat from meat. If necessary, cut meat to fit into a 3½- or 4-quart slow cooker. Sprinkle both sides of meat with Italian seasoning, ⅛ teaspoon salt, and ⅛ teaspoon black pepper. Set aside.

2. In the cooker combine mushrooms, onion, and garlic. Add meat. Pour undrained tomatoes and vinegar over mixture in cooker.

3. Cover and cook on low-heat setting for 7 to 9 hours or on high-heat setting for 3½ to 4½ hours. If using low-heat setting, turn to high-heat setting. Add squash and sweet pepper. Cover and cook for 30 minutes more.

4. Transfer meat to a cutting board. Shred meat by pulling two forks through it in opposite directions.

5. Cut focaccia in half horizontally. Arrange meat on bottom of focaccia. Stir artichoke hearts into vegetable mixture in cooker. Using a slotted spoon, spoon vegetables onto meat. Drizzle with enough of the cooking liquid just to moisten; sprinkle with cheese. Add top of focaccia. Cut into wedges.

Nutrition Facts per serving: 431 cal., 17 g total fat (6 g sat. fat), 58 mg chol., 631 mg sodium, 36 g carbo., 3 g fiber, 33 g pro.

Show off the sophistication of Burgundy with this stew's deep woody taste blended with mellow mushrooms and vegetables. Serve it over a generous helping of noodles or garlic mashed potatoes.

Beef Burgundy

MAKES 6 SERVINGS

Prep: 20 minutes
Cook: Low 7 to 9 hours,
High 3½ to 4½ hours

2	pounds beef stew meat
	Nonstick cooking spray
1	16-ounce package frozen stew vegetables
1	10.75-ounce can condensed golden mushroom soup
⅔	cup Burgundy wine
⅓	cup water
1	tablespoon quick-cooking tapioca
	Hot cooked wide noodles or garlic mashed potatoes (optional)
	Snipped fresh parsley (optional)

1. Trim fat from meat. Cut meat into 2-inch pieces. Lightly coat a large skillet with nonstick cooking spray; heat skillet over medium heat. Brown meat, half at a time, in hot skillet. Drain off fat. Set aside.

2. Place frozen vegetables in a 3½- or 4-quart slow cooker. Add meat. In a medium bowl combine soup, wine, water, and tapioca. Pour over mixture in cooker.

3. Cover and cook on low-heat setting for 7 to 9 hours or on high-heat setting for 3½ to 4½ hours.

4. If desired, serve meat mixture over hot cooked noodles and sprinkle with parsley.

Nutrition Facts per serving: 291 cal., 8 g total fat (3 g sat. fat), 91 mg chol., 535 mg sodium, 14 g carbo., 1 g fiber, 34 g pro.

Beef Stroganoff usually calls for tenderloin or sirloin steak, but this recipe uses less-expensive stew meat and lets the slow cooker work its magic for rich and tender results.

Classic Beef Stroganoff

❧

MAKES 6 SERVINGS

Prep: 25 minutes
Cook: Low 8 to 10 hours,
High 4 to 5 hours,
plus 30 minutes (high)

1½	pounds beef stew meat
1	tablespoon cooking oil
2	cups sliced fresh mushrooms
½	cup sliced green onion (4) or 1 medium onion, chopped (½ cup)
½	teaspoon salt
½	teaspoon dried oregano, crushed
¼	teaspoon dried thyme, crushed
¼	teaspoon black pepper
2	cloves garlic, minced
1	bay leaf
1½	cups lower-sodium beef broth
⅓	cup dry sherry
1	8-ounce carton light dairy sour cream
¼	cup cold water
2	tablespoons cornstarch
	Snipped fresh parsley (optional)

1. Trim fat from meat. Cut meat into 1-inch pieces. In a large skillet brown meat, half at a time, in hot oil over medium heat. Drain off fat. Set aside.

2. In a 3½- or 4-quart slow cooker combine mushrooms, green onion, salt, oregano, thyme, pepper, garlic, and bay leaf. Add meat. Pour broth and sherry over mixture in cooker.

3. Cover and cook on low-heat setting for 8 to 10 hours or on high-heat setting for 4 to 5 hours. Remove bay leaf.

4. If using low-heat setting, turn to high-heat setting. In a medium bowl combine sour cream, water, and cornstarch. Stir about 1 cup of the hot cooking liquid into sour cream mixture. Stir sour cream mixture into mixture in cooker. Cover and cook about 30 minutes more or until thickened.

5. If desired, sprinkle individual servings with parsley.

Nutrition Facts per serving: 248 cal., 9 g total fat (4 g sat. fat), 79 mg chol., 408 mg sodium, 8 g carbo., 1 g fiber, 28 g pro.

A jar of plum sauce, rice vinegar, and grated fresh ginger are your passports to this exotic dish. For a traditional accompaniment to Asian-style cooking, serve hot tea. Jasmine, oolong, pekoe, and green tea are good ones to try.

Plum-Glazed Beef Short Ribs

MAKES 6 SERVINGS

Prep: 20 minutes
Cook: Low 6 to 8 hours,
High 3 to 4 hours

3	pounds boneless beef short ribs
1	7.4-ounce jar plum sauce
⅔	cup ketchup
1	tablespoon rice vinegar
2	teaspoons grated fresh ginger

1. Trim fat from ribs. In a large nonstick skillet brown ribs on all sides over medium-high heat. Drain off fat. Transfer ribs to a 3½- or 4-quart slow cooker. In a medium bowl combine plum sauce, ketchup, vinegar, and ginger; pour over ribs in cooker.

2. Cover and cook on low-heat setting for 6 to 8 hours or on high-heat setting for 3 to 4 hours.

3. Using a slotted spoon, transfer ribs to a serving platter, reserving cooking liquid. Skim fat from liquid. Spoon some of the cooking liquid over ribs; discard remaining liquid.

Nutrition Facts per serving: 245 cal., 8 g total fat (3 g sat. fat), 53 mg chol., 538 mg sodium, 25 g carbo., 0 g fiber, 18 g pro.

Pile this rich, tomatoey beef into toasted hamburger buns or hard rolls and spoon on creamy coleslaw as a zesty topper. For a light dessert, fruit is always a hit. (Photo on page 130.)

Smoky Barbecued Beef Brisket

❦

MAKES 6 SERVINGS

Prep: 30 minutes
Cook: Low 10 to 11 hours, High 5 to 5½ hours

1	2- to 3-pound fresh beef brisket
1	teaspoon chili powder
½	teaspoon garlic powder
¼	teaspoon celery seeds
⅛	teaspoon black pepper
½	cup ketchup
½	cup bottled chili sauce
¼	cup packed brown sugar
2	tablespoons vinegar
2	tablespoons Worcestershire sauce
1½	teaspoons liquid smoke
½	teaspoon dry mustard
⅓	cup cold water
3	tablespoons all-purpose flour

1. Trim fat from meat. In a small bowl combine chili powder, garlic powder, celery seeds, and pepper. Sprinkle mixture evenly over meat; rub in with your fingers. Cut meat to fit into a 3½- or 4-quart slow cooker. Place meat in the cooker.

2. In a medium bowl combine ketchup, chili sauce, brown sugar, vinegar, Worcestershire sauce, liquid smoke, and dry mustard. Pour over meat in cooker.

3. Cover and cook on low-heat setting for 10 to 11 hours or on high-heat setting for 5 to 5½ hours. Transfer meat to a cutting board, reserving cooking liquid. Thinly slice meat across the grain and transfer to a serving platter; cover with foil to keep warm.

4. For sauce, pour the cooking liquid into a glass measuring cup; skim off fat. Measure 2½ cups liquid. In a medium saucepan combine water and flour; stir in the 2½ cups liquid. Cook and stir over medium heat until thickened and bubbly. Cook and stir for 1 minute more. Serve meat with sauce.

Nutrition Facts per serving: 305 cal., 8 g total fat (2 g sat. fat), 87 mg chol., 681 mg sodium, 24 g carbo., 2 g fiber, 34 g pro.

Plan this traditional Irish-American classic for Saint Paddy's Day or any time you're in the mood for the tasty flavors of corned beef paired with cabbage. Enjoy it with a mug of cold beer and a piece of warm Irish soda bread.

Corned Beef and Cabbage

MAKES 6 SERVINGS

Prep: 15 minutes
Cook: Low 10 to 12 hours, High 5 to 6 hours

1	3- to 4-pound corned beef brisket with spice packet
½	of a small head cabbage, cut into 3 wedges
4	medium carrots, cut into 2-inch pieces
2	medium yellow potatoes, cut into 2-inch pieces
1	medium onion, quartered
½	cup water

1. Trim fat from meat. If necessary, cut meat to fit into a 5- to 6-quart slow cooker. Sprinkle spices from packet evenly over meat; rub in with your fingers. Set aside.

2. In the cooker combine cabbage, carrot, potato, and onion. Pour water over vegetables. Place meat on top of vegetables.

3. Cover and cook on low-heat setting for 10 to 12 hours or on high-heat setting for 5 to 6 hours.

4. Transfer meat to a cutting board. Thinly slice meat across the grain. Transfer meat to a serving platter. Using a slotted spoon, transfer vegetables to the serving platter. Discard cooking liquid.

Nutrition Facts per serving: 457 cal., 27 g total fat (7 g sat. fat), 115 mg chol., 1,543 mg sodium, 16 g carbo., 3 g fiber, 35 g pro.

Tex-Mex flavors liven up this meat-and-potato combo. It's perfect for anyone who has a hearty appetite, from teens to tailgaters. Pass the nacho toppings to accent each serving.

Nacho-Style Beef and Potatoes

MAKES 4 SERVINGS

Prep: 15 minutes
Cook: Low 7 to 8 hours,
High 3½ to 4 hours

1 pound lean ground beef
1 large onion, chopped (1 cup)
1 11-ounce can condensed nacho cheese soup
1 cup milk
1 4-ounce can diced green chile peppers, undrained
6 medium red or round white potatoes (2 pounds), cut into wedges
¼ teaspoon garlic salt
  Toppings, such as dairy sour cream, bottled salsa, sliced green onion, and/or shredded cheddar cheese (optional)

1. In a large skillet cook ground beef and onion until meat is brown. Drain off fat. Stir in soup, milk, and undrained chile peppers. Set aside.

2. Place potato wedges in a 3½- or 4-quart slow cooker. Sprinkle with garlic salt. Pour meat mixture over potato wedges in cooker.

3. Cover and cook on low-heat setting for 7 to 8 hours or on high-heat setting for 3½ to 4 hours.

4. Before serving, gently stir potato mixture. If desired, top individual servings with sour cream, salsa, green onion, and/or cheddar cheese.

Nutrition Facts per serving: 550 cal., 23 g total fat (10 g sat. fat), 90 mg chol., 809 mg sodium, 52 g carbo., 6 g fiber, 32 g pro.

Looking for a simpler way to cook? This soul-warming dish is a layered casserole simmered slowly with tomato sauce. For an eye-catching presentation, serve the dish with steamed broccoli.

Hamburger, Potato, and Bean Casserole

MAKES 6 SERVINGS

Prep: 20 minutes
Cook: Low 5 to 6 hours,
High 2½ to 3 hours
Stand: 15 minutes

1	pound lean ground beef
1	medium onion, chopped (½ cup)
2	15-ounce cans dark red kidney beans, rinsed and drained
1	15-ounce can tomato sauce
1	4.5-ounce jar (drained weight) sliced mushrooms, drained
1	tablespoon chili powder
½	teaspoon garlic salt
½	teaspoon black pepper
3	medium red potatoes (1 pound), peeled, if desired, halved lengthwise, and sliced ¼ inch thick
½	cup shredded cheddar or Monterey Jack cheese

1. In a 4-quart Dutch oven cook ground beef and onion until meat is brown. Drain off fat. Stir in drained beans, tomato sauce, drained mushrooms, chili powder, garlic salt, and pepper.

2. Spoon half of the meat mixture (about 3 cups) into a 4-quart slow cooker. Top with potato slices. Add the remaining meat mixture, spreading to cover potato slices.

3. Cover and cook on low-heat setting for 5 to 6 hours or on high-heat setting for 2½ to 3 hours. Sprinkle with cheese. Let stand, covered, for 15 minutes before serving.

Nutrition Facts per serving: 440 cal., 19 g total fat (8 g sat. fat), 64 mg chol., 1,172 mg sodium, 41 g carbo., 13 g fiber, 26 g pro.

Savory meat juices combine with tangy yogurt and fresh dill to make a thick and rich-tasting sauce for this elegant yet hearty lamb and vegetable dish.

Braised Lamb Chops with Dill Sauce

❧

MAKES 6 SERVINGS

Prep: 30 minutes
Cook: Low 7 to 8 hours, High 3½ to 4 hours

6	lamb rib chops (with bone), cut 1 inch thick
2	teaspoons cooking oil
8	or 9 tiny new potatoes (12 ounces)
3	medium carrots, cut into 1-inch pieces
¾	cup water
2	teaspoons snipped fresh dill or ½ teaspoon dried dill
½	teaspoon salt
¼	teaspoon black pepper
½	cup plain low-fat yogurt
4	teaspoons all-purpose flour

1. Trim fat from chops. In a large skillet brown chops, a few at a time, on both sides in hot oil over medium heat. Drain off fat. Set aside.

2. Remove a narrow strip of peel from the middle of each new potato. In a 3½- or 4-quart slow cooker combine potatoes and carrot. Place chops on top of vegetables. Add water, 1 teaspoon of the fresh or ¼ teaspoon of the dried dill, the salt, and pepper.

3. Cover and cook on low-heat setting for 7 to 8 hours or on high-heat setting for 3½ to 4 hours.

4. Transfer chops and vegetables to a serving platter, reserving cooking liquid. Cover chops and vegetables with foil to keep warm.

5. For sauce, strain cooking liquid into a glass measuring cup; skim off fat. Measure ½ cup liquid. In a small saucepan combine yogurt and flour. Stir in the ½ cup liquid and the remaining 1 teaspoon fresh or ¼ teaspoon dried dill. Cook and stir over medium heat until thickened and bubbly. Cook and stir for 1 minute more. Serve chops and vegetables with sauce.

Nutrition Facts per serving: 288 cal., 10 g total fat (3 g sat. fat), 55 mg chol., 510 mg sodium, 29 g carbo., 3 g fiber, 21 g pro.

This main dish comes with a side dish: a crisp, refreshing cabbage slaw that contrasts with the complex flavors of the succulent lamb.

Spiced Lamb with Curried Slaw

MAKES 6 SERVINGS

Prep: 30 minutes
Cook: Low 10 to 12 hours,
High 5 to 6 hours

1	2½- to 3-pound boneless lamb shoulder roast
1	medium onion, cut into thin wedges
¼	teaspoon black pepper
¼	cup apricot jam
¼	cup lower-sodium beef broth
¼	cup soy sauce
1	teaspoon curry powder
1	teaspoon finely shredded lemon peel
½	teaspoon ground cinnamon
¼	teaspoon cayenne pepper
½	cup mayonnaise or salad dressing
3	tablespoons half-and-half or light cream
½	teaspoon curry powder
1	10-ounce package shredded cabbage with carrot (coleslaw mix) or 5 cups packaged shredded cabbage

1. Trim fat from meat. If necessary, cut meat to fit into a 3½- or 4-quart slow cooker. Set aside.

2. Place onion in the cooker. Add meat. Sprinkle meat with black pepper. In a small bowl combine jam, broth, soy sauce, the 1 teaspoon curry powder, the lemon peel, cinnamon, and cayenne pepper. Pour over mixture in cooker.

3. Cover and cook on low-heat setting for 10 to 12 hours or on high-heat setting for 5 to 6 hours.

4. Meanwhile, for slaw, in a large bowl combine mayonnaise, half-and-half, and the ½ teaspoon curry powder. Add cabbage; stir until coated. Cover and chill until ready to serve.

5. Using a slotted spoon, transfer meat to a cutting board and onion to a serving bowl, reserving cooking liquid. Shred meat by pulling two forks through it in opposite directions. Transfer meat to the serving bowl.

6. Skim fat from cooking liquid. Drizzle meat with enough of the liquid to moisten. Serve with slaw.

Nutrition Facts per serving: 441 cal., 24 g total fat (6 g sat. fat), 128 mg chol., 884 mg sodium, 14 g carbo., 2 g fiber, 40 g pro.

The exotic flavors of India's cuisine emerge when you unite lamb, potatoes, and tomatoes with the pleasantly pungent garam masala. Cool yogurt complements the warm, fiery dish.

Indian Lamb and Potatoes

MAKES 6 SERVINGS

Prep: 15 minutes
Cook: Low 8 to 10 hours,
High 4 to 5 hours

2	pounds lean boneless lamb
1	tablespoon garam masala
3	medium round white or yellow potatoes (1 pound), peeled and cubed
¼	teaspoon salt
¼	teaspoon black pepper
1	14.5-ounce can diced tomatoes with garlic and onion, undrained
¼	cup water
1	6-ounce carton plain yogurt (optional)

1. Trim fat from meat. Cut meat into 1-inch pieces. Sprinkle meat with garam masala. Set aside.

2. Place potato in a 3½- or 4-quart slow cooker. Add meat. Sprinkle meat with salt and pepper. Pour undrained tomatoes and water over mixture in cooker.

3. Cover and cook on low-heat setting for 8 to 10 hours or on high-heat setting for 4 to 5 hours.

4. If desired, top individual servings with yogurt.

Nutrition Facts per serving: 282 cal., 8 g total fat (3 g sat. fat), 97 mg chol., 538 mg sodium, 18 g carbo., 1 g fiber, 33 g pro.

Lamb shanks are ideal for the slow cooker—the moist and juicy lamb literally falls off the bone. Infused with orange and spices, this dish is the perfect warming supper for chilly spring days.

Spicy Lamb Shanks

MAKES 4 TO 6 SERVINGS

Prep: 30 minutes
Cook: Low 8 to 9 hours, High 4 to 4½ hours

2	large oranges
5	medium carrots, cut into 2-inch pieces
1½	cups frozen small whole onions
4	large cloves garlic, thinly sliced
4	pounds meaty lamb shanks, cut into 3- to 4-inch pieces
6	inches stick cinnamon, broken into 1-inch pieces
1¼	cups lower-sodium beef broth
1½	teaspoons ground cardamom
1	teaspoon ground cumin
½	teaspoon ground turmeric
½	teaspoon black pepper
2	tablespoons cold water
4	teaspoons cornstarch
⅓	cup pitted kalamata or other black olives, halved (optional)
1	tablespoon snipped fresh cilantro (optional)

1. Using a vegetable peeler, remove the orange part of the peel from one of the oranges. Cut peel into thin strips (you should have about ¼ cup). Squeeze juice from both oranges to make about ⅔ cup. Set aside.

2. In a 5- to 6-quart slow cooker combine carrot, onions, and garlic. Add orange peel strips, the meat, and cinnamon pieces. In a small bowl stir together orange juice, broth, cardamom, cumin, turmeric, and pepper. Pour over mixture in cooker.

3. Cover and cook on low-heat setting for 8 to 9 hours or on high-heat setting for 4 to 4½ hours. Remove cinnamon pieces.

4. Using a slotted spoon, transfer meat and vegetables to a serving platter, reserving cooking liquid. Cover meat and vegetables with foil to keep warm.

5. For sauce, pour cooking liquid into a glass measuring cup; skim off fat. Measure 1½ cups liquid. In a small saucepan combine water and cornstarch; stir in liquid. Cook and stir over medium heat until thickened and bubbly. Cook and stir for 2 minutes more.

6. Serve meat and vegetables with sauce. If desired, sprinkle with olives and cilantro.

Nutrition Facts per serving: 207 cal., 4 g total fat (1 g sat. fat), 85 mg chol., 428 mg sodium, 15 g carbo., 3 g fiber, 28 g pro.

Teamed with apples, parsnips, sweet potatoes, and onion, this pork shoulder is ready when you are and reminiscent of the home-style pot roasts of Pennsylvania Dutch country. Serve tangy sauerkraut on the side.

Pork Pot Roast with Apples

MAKES 6 SERVINGS

Prep: 30 minutes
Cook: Low 7 to 9 hours,
High 3½ to 4½ hours

1	2½- to 3-pound boneless pork shoulder roast
1	tablespoon cooking oil
6	small parsnips, peeled and quartered
2	small sweet potatoes, peeled and quartered
1	small onion, sliced
1	cup beef broth
½	cup apple cider or apple juice
1	teaspoon dried basil, crushed
1	teaspoon dried marjoram, crushed
½	teaspoon salt
¼	teaspoon black pepper
2	small cooking apples, cored and cut into wedges
½	cup cold water
¼	cup all-purpose flour

1. Trim fat from meat. If necessary, cut meat to fit into a 3½- or 4-quart slow cooker. In a large skillet brown meat on all sides in hot oil over medium-high heat. Drain off fat. Set aside.

2. In the cooker combine parsnip, sweet potato, and onion. Add meat. In a medium bowl combine broth, apple cider, basil, marjoram, salt, and pepper. Pour over mixture in cooker.

3. Cover and cook on low-heat setting for 7 to 9 hours or on high-heat setting for 3½ to 4½ hours, adding apple wedges during the last 30 minutes of cooking.

4. Transfer meat, vegetables, and apple to a serving platter, reserving cooking liquid. Cover meat, vegetables, and apple with foil to keep warm.

5. For gravy, strain cooking liquid into a glass measuring cup; skim off fat. Measure 1¾ cups liquid. In a medium saucepan combine water and flour; stir in the 1¾ cups liquid. Cook and stir over medium heat until thickened and bubbly. Cook and stir for 1 minute more. Serve meat, vegetables, and apple with gravy.

Nutrition Facts per serving: 485 cal., 16 g total fat (5 g sat. fat), 126 mg chol., 492 mg sodium, 45 g carbo., 8 g fiber, 40 g pro.

*For a truly German meal, serve this well-seasoned
pork roast and tangy gravy with sauerkraut, dark rye bread,
and mugs of cold beer.*

Bavarian Pork Roast

MAKES 6 SERVINGS

Prep: 20 minutes
Cook: Low 7 to 8 hours,
High 3½ to 4 hours

1	1½- to 2-pound boneless pork shoulder roast
2	teaspoons caraway seeds
1	teaspoon dried marjoram, crushed
¾	teaspoon salt
½	teaspoon black pepper
1	tablespoon olive oil or cooking oil
½	cup water
1	tablespoon white wine vinegar
1	8-ounce carton dairy sour cream
4	teaspoons cornstarch

1. Trim fat from meat. In a small bowl combine caraway seeds, marjoram, salt, and pepper. Sprinkle mixture evenly over meat; rub in with your fingers. If necessary, cut meat to fit into a 3½- or 4-quart slow cooker.

2. In a large skillet brown meat on all sides in hot oil over medium-high heat. Drain off fat. Transfer meat to cooker. Add water to skillet. Bring to a gentle boil over medium heat, stirring to loosen brown bits in bottom of skillet. Pour skillet juices and vinegar over meat in cooker.

3. Cover and cook on low-heat setting for 7 to 8 hours or on high-heat setting for 3½ to 4 hours. Transfer meat to a serving platter, reserving cooking liquid. Cover meat with foil to keep warm.

4. For gravy, pour cooking liquid into a glass measuring cup; skim off fat. Measure 1¼ cups liquid (add water, if necessary). Pour cooking liquid into a small saucepan; bring to boiling. In a small bowl combine sour cream and cornstarch; stir into cooking liquid. Cook and stir over medium heat until thickened and bubbly. Cook and stir for 2 minutes more. Serve meat with gravy.

Nutrition Facts per serving: 277 cal., 18 g total fat (8 g sat. fat), 92 mg chol., 398 mg sodium, 4 g carbo., 0 g fiber, 24 g pro.

Orange marmalade and honey mustard combine to form a piquant, glistening sauce for chops and winter squash. Steam green beans or baby carrots to serve on the side.

Orange Pork Chops with Squash

❧

MAKES 6 SERVINGS

Prep: 20 minutes
Cook: Low 5 to 6 hours,
High 2½ to 3 hours

2	small or medium acorn squash (about 2 pounds)
1	large onion, halved lengthwise and sliced
6	pork loin chops (with bone), cut ¾ inch thick
¼	teaspoon salt
¼	teaspoon black pepper
½	cup chicken broth
⅓	cup orange marmalade
1	tablespoon honey mustard or Dijon-style mustard
1	teaspoon dried marjoram or thyme, crushed
¼	teaspoon black pepper
2	tablespoons cornstarch
2	tablespoons cold water

1. Cut squash in half lengthwise; discard seeds. Cut squash into 2-inch chunks. In a 5- to 6-quart slow cooker combine squash and onion. Trim fat from chops. Sprinkle chops with salt and ¼ teaspoon pepper. Place chops on top of squash and onion.

2. In a small bowl combine broth, marmalade, mustard, marjoram, and ¼ teaspoon pepper. Pour over mixture in cooker.

3. Cover and cook on low-heat setting for 5 to 6 hours or on high-heat setting for 2½ to 3 hours. Transfer chops and vegetables to a serving platter, reserving cooking liquid. Cover chops and vegetables with foil to keep warm.

4. For gravy, strain cooking liquid into a glass measuring cup; skim off fat. Measure 1¾ cups liquid (add water, if necessary). In a medium saucepan combine cornstarch and the 2 tablespoons water; stir in 1¾ cups liquid. Cook and stir over medium heat until thickened and bubbly. Cook and stir for 2 minutes more. Serve chops and vegetables with gravy.

Nutrition Facts per serving: 339 cal., 8 g total fat (3 g sat. fat), 100 mg chol., 300 mg sodium, 30 g carbo., 2 g fiber, 37 g pro.

Try this Southern-style meal when you have a craving for holiday fare. Browned pork chops slow-cook on top of corn bread stuffing studded with vegetables, yielding a savory meal.

Pork Chops and Corn Bread Stuffing

MAKES 4 SERVINGS

Prep: 20 minutes
Cook: Low 5 to 6 hours,
High 2½ to 3 hours

4   pork rib chops (with bone),
    cut ¾ inch thick
    Nonstick cooking spray

1   10.75-ounce can
    condensed golden
    mushroom or cream of
    mushroom soup

¼   cup butter or margarine,
    melted

1   16-ounce package frozen
    broccoli, cauliflower, and
    carrots

½   of a 16-ounce package
    (about 3 cups) corn bread
    stuffing mix

1. Trim fat from chops. Lightly coat the inside of a 5½- or 6-quart slow cooker and a large skillet with nonstick cooking spray. Set cooker aside; heat skillet over medium heat. Brown chops, half at a time, on both sides in hot skillet. Drain off fat. Set aside.

2. In a very large bowl combine soup and melted butter. Stir in frozen vegetables and stuffing mix. Transfer stuffing mixture to the prepared cooker. Add chops.

3. Cover and cook on low-heat setting for 5 to 6 hours or on high-heat setting for 2½ to 3 hours.

Nutrition Facts per serving: 558 cal., 22 g total fat (10 g sat. fat), 89 mg chol., 1,533 mg sodium, 56 g carbo., 7 g fiber, 30 g pro.

This might remind you a little of one of those charming skillet dinners served at popular restaurants. The lovely timesaving recipe, adapted for the slow cooker, brings the specialty home.

Pork Chops O'Brien

MAKES 4 SERVINGS

Prep: 20 minutes
Cook: Low 7 to 9 hours,
High 3½ to 4½ hours

Nonstick cooking spray

5 cups frozen diced hash brown potatoes with onions and peppers, thawed

1 10.75-ounce can reduced-fat and reduced-sodium condensed cream of mushroom soup

½ cup bottled roasted red sweet peppers, drained and chopped

½ cup dairy sour cream

½ cup shredded Colby Jack cheese

¼ teaspoon black pepper

4 pork loin chops (with bone), cut ¾ inch thick

1 tablespoon cooking oil

1 2.8-ounce can French-fried onions

1. Lightly coat the inside of a 3½- or 4-quart slow cooker with nonstick cooking spray; set aside. In a large bowl combine hash brown potatoes, soup, roasted red pepper, sour cream, cheese, and black pepper. Transfer potato mixture to the prepared cooker.

2. Trim fat from chops. In a large skillet brown chops on both sides in hot oil over medium heat. Drain off fat. Place chops on top of mixture in cooker.

3. Cover and cook on low-heat setting for 7 to 9 hours or on high-heat setting for 3½ to 4½ hours. Sprinkle individual servings with French-fried onions.

Nutrition Facts per serving: 670 cal., 29 g total fat (9 g sat. fat), 92 mg chol., 639 mg sodium, 64 g carbo., 4 g fiber, 37 g pro.

Test Kitchen Tip: Browning meat before adding it to a slow cooker adds a bit of color and flavor. But if you're in a hurry, you can skip this step—except for ground meat. Browning ground meat helps remove fat, keeps the pieces from clumping, and adds appetizing color.

Bake a batch of corn muffins (or pick some up at the supermarket) to serve with these tender pork loin chops accented with thyme.

Fruited Pork Chops

MAKES 6 SERVINGS

Prep: 15 minutes
Cook: Low 4 to 4½ hours,
High 2 to 2½ hours

6   boneless pork loin chops,
    cut 1 inch thick
1   teaspoon dried thyme,
    crushed
2   7-ounce packages mixed
    dried fruit
1   medium red or yellow
    sweet pepper, sliced
1   cup bottled barbecue
    sauce

1. Trim fat from chops. Place chops in a 3½- or 4-quart slow cooker. Sprinkle chops with thyme. Add dried fruit and sweet pepper. Pour barbecue sauce over mixture in cooker.

2. Cover and cook on low-heat setting for 4 to 4½ hours or on high-heat setting for 2 to 2½ hours.

3. Transfer chops to a serving platter. Skim fat from sauce. Spoon some of the sauce over chops; pass the remaining sauce.

Nutrition Facts per serving: 450 cal., 11 g total fat (4 g sat. fat), 92 mg chol., 421 mg sodium, 49 g carbo., 3 g fiber, 40 g pro.

The trio of fennel, Italian seasoning, and balsamic vinegar lends authentic Italian flavor to these meaty chops. A generous side serving of orzo, which is small rice-shape pasta, makes the dish absolutely irresistible.

Italian Pork Chops

MAKES 6 SERVINGS

Prep: 25 minutes
Cook: Low 7 to 8 hours,
High 3½ to 4 hours

1   large fennel bulb, trimmed and cut into thin wedges

1   medium onion, chopped (½ cup)

6   pork rib chops (with bone), cut ¾ inch thick

1   teaspoon dried Italian seasoning, crushed

¼   teaspoon salt

¼   teaspoon black pepper

2   cloves garlic, minced

2   14.5-ounce cans diced tomatoes with basil, garlic, and oregano, undrained

2   tablespoons balsamic vinegar

1   large zucchini, cut into 1-inch pieces

2   tablespoons cornstarch

2   tablespoons cold water

3   cups hot cooked orzo pasta

2   tablespoons pine nuts or slivered almonds, toasted (see tip, page 29)

1. In a 5- to 6-quart slow cooker combine fennel and onion. Trim fat from chops. Place chops on top of vegetables. Sprinkle chops with Italian seasoning, salt, pepper, and garlic. Pour undrained tomatoes and balsamic vinegar over chops. Add zucchini to mixture in cooker.

2. Cover and cook on low-heat setting for 7 to 8 hours or on high-heat setting for 3½ to 4 hours. Using a slotted spoon, transfer chops and vegetables to a serving platter, reserving cooking liquid. Cover chops and vegetables with foil to keep warm.

3. For sauce, in a medium saucepan combine cornstarch and water; stir in cooking liquid. Cook and stir over medium heat until thickened and bubbly. Cook and stir for 2 minutes more. Serve chops and vegetables with sauce and hot cooked orzo. Sprinkle with nuts.

Nutrition Facts per serving: 396 cal., 10 g total fat (3 g sat. fat), 71 mg chol., 879 mg sodium, 41 g carbo., 3 g fiber, 36 g pro.

Choucroute garni (pronounced shoo-KROOT gar-NEE) means "garnished sauerkraut" in French and hails from the Alsatian region. The hearty dish traditionally features sauerkraut topped with meats, such as sausage and pork, and potatoes.

Choucroute Garni

MAKES 4 SERVINGS

Prep: 15 minutes
Cook: Low 9 to 10 hours,
High 4½ to 5 hours

2	medium red or round white potatoes, quartered
2	medium carrots, cut into ½-inch pieces
1	medium onion, chopped (½ cup)
1	bay leaf
2	cooked smoked pork chops, cut ¾ inch thick, or one 8-ounce cooked ham slice, cut into pieces
1	14-ounce can sauerkraut, drained
2	small cooking apples, cored and quartered
2	cooked knockwurst, scored diagonally
½	cup water
½	cup dry white wine or apple juice
1	teaspoon instant chicken bouillon granules
⅛	teaspoon ground cloves
⅛	teaspoon black pepper

1. In a 3½- to 4½-quart slow cooker layer potato, carrot, onion, and bay leaf. Add chops, drained sauerkraut, apple, and knockwurst.

2. In a small bowl combine water, wine, bouillon granules, cloves, and pepper. Pour over mixture in cooker.

3. Cover and cook on low-heat setting for 9 to 10 hours or on high-heat setting for 4½ to 5 hours. Remove bay leaf.

Nutrition Facts per serving: 380 cal., 21 g total fat (8 g sat. fat), 58 mg chol., 1,753 mg sodium, 28 g carbo., 4 g fiber, 18 g pro.

Did you know you'll get more juice out of fresh lemons if they're at room temperature? Take them out of the refrigerator and let them sit on the counter awhile before squeezing.

Hawaiian Pork

MAKES 6 SERVINGS

Prep: 20 minutes
Cook: Low 8 to 10 hours,
High 4 to 5 hours,
plus 15 minutes (high)

2	pounds boneless pork shoulder roast
½	teaspoon salt
¼	teaspoon black pepper
1	tablespoon cooking oil
1	20-ounce can pineapple tidbits (juice pack), undrained
1	large onion, cut into thick wedges
2	tablespoons grated fresh ginger
1	tablespoon lemon juice
½	teaspoon crushed red pepper
2	tablespoons cornstarch
2	tablespoons cold water
2	medum red sweet peppers, chopped (1½ cups)

1. Trim fat from meat. Cut meat into 1½-inch pieces. Sprinkle meat with salt and black pepper. In a large skillet brown meat, half at a time, in hot oil over medium heat. Drain off fat. Transfer meat to a 3½- or 4-quart slow cooker. Stir in undrained pineapple, onion, ginger, lemon juice, and crushed red pepper.

2. Cover and cook on low-heat setting for 8 to 10 hours or on high-heat setting for 4 to 5 hours.

3. If using low-heat setting, turn to high-heat setting. In a small bowl combine cornstarch and water; stir into mixture in cooker. Stir in sweet pepper.

4. Cover and cook for 15 to 30 minutes more or until the mixture is slightly thickened and sweet pepper is crisp-tender, stirring once.

Nutrition Facts per serving: 359 cal., 16 g total fat (4 g sat. fat), 98 mg chol., 321 mg sodium, 23 g carbo., 2 g fiber, 31 g pro.

Marengo refers to the battle Napoléon Bonaparte won against Austria in 1800. To celebrate the victory, Napoléon's chef invented a dish similar to this one.

Pork and Mushroom Marengo

❈

MAKES 6 SERVINGS

Prep: 25 minutes
Cook: Low 8 to 10 hours,
High 4 to 5 hours,
plus 15 minutes (high)

1½	pounds boneless pork shoulder roast
3	cups sliced fresh mushrooms (8 ounces)
1	medium onion, chopped (½ cup)
1	14.5-ounce can diced tomatoes, undrained
1	cup water
1	teaspoon dried marjoram, crushed
1	teaspoon dried thyme, crushed
1	teaspoon instant chicken bouillon granules
¼	teaspoon salt
	Dash black pepper
3	tablespoons cornstarch
3	tablespoons cold water
	Hot cooked brown rice (optional)

1. Trim fat from meat. Cut meat into 1-inch pieces. Set aside.

2. In a 3½- or 4-quart slow cooker combine mushrooms and onion. Add meat. In a medium bowl combine undrained tomatoes, the 1 cup water, the marjoram, thyme, bouillon granules, salt, and pepper. Pour over mixture in cooker.

3. Cover and cook on low-heat setting for 8 to 10 hours or on high-heat setting for 4 to 5 hours.

4. If using low-heat setting, turn to high-heat setting. In a small bowl combine cornstarch and the 3 tablespoons water; stir into mixture in cooker. Cover and cook about 15 minutes more or until thickened. If desired, serve meat mixture with hot cooked brown rice.

Nutrition Facts per serving: 208 cal., 7 g total fat (2 g sat. fat), 73 mg chol., 452 mg sodium, 10 g carbo., 1 g fiber, 24 g pro.

Pork shoulder roast—sometimes called Boston butt—is a wonderful cut of meat. The streaks of fat melt away during cooking, bringing rich, bold flavors to the appealing dish. The added value: It's inexpensive.

Cherry and Port-Sauced Pork

MAKES 6 SERVINGS

Prep: 20 minutes
Cook: Low 7 to 8 hours,
High 3½ to 4 hours,
plus 15 minutes (high)

2½	pounds boneless pork shoulder roast
½	cup dried tart cherries
1	8-ounce can tomato sauce
1	medium onion, chopped (½ cup)
½	cup port
½	cup water
1	tablespoon Worcestershire sauce
1	teaspoon dried marjoram, crushed
½	teaspoon dried oregano, crushed
2	cloves garlic, minced
2	tablespoons cornstarch
2	tablespoons cold water
3	cups hot cooked pasta (optional)

1. Trim fat from meat. Cut meat into 1-inch pieces. In a 3½- or 4-quart slow cooker combine meat and dried cherries. In a small bowl combine tomato sauce, onion, port, the ½ cup water, the Worcestershire sauce, marjoram, oregano, and garlic. Pour over mixture in cooker.

2. Cover and cook on low-heat setting for 7 to 8 hours or on high-heat setting for 3½ to 4 hours.

3. If using low-heat setting, turn to high-heat setting. In a small bowl combine cornstarch and the 2 tablespoons water. Stir into mixture in cooker. Cover and cook about 15 minutes more or until thickened.

4. If desired, serve meat mixture over hot cooked pasta.

Nutrition Facts per serving: 347 cal., 11 g total fat (4 g sat. fat), 122 mg chol., 364 mg sodium, 15 g carbo., 1 g fiber, 38 g pro.

While lo mein gets its name from the type of Chinese noodle traditionally used in the dish, many other types of thin noodles, including angel hair pasta and vermicelli, are substitutes for curly thin egg noodles. (Photo on page 261.)

Pork lo Mein

MAKES 6 SERVINGS

Prep: 20 minutes
Cook: Low 6½ to 7 hours,
High 3½ to 4 hours,
plus 10 minutes (high)

1½	pounds boneless pork shoulder roast
2	cups frozen sliced carrots
2	medium onions, cut into wedges
2	stalks celery, thinly bias-sliced (1 cup)
1	12-ounce jar teriyaki glaze
1	8-ounce can sliced water chestnuts, drained
1	5-ounce can sliced bamboo shoots, drained
1	teaspoon grated fresh ginger
1	6-ounce package frozen snow pea pods
1	cup broccoli florets
9	ounces dried curly thin egg noodles
¼	cup cashews

1. Trim fat from meat. Cut meat into ¾-inch pieces. In a 3½- or 4-quart slow cooker combine meat, frozen carrots, onion, celery, teriyaki glaze, drained water chestnuts, drained bamboo shoots, and ginger.

2. Cover and cook on low-heat setting for 6½ to 7 hours or on high-heat setting for 3½ to 4 hours.

3. If using low-heat setting, turn to high-heat setting. Stir in frozen pea pods and broccoli. Cover and cook for 10 to 15 minutes more or until pea pods are crisp-tender.

4. Meanwhile, cook noodles according to package directions; drain. Serve meat mixture over hot cooked noodles. Sprinkle with cashews.

Nutrition Facts per serving: 509 cal., 12 g total fat (3 g sat. fat), 73 mg chol., 2,274 mg sodium, 66 g carbo., 6 g fiber, 33 g pro.

By substituting brown lentils for white beans that are in a traditional French cassoulet, you skip the step of precooking and soaking the dried beans. Lentils are added to the slow cooker straight from the package. How easy is that?

Pork and Lentil Cassoulet

MAKES 6 SERVINGS

Prep: 25 minutes
Cook: Low 10 to 12 hours,
High 4½ to 5½ hours

1	pound boneless pork shoulder roast
1	large onion, cut into wedges
2	cloves garlic, minced
1	tablespoon cooking oil
2½	cups beef broth
1	14.5-ounce can diced tomatoes, undrained
4	medium carrots and/or parsnips, cut into ½-inch pieces
2	stalks celery, thinly sliced (1 cup)
¾	cup brown lentils, rinsed and drained
1	teaspoon dried rosemary, crushed
¼	teaspoon black pepper

1. Trim fat from meat. Cut meat into ¾-inch pieces. In a very large skillet cook meat, onion, and garlic in hot oil over medium-high heat until meat is brown. Drain off fat.

2. Transfer meat mixture to a 3½- or 4-quart slow cooker. Stir in broth, undrained tomatoes, carrot and/or parsnip, celery, lentils, rosemary, and pepper.

3. Cover and cook on low-heat setting for 10 to 12 hours or on high-heat setting for 4½ to 5½ hours.

Nutrition Facts per serving: 263 cal., 7 g total fat (2 g sat. fat), 49 mg chol., 586 mg sodium, 25 g carbo., 9 g fiber, 23 g pro.

Tender red beans go from tame to lively when mixed with the distinctively heady aroma and slightly smoky flavor of ground cumin. Serve sliced hot peppers and lime wedges on the side for an extra flavor twist.

Red Beans over Spanish Rice

MAKES 6 SERVINGS

Prep: 30 minutes
Stand: 1 hour
Cook: Low 10 to 11 hours, High 5 to 5½ hours

2   cups dried red beans or red kidney beans
     Nonstick cooking spray
12   ounces boneless pork shoulder roast
1   tablespoon cooking oil
4   cups water
2½   cups chopped onion
1   tablespoon ground cumin
6   cloves garlic, minced
1   6.75-ounce package Spanish rice mix
     Fresh jalapeño chile peppers, sliced (optional) (see tip, page 10)
     Lime wedges (optional)

1. Rinse beans. In a large saucepan combine beans and enough water to cover beans by 2 inches. Bring to boiling; reduce heat. Simmer, uncovered, for 10 minutes. Remove from heat. Cover and let stand for 1 hour. Drain and rinse beans. Set aside.

2. Lightly coat the inside of a 3½- or 4-quart slow cooker with nonstick cooking spray; set aside. Trim fat from meat. Cut meat into 1-inch pieces. In a large skillet brown meat, half at a time, in hot oil over medium heat. Drain off fat. In the prepared cooker combine beans, meat, the 4 cups water, the onion, cumin, and garlic.

3. Cover and cook on low-heat setting for 10 to 11 hours or on high-heat setting for 5 to 5½ hours.

4. Before serving, prepare the rice mix according to package directions. Spoon cooked rice onto a serving platter. Using a slotted spoon, spoon bean mixture over rice. Drizzle enough of the cooking liquid over bean mixture and rice to moisten. If desired, garnish with jalapeño pepper slices and lime wedges.

Nutrition Facts per serving: 344 cal., 1 g total fat (0 g sat. fat), 0 mg chol., 450 mg sodium, 68 g carbo., 17 g fiber, 19 g pro.

Busy cooks can save time by calling ahead and asking the butcher to cut up the pork shoulder. Colorful mandarin orange sections add a fresh note to the dish.

Sweet-and-Sour Pork with Peppers

MAKES 6 SERVINGS

Prep: 20 minutes
Cook: Low 7 to 8 hours,
High 3½ to 4 hours
Stand: 10 minutes

2	pounds boneless pork shoulder roast
1	8-ounce can sliced bamboo shoots, drained
1	16-ounce package frozen (yellow, green, and red) pepper and onion stir-fry vegetables
¼	cup frozen orange juice concentrate, thawed
¼	cup cider vinegar
¼	cup water
2	tablespoons packed brown sugar
2	tablespoons soy sauce
½	teaspoon salt
1½	cups uncooked instant white rice
1	11-ounce can mandarin orange sections, drained

1. Trim fat from meat. Cut meat into 1-inch pieces. In a 3½- or 4-quart slow cooker combine meat and drained bamboo shoots. Add frozen stir-fry vegetables.

2. In a small bowl combine orange juice concentrate, vinegar, water, brown sugar, soy sauce, and salt. Pour over mixture in cooker.

3. Cover and cook on low-heat setting for 7 to 8 hours or on high-heat setting for 3½ to 4 hours.

4. Stir in rice. Let stand, covered, for 10 minutes. Before serving, stir in drained mandarin oranges.

Nutrition Facts per serving: 406 cal., 10 g total fat (3 g sat. fat), 98 mg chol., 928 mg sodium, 40 g carbo., 2 g fiber, 34 g pro.

This delightful blend of slow-simmered pork and enchilada sauce boasts a pronounced Mexican flavor. Even for the pickiest of eaters, these top-your-own-tacos will be a sure hit.

Shredded Pork Tacos

MAKES 4 SERVINGS

Prep: 30 minutes
Cook: Low 8 to 10 hours,
High 4 to 5 hours

1   2½- to 3-pound boneless pork shoulder roast
1   cup chicken broth
½   cup enchilada sauce or bottled salsa
4   taco shells
     Toppers (such as shredded lettuce, shredded Mexican-blend cheeses, chopped tomato, sliced pitted ripe olives, and/or chopped avocado)
     Dairy sour cream (optional)

1. Trim fat from meat. If necessary, cut meat to fit into a 3½- or 4-quart slow cooker. Place meat in cooker. Add broth. Cover and cook on low-heat setting for 8 to 10 hours or on high-heat setting for 4 to 5 hours.

2. Transfer meat to a cutting board; discard broth. Shred meat by pulling two forks through it in opposite directions. Reserve 2 cups of the meat. (Place the remaining meat in an airtight container for another use; chill for up to 3 days or freeze for up to 3 months.)

3. In a medium saucepan combine the reserved 2 cups meat and the enchilada sauce. Cover and cook over medium-low heat about 10 minutes or until heated through, stirring occasionally. Meanwhile, warm taco shells according to package directions.

4. To serve, fill taco shells with meat mixture. Top with lettuce, cheese, tomato, olives, and/or avocado. If desired, serve tacos with sour cream.

Nutrition Facts per serving: 307 cal., 16 g total fat (5 g sat. fat), 80 mg chol., 538 mg sodium, 14 g carbo., 3 g fiber, 27 g pro.

These pork ribs sing with Asian flavor. An aromatic, sweet, dark hoisin sauce glazes the lip-smacking meat. Serve with a side of hot cooked brown rice and sprinkle with toasted sesame seeds, if you like.

Orange Sesame Ribs

MAKES 4 SERVINGS

Prep: 15 minutes
Cook: Low 8 to 10 hours, High 4 to 5 hours

	Nonstick cooking spray
2½	to 3 pounds boneless pork country-style ribs
1	10-ounce jar orange marmalade
1	7.25-ounce jar hoisin sauce
1	teaspoon toasted sesame oil
3	cloves garlic, minced
	Hot cooked brown rice (optional)

1. Lightly coat a large skillet with nonstick cooking spray; heat skillet over medium heat. Brown ribs on all sides in hot skillet. Drain off fat. Transfer ribs to a 3½- or 4-quart slow cooker.

2. In a medium bowl combine marmalade, hoisin sauce, sesame oil, and garlic. Pour over ribs in cooker; stir to coat ribs with sauce.

3. Cover and cook on low-heat setting for 8 to 10 hours or on high-heat setting for 4 to 5 hours. Transfer ribs to a serving platter.

4. Skim fat from sauce. Spoon some of the sauce over ribs; pass the remaining sauce. If desired, serve with rice.

Nutrition Facts per serving: 532 cal., 16 g total fat (5 g sat. fat), 101 mg chol., 696 mg sodium, 66 g carbo., 0 g fiber, 33 g pro.

Grab extra napkins. These boneless pork ribs simmered in a scrumptious barbecue sauce will have your family and friends licking their fingers with delight. Use a little more hot sauce if you like more heat.

Tomato-Sauced Pork Ribs

MAKES 6 SERVINGS

Prep: 20 minutes
Cook: Low 8 to 10 hours,
High 4 to 5 hours

1	28-ounce can crushed tomatoes
2	stalks celery, chopped (1 cup)
1	medium green sweet pepper, chopped (¾ cup)
1	medium onion, chopped (½ cup)
2	tablespoons quick-cooking tapioca
2	teaspoons dried Italian seasoning, crushed
¾	teaspoon salt
¼	to ½ teaspoon bottled hot pepper sauce
¼	teaspoon black pepper
1	clove garlic, minced
2	pounds boneless pork country-style ribs
	Hot cooked pasta or polenta (optional)

1. For sauce, in a 3½- or 4-quart slow cooker combine tomatoes, celery, sweet pepper, onion, tapioca, Italian seasoning, salt, hot pepper sauce, black pepper, and garlic. Add ribs; stir to coat ribs with sauce.

2. Cover and cook on low-heat setting for 8 to 10 hours or on high-heat setting for 4 to 5 hours.

3. Transfer ribs to a serving platter. Skim fat from sauce. Spoon some of the sauce over ribs; pass the remaining sauce. If desired, serve with hot cooked pasta.

Nutrition Facts per serving: 304 cal., 12 g total fat (4 g sat. fat), 96 mg chol., 583 mg sodium, 16 g carbo., 3 g fiber, 32 g pro.

Red raspberry preserves and balsamic vinegar add just the right hint of sweetness to these spunky country-style ribs spiked with chipotle chiles.

Ribs in Raspberry-Chipotle Sauce

MAKES 4 TO 6 SERVINGS

Prep: 20 minutes
Cook: Low 8 to 10 hours,
High 4 to 5 hours

2	medium onions, sliced and separated into rings
3	pounds pork country-style ribs
1	18-ounce jar (1½ cups) seedless red raspberry preserves
⅓	cup apple cider or apple juice
2	tablespoons balsamic vinegar
1	canned chipotle pepper in adobo sauce

1. Place onion in a 4- to 5-quart slow cooker. Add ribs. In a blender combine preserves, apple cider, balsamic vinegar, and chipotle pepper. Cover and blend until smooth. Reserve 1¼ cups of the mixture for sauce; cover and chill until needed. Pour the remaining preserves mixture over ribs in cooker.

2. Cover and cook on low-heat setting for 8 to 10 hours or on high-heat setting for 4 to 5 hours.

3. For sauce, in a medium saucepan bring the reserved preserves mixture to boiling; reduce heat. Simmer, uncovered, for 5 minutes.

4. Using a slotted spoon, transfer ribs and onion to a serving dish; discard cooking liquid. Spoon some of the sauce over ribs and onion; pass the remaining sauce.

Nutrition Facts per serving: 689 cal., 15 g total fat (5 g sat. fat), 121 mg chol., 211 mg sodium, 97 g carbo., 2 g fiber, 38 g pro.

Anyone who loves ribs will adore this tantalizing recipe that's jazzed up with molasses and mustard. These pork country-style ribs offer more meat with less mess.

Country-Style Ribs with Molasses Sauce

MAKES 4 TO 6 SERVINGS

Prep: 25 minutes
Cook: Low 10 to 12 hours,
High 5 to 6 hours

1	large onion, sliced
2½	to 3 pounds pork country-style ribs
1½	cups vegetable juice
½	of a 6-ounce can (⅓ cup) tomato paste
¼	cup molasses
3	tablespoons vinegar
1	teaspoon dry mustard
¼	teaspoon salt
¼	teaspoon black pepper
⅛	teaspoon dried thyme, crushed
⅛	teaspoon dried rosemary, crushed

1. Place onion in a 3½- to 6-quart slow cooker. Place ribs on top of onion. In a medium bowl combine vegetable juice, tomato paste, molasses, vinegar, dry mustard, salt, pepper, thyme, and rosemary. Reserve 1 cup of the mixture for sauce; cover and chill until needed. Pour the remaining mixture over ribs.

2. Cover and cook on low-heat setting for 10 to 12 hours or on high-heat setting for 5 to 6 hours.

3. For sauce, in a small saucepan bring the reserved tomato mixture to boiling; reduce heat. Simmer, uncovered, for 10 minutes.

4. Using a slotted spoon, transfer ribs to a serving platter. Discard cooking liquid. Serve ribs with sauce.

Nutrition Facts per serving: 354 cal., 13 g total fat (4 g sat. fat), 101 mg chol., 518 mg sodium, 26 g carbo., 2 g fiber, 33 g pro.

This is not your mama's Tex-Mex, but she'd like this creamy version just the same—as will your kids. Hash brown potatoes are mixed with Canadian-style bacon, broccoli, nacho cheese soup, and Monterey Jack cheese.

Tex-Mex Casserole

MAKES 6 SERVINGS

Prep: 15 minutes
Cook: Low 5 to 6 hours,
High 2½ to 3 hours
Stand: 15 minutes

Nonstick cooking spray
1   10.75-ounce can condensed nacho cheese soup
⅔   cup half-and-half, light cream, or milk
1   teaspoon bottled hot pepper sauce (optional)
1   24-ounce package frozen diced hash brown potatoes with onions and peppers
2   6-ounce packages sliced Canadian-style bacon, quartered
1   10-ounce package frozen broccoli in cheese sauce
½   cup shredded Monterey Jack cheese with jalapeño chile peppers or Monterey Jack cheese
    Bottled cilantro salsa (optional)

1. Lightly coat the inside of a 3½- or 4-quart slow cooker with nonstick cooking spray.

2. In the prepared cooker combine soup, half-and-half, and, if desired, hot pepper sauce. Stir in potatoes and Canadian-style bacon. Place frozen broccoli, cheese side up, on top of potato mixture.

3. Cover and cook on low-heat setting for 5 to 6 hours or on high-heat setting for 2½ to 3 hours.

4. Remove liner from cooker, if possible, or turn off cooker. Stir mixture in cooker. Sprinkle with cheese. Let stand, covered, about 15 minutes before serving. If desired, serve with salsa.

Nutrition Facts per serving: 343 cal., 13 g total fat (7 g sat. fat), 52 mg chol., 1,464 mg sodium, 38 g carbo., 3 g fiber, 18 g pro.

Jazz up the taste of au gratin potatoes from a mix by stirring in ham, roasted red pepper, and cheddar cheese soup. Dinner's set!

5
Ingredient
Recipe

Ham and Potatoes au Gratin

MAKES 6 SERVINGS

Prep: 15 minutes
Cook: Low 7 to 8 hours,
High 3½ to 4 hours

	Nonstick cooking spray
2	5.1-ounce packages dry au gratin potato mix
2	cups diced cooked ham
¼	cup bottled roasted red sweet peppers, drained and chopped
3	cups water
1	10.75-ounce can condensed cheddar cheese soup
	Snipped fresh chives (optional)

1. Lightly coat the inside of a 3½- or 4-quart slow cooker with nonstick cooking spray. In the cooker combine potato from mixes, the contents of the seasoning packets from mixes, the ham, and roasted red pepper. In a medium bowl stir water into soup. Pour over potato mixture in cooker.

2. Cover and cook on low-heat setting for 7 to 8 hours or on high-heat setting for 3½ to 4 hours.

3. If desired, sprinkle individual servings with fresh chives.

Nutrition Facts per serving: 255 cal., 7 g total fat (3 g sat. fat), 29 mg chol., 2,087 mg sodium, 45 g carbo., 3 g fiber, 15 g pro.

Red kidney beans, broth, and mushrooms cook with raisins, curry, and sliced apple in this hearty medley. Chutney lends sweetness and a touch of heat while the nuts add crunch.

Curried Beans

MAKES 6 SERVINGS

Prep: 25 minutes
Cook: Low 8 to 9 hours,
High 4 to 5 hours,
plus 15 minutes (high)
Stand: 1 hour

3½	cups dried red kidney beans
1	14-ounce can vegetable broth
¾	cup water
1	medium onion, cut into thin wedges
1	4.5-ounce jar (drained weight) sliced mushrooms, drained
½	cup golden raisins
1	tablespoon curry powder
¼	teaspoon black pepper
1	large red or green apple, peeled, if desired, cored, and sliced
	Hot cooked couscous (optional)
	Bottled chutney (optional)
	Chopped almonds, toasted (optional) (see tip, page 29)

1. Rinse beans. In a large saucepan combine beans and enough water to cover beans by 2 inches. Bring to boiling; reduce heat. Simmer, uncovered, for 10 minutes. Remove from heat. Cover and let stand for 1 hour. Drain and rinse beans.

2. Transfer beans to a 3½- or 4-quart slow cooker. Stir in broth, water, onion, drained mushrooms, raisins, curry powder, and pepper.

3. Cover and cook on low-heat setting for 8 to 9 hours or on high-heat setting for 4 to 5 hours. If desired, mash beans slightly.

4. If using low-heat setting, turn to high-heat setting. Stir in apple. Cover and cook for 15 minutes more. If desired, serve bean mixture over hot cooked couscous, top with chutney, and sprinkle with almonds.

Nutrition Facts per serving: 325 cal., 1 g total fat (0 g sat. fat), 0 mg chol., 350 mg sodium, 64 g carbo., 21 g fiber, 20 g pro.

Test Kitchen Tip: Dried beans cook more slowly in a slow cooker than in a saucepan. Therefore, the beans must be precooked for 10 minutes. Soaking dried beans overnight doesn't work for slow-cooker recipes—the beans never get tender.

*With its slightly sweet, cornlike flavor, golden hominy provides
its own special touch to this stuffed-pepper meal. For additional
flavor, top the cooked peppers with the salsa mixture and
cheddar cheese just before serving.*

Peppers Stuffed with Hominy and Black Beans

❋

MAKES 4 SERVINGS

Prep: 15 minutes
Cook: Low 6 to 6½ hours,
High 3 to 3½ hours

4	medium green and/or yellow sweet peppers
2	cups bottled thick and chunky salsa
½	of a 6-ounce can (⅓ cup) tomato paste
½	teaspoon ground cumin
1	15.5-ounce can golden hominy, drained
1	15-ounce can black beans, rinsed and drained
1	cup shredded cheddar cheese

1. Remove tops, seeds, and membranes from sweet peppers; set peppers aside. In a medium bowl combine salsa, tomato paste, and cumin. In another medium bowl combine ¾ cup of the salsa mixture, the drained hominy, drained beans, and ½ cup of the cheese. Spoon bean mixture into pepper shells.

2. Pour the remaining salsa mixture into a 5- to 6-quart slow cooker. Place peppers, filled sides up, in the cooker.

3. Cover and cook on low-heat setting for 6 to 6½ hours or on high-heat setting for 3 to 3½ hours.

4. Transfer sweet peppers to dinner plates. Spoon salsa mixture over sweet peppers and sprinkle with the remaining ½ cup cheese.

Nutrition Facts per serving: 349 cal., 11 g total fat (6 g sat. fat), 30 mg chol., 1,752 mg sodium, 50 g carbo., 11 g fiber, 17 g pro.

*Raisins and brown sugar sweeten purchased marinara sauce,
and a splash of lemon juice adds a pleasing tartness.
The resulting tangy-sweet sauce complements these
cabbage rolls filled with beans and rice.*

Sweet-and-Sour Cabbage Rolls

❋

MAKES 4 SERVINGS

Prep: 45 minutes
Cook: Low 6 to 7 hours,
High 3 to 3½ hours

1	large head green cabbage
3½	cups purchased marinara sauce or meatless spaghetti sauce
1	15-ounce can black beans or red kidney beans, rinsed and drained
1	cup cooked brown rice
1	medium carrot, chopped (½ cup)
1	stalk celery, chopped (½ cup)
1	medium onion, chopped (½ cup)
1	clove garlic, minced
⅓	cup raisins
3	tablespoons lemon juice
1	tablespoon packed brown sugar

1. Remove 8 large outer leaves from cabbage. In a Dutch oven cook cabbage leaves in boiling water for 4 to 5 minutes or just until limp; drain. Trim the heavy vein from each leaf; set leaves aside. Shred 4 cups of the remaining cabbage; place shredded cabbage in a 5- to 6-quart slow cooker.

2. In a medium bowl combine ½ cup of the marinara sauce, the drained beans, cooked rice, carrot, celery, onion, and garlic. Spoon about ⅓ cup of the bean mixture onto each cabbage leaf. Fold in sides; roll up each leaf.

3. In another medium bowl combine the remaining 3 cups marinara sauce, the raisins, lemon juice, and brown sugar. Stir about half of the sauce mixture into shredded cabbage in cooker. Place cabbage rolls on top of shredded cabbage. Add the remaining sauce mixture.

4. Cover and cook on low-heat setting for 6 to 7 hours or on high-heat setting for 3 to 3½ hours. Carefully remove cabbage rolls and serve with the shredded cabbage mixture.

Nutrition Facts per serving: 387 cal., 6 g total fat (1 g sat. fat), 0 mg chol., 1,368 mg sodium, 76 g carbo., 11 g fiber, 15 g pro.

There's no missing the meat when you have such a thick, rich bean-and-vegetable mixture topping penne pasta! Add color by cooking with both green and red sweet peppers.

Pesto Beans and Pasta

MAKES 6 SERVINGS

Prep: 20 minutes
Cook: Low 7 to 9 hours,
High 3½ to 4½ hours

2	19-ounce cans cannellini beans (white kidney beans), rinsed and drained
1	14.5-ounce can Italian-style stewed tomatoes, undrained
1	medium green sweet pepper, chopped (¾ cup)
1	medium red sweet pepper, chopped (¾ cup)
1	medium onion, cut into thin wedges
2	teaspoons dried Italian seasoning, crushed
½	teaspoon cracked black pepper
4	cloves garlic, minced
½	cup vegetable broth
½	cup dry white wine or vegetable broth
1	7-ounce container refrigerated basil pesto
12	ounces dried multigrain or whole wheat penne pasta
½	cup finely shredded Parmesan or Romano cheese

1. In a 3½- or 4-quart slow cooker combine drained beans, undrained tomatoes, sweet peppers, onion, Italian seasoning, black pepper, and garlic. Pour broth and wine over mixture in cooker.

2. Cover and cook on low-heat setting for 7 to 9 hours or on high-heat setting for 3½ to 4½ hours. Using a slotted spoon, transfer bean mixture to a very large serving bowl, reserving cooking liquid. Stir pesto into bean mixture.

3. Meanwhile, cook pasta according to package directions; drain. Add pasta to bean mixture; gently toss to combine, adding enough of the cooking liquid to moisten. Sprinkle individual servings with cheese.

Nutrition Facts per serving: 580 cal., 20 g total fat (2 g sat. fat), 10 mg chol., 843 mg sodium, 80 g carbo., 11 g fiber, 25 g pro.

Golden raisins and mixed dried fruit bits add a little sweetness to this combo of beans and couscous. Loaded with fiber and protein, this dish is ideal when you need a robust meal to serve at the end of a busy day.

Fruited Couscous and Beans

MAKES 6 SERVINGS

Prep: 20 minutes
Cook: Low 6 to 7 hours,
High 3 to 3½ hours
Stand: 5 minutes

2	15-ounce cans Great Northern beans or pinto beans, rinsed and drained
1	large onion, finely chopped (1 cup)
1	cup golden raisins
1	cup mixed dried fruit bits
2	teaspoons grated fresh ginger
¾	teaspoon salt
¼	teaspoon crushed red pepper
1	14-ounce can vegetable broth
1¾	cups unsweetened pineapple juice
1	10-ounce package couscous
1	tablespoon olive oil
½	cup sliced almonds, toasted (see tip, page 29)
	Sliced green onion (optional)

1. In a 3½- or 4-quart slow cooker combine drained beans, onion, raisins, dried fruit bits, ginger, salt, and crushed red pepper. Pour broth and pineapple juice over mixture in cooker.

2. Cover and cook on low-heat setting for 6 to 7 hours or on high-heat setting for 3 to 3½ hours. Stir in couscous and oil.

3. Remove liner from cooker, if possible, or turn off cooker. Cover and let stand for 5 to 10 minutes or until couscous is tender. Fluff with a fork. Sprinkle individual servings with almonds and, if desired, green onion.

Nutrition Facts per serving: 623 cal., 9 g total fat (1 g sat. fat), 0 mg chol., 596 mg sodium, 120 g carbo., 14 g fiber, 22 g pro.

Elegant and superbly flavored, this pasta dish is quite impressive. Round out the menu with salad greens tossed with a light vinaigrette, steamed sugar snap peas, and breadsticks.

Ravioli with Mushroom-Wine Sauce

MAKES 4 SERVINGS

Prep: 20 minutes
Cook: Low 4 to 6 hours,
High 2 to 3 hours,
plus 20 minutes (high)

4	cups sliced fresh button mushrooms
4	cups sliced fresh portobello, stemmed shiitake, and/or cremini mushrooms
2	14.5-ounce cans diced tomatoes, undrained
½	cup water
⅓	cup dry red wine
½	teaspoon salt
¼	teaspoon dried rosemary, crushed
¼	teaspoon crushed red pepper
4	cloves garlic, minced
1	9-ounce package refrigerated cheese-filled ravioli
	Finely shredded Parmesan cheese (optional)

1. In a 4- to 5-quart slow cooker combine mushrooms, undrained tomatoes, water, wine, salt, rosemary, crushed red pepper, and garlic.

2. Cover and cook on low-heat setting for 4 to 6 hours or on high-heat setting for 2 to 3 hours.

3. If using low-heat setting, turn to high-heat setting. Stir in ravioli. Cover and cook for 20 minutes more.

4. If desired, sprinkle individual servings with Parmesan cheese.

Nutrition Facts per serving: 277 cal., 4 g total fat (2 g sat. fat), 23 mg chol., 848 mg sodium, 44 g carbo., 4 g fiber, 13 g pro.

Another time, try this option to make a meat sauce. Brown ground beef in a skillet, drain, and stir into the tomato mixture before turning on the slow cooker.

Herbed Tomato Sauce with Spaghetti

❧

MAKES 6 SERVINGS

Prep: 15 minutes
Cook: Low 8 to 10 hours,
High 4 to 5 hours

2 14.5-ounce cans whole peeled tomatoes, undrained and cut up

3 cups sliced fresh mushrooms (8 ounces)

1 6-ounce can tomato paste

1 medium onion, chopped (½ cup)

2 tablespoons grated Parmesan cheese

2 teaspoons packed brown sugar

2 teaspoons dried oregano, crushed

1½ teaspoons dried basil, crushed

½ teaspoon salt

½ teaspoon fennel seeds, crushed

¼ teaspoon crushed red pepper (optional)

2 cloves garlic, minced

1 bay leaf

12 ounces dried spaghetti, linguine, or other pasta

Grated Parmesan cheese (optional)

1. In a 3½- or 4-quart slow cooker combine undrained tomatoes, mushrooms, tomato paste, onion, the 2 tablespoons Parmesan cheese, the brown sugar, oregano, basil, salt, fennel seeds, crushed red pepper (if desired), garlic, and bay leaf.

2. Cover and cook on low-heat setting for 8 to 10 hours or on high-heat setting for 4 to 5 hours. Remove bay leaf.

3. Before serving, cook pasta according to package directions; drain. Serve herbed tomato sauce over hot cooked pasta. If desired, sprinkle with additional Parmesan cheese.

Nutrition Facts per serving: 302 cal., 2 g total fat (1 g sat. fat), 1 mg chol., 679 mg sodium, 59 g carbo., 4 g fiber, 11 g pro.

Herb-infused tomatoes blend with garlic, artichokes, and whipping cream for a sensational sauce to serve over any favorite pasta. The sliced olives and feta cheese sprinkled on top add a Mediterranean touch. (Photo on page 143.)

Garlic and Artichoke Pasta

MAKES 6 SERVINGS

Prep: 15 minutes
Cook: Low 6 to 8 hours, High 3 to 4 hours
Stand: 5 minutes

Nonstick cooking spray

3 14.5-ounce cans diced tomatoes with basil, garlic, and oregano, undrained

2 14-ounce cans artichoke hearts, drained and quartered

6 cloves garlic, minced

½ cup whipping cream

12 ounces dried linguine, fettuccine, or other pasta

Sliced pimiento-stuffed green olives and/or sliced pitted ripe olives (optional)

Crumbled feta cheese or finely shredded Parmesan cheese (optional)

1. Lightly coat the inside of a 3½- or 4-quart slow cooker with nonstick cooking spray. Drain 2 of the cans of tomatoes (do not drain remaining can). In the prepared cooker combine drained and undrained tomatoes, artichoke hearts, and garlic.

2. Cover and cook on low-heat setting for 6 to 8 hours or on high-heat setting for 3 to 4 hours. Stir in cream. Let stand, covered, about 5 minutes or until heated through.

3. Meanwhile, cook pasta according to package directions; drain. Serve artichoke sauce over hot cooked pasta. If desired, top with olives and feta cheese.

Nutrition Facts per serving: 403 cal., 8 g total fat (5 g sat. fat), 27 mg chol., 1,513 mg sodium, 68 g carbo., 7 g fiber, 13 g pro.

Mild tofu soaks up the enchanting blend of peanut sauce, soy sauce, fresh ginger, and toasted sesame oil in this easy Asian-inspired dish. Look for the Vietnamese noodles in the Asian section of your supermarket or at a specialty market.

Sesame Vegetables and Tofu

MAKES 6 SERVINGS

Prep: 20 minutes
Cook: Low 3½ to 4½ hours, plus 30 minutes (high)

1	16-ounce package frozen (yellow, green, and red) pepper and onion stir-fry vegetables
1	10-ounce package frozen cut green beans
1	8-ounce can sliced bamboo shoots, drained
1	cup vegetable broth
1	4.5-ounce jar (drained weight) sliced mushrooms, drained
¼	cup bottled peanut sauce
2	tablespoons soy sauce
1	tablespoon grated fresh ginger
2	teaspoons toasted sesame oil
2	cups broccoli florets
4	ounces banh pho (Vietnamese wide rice noodles)
8	ounces firm, tub-style tofu (fresh bean curd), drained and cut into bite-size strips
½	cup coarsely chopped peanuts

1. In a 4- to 5-quart slow cooker combine frozen stir-fry vegetables, frozen green beans, drained bamboo shoots, broth, drained mushrooms, peanut sauce, soy sauce, ginger, and sesame oil.

2. Cover and cook on low-heat setting (do not use high-heat setting) for 3½ to 4½ hours.

3. Turn cooker to high-heat setting. Stir in broccoli. Cover and cook for 30 minutes more.

4. Meanwhile, cook banh pho according to package directions; drain. Before serving, stir noodles and tofu into vegetable mixture in cooker. Sprinkle individual servings with peanuts.

Nutrition Facts per serving: 277 cal., 11 g total fat (2 g sat. fat), 0 mg chol., 735 mg sodium, 34 g carbo., 6 g fiber, 11 g pro.

Tubes of refrigerated cooked polenta usually are found in the produce section of the supermarket. Choose the flavor that appeals to you.

Polenta and Vegetable Ragoût

MAKES 5 SERVINGS

Prep: 20 minutes
Cook: Low 8 to 10 hours,
High 4 to 5 hours,
plus 15 minutes (high)

1	medium eggplant (about 1 pound), peeled and cubed
1	26- to 28-ounce jar meatless tomato pasta sauce
8	ounces fresh mushrooms, quartered
1	medium zucchini, halved lengthwise and cut into ½-inch pieces (1¼ cups)
1	cup vegetable broth
1	medium onion, chopped (½ cup)
¼	cup dry red wine (optional)
1	16-ounce tube refrigerated cooked polenta, cut into 1-inch pieces
⅓	cup grated or finely shredded Parmesan cheese

1. In a 5- to 6-quart slow cooker combine eggplant, pasta sauce, mushrooms, zucchini, broth, onion, and, if desired, wine.

2. Cover and cook on low-heat setting for 8 to 10 hours or on high-heat setting for 4 to 5 hours.

3. If using low-heat setting, turn to high-heat setting. Gently stir in polenta. Cover and cook for 15 minutes more. Sprinkle individual servings with Parmesan cheese.

Nutrition Facts per serving: 296 cal., 7 g total fat (2 g sat. fat), 5 mg chol., 1,341 mg sodium, 49 g carbo., 10 g fiber, 10 g pro.

Traditional moussaka is a layered eggplant and meat casserole. This meatless slow-cooker adaptation mixes many of the same flavors with eggplant, lentils, and potatoes.

Lentil "Moussaka"

MAKES 6 SERVINGS

Prep: 20 minutes
Cook: Low 6 hours,
High 3 hours,
plus 30 minutes (high)

2	medium red potatoes, cut into ½-inch cubes
1	cup vegetable broth
¾	cup brown or yellow lentils, rinsed and drained
½	teaspoon salt
¼	teaspoon ground cinnamon
¼	teaspoon black pepper
2	cloves garlic, minced
1	medium eggplant (about 1 pound), cubed
3	medium carrots, thinly sliced (1½ cups)
1	14.5-ounce can diced tomatoes with basil, garlic, and oregano, undrained
2	eggs, slightly beaten
1	8-ounce package cream cheese, softened

1. In a 3½- or 4-quart slow cooker combine potato, broth, lentils, salt, cinnamon, pepper, and garlic. Place eggplant and carrot on top of potato mixture.

2. Cover and cook on low-heat setting for 6 hours or on high-heat setting for 3 hours. Stir in undrained tomatoes.

3. If using low-heat setting, turn to high-heat setting. In a medium bowl combine eggs and cream cheese. Beat with an electric mixer on low speed until combined. Spoon cream cheese mixture over lentil mixture in cooker. Cover and cook for 30 minutes more.

Nutrition Facts per serving: 333 cal., 15 g total fat (9 g sat. fat), 112 mg chol., 868 mg sodium, 36 g carbo., 11 g fiber, 15 g pro.

Greek seasonings impart a zesty, fresh flavor that is pleasing with lentils. If you like, serve them on toasted pita wedges with a sprinkling of sliced green onion and chopped tomato or a spoonful of sour cream.

Greek-Seasoned Lentils

MAKES 6 SERVINGS

Prep: 15 minutes
Cook: Low 6 to 7 hours,
High 3 to 3½ hours

Nonstick cooking spray

3   14-ounce cans vegetable broth

2   cups dry brown lentils, rinsed and drained

4   medium carrots, shredded (2 cups)

1   large onion, chopped (1 cup)

2   teaspoons Greek seasoning

1. Lightly coat the inside of a 3½- to 5-quart slow cooker with nonstick cooking spray. In the prepared cooker combine broth, lentils, carrot, onion, and Greek seasoning.

2. Cover and cook on low-heat setting for 6 to 7 hours or on high-heat setting for 3 to 3½ hours. Use a slotted spoon to serve lentils.

Nutrition Facts per serving: 260 cal., 2 g total fat (0 g sat. fat), 0 mg chol., 874 mg sodium, 45 g carbo., 21 g fiber, 20 g pro.

In this appetizing main dish, barley with its slightly chewy texture and mild nutty flavor pairs nicely with the naturally sweet taste of butternut squash. The savory gratin also is terrific as a side dish for a party of twelve.

Barley and Squash Gratin

MAKES 6 SERVINGS

Prep: 15 minutes
Cook: Low 6 to 7 hours,
High 3 to 3½ hours
Stand: 10 minutes

1	2-pound butternut squash, halved, seeded, peeled, and cubed (about 5 cups)
1	10-ounce package frozen chopped spinach, thawed and well drained
1	cup regular barley
1	medium onion, cut into wedges
¾	teaspoon salt
¼	teaspoon black pepper
3	cloves garlic, minced
1	14-ounce can vegetable broth
½	cup water
½	cup finely shredded Parmesan cheese

1. In a 3½- or 4-quart slow cooker combine squash, spinach, barley, onion, salt, pepper, and garlic. Pour broth and water over mixture in cooker.

2. Cover and cook on low-heat setting for 6 to 7 hours or on high-heat setting for 3 to 3½ hours.

3. Remove liner from cooker, if possible, or turn off cooker. Sprinkle with Parmesan cheese. Let stand, covered, for 10 minutes before serving.

Nutrition Facts per serving: 196 cal., 3 g total fat (1 g sat. fat), 5 mg chol., 737 mg sodium, 36 g carbo., 8 g fiber, 9 g pro.

Nothing says fall like the time-honored preparation of a hot and hearty vegetable dish. Here fresh mushrooms, sweet potatoes, and onions contrast with the thyme-flavored sauce.

Mushrooms and Sweet Potatoes on Rice

❧

MAKES 6 SERVINGS

Prep: 20 minutes
Cook: Low 5 to 6 hours,
High 2½ to 3 hours

4	medium sweet potatoes (1½ to 2 pounds), peeled and cut into 1-inch pieces
8	ounces assorted fresh mushrooms (such as button, stemmed shiitake, and/or cremini), quartered
2	medium onions, cut into wedges
1	12-ounce jar mushroom gravy
½	cup vegetable broth
1	tablespoon quick-cooking tapioca
1	teaspoon dried thyme, crushed
¼	teaspoon salt
¼	teaspoon black pepper
3	cups hot cooked brown rice
1½	cups shredded Gruyère or Swiss cheese

1. In a 4- to 6-quart slow cooker combine sweet potato, mushrooms, onion, gravy, broth, tapioca, thyme, salt, and pepper.

2. Cover and cook on low-heat setting for 5 to 6 hours or on high-heat setting for 2½ to 3 hours.

3. Serve potato mixture over hot cooked brown rice. Sprinkle with cheese.

Nutrition Facts per serving: 413 cal., 12 g total fat (6 g sat. fat), 31 mg chol., 695 mg sodium, 62 g carbo., 7 g fiber, 16 g pro.

Three kinds of grains—wheat berries, barley, and wild rice—
make this dish wholesome, filling, and infinitely interesting.
Round out the meal with coleslaw and hearty rolls.

Multigrain Pilaf

MAKES 6 SERVINGS

Prep: 15 minutes
Cook: Low 6 to 8 hours,
High 3 to 4 hours

⅔ cup wheat berries

½ cup regular barley

½ cup uncooked wild rice

2 14-ounce cans vegetable broth

2 cups frozen shelled sweet soybeans (edamame) or baby lima beans

1 medium red sweet pepper, chopped (¾ cup)

1 medium onion, finely chopped (½ cup)

1 tablespoon butter or margarine

¾ teaspoon dried sage, crushed

½ teaspoon salt

¼ teaspoon black pepper

4 cloves garlic, minced

Grated Parmesan cheese (optional)

1. Rinse and drain wheat berries, barley, and wild rice. In a 3½- or 4-quart slow cooker combine wheat berries, barley, wild rice, broth, frozen soybeans, sweet pepper, onion, butter, sage, salt, black pepper, and garlic.

2. Cover and cook on low-heat setting for 6 to 8 hours or on high-heat setting for 3 to 4 hours. Stir before serving.

3. If desired, sprinkle individual servings with Parmesan cheese.

Nutrition Facts per serving: 342 cal., 9 g total fat (2 g sat. fat), 5 mg chol., 814 mg sodium, 50 g carbo., 10 g fiber, 20 g pro.

Flecks of colorful zucchini, sweet peppers, and tomatoes dress up the brown rice in this one-dish meal. The addition of feta cheese at the end lends a tangy note.

Brown Rice Primavera

MAKES 6 SERVINGS

Prep: 20 minutes
Cook: High 2 to 2½ hours, plus 30 minutes (high)

1	medium eggplant (about 1 pound), peeled, if desired, and cubed
2	medium zucchini, halved lengthwise and cut into ½-inch pieces (2½ cups)
1	medium onion, cut into thin wedges
1	14-ounce can vegetable broth
2	medium red and/or yellow sweet peppers, cut into thin bite-size strips
1	14.5-ounce can diced tomatoes with basil, garlic, and oregano, drained
1	cup uncooked instant brown rice
2	cups crumbled feta cheese

1. In a 5- to 6-quart slow cooker combine eggplant, zucchini, and onion. Pour broth over mixture in cooker.

2. Cover and cook on high-heat setting (do not use low-heat setting) for 2 to 2½ hours.

3. Stir in sweet pepper, drained tomatoes, and brown rice. Cover and cook for 30 minutes more. Sprinkle individual servings with feta cheese.

Nutrition Facts per serving: 212 cal., 9 g total fat (6 g sat. fat), 34 mg chol., 1,045 mg sodium, 26 g carbo., 5 g fiber, 9 g pro.

Root vegetables and balsamic vinegar are two very popular ingredients on trendy bistro menus. Take the idea on home with this creative side dish.

Balsamic Root Vegetables

MAKES 4 TO 6 SERVINGS

Prep: 15 minutes
Cook: Low 10 to 11 hours, High 5 to 5½ hours

2	small red or yellow potatoes, peeled and cut into 1-inch pieces
2	small parsnips, peeled and cut into 1-inch pieces
1	cup packaged peeled baby carrots
1	medium onion, cut into thin wedges
½	cup chicken broth
1	tablespoon packed brown sugar
¼	teaspoon salt
⅛	teaspoon black pepper
1	clove garlic, minced
2	tablespoons balsamic vinegar

1. In a 1½- or 2-quart slow cooker combine potato, parsnip, carrots, onion, broth, brown sugar, salt, pepper, and garlic.

2. Cover and cook on low-heat setting for 10 to 11 hours or on high-heat setting for 5 to 5½ hours. If no heat setting is available, cook for 8½ to 9 hours. Stir in balsamic vinegar.

Nutrition Facts per serving: 99 cal., 0 g total fat (0 g sat. fat), 0 mg chol., 296 mg sodium, 23 g carbo., 3 g fiber, 2 g pro.

Rich and full-flavored, these vegetables accented with curry are best served with plain meats and poultry. You'll find coconut milk in the ethnic food section of supermarkets or at Asian food stores.

Curried Vegetables and Garbanzo Beans

❧

MAKES 4 TO 6 SERVINGS

Prep: 15 minutes
Cook: Low 5 to 6 hours,
High 2½ to 3 hours

3	cups cauliflower florets
1	15-ounce can garbanzo beans (chickpeas), rinsed and drained
1	cup frozen cut green beans
2	medium carrots, sliced (1 cup)
1	medium onion, chopped (½ cup)
1	14-ounce can vegetable broth
2	to 3 teaspoons curry powder
1	14-ounce can unsweetened light coconut milk
¼	cup finely shredded fresh basil

1. In a 3½- or 4-quart slow cooker combine cauliflower, drained garbanzo beans, frozen green beans, carrot, and onion. Stir in broth and curry powder.

2. Cover and cook on low-heat setting for 5 to 6 hours or on high-heat setting for 2½ to 3 hours. Stir in coconut milk and basil.

Nutrition Facts per serving: 219 cal., 7 g total fat (4 g sat. fat), 0 mg chol., 805 mg sodium, 32 g carbo., 9 g fiber, 8 g pro.

*Enjoy a new version of this sweet and tangy recipe
each time you make it by mixing and matching different
combinations of beans.*

Molasses Baked Beans

MAKES 6 SERVINGS

Prep: 15 minutes
Cook: Low 5 to 6 hours,
High 2½ to 3 hours

2	15-ounce cans Great Northern beans, red kidney beans, black beans, and/or butter beans, rinsed and drained
½	cup tomato sauce
⅓	cup diced cooked ham or Canadian-style bacon
¼	cup water
2	tablespoons molasses
1	tablespoon cider vinegar
1	teaspoon dry mustard
⅛	teaspoon ground ginger
⅛	teaspoon black pepper

1. In a 1½- or 2-quart slow cooker combine drained beans, tomato sauce, ham, water, molasses, vinegar, dry mustard, ginger, and pepper.

2. Cover and cook on low-heat setting for 5 to 6 hours or on high-heat setting for 2½ to 3 hours. If no heat setting is available, cook for 3½ to 4 hours.

Nutrition Facts per serving: 198 cal., 1 g total fat (0 g sat. fat), 4 mg chol., 271 mg sodium, 36 g carbo., 7 g fiber, 13 g pro.

This savory baked bean dish is a real filler-upper! If you serve this with creamy coleslaw, corn bread, and cookies and ice cream for dessert, it's also a hassle-free meal.

Meaty Baked Beans

MAKES 6 SERVINGS

Prep: 20 minutes
Cook: Low 5 to 6 hours,
High 2½ to 3 hours

8	ounces bulk pork sausage
1	medium onion, chopped (½ cup)
1	clove garlic, minced
1	15-ounce can pork and beans in tomato sauce, undrained
1	15-ounce can butter beans or black beans, rinsed and drained
½	cup bottled barbecue sauce
¼	cup packed brown sugar
2	slices bacon, crisp-cooked, drained, and crumbled
2	tablespoons water
1	tablespoon yellow mustard
½	teaspoon chili powder
⅛	teaspoon black pepper

1. In a large skillet cook sausage, onion, and garlic until meat is brown. Drain off fat. Transfer meat mixture to a 1½- or 2-quart slow cooker.

2. Stir in undrained pork and beans, drained butter beans, barbecue sauce, brown sugar, bacon, water, mustard, chili powder, and pepper.

3. Cover and cook on low-heat setting for 5 to 6 hours or on high-heat setting for 2½ to 3 hours. If no heat setting is available, cook for 4½ to 5 hours.

Nutrition Facts per serving: 367 cal., 14 g total fat (5 g sat. fat), 35 mg chol., 1,073 mg sodium, 43 g carbo., 7 g fiber, 14 g pro.

Brilliantly colored beets sparkle in this tangy side dish.
It's just the recipe to perk up the Thanksgiving table.

Beets with Cranberry-Orange Sauce

MAKES 4 TO 6 SERVINGS

Prep: 15 minutes
Cook: Low 6 to 7 hours,
High 3 to 3½ hours,
plus 15 minutes (high)

4	medium beets (1 pound), peeled and quartered
¼	teaspoon ground nutmeg
½	cup cranberry juice
1	teaspoon finely shredded orange peel
¼	teaspoon salt
1	tablespoon butter or margarine, cut into small pieces
1	tablespoon sugar
2	teaspoons cornstarch

1. Place beets in a 1½- or 2-quart slow cooker. Sprinkle with nutmeg. Add cranberry juice, orange peel, and salt; dot with butter.

2. Cover and cook on low-heat setting for 6 to 7 hours or on high-heat setting for 3 to 3½ hours. If no heat setting is available, cook for 5 to 5½ hours.

3. If using low-heat setting, turn to high-heat setting (or if no heat setting is available, continue cooking). In a small bowl combine sugar and cornstarch; stir into mixture in cooker. Cover and cook for 15 to 30 minutes more or until thickened.

Nutrition Facts per serving: 91 cal., 3 g total fat (2 g sat. fat), 8 mg chol., 226 mg sodium, 16 g carbo., 2 g fiber, 1 g pro.

It's more convenient to stir together the ingredients for this cheesy vegetable side in a bowl before you place the mixture in a slow cooker. Serve the saucy side dish in small bowls.

Creamy Corn and Broccoli

MAKES 4 SERVINGS

Prep: 10 minutes
Cook: Low 5 to 6 hours, High 2½ to 3 hours

    Nonstick cooking spray
2   cups frozen cut broccoli
2   cups frozen whole kernel corn
1   10.75-ounce can condensed cheddar cheese soup
½   cup shredded cheddar cheese
2   tablespoons milk

1. Lightly coat the inside of a 1½- or 2-quart slow cooker with nonstick cooking spray. In a medium bowl combine frozen broccoli, frozen corn, soup, cheese, and milk. Spoon broccoli mixture into cooker.

2. Cover and cook on low-heat setting for 5 to 6 hours or on high-heat setting for 2½ to 3 hours. If no heat setting is available, cook for 4 to 4½ hours. Before serving, gently stir vegetable mixture.

Nutrition Facts per serving: 215 cal., 8 g total fat (4 g sat. fat), 22 mg chol., 696 mg sodium, 29 g carbo., 5 g fiber, 10 g pro.

*Brussels sprouts are peppery and nutty—and so very good.
They are divine cooked with chicken broth, spicy brown
mustard, half-and-half, and shredded Swiss.*

Mustard-Sauced Brussels Sprouts

MAKES 6 SERVINGS

Prep: 20 minutes
Cook: Low 4 to 4½ hours,
High 2½ to 3 hours,
plus 15 minutes (high)

2	pounds Brussels sprouts, trimmed and large sprouts halved (about 8 cups)
¼	teaspoon salt
¼	teaspoon black pepper
¾	cup reduced-sodium chicken broth
3	tablespoons spicy brown mustard
½	cup half-and-half or light cream
1	tablespoon cornstarch
⅓	cup shredded Swiss cheese

1. Place Brussels sprouts in a 3½- or 4-quart slow cooker. Sprinkle sprouts with salt and pepper. In a small bowl combine broth and mustard; pour over sprouts in cooker.

2. Cover and cook on low-heat setting for 4 to 4½ hours or on high-heat setting for 2½ to 3 hours.

3. Using a slotted spoon, transfer Brussels sprouts to a serving dish, reserving cooking liquid. Cover sprouts with foil to keep warm.

4. If using low-heat setting, turn to high-heat setting. For sauce, in a small bowl combine half-and-half and cornstarch. Stir into liquid in cooker. Cover and cook about 15 minutes more or until thickened. Whisk cheese into liquid in cooker until smooth. Spoon sauce over sprouts.

Nutrition Facts per serving: 127 cal., 5 g total fat (3 g sat. fat), 14 mg chol., 344 mg sodium, 15 g carbo., 5 g fiber, 8 g pro.

This flavorful cauliflower dish is made super easy by using a jar of cheddar cheese pasta sauce. Cracked black pepper adds a bit of a bite to the creamy veggies.

Cheesy Cauliflower

MAKES 6 SERVINGS

Prep: 15 minutes
Cook: Low 5 to 5½ hours, High 2½ to 2¾ hours

    Nonstick cooking spray
4   cups cauliflower florets (1 small head)
1   medium onion, cut into thin wedges
1   cup bottled cheddar cheese pasta sauce
    Cracked black pepper

1. Coat the inside of a 1½- or 2-quart slow cooker with nonstick cooking spray. In the prepared cooker combine cauliflower and onion. Pour pasta sauce over mixture in cooker.

2. Cover and cook on low-heat setting for 5 to 5½ hours or on high-heat setting for 2½ to 2¾ hours. If no heat setting is available, cook for 4 to 4½ hours.

3. Before serving, gently stir mixture. Sprinkle with pepper.

Nutrition Facts per serving: 97 cal., 6 g total fat (3 g sat. fat), 12 mg chol., 369 mg sodium, 8 g carbo., 2 g fiber, 4 g pro.

Lots of time and low heat transform sliced onions into a golden, sweet, edible heaven. Tangling them with creamy potatoes makes a perfect match for full-flavored meat and seafood such as beef tenderloin, pork chops, and salmon.

Caramelized Potatoes and Onion

MAKES 4 SERVINGS

Prep: 15 minutes
Cook: Low 7 to 8 hours,
High 3½ to 4 hours

8	or 9 tiny new potatoes (12 ounces), halved
2	medium sweet onions (such as Vidalia, Maui, or Walla Walla), thinly sliced (1 cup)
¼	cup beef broth or chicken broth
2	tablespoons butter or margarine, melted
1	tablespoon packed brown sugar
¼	teaspoon salt
⅛	teaspoon black pepper
	Black pepper (optional)

1. In a 1½- or 2-quart slow cooker combine potato and onion. In a small bowl stir together broth, butter, brown sugar, salt, and the ⅛ teaspoon pepper. Pour over mixture in cooker.

2. Cover and cook on low-heat setting for 7 to 8 hours or on high-heat setting for 3½ to 4 hours. If no heat setting is available, cook for 6 to 6½ hours.

3. Before serving, gently stir mixture. If desired, sprinkle with additional pepper. Serve vegetables with a slotted spoon.

Nutrition Facts per serving: 147 cal., 6 g total fat (4 g sat. fat), 15 mg chol., 250 mg sodium, 22 g carbo., 3 g fiber, 2 g pro.

Asiago cheese spikes a blend of cream cheese and sour cream chive dip to make a velvety coating for refrigerated potato wedges. This side dish is special enough for company and is delicious with pork or beef.

5 Ingredient Recipe

Creamy Potato Wedges

MAKES 6 SERVINGS

Prep: 10 minutes
Cook: Low 5½ to 6½ hours, High 2¼ to 2¾ hours

1 8-ounce container dairy sour cream chive-flavor dip

½ cup finely shredded Asiago cheese

1 3-ounce package cream cheese, cubed

2 tablespoons mayonnaise or salad dressing

1 20-ounce package refrigerated red potato wedges

   Snipped fresh chives (optional)

1. In a 1½- or 2-quart slow cooker stir together sour cream dip, Asiago cheese, cream cheese, and mayonnaise. Stir in potato wedges.

2. Cover and cook on low-heat setting for 5½ to 6½ hours or on high-heat setting for 2¼ to 2¾ hours. If no heat setting is available, cook for 3½ to 4 hours.

3. Before serving, gently stir potato mixture. If desired, sprinkle with chives.

Nutrition Facts per serving: 294 cal., 19 g total fat (10 g sat. fat), 54 mg chol., 408 mg sodium, 22 g carbo., 1 g fiber, 6 g pro.

Kidney and black beans elevate scalloped potatoes from a supporting role to the main attraction. To cut down on prep time and to boost fiber, leave the peels on the potatoes.

Scalloped Potatoes and Beans

MAKES 5 SERVINGS

Prep: 15 minutes
Cook: Low 8 to 10 hours, High 4 to 5 hours

1   15-ounce can red kidney beans, rinsed and drained

1   15-ounce can black beans, rinsed and drained

1   10.75-ounce can condensed cream of mushroom soup

1   large green sweet pepper, chopped (1 cup)

2   stalks celery, sliced ¼ inch thick (1 cup)

1   large onion, chopped (1 cup)

1   teaspoon dried thyme, crushed

¼   teaspoon black pepper

4   cloves garlic, minced

3   medium red or round white potatoes (1 pound), sliced ¼ inch thick

1   cup frozen peas

1   cup shredded cheddar cheese (optional)

1. In a large bowl combine drained kidney beans, drained black beans, soup, sweet pepper, celery, onion, thyme, black pepper, and garlic.

2. Spoon half of the bean mixture into a 3½- or 4-quart slow cooker. Top with potato, frozen peas, and the remaining bean mixture.

3. Cover and cook on low-heat setting for 8 to 10 hours or on high-heat setting for 4 to 5 hours. If desired, sprinkle individual servings with cheese.

Nutrition Facts per serving: 289 cal., 4 g total fat (1 g sat. fat), 0 mg chol., 796 mg sodium, 55 g carbo., 13 g fiber, 17 g pro.

To everyone who loves potatoes: You'll love them even more with the added flavor of bacon, green onion, and three kinds of cheese—smoked Gouda, provolone, and cream cheese.

Easy Cheesy Potatoes

MAKES 6 SERVINGS

Prep: 15 minutes
Cook: Low 6 hours

½ of a 28-ounce package frozen diced hash brown potatoes with onions and peppers, thawed

1 10.75-ounce can condensed cream of chicken with herbs soup

1 3-ounce package cream cheese, cut into small cubes

½ cup finely shredded smoked Gouda cheese

½ cup finely shredded provolone cheese

⅓ cup milk

2 tablespoons thinly sliced green onion (1)

¼ teaspoon black pepper

2 slices bacon, crisp-cooked, drained, and crumbled

1. In a 1½- or 2-quart slow cooker combine potatoes, soup, cream cheese, Gouda cheese, provolone cheese, milk, green onion, and pepper (a 1½-quart cooker will be full).

2. Cover and cook on low-heat setting (do not use high-heat setting) for 6 hours. If no heat setting is available, cook for 4½ to 5 hours.

3. Before serving, gently stir mixture. Sprinkle individual servings with bacon.

Nutrition Facts per serving: 261 cal., 17 g total fat (9 g sat. fat), 44 mg chol., 781 mg sodium, 17 g carbo., 1 g fiber, 9 g pro.

Accompany this slow-cooker version of the old-world favorite with pork or sausage links. For the best contrast of textures, spoon the zesty, hot potatoes over the spinach leaves just before serving.

Hot German Potato Salad

MAKES 6 SERVINGS

Prep: 20 minutes
Cook: Low 8 to 10 hours,
High 4 to 5 hours

3	medium red potatoes (1 pound), peeled, if desired, and cut into ¼-inch-thick slices
1	medium onion, chopped (½ cup)
1	stalk celery, chopped (½ cup)
⅓	cup water
¼	cup cider vinegar
2	tablespoons sugar
½	teaspoon salt
⅛	to ¼ teaspoon celery seeds
⅛	teaspoon black pepper
3	slices bacon, crisp-cooked, drained, and crumbled
2	tablespoons snipped fresh parsley
4	cups shredded fresh spinach

1. In a 1½- or 2-quart slow cooker combine potato, onion, and celery. In a small bowl combine water, vinegar, sugar, salt, celery seeds, and pepper. Pour over mixture in cooker.

2. Cover and cook on low-heat setting for 8 to 10 hours or on high-heat setting for 4 to 5 hours. If no heat setting is available, cook for 3½ to 4 hours.

3. Stir in bacon and parsley. Serve the hot potato mixture over spinach.

Nutrition Facts per serving: 176 cal., 9 g total fat (3 g sat. fat), 13 mg chol., 381 mg sodium, 20 g carbo., 3 g fiber, 4 g pro.

You'll love the extra dimensions of sweetness and tang that
orange juice and apricots bring to the unassuming sweet potato.

Maple-Orange Sweet Potatoes

MAKES 4 SERVINGS

Prep: 20 minutes
Cook: Low 8 to 9 hours,
High 4 to 4½ hours

Nonstick cooking spray
1   to 1½ pounds sweet
      potatoes, peeled and cut
      into 1½-inch pieces*
½   cup snipped dried apricots
¼   cup maple syrup
2   tablespoons water
2   tablespoons frozen orange
      juice concentrate, thawed
1   tablespoon butter or
      margarine, melted
¼   teaspoon salt
⅛   teaspoon ground cinnamon
⅛   teaspoon black pepper

1. Lightly coat the inside of a 1½- or 2-quart slow cooker with nonstick cooking spray. In the prepared cooker combine sweet potato and dried apricots. In a small bowl combine maple syrup, water, orange juice concentrate, butter, salt, cinnamon, and pepper. Pour over mixture in cooker.

2. Cover and cook on low-heat setting for 8 to 9 hours or on high-heat setting for 4 to 4½ hours. If no heat setting is available, cook for 7½ to 8 hours.

3. Using a slotted spoon, transfer sweet potato and apricots to a serving dish, reserving cooking liquid. If desired, drizzle some of the cooking liquid over sweet potato and apricots; discard the remaining liquid.

Nutrition Facts per serving: 202 cal., 3 g total fat (2 g sat. fat), 8 mg chol., 215 mg sodium, 44 g carbo., 4 g fiber, 2 g pro.

*Note: If using a 2-quart slow cooker, use 1½ pounds sweet potatoes.

Deep-orange mashed sweet potatoes are beautiful on the table and plate; the addition of a few parsnips adds a sophisticated taste.

Mashed Sweet Potatoes and Parsnips

MAKES 6 SERVINGS

Prep: 20 minutes
Cook: Low 7 to 8 hours, High 3½ to 4 hours

	Nonstick cooking spray
1½	pounds sweet potatoes, peeled and cubed (about 4 cups)
3	medium parsnips, peeled and cubed (about 2½ cups)
½	cup chicken broth
2	tablespoons butter or margarine, melted
½	teaspoon onion salt
½	teaspoon ground sage

1. Lightly coat the inside of a 3½- or 4-quart slow cooker with nonstick cooking spray. Add sweet potato, parsnip, broth, butter, onion salt, and sage.

2. Cover and cook on low-heat setting for 7 to 8 hours or on high-heat setting for 3½ to 4 hours. Mash vegetables with a potato masher.

Nutrition Facts per serving: 166 cal., 5 g total fat (3 g sat. fat), 11 mg chol., 273 mg sodium, 30 g carbo., 5 g fiber, 2 g pro.

With only a few ingredients, this side dish has amazing flavor. No matter whether you serve the festive cranberry-sauced squash with roasted pork, grilled poultry, or broiled fish, it's a top-notch way to round out a meal. (Photo on page 142.)

Acorn Squash with Orange-Cranberry Sauce

MAKES 4 TO 6 SERVINGS

Prep: 15 minutes
Cook: Low 6 to 7 hours,
High 3 to 3½ hours

2	medium acorn squash (about 2 pounds)
1	16-ounce can jellied cranberry sauce
¼	cup orange marmalade
¼	cup raisins
¼	teaspoon ground cinnamon
	Salt
	Black pepper

1. Cut each squash in half lengthwise; remove seeds. Cut squash into 1-inch-thick wedges. Arrange squash in a 3½- or 4-quart slow cooker.

2. In a small saucepan combine cranberry sauce, marmalade, raisins, and cinnamon. Cook and stir over medium heat until smooth. Pour over squash in cooker.

3. Cover and cook on low-heat setting for 6 to 7 hours or on high-heat setting for 3 to 3½ hours. Season to taste with salt and pepper.

Nutrition Facts per serving: 328 cal., 0 g total fat (0 g sat. fat), 0 mg chol., 220 mg sodium, 83 g carbo., 5 g fiber, 2 g pro.

If you've passed on risotto recipes because they require too much stirring, take a look at this recipe! Here the rice cooks up to the traditional moist and creamy risotto consistency without all that effort.

Slow-Cooker Mushroom Risotto

MAKES 4 TO 6 SERVINGS

Prep: 20 minutes
Cook: Low 5 to 5½ hours
Stand: 15 minutes

Nonstick cooking spray

3 cups sliced fresh mushrooms (such as cremini, button, and/or shiitake) (8 ounces)

1 14-ounce can vegetable broth

¾ cup uncooked converted rice (do not substitute long grain rice)

½ cup water

3 tablespoons dry white wine or vegetable broth

3 tablespoons chopped shallot

¼ teaspoon dried thyme, crushed

⅛ teaspoon salt

⅛ teaspoon black pepper

1 clove garlic, minced

½ cup finely shredded Parmesan cheese

2 tablespoons butter or margarine, cut into small pieces

1. Lightly coat the inside of a 2-quart slow cooker with nonstick cooking spray. In the prepared cooker combine mushrooms, broth, rice, water, wine, shallot, thyme, salt, pepper, and garlic.

2. Cover and cook on low-heat setting (do not use high-heat setting) for 5 to 5½ hours. If no heat setting is available, cook for 4½ to 5 hours. Stir in Parmesan cheese and butter.

3. Remove liner from cooker, if possible, or turn off cooker. Let stand, covered, for 15 minutes before serving.

Nutrition Facts per serving: 261 cal., 10 g total fat (6 g sat. fat), 23 mg chol., 677 mg sodium, 34 g carbo., 0 g fiber, 9 g pro.

If you're searching for a recipe with bold flavors, awaken your taste buds with this moist, lightly herbed side dish. Topped with chopped pecans, it adds up to a delicious reason to embrace eating more wild rice.

Wild Rice with Pecans and Cherries

❧

MAKES 6 SERVINGS

Prep: 20 minutes
Cook: Low 5 to 6 hours
Stand: 10 minutes

2⅓	cups chicken broth
¾	cup uncooked wild rice, rinsed and drained
1	medium carrot, coarsely shredded (½ cup)
1	2.5-ounce jar (drained weight) sliced mushrooms, drained
1	tablespoon butter or margarine
1	teaspoon dried marjoram, crushed
⅛	teaspoon salt
⅛	teaspoon black pepper
⅓	cup dried tart cherries
⅓	cup sliced green onion (3)
¼	cup broken pecans, toasted (see tip, page 29)

1. In a 1½- or 2-quart slow cooker stir together broth, wild rice, carrot, drained mushrooms, butter, marjoram, salt, and pepper.

2. Cover and cook on low-heat setting (do not use high-heat setting) for 5 to 6 hours. If no heat setting is available, cook for 4½ to 5 hours.

3. Turn off cooker. Stir in dried cherries and green onion. Let stand, covered, for 10 minutes. Before serving, sprinkle with pecans.

Nutrition Facts per serving: 166 cal., 6 g total fat (2 g sat. fat), 6 mg chol., 491 mg sodium, 26 g carbo., 3 g fiber, 4 g pro.

Preparing the stuffing in the slow cooker leaves space in the oven for other dishes—a lifesaver when you're making a traditional holiday meal.

Savory Stuffing with Fruit and Pecans

MAKES 6 SERVINGS

Prep: 20 minutes
Cook: Low 4 to 4½ hours,
High 2 to 2¼ hours

¼	cup apple juice
⅔	cup mixed dried fruit bits
1	stalk celery, finely chopped (½ cup)
¼	cup sliced green onion (2)
¼	cup butter or margarine
1	tablespoon snipped fresh parsley
½	teaspoon dried sage, crushed
¼	teaspoon salt
¼	teaspoon dried thyme, crushed
¼	teaspoon dried marjoram, crushed
⅛	teaspoon black pepper
5	cups dried ½-inch bread cubes (7 to 8 slices) (see tip, page 225)
¼	cup broken pecans, toasted (see tip, page 29)
½	to ¾ cup chicken broth

1. In a small saucepan bring apple juice to boiling. Stir in dried fruit bits; remove from heat. Cover and let stand until needed.

2. Meanwhile, in a medium saucepan cook and stir celery and green onion in hot butter over medium heat until tender. Remove from heat. Stir in parsley, sage, salt, thyme, marjoram, and pepper.

3. Place bread cubes in a large bowl. Add dried fruit mixture, celery mixture, and pecans. Drizzle with enough of the broth to moisten, tossing gently to combine. Transfer bread mixture to a 1½- or 2-quart slow cooker.

4. Cover and cook on low-heat setting for 4 to 4½ hours or on high-heat setting for 2 to 2¼ hours. If no heat setting is available, cook for 3 to 3½ hours.

Nutrition Facts per serving: 231 cal., 12 g total fat (5 g sat. fat), 21 mg chol., 454 mg sodium, 29 g carbo., 3 g fiber, 5 g pro.

Make this fancy oatmeal anytime you want a hot, no-fuss breakfast. Use steel-cut oats; no other type stands up to long cooking.

Fruited Irish Oatmeal

MAKES 6 SERVINGS

Prep: 10 minutes
Cook: Low 6 to 7 hours,
High 3 to 3½ hours

2½	cups water
1	cup steel-cut oats
½	cup apple juice
½	cup mixed dried fruit bits
2	tablespoons maple syrup
½	teaspoon ground cinnamon
¼	teaspoon salt
	Brown sugar or maple syrup
	Chopped walnuts or pecans, toasted (see tip, page 29)
	Milk

1. In a 1½- or 2-quart slow cooker combine water, oats, apple juice, dried fruit bits, the 2 tablespoons maple syrup, the cinnamon, and salt.

2. Cover and cook on low-heat setting for 6 to 7 hours or on high-heat setting for 3 to 3½ hours. If no heat setting is available, cook for 5½ to 6 hours.

3. Serve oatmeal with brown sugar, toasted nuts, and milk.*

Nutrition Facts per serving: 220 cal., 5 g total fat (0 g sat. fat), 1 mg chol., 116 mg sodium, 39 g carbo., 6 g fiber, 6 g pro.

*Note: To reheat, place a single serving of oatmeal in a microwave-safe bowl. Cover and microwave on 100 percent power (high) for 30 seconds; stir. Microwave, covered, for 15 to 30 seconds more or until heated through.

You can't beat this decadent dessert. It's a classic combo: moist, tender cake and crunchy pecans smothered in rich caramel sauce.

Orange Pudding Caramel Cake

MAKES 6 SERVINGS

Prep: 25 minutes
Cook: Low 4½ to 5 hours
Stand: 45 minutes

Nonstick cooking spray or 1 disposable slow-cooker liner
1 cup all-purpose flour
⅓ cup granulated sugar
1 teaspoon baking powder
½ teaspoon ground cinnamon
¼ teaspoon salt
½ cup milk
2 tablespoons butter, melted
½ cup chopped pecans
¼ cup dried currants or raisins
¾ cup water
½ teaspoon finely shredded orange peel
¾ cup orange juice
⅔ cup packed brown sugar
1 tablespoon butter
Caramel ice cream topping
Chopped pecans

1. Lightly coat the inside of a 3½- or 4-quart slow cooker with nonstick cooking spray or line with a slow cooker liner; set aside.

2. In a medium bowl combine flour, granulated sugar, baking powder, cinnamon, and salt. Add milk and the melted butter; stir just until combined. Stir in the ½ cup pecans and the currants. Spread evenly in the bottom of the prepared cooker.

3. In a medium saucepan combine water, orange peel, orange juice, brown sugar, and the 1 tablespoon butter. Bring to boiling, stirring to dissolve sugar; reduce heat. Boil gently, uncovered, for 2 minutes. Carefully pour over mixture in cooker.

4. Cover and cook on low-heat setting (do not use high-heat setting) for 4½ to 5 hours. Remove stoneware liner from cooker, if possible, or turn off cooker. Let stand, uncovered, about 45 minutes to cool slightly before serving.

5. To serve, spoon pudding cake into dessert dishes. Top with caramel topping and additional chopped pecans.

Nutrition Facts per serving: 390 cal., 15 g total fat (6 g sat. fat), 23 mg chol., 255 mg sodium, 61 g carbo., 2 g fiber, 5 g pro.

With caramel apple "pudding" on the bottom and a moist walnut cake layer on top, this dessert has an irresistible homespun appeal.

Dutch Apple Pudding Cake

MAKES 6 SERVINGS

Prep: 20 minutes
Cook: High 2 to 2½ hours
Stand: 30 minutes

	Nonstick cooking spray
1	21-ounce can apple pie filling
½	cup dried cherries, dried cranberries, or raisins
1	cup all-purpose flour
¼	cup granulated sugar
1	teaspoon baking powder
¼	teaspoon salt
½	cup milk
2	tablespoons butter or margarine, melted
½	cup chopped walnuts, toasted (see tip, page 29)
1¼	cups apple juice or apple cider
⅓	cup packed brown sugar
1	tablespoon butter or margarine
	Sweetened whipped cream (optional)

1. Lightly coat the inside of a 3½- or 4-quart slow cooker with nonstick cooking spray; set aside. In a small saucepan bring apple pie filling to boiling. Stir in dried cherries. Transfer apple mixture to the prepared cooker.

2. In a medium bowl stir together flour, granulated sugar, baking powder, and salt. Add milk and the 2 tablespoons melted butter; stir just until combined. Stir in walnuts. Pour over mixture in cooker, spreading evenly.

3. In the same small saucepan combine apple juice, brown sugar, and the 1 tablespoon butter. Bring to boiling; reduce heat. Boil gently, uncovered, for 2 minutes. Carefully pour over mixture in cooker.

4. Cover and cook on high-heat setting (do not use low-heat setting) for 2 to 2½ hours or until a toothpick inserted into center of cake comes out clean.

5. Remove liner from cooker, if possible, or turn off cooker. Let stand, uncovered, for 30 to 45 minutes to cool slightly before serving.

6. To serve, spoon warm cake into dessert dishes; spoon apple mixture over cake. If desired, top with sweetened whipped cream.

Nutrition Facts per serving: 435 cal., 13 g total fat (5 g sat. fat), 18 mg chol., 284 mg sodium, 77 g carbo., 3 g fiber, 5 g pro.

Snipped apricots soften to yield a mellow, sweet flavor and a bright jewel hue in this luscious spiced dessert. It's a lovely reward to share after a light dinner or with friends invited for dessert and coffee.

White Chocolate-Apricot Bread Pudding

MAKES 6 SERVINGS

Prep: 30 minutes
Cook: Low 4 hours,
High 2 hours

1½	cups half-and-half or light cream
½	of a 6-ounce package white chocolate baking squares (with cocoa butter), coarsely chopped
⅓	cup snipped dried apricots
2	eggs, slightly beaten
½	cup sugar
½	teaspoon ground cardamom
3	cups dried ½-inch bread cubes (about 4½ slices) (see tip, page 225)
¼	cup coarsely chopped almonds
1	cup warm water
	Whipped cream (optional)
	Grated white chocolate baking squares (with cocoa butter) (optional)

1. Tear off an 18x12-inch piece of heavy foil; cut in half lengthwise. Fold each piece lengthwise into thirds. Crisscross the foil strips and place a 4- to 5-cup soufflé dish in the center of the foil cross; set aside.

2. In a small saucepan heat half-and-half over medium heat until very warm but not boiling. Remove from heat. Add the chopped white chocolate and the dried apricots; stir until chocolate is melted.

3. In a medium bowl combine eggs, sugar, and cardamom. Whisk in half-and-half mixture. Gently stir in bread cubes and almonds. Transfer mixture to the soufflé dish (dish may be full). Cover dish tightly with another piece of foil.

4. Pour warm water into a 3½- to 5-quart slow cooker. Bringing up the foil strips, lift the ends of the strips to transfer the dish and foil to cooker. Leave foil strips under dish.

5. Cover and cook on low-heat setting for 4 hours or on high-heat setting for 2 hours. Using the foil strips, carefully lift soufflé dish out of cooker; discard foil strips.

6. To serve, spoon bread pudding into dessert dishes. If desired, top with whipped cream and the grated white chocolate.

Nutrition Facts per serving: 345 cal., 17 g total fat (8 g sat. fat), 98 mg chol., 191 mg sodium, 42 g carbo., 2 g fiber, 8 g pro.

Chunky apple pie filling and cinnamon-raisin bread are the star attractions. You can substitute white bread, ⅓ cup raisins, and ⅛ teaspoon cinnamon to save a trip to the store.

Apple Pie Bread Pudding

MAKES 6 SERVINGS

Prep: 10 minutes
Cook: Low 3 hours
Stand: 30 minutes

	Nonstick cooking spray
3	eggs, slightly beaten
2	cups milk, half-and-half, or light cream
½	cup sugar
1	21-ounce can chunky apple pie filling (more fruit)
4½	cups dried ½-inch cinnamon-raisin bread cubes (8 or 9 slices) (see tip, right)
	Whipped cream or vanilla ice cream (optional)

1. Lightly coat the inside of a 3½- or 4-quart slow cooker with nonstick cooking spray; set aside.

2. In a large bowl whisk together eggs, milk, and sugar. Stir in pie filling; gently stir in bread cubes. Transfer mixture to the prepared cooker.

3. Cover and cook on low-heat setting (do not use high-heat setting) about 3 hours or until a knife inserted near the center comes out clean (mixture will puff).

4. Remove liner from cooker, if possible, or turn off cooker. Let stand, uncovered, for 30 to 45 minutes to cool slightly before serving (pudding will fall as it cools).

5. To serve, spoon bread pudding into dessert dishes. If desired, top with whipped cream.

Nutrition Facts per serving: 548 cal., 6 g total fat (2 g sat. fat), 113 mg chol., 133 mg sodium, 114 g carbo., 8 g fiber, 16 g pro.

Test Kitchen Tip: To make dried bread cubes, cut fresh bread into ½-inch cubes. Spread in a single layer in a 15x10x1-inch baking pan. Bake in a 300°F oven for 10 to 15 minutes or until cubes are dry, stirring twice; cool. Or let bread cubes stand loosely covered at room temperature for 8 to 12 hours.

Bread pudding most likely was developed as a way to recycle what was left of yesterday's loaf of bread. The result is truly sublime.

Raisin Bread Pudding

MAKES 4 SERVINGS

Prep: 10 minutes
Cook: Low 3 hours
Stand: 30 minutes

Nonstick cooking spray
1 egg, slightly beaten
⅓ cup sugar
1 teaspoon ground cinnamon
1 teaspoon vanilla
⅛ teaspoon ground nutmeg
1 12-ounce can evaporated milk
3 cups dried ½-inch French bread cubes (3 to 4 ounces) (see tip, page 225)
⅓ cup raisins
Caramel ice cream topping (optional)

1. Lightly coat the inside of a 1½-quart slow cooker with nonstick cooking spray. In a medium bowl combine egg, sugar, cinnamon, vanilla, and nutmeg. Whisk in evaporated milk. Gently stir in bread cubes and raisins. Transfer mixture to the prepared cooker.

2. Cover and cook on low-heat setting (do not use high-heat setting) about 3 hours or until a knife inserted in the center comes out clean. If no heat setting is available, cook for 2½ hours. Turn off cooker. Let stand, uncovered, for 30 to 60 minutes to cool slightly before serving.

3. To serve, spoon bread pudding into dessert dishes. If desired, drizzle with caramel topping.

Nutrition Facts per serving: 298 cal., 8 g total fat (4 g sat. fat), 78 mg chol., 248 mg sodium, 47 g carbo., 1 g fiber, 11 g pro.

What apple variety works best in baked recipes? Look for
Golden Delicious, Granny Smith, or Jonathan apples.

Apple-Cherry Cobbler

MAKES 6 SERVINGS

Prep: 15 minutes
Cook: Low 5 to 6 hours,
High 2½ to 3 hours

½	cup sugar
4	teaspoons quick-cooking tapioca
1	teaspoon apple pie spice
1½	pounds cooking apples, peeled, cored, and cut into ½-inch-thick slices (4½ cups)
1	16-ounce can pitted tart red cherries, undrained
½	cup dried cherries
1	recipe Spiced Triangles
	Ice cream (such as butter pecan or cinnamon) (optional)

1. In a 3½- or 4-quart slow cooker combine sugar, tapioca, and apple pie spice. Stir in apple slices, undrained canned cherries, and dried cherries.

2. Cover and cook on low-heat setting for 5 to 6 hours or on high-setting for 2½ to 3 hours.

3. To serve, spoon the apple mixture into dessert dishes. Top with Spiced Triangles and, if desired, ice cream.

Spiced Triangles: Preheat oven to 375°F. In a small bowl combine 1 tablespoon sugar and ½ teaspoon apple pie spice. Unroll one 8-ounce package (8) refrigerated crescent rolls. Separate triangles. Brush 1 tablespoon melted butter or margarine over dough triangles; lightly sprinkle with sugar mixture. Cut each triangle into three smaller triangles. Place on an ungreased baking sheet. Bake for 8 to 10 minutes or until bottoms are lightly browned. Transfer triangles to a wire rack and let cool. Makes 24 triangles.

Nutrition Facts per serving: 414 cal., 10 g total fat (4 g sat. fat), 5 mg chol., 317 mg sodium, 79 g carbo., 5 g fiber, 7 g pro.

The toasted coconut and crunchy granola topping takes your palate to warmer climates. Tropical dried fruit bits intensify the flavor of the apricot pie filling.

Tropical Apricot Crisp

MAKES 6 SERVINGS

Prep: 10 minutes
Cook: Low 2½ hours
Cool: 30 minutes

Nonstick cooking spray
2 21-ounce cans apricot pie filling
1 7-ounce package tropical blend mixed dried fruit bits
1 cup granola
⅓ cup coconut, toasted (see tip, page 29)
1 pint vanilla ice cream

1. Lightly coat the inside of a 3½- or 4-quart slow cooker with nonstick cooking spray. In the prepared cooker combine the pie filling and dried fruit bits.

2. Cover and cook on low-heat setting (do not use high-heat setting) for 2½ hours.

3. Remove liner from cooker, if possible, or turn off cooker. In a small bowl combine granola and coconut. Sprinkle over mixture in cooker. Let stand, uncovered, about 30 minutes to cool slightly before serving.

4. To serve, spoon apricot mixture into dessert dishes. Top with scoops of vanilla ice cream.

Nutrition Facts per serving: 587 cal., 13 g total fat (8 g sat. fat), 45 mg chol., 144 mg sodium, 109 g carbo., 7 g fiber, 6 g pro.

5
Ingredient
Recipe

Celebrate autumn with a visit to a local orchard and turn your finds into an apple betty. Tart apples and apple butter cook with brown sugar and cinnamon-raisin bread to produce a full-flavored comfort food.

Slow-Cooked Apple Betty

MAKES 6 SERVINGS

Prep: 20 minutes
Cook: Low 4 hours
Stand: 30 minutes

Nonstick cooking spray
5   medium tart cooking apples, peeled, cored, and sliced (5 cups)
¾   cup packed brown sugar
⅔   cup apple butter
½   cup water
5   cups soft ½-inch cinnamon-raisin bread cubes (about 5 slices)
⅓   cup butter or margarine, melted
Caramel ice cream topping and/or vanilla ice cream (optional)

1. Lightly coat the inside of a 3½- or 4-quart slow cooker with nonstick cooking spray; set aside.

2. In a large bowl combine apple slices, brown sugar, apple butter, and water. Stir gently to coat apples. Place bread cubes in a medium bowl. Drizzle with melted butter; toss gently to combine.

3. Place half of the buttered bread cubes in the prepared cooker. Pour all of the apple mixture over bread cubes. Sprinkle with the remaining buttered bread cubes.

4. Cover and cook on low-heat setting (do not use high-heat setting) for 4 hours.

5. Remove liner from cooker, if possible, or turn off cooker. Let stand, uncovered, about 30 minutes to cool slightly before serving.

6. To serve, spoon the apple mixture into dessert dishes. If desired, top with caramel topping and/or ice cream.

Nutrition Facts per serving: 492 cal., 12 g total fat (7 g sat. fat), 29 mg chol., 209 mg sodium, 97 g carbo., 5 g fiber, 2 g pro.

These velvety and lemony sauced pears make a captivating finish to a dinner party. If you'd like something more substantial, add angel food or pound cake slices in place of the sugar-cookie garnish.

Pears in Lemon Cream Sauce

MAKES 6 SERVINGS

Prep: 20 minutes
Cook: High 1½ to 2 hours

6	medium ripe yet firm pears
1	teaspoon finely shredded lemon peel
2	tablespoons lemon juice
⅓	cup packed brown sugar
¼	teaspoon ground nutmeg
½	of an 8-ounce package cream cheese, cubed and softened
¼	cup whipping cream
3	tablespoons broken pecans, toasted (see tip, page 29)
6	sugar cookies (optional)

1. If desired, peel pears; halve pears lengthwise and remove cores. Place pears in a medium bowl. Add lemon peel and lemon juice; toss gently to coat. Add brown sugar and nutmeg; toss gently to combine. Transfer pear mixture to a 3½- or 4-quart slow cooker.

2. Cover and cook on high-heat setting (do not use low-heat setting) for 1½ to 2 hours. Using a slotted spoon, transfer pears to dessert dishes, reserving cooking liquid.

3. For sauce, add cream cheese and whipping cream to liquid in cooker. Cook and stir with a wire whisk until cream cheese is melted. Spoon the sauce over pears. Sprinkle with pecans. If desired, garnish with sugar cookies.

Nutrition Facts per serving: 273 cal., 13 g total fat (7 g sat. fat), 34 mg chol., 65 mg sodium, 40 g carbo., 4 g fiber, 3 g pro.

Added sugar isn't needed for this dessert.
Grape juice and dried cranberries add sweetness.

Poached Pears and Cranberry Syrup

MAKES 6 SERVINGS

Prep: 20 minutes
Cook: Low 4 to 5 hours,
High 2 to 2½ hours

¾	cup dried cranberries
6	medium ripe yet firm pears
1½	cups white grape juice
½	teaspoon almond extract (optional)
3	cups frozen vanilla yogurt

1. Place dried cranberries in a 3½- or 4-quart slow cooker. Peel pears; halve pears lengthwise and remove cores. Add pears to cooker. Pour juice and, if desired, almond extract over pears.

2. Cover and cook on low-heat setting for 4 to 5 hours or on high-heat setting for 2 to 2½ hours.

3. Using a slotted spoon, transfer pears to dessert dishes. Spoon cranberry mixture over pears. Serve with scoops of frozen yogurt.

Nutrition Facts per serving: 297 cal., 4 g total fat (2 g sat. fat), 1 mg chol., 74 mg sodium, 64 g carbo., 6 g fiber, 4 g pro.

5 Ingredient Recipe

*This classic, old-fashioned dessert
is a real family pleaser.*

Stuffed Apples

MAKES 4 SERVINGS

Prep: 20 minutes
Cook: Low 5 hours,
High 2½ hours

4	medium tart baking apples (such as Granny Smith)
⅓	cup snipped dried figs or raisins
¼	cup packed brown sugar
½	teaspoon apple pie spice or ground cinnamon
¼	cup apple juice
1	tablespoon butter or margarine, cut into 4 pieces

1. Core apples; peel a strip from the top of each apple. Place apples, top sides up, in a 3½- or 4-quart slow cooker.

2. In a small bowl combine figs, brown sugar, and apple pie spice. Spoon mixture into centers of apples, patting in with a knife or narrow metal spatula. Pour apple juice around apples in cooker. Top each apple with a piece of butter.

3. Cover and cook on low-heat setting for 5 hours or on high-heat setting for 2½ hours.

4. Using a large spoon, transfer apples to dessert dishes. Spoon the cooking liquid from cooker over apples. Serve warm.

Nutrition Facts per serving: 200 cal., 3 g total fat (2 g sat. fat), 8 mg chol., 31 mg sodium, 45 g carbo., 5 g fiber, 1 g pro.

Big-Batch Recipes for a Crowd

*These slow-cooked "loose-meat" sandwiches get their extra
special firepower from a Scotch bonnet chile pepper
(one of the smallest and hottest peppers in the world)
along with chili powder and black pepper.*

Hot and Spicy Sloppy Joes

**MAKES 12 TO 14
SANDWICHES**

Prep: 25 minutes
Cook: Low 8 to 10 hours,
High 4 to 5 hours

2 pounds lean ground beef
4 medium onions, cut into strips
4 medium green sweet peppers, cut into strips
2 medium red sweet peppers, cut into strips
1 cup ketchup
¼ cup cider vinegar
1 fresh Scotch bonnet chile pepper, seeded and finely chopped (see tip, page 10), or ¼ teaspoon cayenne pepper
1 tablespoon chili powder
½ teaspoon salt
½ teaspoon black pepper
12 to 14 hoagie buns or hamburger buns, split and toasted

1. In a very large skillet or Dutch oven, cook ground beef and onion until meat is brown and onion is tender. Drain off fat. Transfer meat mixture to a 5- to 6-quart slow cooker.

2. Stir in sweet peppers, ketchup, vinegar, chile pepper, chili powder, salt, and black pepper.

3. Cover and cook on low-heat setting for 8 to 10 hours or on high-heat setting for 4 to 5 hours. Serve meat mixture in buns.

Nutrition Facts per serving: 592 cal., 18 g total fat (6 g sat. fat), 48 mg chol., 1,051 mg sodium, 83 g carbo., 6 g fiber, 27 g pro.

Test Kitchen Tip: To carry a slow cooker full of hot food to a party, wrap it in several layers of newspaper or a thick towel, then place the cooker in an insulated container. If electricity is available at the site, take along a heavy extension cord and plug in the cooker. The food will stay warm for several hours on the low setting. If there's no electricity, serve the food within two hours.

Ground beef slow-cooks with tomatoes, chile peppers, lots of spices, and hot dogs before joining cheese and onions on toasted buns for a hearty sandwich meal.

Beefy Chili Dogs

MAKES 10 SANDWICHES

Prep: 25 minutes
Cook: Low 4 to 4½ hours,
High 2 to 2½ hours

12	ounces lean ground beef
1	large onion, chopped (1 cup)
3	cloves garlic, minced
1	14.5-ounce can diced tomatoes, undrained
1	4-ounce can diced green chile peppers, drained
1	tablespoon chili powder
1	tablespoon yellow mustard
1	teaspoon sugar
1	teaspoon paprika
1	teaspoon Worcestershire sauce
½	teaspoon ground cumin
½	teaspoon celery seeds
¼	teaspoon salt
¼	teaspoon black pepper
10	hot dogs
10	hot dog buns, split and toasted
	Shredded cheddar cheese (optional)
	Chopped onion (optional)
	Yellow mustard (optional)

1. For meat sauce, in a large skillet cook ground beef, the 1 cup onion, and the garlic until meat is brown and onion is tender. Drain off fat. Stir in undrained tomatoes, drained chile peppers, chili powder, the 1 tablespoon mustard, the sugar, paprika, Worcestershire sauce, cumin, celery seeds, salt, and black pepper.

2. Place hot dogs in the bottom of a 2½- to 3½-quart slow cooker. Spoon meat mixture over hot dogs.

3. Cover and cook on low-heat setting for 4 to 4½ hours or on high-heat setting for 2 to 2½ hours.

4. Using tongs, remove hot dogs from meat sauce. Place hot dogs in buns. Top each with about ⅓ cup of the meat sauce. If desired, serve sandwiches with cheese and additional onion and mustard.

Nutrition Facts per serving: 360 cal., 20 g total fat (7 g sat. fat), 46 mg chol., 923 mg sodium, 28 g carbo., 2 g fiber, 17 g pro.

These perfectly seasoned sloppy joe–style sandwiches are just the right consistency thanks to of the addition of a can of tomato soup.

Saucy Cheeseburger Sandwiches

MAKES 12 TO 15 SANDWICHES

Prep: 20 minutes
Cook: Low 6 to 8 hours,
High 3 to 4 hours,
plus 5 minutes (low)

2½	pounds lean ground beef
1	10.75-ounce can condensed tomato soup
1	large onion, finely chopped (1 cup)
¼	cup water
2	tablespoons tomato paste
1	tablespoon Worcestershire sauce
1	tablespoon yellow mustard
2	teaspoons dried Italian seasoning, crushed
¼	teaspoon black pepper
2	cloves garlic, minced
6	ounces American cheese, cut into cubes
12	to 15 hamburger buns, split and toasted

1. In a 12-inch skillet cook ground beef until brown. Drain off fat. Transfer meat to a 3½- or 4-quart slow cooker. Stir in soup, onion, water, tomato paste, Worcestershire sauce, mustard, Italian seasoning, pepper, and garlic.

2. Cover and cook on low-heat setting for 6 to 8 hours or on high-heat setting for 3 to 4 hours.

3. If using high-heat setting, turn to low-heat setting. Stir in cheese. Cover and cook for 5 to 10 minutes more or until cheese is melted. Spoon meat mixture into buns.

Nutrition Facts per serving: 357 cal., 16 g total fat (7 g sat. fat), 73 mg chol., 664 mg sodium, 28 g carbo., 2 g fiber, 25 g pro.

These finger-lickin' sandwiches will draw a hungry crowd. An old Southern trick is toasting the buns to keep them from getting soggy when the barbecue meat is piled on.

Down South Barbecue

MAKES 16 SANDWICHES

Prep: 20 minutes
Cook: Low 10 to 12 hours, High 5 to 6 hours

1½	pounds boneless pork shoulder roast
1½	pounds boneless beef chuck roast
1	6-ounce can tomato paste
½	cup sugar
¼	cup cider vinegar
¼	cup water
2	tablespoons chili powder
2	teaspoons Worcestershire sauce
1	teaspoon dry mustard
½	teaspoon salt
16	whole-grain hamburger buns, split and toasted

1. Trim fat from meat. Place meat in a 3½- or 4-quart slow cooker. In a small bowl combine tomato paste, sugar, vinegar, water, chili powder, Worcestershire sauce, dry mustard, and salt. Pour over meat in cooker.

2. Cover and cook on low-heat setting for 10 to 12 hours or on high-heat setting for 5 to 6 hours.

3. Transfer meat to a cutting board. Shred meat by pulling two forks through it in opposite directions. Return meat to cooker; stir to combine with cooking liquid.

4. Using a slotted spoon, spoon meat mixture into buns.

Nutrition Facts per serving: 241 cal., 7 g total fat (2 g sat. fat), 53 mg chol., 430 mg sodium, 23 g carbo., 2 g fiber, 22 g pro.

In eastern North Carolina, home of vinegar-sauced barbecued pork, coleslaw is a must-have accompaniment. Try spooning some coleslaw onto the roll with the meat instead of serving it alongside.

Pork and Slaw Barbecue Rolls

MAKES 16 SANDWICHES

Prep: 20 minutes
Cook: Low 10 to 12 hours,
High 5 to 6 hours

4   to 5 pounds boneless pork shoulder roast
¾   cup cider vinegar
2   tablespoons packed brown sugar
½   teaspoon salt
½   teaspoon crushed red pepper
¼   teaspoon black pepper
16   kaiser rolls, split and toasted
     Purchased deli coleslaw

1. Trim fat from meat. Cut meat to fit into a 4- to 6-quart slow cooker. Place meat in cooker. In a small bowl combine vinegar, brown sugar, salt, crushed red pepper, and black pepper. Pour over meat in cooker.

2. Cover and cook on low-heat setting for 10 to 12 hours or on high-heat setting for 5 to 6 hours.

3. Transfer meat to a cutting board, reserving cooking liquid. Shred or coarsely chop meat.

4. In a medium bowl combine meat and enough of the cooking liquid to moisten. Spoon meat and coleslaw into rolls.

Nutrition Facts per serving: 272 cal., 6 g total fat (2 g sat. fat), 41 mg chol., 563 mg sodium, 34 g carbo., 1 g fiber, 18 g pro.

*Cola-simmered pork roast and sliced onion join forces with a
fiery tomato topper in these hefty south-of-the-border hoagies.*

Slow-Simmered Pork Sandwiches

MAKES 12 SANDWICHES

Prep: 30 minutes
Cook: Low 9 to 10 hours,
High 4½ to 5 hours

4	pounds boneless pork shoulder roast
5	teaspoons cumin seeds, toasted*
2	tablespoons packed brown sugar
1½	teaspoons salt
¾	teaspoon black pepper
½	teaspoon cayenne pepper
1	medium onion, sliced
3	cloves garlic, minced
1	12-ounce can cola
1	cup chicken broth
¼	cup cooking oil
1	pound roma tomatoes, seeded and chopped
1	12- or 16-ounce jar sliced pickled jalapeño chile peppers
⅔	cup coarsely snipped fresh cilantro
12	hoagie buns, Mexican torta rolls, or other hard rolls, split and toasted
2	limes, cut into wedges

1. Trim fat from meat. Set meat aside. Crush cumin seeds with a mortar and pestle or blender. In a small bowl combine crushed cumin seed, brown sugar, 1 teaspoon of the salt, ½ teaspoon of the black pepper, and the cayenne pepper. Sprinkle evenly over meat; rub in with your fingers. If necessary, cut meat to fit into a 3½- to 5-quart slow cooker. Set aside.

2. In the cooker combine onion and garlic. Add meat. Pour cola and broth over mixture in cooker.

3. Cover and cook on low-heat setting for 9 to 10 hours or on high-heat setting for 4½ to 5 hours.

4. Meanwhile, in a large skillet heat oil over medium heat. Add tomato. Cook, uncovered, for 4 minutes, stirring occasionally. Drain jalapeño peppers, reserving ½ cup of the liquid; set peppers aside. Add the reserved liquid, the cilantro, the remaining ½ teaspoon salt, and the remaining ¼ teaspoon black pepper to tomato in skillet. Bring to boiling; reduce heat. Cook, uncovered, for 3 to 4 minutes or until slightly thickened, stirring occasionally. Set aside.

5. Using a slotted spoon, remove meat and onion from cooker; discard cooking liquid. Shred meat by pulling two forks through it in opposite directions.

6. Spoon meat, onion, and tomato mixture into buns. Serve with jalapeño peppers and lime wedges.

Nutrition Facts per serving: 683 cal., 22 g total fat (6 g sat. fat), 98 mg chol., 1,265 mg sodium, 80 g carbo., 5 g fiber, 42 g pro.

*Note: To toast cumin seeds, place seeds in a dry skillet. Cook over medium heat for 2 to 3 minutes or until cumin becomes fragrant, shaking skillet occasionally. (Avoid overcooking cumin seeds; they become bitter.) Let cool before crushing.

Adjust the spiciness by varying the number of jalapeño chile peppers you use. Want to turn up the heat even more? Don't seed the peppers. Use leftover shredded meat as a filling for quesadillas.

Southwestern Shredded Pork Sandwiches

❦

MAKES 10 SANDWICHES

Prep: 20 minutes
Cook: Low 10 to 11 hours, High 5 to 5½ hours

2½	to 3 pounds boneless pork shoulder roast
1	medum onion, finely chopped (½ cup)
1	or 2 fresh jalapeño chile peppers, seeded (if desired) and finely chopped (see tip, page 10), or 1 large green or red sweet pepper, cut into bite-size strips
½	teaspoon ground cumin
¼	teaspoon dried oregano, crushed
2	cloves garlic, minced
2	10-ounce cans enchilada sauce
10	whole-grain hamburger buns, split and toasted

1. Trim fat from meat. If necessary, cut meat to fit into a 3½- or 4-quart slow cooker. Place meat in cooker. Add onion, jalapeño pepper, cumin, oregano, and garlic. Pour enchilada sauce over mixture in cooker.

2. Cover and cook on low-heat setting for 10 to 11 hours or on high-heat setting for 5 to 5½ hours.

3. Transfer meat to a cutting board. Shred meat by pulling two forks through it in opposite directions. Skim fat from cooking liquid. Return meat to cooker; stir to combine with cooking liquid. Using a slotted spoon, spoon meat mixture into buns.

Nutrition Facts per serving: 348 cal., 12 g total fat (3 g sat. fat), 76 mg chol., 526 mg sodium, 30 g carbo., 2 g fiber, 28 g pro.

Here's a yummy recipe to serve kids at the potluck.
Mac and cheese with taco flavorings combine two of
their favorite foods into one scrumptious dish.

Mexicali Mac and Cheese

MAKES 10 SERVINGS

Prep: 20 minutes
Cook: Low 5½ to 6 hours

2	pounds lean ground beef
1	large onion, chopped (1 cup)
3	cups shredded Mexican-blend cheeses
1	16-ounce jar salsa
1	15-ounce jar cheese dip
1	4-ounce can diced green chile peppers, undrained
1	2.25-ounce can sliced pitted ripe olives, drained
12	ounces dried elbow macaroni

1. In a very large skillet or Dutch oven cook ground beef and onion until meat is brown and onion is tender. Drain off fat. Transfer meat mixture to a 4½- to 6-quart slow cooker. Stir in shredded cheese, salsa, cheese dip, undrained chile peppers, and drained olives.

2. Cover and cook on low-heat setting (do not use high-heat setting) for 5½ to 6 hours.

3. Before serving, cook macaroni according to package directions; drain. Stir cooked macaroni into mixture in cooker.

Nutrition Facts per serving: 577 cal., 32 g total fat (17 g sat. fat), 113 mg chol., 1,337 mg sodium, 36 g carbo., 2 g fiber, 35 g pro.

In Cincinnati chili parlors, meaty chili is spooned over spaghetti and topped with cheddar cheese and chopped onion. Great for potluck dinners, this version—with ziti (thick tube shapes) or gemelli (short twists)—has the consistency of a saucy casserole.

Cincinnati-Style Chili Casserole

MAKES 16 SERVINGS

Prep: 25 minutes
Cook: Low 8 to 10 hours,
High 4 to 5 hours

2	pounds lean ground beef
2	large onions, chopped (2 cups)
1	26-ounce jar tomato and garlic pasta sauce
1	15-ounce can red kidney beans, rinsed and drained
½	cup water
2	tablespoons chili powder
2	tablespoons semisweet chocolate pieces
1	tablespoon vinegar
1	teaspoon ground cinnamon
1	teaspoon instant beef bouillon granules
¼	teaspoon cayenne pepper
¼	teaspoon ground allspice
1	pound dried cut ziti or gemelli pasta
	Shredded cheddar cheese (optional)
	Chopped onion (optional)

1. In a very large skillet or Dutch oven cook ground beef and the 2 cups onion until meat is brown and onion is tender. Drain off fat. Transfer meat mixture to a 4- to 5-quart slow cooker.

2. Stir in pasta sauce, drained kidney beans, water, chili powder, chocolate pieces, vinegar, cinnamon, bouillon granules, cayenne pepper, and allspice.

3. Cover and cook on low-heat setting for 8 to 10 hours or on high-heat setting for 4 to 5 hours.

4. Before serving, cook pasta according to package directions; drain. Add cooked pasta to meat mixture in cooker; toss gently to combine. If desired, sprinkle individual servings with cheese and additional onion.

Nutrition Facts per serving: 257 cal., 7 g total fat (2 g sat. fat), 36 mg chol., 277 mg sodium, 33 g carbo., 4 g fiber, 17 g pro.

Put together three of the all-time favorite Italian convenience products—spaghetti sauce, frozen ravioli, and frozen Italian meatballs—and you have a super-speedy potluck dish that promises to please.

Saucy Ravioli with Meatballs

MAKES 10 TO 12 SERVINGS

Prep: 20 minutes
Cook: Low 4½ to 5 hours, High 2½ to 3 hours
Stand: 15 minutes

Nonstick cooking spray

2   26-ounce jars spaghetti sauce with mushrooms and onions

2   20- or 24-ounce packages frozen ravioli

1   16-ounce package (32) frozen cooked Italian-style meatballs, thawed

2   cups shredded mozzarella cheese

½   cup finely shredded Parmesan cheese

1. Lightly coat the inside of a 5½- or 6-quart slow cooker with nonstick cooking spray. Add 1 cup of the spaghetti sauce.

2. Add one package of the frozen ravioli and all of the meatballs. Sprinkle with 1 cup of the mozzarella cheese. Top with the remaining spaghetti sauce from first jar. Add the remaining package of frozen ravioli and the remaining 1 cup mozzarella cheese. Pour spaghetti sauce from the second jar over mixture in cooker.

3. Cover and cook on low-heat setting for 4½ to 5 hours or on high-heat setting for 2½ to 3 hours.

4. Turn off cooker. Sprinkle mixture with Parmesan cheese. Let stand, covered, about 15 minutes before serving.

Nutrition Facts per serving: 494 cal., 18 g total fat (9 g sat. fat), 81 mg chol., 1,566 mg sodium, 60 g carbo., 5 g fiber, 26 g pro.

Lasagna in the slow cooker? Who knew? Pop garlic bread into the oven 15 to 30 minutes before serving while the cheesy layers of the robust lasagna set up.

Sweet Italian Sausage Lasagna

MAKES 8 TO 10 SERVINGS

Prep: 20 minutes
Cook: Low 4 to 6 hours,
High 2 to 3 hours
Stand: 15 minutes

	Nonstick cooking spray
1	pound bulk sweet Italian sausage
1	26-ounce jar chunky tomato, basil, and cheese pasta sauce
¾	cup water
12	no-boil lasagna noodles
1	15-ounce carton ricotta cheese
2	cups shredded Italian-blend cheeses

1. Lightly coat the inside of a 3½- or 4-quart slow cooker with nonstick cooking spray; set aside. In a large skillet cook sausage until brown. Drain off fat. Stir in pasta sauce and water.

2. Place ½ cup of the meat mixture in the bottom of the prepared cooker. Layer 4 of the noodles on top of the meat mixture (break noodles to fit, if necessary). Top with one-third of the ricotta cheese, one-third of the remaining meat mixture, and one-third of the cheese. Repeat layers 2 more times, starting with noodles and ending with meat mixture. Cover and chill the remaining cheese until ready to serve.

3. Cover and cook on low-heat setting for 4 to 6 hours or on high-heat setting for 2 to 3 hours or until noodles are tender and center is heated through.

4. Turn off cooker. Sprinkle lasagna with the reserved cheese. Let stand, covered, for 15 minutes before serving.

Nutrition Facts per serving: 497 cal., 30 g total fat (14 g sat. fat), 87 mg chol., 909 mg sodium, 26 g carbo., 1 g fiber, 26 g pro.

Have this robust veggie filling ready in your slow cooker for a crowd-pleasing meal. For easy side dishes, fix a Mexican-style rice mix and pick up fruit salad from the deli.

Meatless Burritos

MAKES 16 SERVINGS

Prep: 20 minutes
Cook: Low 6 to 8 hours,
High 3 to 4 hours

3	15-ounce cans red kidney beans and/or black beans, rinsed and drained
1	14.5-ounce can diced tomatoes, undrained
1½	cups bottled salsa or picante sauce
1	11-ounce can whole kernel corn with sweet peppers, drained
1	fresh jalapeño chile pepper, seeded and finely chopped (optional) (see tip, page 10)
2	teaspoons chili powder
2	cloves garlic, minced
16	8- to 10-inch flour tortillas, warmed (see tip, page 118)
2	cups shredded lettuce
1	cup shredded taco cheese or cheddar cheese
	Sliced green onion (optional)
	Dairy sour cream (optional)

1. In a 3½- or 4-quart slow cooker combine drained beans, undrained tomatoes, salsa, drained corn, jalapeño pepper (if desired), chili powder, and garlic.

2. Cover and cook on low-heat setting for 6 to 8 hours or on high-heat setting for 3 to 4 hours.

3. To serve, spoon bean mixture onto warm tortillas just below the centers. Top with lettuce and cheese. If desired, add green onion and sour cream. Fold the bottom edge of each tortilla up and over filling. Fold in opposite sides; roll up from bottom.

Nutrition Facts per serving: 205 cal., 3 g total fat (2 g sat. fat), 7 mg chol., 471 mg sodium, 34 g carbo., 6 g fiber, 8 g pro.

Wrapped and ready to serve when your guests walk through the door, these appetizers are good-looking, bite-size, savory, and filling. That's the key to getting a party started right!

Spicy Chicken Fajita Bites

MAKES ABOUT 25 SERVINGS

Prep: 25 minutes
Cook: Low 6 to 7 hours

Nonstick cooking spray
1 pound packaged chicken or beef stir-fry strips
½ cup spicy brown mustard
½ cup water
4 teaspoons fajita seasoning
5 7- to 8-inch whole wheat flour tortillas, warmed (see tip, page 118)
1 medium red, green, or yellow sweet pepper, cut into thin strips
¼ cup sliced green onion (2)
2 tablespoons snipped fresh cilantro

1. Lightly coat a large skillet with nonstick cooking spray; heat skillet over medium-high heat. Cook chicken in hot skillet until brown. Drain off fat. Set aside.

2. In a 1½-quart slow cooker combine mustard, water, and fajita seasoning. Add chicken; stir to coat with mustard mixture.

3. Cover and cook on low-heat setting (do not use high-heat setting) for 6 to 7 hours. If no heat setting is available, cook for 5 to 6 hours. Using a slotted spoon, remove chicken from cooker; discard mustard mixture.

4. Divide chicken evenly among warm tortillas. Top with sweet pepper, green onion, and cilantro. Roll up tortillas.

5. Using a serrated knife, cut filled tortillas crosswise into bite-size pieces. Secure with decorative toothpicks.

Nutrition Facts per serving: 47 cal., 1 g total fat (0 g sat. fat), 13 mg chol., 131 mg sodium, 4 g carbo., 0 g fiber, 5 g pro.

Thai restaurant servers often ask customers how they want their curry based on a scale of stars. One star is a little lip tingling; four stars designate a four-alarm experience. This curry paste amount is one to two stars. (Photo on page 144.)

Red Curry Chicken Wings

MAKES 16 SERVINGS

Prep: 30 minutes
Cook: Low 3 to 4 hours,
High 1½ to 2 hours

3	pounds chicken wings (about 16)
¾	cup unsweetened coconut milk
3	tablespoons fish sauce
2	to 3 tablespoons red curry paste
1	small onion, finely chopped (⅓ cup)
2	tablespoons cornstarch
2	tablespoons cold water
¼	cup finely shredded fresh basil (optional)

1. Preheat broiler. If desired, use a sharp knife to carefully cut off tips of the wings; discard tips. Cut each wing at joint to make 2 pieces. Place wing pieces in a single layer on the unheated rack of a foil-lined broiler pan. Broil 4 to 5 inches from the heat for 10 to 12 minutes or until chicken is brown, turning once. Drain off fat.

2. Meanwhile, in a 3½- or 4-quart slow cooker combine coconut milk, fish sauce, and curry paste. Add wing pieces and onion, stirring to coat with curry mixture.

3. Cover and cook on low-heat setting for 3 to 4 hours or on high-heat setting for 1½ to 2 hours.

4. Using a slotted spoon, remove chicken from cooker; cover with foil to keep warm. Skim fat from curry mixture.

5. For sauce, in a medium saucepan combine cornstarch and water; stir in curry mixture. Cook and stir over medium heat until thickened and bubbly. Cook and stir for 2 minutes more. Stir in basil, if desired. Serve chicken wings with sauce.

Nutrition Facts per serving: 183 cal., 14 g total fat (5 g sat. fat), 47 mg chol., 488 mg sodium, 3 g carbo., 0 g fiber, 12 g pro.

For many people the best thing about a party is the tempting sampling of appetizers. Orange marmalade and fresh ginger make these tender, slow-simmered riblets irresistible.

Orange-Glazed Ribs

MAKES ABOUT 16 (2-RIB) SERVINGS

....

Prep: 20 minutes
Cook: Low 5 to 6 hours,
High 2½ to 3 hours

....

4	pounds pork loin back ribs*
1	medium onion, chopped (½ cup)
½	cup chopped dried apricots or figs
¾	cup orange marmalade
¼	cup lemon juice
¼	cup water
1	tablespoon grated fresh ginger
⅓	cup bottled barbecue sauce
⅓	cup orange marmalade

1. Cut ribs into single-rib portions. Place ribs in a 5- to 6-quart slow cooker. Add onion and dried apricots. In a small bowl stir together the ¾ cup marmalade, the lemon juice, water, and ginger. Pour over mixture in cooker.

2. Cover and cook on low-heat setting for 5 to 6 hours or on high-heat setting for 2½ to 3 hours.

3. Using a slotted spoon or tongs, transfer ribs to a serving dish. For sauce, in a small saucepan stir together barbecue sauce and the ⅓ cup marmalade; heat through. Serve ribs with sauce.

Nutrition Facts per serving: 177 cal., 6 g total fat (2 g sat. fat), 48 mg chol., 89 mg sodium, 12 g carbo., 1 g fiber, 20 g pro.

*Note: To make eating the ribs easier, have your butcher saw them in half crosswise (across the bone) for smaller rib portions.

Partygoers (especially the younger set) will rave about this fondue spin on one of everyone's favorite: pizza! For a super version, use a combination of Italian sausage, pepperoni, and Canadian-style bacon.

Supreme Pizza Fondue

MAKES 16 SERVINGS

Prep: 20 minutes
Cook: Low 3 hours,
plus 15 minutes (low)

8	ounces bulk Italian sausage
1	medium onion, finely chopped (½ cup)
2	cloves garlic, minced
2	28-ounce jars meatless spaghetti sauce
2	cups sliced fresh mushrooms
1	3.5-ounce package sliced pepperoni or Canadian-style bacon, chopped
2	teaspoons dried basil or oregano, crushed
1	cup sliced pitted ripe olives (optional)
1	small green sweet pepper, chopped (½ cup)
1	recipe Fried Stuffed Pasta Dippers, soft breadsticks, and/or sticks of mozzarella (string) cheese

1. In a large skillet cook sausage, onion, and garlic until meat is brown. Drain off fat. Set aside.

2. In a 3½- or 4-quart slow cooker combine spaghetti sauce, mushrooms, pepperoni, and basil. Stir in sausage mixture.

3. Cover and cook on low-heat setting (do not use high-heat setting) for 3 hours. Stir in olives (if desired) and sweet pepper. Cover and cook for 15 minutes more.

4. Meanwhile, prepare Fried Stuffed Pasta Dippers, if using.

5. Spear pasta, breadsticks, and/or mozzarella sticks with fondue forks. Dip into sausage mixture, swirling as you dip.

Fried Stuffed Pasta Dippers: In a large skillet heat ½ inch of cooking oil until oil sizzles when pasta is dropped into the fat. Cook refrigerated cheese ravioli and/or tortellini, a few at a time, in hot oil for 2 to 3 minutes or until golden, turning once. Drain on paper towels. While pasta is still hot, sprinkle with grated Parmesan cheese and black pepper. Keep warm in a 250°F oven while frying remaining pasta.

Nutrition Facts per serving fondue: 140 cal., 8 g total fat (3 g sat. fat), 18 mg chol., 692 mg sodium, 14 g carbo., 3 g fiber, 5 g pro.

Take this classic to a party and you'll be a hit—it's a reliable favorite. Chopped red sweet pepper gives the dip a festive confetti look and a sweet crunch. Mediterranean seasoning and Parmesan cheese deliver awesome flavor.

Hot Artichoke Dip

MAKES ABOUT 20 SERVINGS

Prep: 20 minutes
Cook: Low 3 to 4 hours

2	medium leeks, thinly sliced (⅔ cup)
1	tablespoon olive oil
2	14-ounce cans artichoke hearts, drained and coarsely chopped
2	cups light mayonnaise (do not use regular mayonnaise)
1	large red sweet pepper, chopped (1 cup)
1	cup finely shredded Parmesan cheese
1	teaspoon Mediterranean seasoning or lemon-pepper seasoning
	Finely shredded Parmesan cheese
	Toasted pita wedges

1. In a large skillet cook leek in hot oil over medium heat until tender. Transfer to a 2-quart slow cooker. Stir in artichoke hearts, light mayonnaise, sweet pepper, the 1 cup Parmesan cheese, and the Mediterranean seasoning.

2. Cover and cook on low-heat setting (do not use high-heat setting) for 3 to 4 hours or until cheese is melted and mixture is heated through. If no heat setting is available, cook for 2½ to 3 hours.

3. Stir mixture before serving. Sprinkle with additional Parmesan cheese. Serve immediately or keep warm, covered, on warm setting or low-heat setting for up to 1 hour. Stir occasionally. Serve dip with pita wedges.

Nutrition Facts per ¼ cup dip: 123 cal., 10 g total fat (2 g sat. fat), 11 mg chol., 406 mg sodium, 6 g carbo., 2 g fiber, 3 g pro.

Cheese and more cheese—American, Monterey Jack, and cream cheese—cook slowly with salsa and beer to create a tangy appetizer. To treat the spice lovers at your party with even more kick, use a salsa with plenty of heat.

Cheesy Beer and Salsa Dip

MAKES ABOUT 22 SERVINGS

Prep: 15 minutes
Cook: Low 3 to 4 hours,
High 1½ to 2 hours

1	16-ounce jar salsa
1	pound pasteurized prepared cheese product, cut into cubes (4 cups)
2	cups shredded Monterey Jack cheese
1	8-ounce package cream cheese, cut into cubes
⅔	cup beer
	Vegetable dippers and/or crackers

1. In a 3½- or 4-quart slow cooker combine salsa, cheese product, Monterey Jack cheese, cream cheese, and beer.

2. Cover and cook on low-heat setting for 3 to 4 hours or on high-heat setting for 1½ to 2 hours.

3. Serve immediately or keep warm, covered, on warm setting or low-heat setting for up to 2 hours. Stir occasionally. Serve dip with vegetables and/or crackers.

Nutrition Facts per ¼ cup dip: 160 cal., 13 g total fat (8 g sat. fat), 40 mg chol., 517 mg sodium, 2 g carbo., 0 g fiber, 8 g pro.

Test Kitchen Tip: With the help of your slow cooker, you can entertain without spending hours in the kitchen. Start with one or two of the recipes in this chapter. (If you want to make two recipes, consider buying another slow cooker or borrow one from a friend.) Then round out the menu with store-bought chips, crackers, cheese, and cut-up fresh fruits or vegetables.

This rich, opulent crab dip—perfectly spiced with Worcestershire sauce and horseradish—will be a knockout addition to your appetizer buffet. Plan on everyone coming back for seconds.

Horseradish Crab Dip

MAKES 10 SERVINGS

Prep: 15 minutes
Cook: Low 2½ to 3½ hours, High 1¼ to 1¾ hours

Nonstick cooking spray

2 6-ounce cans crabmeat, drained, flaked, and cartilage removed

1 8-ounce package cream cheese, cubed

1 4-ounce can (drained weight) mushroom stems and pieces, drained and chopped

¼ cup finely chopped onion

2 slices bacon, crisp-cooked, drained, and crumbled

1 teaspoon Worcestershire sauce

2 to 3 teaspoons prepared horseradish

Rich round crackers and/or celery sticks

1. Lightly coat the inside of a 1½- or 2-quart slow cooker with nonstick cooking spray. In the prepared cooker combine crabmeat, cream cheese, drained mushrooms, onion, bacon, and Worcestershire sauce.

2. Cover and cook on low-heat setting for 2½ to 3½ hours or on high-heat setting for 1¼ to 1¾ hours. If no heat setting is available, cook for 1½ to 2½ hours.

3. Before serving, stir in horseradish. Serve dip with crackers and/or celery.

Nutrition Facts per ¼ cup dip: 127 cal., 9 g total fat (5 g sat. fat), 57 mg chol., 275 mg sodium, 2 g carbo., 0 g fiber, 10 g pro.

This recipe is super easy and a surefire hit with any crowd.
Place toasted nuts and a few other ingredients in the
slow cooker for a couple of hours to create this
delicious glazed snack.

Sweet Spiced Nuts

MAKES 14 SERVINGS

Prep: 20 minutes
Cook: Low 2 hours
Cool: 1 hour

1⅓	cups whole almonds, toasted (see tip, page 29)
1⅓	cups pecan halves, toasted (see tip, page 29)
1⅓	cups walnut halves, toasted (see tip, page 29)
½	cup sugar
⅓	cup butter or margarine, melted
2	teaspoons apple pie spice or ground cinnamon
½	teaspoon salt

1. In a 1½- to 3-quart slow cooker combine almonds, pecans, and walnuts. In a small bowl combine sugar, butter, apple pie spice, and salt. Sprinkle mixture over nuts in cooker; stir to coat nuts.

2. Cover and cook on low-heat setting (do not use high-heat setting) for 2 hours, stirring after 1 hour. If no heat setting is available, cook for 2 hours, stirring after 1 hour.

3. Stir nuts again. Spread in a single layer on waxed paper or foil; cool for 1 hour. (Nuts may appear soft after cooking, but will crisp upon cooling.) Store in a tightly covered container at room temperature for up to 3 days.

Nutrition Facts per serving: 248 cal., 22 g total fat (4 g sat. fat), 10 mg chol., 100 mg sodium, 11 g carbo., 3 g fiber, 5 g pro.

For a change of pace, enjoy chai in place of tea or coffee. It's a great way to lift the spirits and wind down. You'll find this traditional recipe produces a lighter, less rich cup of chai than most American coffee shop versions.

Chai

MAKES ABOUT 12 SERVINGS

Prep: 15 minutes
Cook: Low 4 to 6 hours,
High 2 to 2½ hours,
plus 30 minutes

6	inches stick cinnamon, broken into 1-inch pieces
6	slices fresh ginger
1	teaspoon whole cloves
5	cups cold water
1	cup sugar
1½	teaspoons ground nutmeg
½	teaspoon ground cardamom
6	cups milk
12	tea bags

1. For spice bag, cut a 6-inch square from a double thickness of 100-percent-cotton cheesecloth. Place cinnamon, ginger, and cloves on the cheesecloth. Bring up corners of cheesecloth and tie closed with clean 100-percent-cotton kitchen string.

2. In a 3½- to 5-quart slow cooker combine spice bag, water, sugar, nutmeg, and cardamom.

3. Cover and cook on low-heat setting for 4 to 6 hours or on high-heat setting for 2 to 2½ hours.

4. Add milk and tea bags.* Cover and cook for 30 minutes more. Remove spice bag and tea bags, squeezing gently to remove liquid.

Iced Chai: Prepare as directed. Transfer to two 2-quart containers. Cover and chill for 2 to 24 hours. Serve over ice.

Nutrition Facts per serving regular or iced variation: 124 cal., 2 g total fat (1 g sat. fat), 10 mg chol., 57 mg sodium, 22 g carbo., 0 g fiber, 4 g pro.

*Note: For easy removal, allow the strings of the tea bags to hang over the side of the slow cooker and use the lid to hold the tea bags in place inside the cooker.

Vary this rich and delicious drink with flavored creamers and liqueurs. It will hold up to one hour in the slow cooker.

Chocolate Cream Cocoa

MAKES ABOUT 12 SERVINGS

Prep: 10 minutes
Cook: Low 3 to 4 hours,
High 1½ to 2 hours

3½ cups nonfat dry milk powder
1 cup powdered sugar
1 cup plain powdered nondairy creamer
¾ cup unsweetened cocoa powder
8 cups water
½ cup crème de cacao (optional)
Sweetened whipped cream

1. In a 3½- to 5-quart slow cooker combine dry milk powder, powdered sugar, nondairy creamer, and cocoa powder. Gradually add water, stirring to dissolve milk powder.

2. Cover and cook on low-heat setting for 3 to 4 hours or on high-heat setting for 1½ to 2 hours. If desired, stir in crème de cacao.

3. Stir mixture before serving. Serve immediately or keep warm, covered, on warm setting or low-heat setting for up to 1 hour. Stir occasionally. Top individual servings with sweetened whipped cream.

Nutrition Facts per serving: 210 cal., 6 g total fat (4 g sat. fat), 14 mg chol., 132 mg sodium, 29 g carbo., 0 g fiber, 9 g pro.

Tweak classic spiced cider by mixing it with tart and sweet cranberry-raspberry juice. Garnish with thinly sliced apple. The fruit soaked in cider makes a nice crunchy finish when the mug's empty.

Berry-Apple Cider

MAKES 8 SERVINGS

Prep: 10 minutes
Cook: Low 4 to 6 hours, High 2 to 2½ hours

4	inches stick cinnamon, broken into 1-inch pieces
1½	teaspoons whole cloves
4	cups apple cider or apple juice
4	cups cranberry-raspberry juice
	Thinly sliced apple (optional)

1. For spice bag, cut a 6-inch square from a double thickness of 100-percent-cotton cheesecloth. Place cinnamon and cloves on the cheesecloth. Bring up corners of cheesecloth and tie closed with clean 100-percent-cotton kitchen string.

2. In a 3½- to 5-quart slow cooker combine spice bag, apple cider, and cranberry-raspberry juice.

3. Cover and cook on low-heat setting for 4 to 6 hours or on high-heat setting for 2 to 2½ hours. Discard spice bag.

4. Serve immediately or keep warm, covered, on warm setting or low-heat setting for up to 2 hours. Stir occasionally. If desired, garnish individual servings with apple.

Nutrition Facts per serving: 128 cal., 0 g total fat (0 g sat. fat), 0 mg chol., 21 mg sodium, 31 g carbo., 0 g fiber, 0 g pro.

Chicken and Stuffing Casserole
(Recipe on page 305)

Mediterranean Beef Ragoût
(Recipe on page 72)

Cranberry Pork Roast
(Recipe on page 298)

Wine-Braised Beef Brisket
(Recipe on page 356)

Brisket Pie
(Recipe on page 357)

Pork lo Mein
(Recipe on page 175)

Ratatouille
(Recipe on page 392)

Southwest Vegetable Empanadas
(Recipe on page 393)

263

Fruit and Nut Chili
(Recipe on page 274)

Sage-Scented Pork Chops
(Recipe on page 366)

**Pork and Potato Gratin
with Gruyère Cheese**
(Recipe on page 367)

Cacciatore-Style Chicken
(Recipe on page 110)

Crock Posole
(Recipe on page 11)

Thai Chicken over Rice Noodles
(Recipe on page 328)

Thai Chicken and Coconut-Red Curry Soup
(Recipe on page 329)

Chinese Chicken Salad
(Recipe on page 121)

Fire-Roasted Tomato and Italian Sausage Grinders
(Recipe on page 370)

Sausage-Stuffed Manicotti
(Recipe on page 371)

Fireside Chili for Two
(Recipe on page 21)

If you like your chili seriously hot, this tongue-tingling recipe is for you. For an even bigger kick use a whole teaspoon of cayenne pepper.

Kickin' Hot Chili

MAKES 8 SERVINGS

Prep: 25 minutes
Cook: Low 8 to 10 hours,
High 4 to 5 hours

1½	pounds lean ground beef
2	large onions, chopped (2 cups)
3½	cups water
1	15-ounce can dark red kidney beans, rinsed and drained
1	14.5-ounce can diced tomatoes, undrained
2	6-ounce cans tomato paste
1	small green or red sweet pepper, chopped (½ cup)
1	4-ounce can diced green chile peppers, undrained
1	tablespoon yellow mustard
1	teaspoon chili powder
1	teaspoon black pepper
½	teaspoon ground cumin
¼	teaspoon salt
¼	teaspoon cayenne pepper
6	cloves garlic, minced

1. In a 12-inch skillet or Dutch oven cook ground beef and onion until meat is brown and onion is tender. Drain off fat. Transfer meat mixture to a 4- to 5-quart slow cooker.

2. Stir in water, drained beans, undrained tomatoes, tomato paste, sweet pepper, undrained chile peppers, mustard, chili powder, black pepper, cumin, salt, cayenne pepper, and garlic.

3. Cover and cook on low-heat setting for 8 to 10 hours or on high-heat setting for 4 to 5 hours.

Nutrition Facts per serving: 296 cal., 13 g total fat (5 g sat. fat), 58 mg chol., 724 mg sodium, 25 g carbo., 7 g fiber, 23 g pro.

Chocolate and spicy ingredients are a common pairing in chili creations. With the addition of curry, almonds, and apples, this version is a recipe you must try. (Photo on page 264.)

Fruit and Nut Chili

MAKES 8 SERVINGS

Prep: 25 minutes
Cook: Low 8 to 10 hours,
High 4 to 5 hours

1½	pounds lean ground beef
2	large onions, chopped (2 cups)
3	cloves garlic, minced
2	14.5-ounce cans diced tomatoes, undrained
1	15-ounce can red kidney beans, rinsed and drained
1	15-ounce can tomato sauce
1	14-ounce can chicken broth
3	medium sweet peppers, chopped (2¼ cups)
2	medium cooking apples, cored and chopped (1⅓ cups)
2	4-ounce cans diced green chile peppers, drained
3	tablespoons chili powder
2	tablespoons unsweetened cocoa powder
1	tablespoon curry powder
1	teaspoon ground cinnamon
⅔	cup slivered almonds
	Shredded cheddar cheese, raisins, and/or plain yogurt or dairy sour cream (optional)

1. In a 12-inch skillet cook ground beef, onion, and garlic until meat is brown and onion is tender. Drain off fat. Transfer meat mixture to a 6-quart slow cooker.

2. Add undrained tomatoes, drained beans, tomato sauce, and broth. Stir in sweet pepper, apple, drained chile peppers, chili powder, cocoa powder, curry powder, and cinnamon.

3. Cover and cook on low-heat setting for 8 to 10 hours or on high-heat setting for 4 to 5 hours.

4. Serve with almonds and, if desired, cheese, raisins, and/or yogurt or sour cream.

Nutrition Facts per serving: 357 cal., 16 g total fat (4 g sat. fat), 54 mg chol., 782 mg sodium, 34 g carbo., 10 g fiber, 26 g pro.

This recipe makes a whole mess of chili. If your gathering is small, freeze the leftovers for the next roundup. And if you like your chili spicy, add the greater amount of cayenne pepper.

Giddyap Chili

MAKES 10 SERVINGS

Prep: 20 minutes
Cook: Low 8 to 10 hours,
High 4 to 5 hours

2	pounds lean ground beef
2	large onions, chopped (2 cups)
1	medium green or red sweet pepper, chopped (¾ cup)
3	cloves garlic, minced
2	15-ounce cans dark red kidney beans, rinsed and drained
2	14-ounce cans chicken broth
1	15-ounce can Great Northern beans, rinsed and drained
1	14.5-ounce can diced tomatoes, undrained
1	6-ounce can tomato paste
1	tablespoon yellow mustard
2	teaspoons chili powder
1	teaspoon ground cumin
½	teaspoon salt
¼	to ½ teaspoon cayenne pepper
¼	teaspoon black pepper
	Shredded cheddar cheese

1. In a very large skillet cook ground beef, onion, sweet pepper, and garlic until meat is brown. Drain off fat. Transfer meat mixture to a 5- to 6-quart slow cooker.

2. Stir in drained kidney beans, broth, drained Great Northern beans, undrained tomatoes, tomato paste, mustard, chili powder, cumin, salt, cayenne pepper, and black pepper.

3. Cover and cook on low-heat setting for 8 to 10 hours or on high-heat setting for 4 to 5 hours.

4. Sprinkle individual servings with cheddar cheese.

Nutrition Facts per serving: 411 cal., 17 g total fat (8 g sat. fat), 75 mg chol., 827 mg sodium, 34 g carbo., 9 g fiber, 33 g pro.

It's easy to feed a famished crowd with this great-tasting recipe. Prepare the chili sides and simmer the lively combo of meat and beans in advance. Come serving time set out the accompaniments and a stack of bowls.

Game Day Chili

MAKES 10 TO 12 SERVINGS

Prep: 25 minutes
Cook: Low 10 to 12 hours, High 5 to 6 hours

- 2 pounds boneless beef round steak or pork shoulder roast
- 2 15-ounce cans chili beans in chili gravy, undrained
- 2 14.5-ounce cans Mexican-style stewed tomatoes, undrained and cut up
- 2 large sweet peppers, chopped (2 cups)
- 2 large onions, chopped (2 cups)
- 1 15-ounce can red kidney beans or pinto beans, rinsed and drained
- 1 cup beer or beef broth
- 1 to 2 tablespoons chopped canned chipotle pepper in adobo sauce (see tip, page 10)
- 2 teaspoons garlic salt
- 2 teaspoons ground cumin
- 1 teaspoon dried oregano, crushed
-    Dairy sour cream, lime wedges, and/or snipped fresh cilantro (optional)

1. Trim fat from meat. Cut meat into ½-inch pieces. Transfer meat to a 5½- or 6-quart slow cooker.

2. Stir in undrained chili beans in chili gravy, undrained tomatoes, sweet pepper, onion, drained kidney beans, beer, chipotle pepper, garlic salt, cumin, and oregano.

3. Cover and cook on low-heat setting for 10 to 12 hours or on high-heat setting for 5 to 6 hours. Spoon off fat.

4. If desired, serve chili with sour cream, lime wedges, and/or cilantro.

Nutrition Facts per serving: 294 cal., 5 g total fat (1 g sat. fat), 52 mg chol., 823 mg sodium, 32 g carbo., 8 g fiber, 29 g pro.

This hearty chili flavored with enchilada sauce can be made ahead. Stir it frequently while reheating so the cornmeal does not settle to the bottom of the pan.

Enchilada Chili

MAKES 8 SERVINGS

Prep: 20 minutes
Cook: Low 10 to 12 hours,
High 6 to 7 hours,
plus 15 minutes (high)

2½	pounds boneless beef chuck roast
2	tablespoons cooking oil
2	15-ounce cans pinto beans and/or red kidney beans, rinsed and drained
2	14.5-ounce cans diced tomatoes, undrained
1	10.5-ounce can condensed beef broth
1	10-ounce can enchilada sauce
1	medium onion, chopped (½ cup)
4	cloves garlic, minced
½	cup water
⅓	cup cornmeal
¼	cup snipped fresh cilantro
1	recipe Fry Bread or 8 flour tortillas (optional)
½	cup shredded queso blanco or Monterey Jack cheese

1. Trim fat from meat. Cut meat into ¾-inch pieces. In a large skillet brown meat, half at a time, in hot oil over medium-high heat. Drain off fat. Transfer meat to a 5- to 6-quart slow cooker. Stir in drained beans, undrained tomatoes, broth, enchilada sauce, onion, and garlic.

2. Cover and cook on low-heat setting for 10 to 12 hours or on high-heat setting for 6 to 7 hours.

3. If using low-heat setting, turn to high-heat setting. In a small bowl stir together water and cornmeal; stir into meat mixture. Cover and cook for 15 minutes more.

4. Before serving, stir in cilantro. If desired, serve chili with Fry Bread. Sprinkle with cheese.

Fry Bread: In a large bowl combine 1½ cups all-purpose flour, ½ cup cornmeal, 1 teaspoon salt, and ¼ teaspoon baking powder. Using a pastry blender, cut in ¼ cup shortening until pieces are pea size. Add ¾ cup water and ⅓ cup snipped fresh cilantro; stir just until a ball forms (dough will be slightly sticky). Divide into 8 portions. On a floured surface, roll each portion into a 5- to 6-inch circle.

In a 10-inch heavy skillet heat 1 tablespoon shortening over medium heat. Cook dough circles, one at a time, in hot shortening for 4 to 6 minutes or until golden, turning once. Add more shortening during cooking as needed. If bread browns too quickly, reduce heat to medium-low.

Nutrition Facts per serving: 387 cal., 12 g total fat (3 g sat. fat), 84 mg chol., 1,164 mg sodium, 29 g carbo., 7 g fiber, 39 g pro.

Serve this chili at an open house during or after a bowl game.
Set out an assortment of toppers so guests can personalize it.

Hearty Pork Chili

MAKES 8 SERVINGS

Prep: 20 minutes
Cook: Low 8 to 10 hours,
High 4 to 5 hours

1½	pounds boneless pork shoulder roast
2	15-ounce cans black beans and/or garbanzo beans (chickpeas), rinsed and drained
2	14.5-ounce cans diced tomatoes with onion and garlic, undrained
2	cups vegetable juice or tomato juice
1	10-ounce can diced tomatoes and green chile peppers, undrained
3	stalks celery, chopped (1½ cups)
1	large green sweet pepper, chopped (1 cup)
1	tablespoon chili powder
1	teaspoon ground cumin
1	teaspoon dried oregano, crushed
3	cloves garlic, minced
	Shredded Mexican-blend cheeses, dairy sour cream, sliced green onion, and/or sliced pitted ripe olives (optional)

1. Trim fat from meat. Cut meat into 1-inch pieces. Transfer meat to a 5- to 6-quart slow cooker.

2. Add drained beans, undrained diced tomatoes, vegetable juice, and undrained tomatoes and chile peppers. Stir in celery, sweet pepper, chili powder, cumin, oregano, and garlic.

3. Cover and cook on low-heat setting for 8 to 10 hours or on high-heat setting for 4 to 5 hours.

4. If desired, top individual servings with cheese, sour cream, green onion, and/or olives.

Nutrition Facts per serving: 251 cal., 6 g total fat (2 g sat. fat), 55 mg chol., 1,126 mg sodium, 28 g carbo., 8 g fiber, 27 g pro.

This white chili touts a touch of heat due to green chiles, which will warm you up during a fall tailgating event— or in your kitchen all winter long.

Turkey and Wild Rice Chili

MAKES 8 SERVINGS

Prep: 20 minutes
Cook: Low 7 to 8 hours,
High 3½ to 4 hours

1	pound turkey breast tenderloin or skinless, boneless chicken breast, cut into ½-inch pieces
1	15.25-ounce can whole kernel corn, drained
1	15-ounce can Great Northern beans, rinsed and drained
⅔	cup uncooked wild rice, rinsed and drained
2	4-ounce cans diced green chile peppers, undrained
1	medium onion, chopped (½ cup)
1	tablespoon chili powder
1	teaspoon ground cumin
	Few dashes bottled hot pepper sauce
2	cloves garlic, minced
2	14-ounce cans chicken broth
1¼	cups water
½	cup shredded Monterey Jack cheese
½	cup dairy sour cream
	Snipped fresh parsley (optional)

1. In a 4- to 5-quart slow cooker combine turkey, drained corn, drained beans, wild rice, undrained chile peppers, onion, chili powder, cumin, hot pepper sauce, and garlic. Stir in broth and water.

2. Cover and cook on low-heat setting for 7 to 8 hours or on high-heat setting for 3½ to 4 hours.

3. Top individual servings with cheese, sour cream, and, if desired, parsley.

Nutrition Facts per serving: 303 cal., 9 g total fat (5 g sat. fat), 53 mg chol., 676 mg sodium, 32 g carbo., 5 g fiber, 25 g pro.

Taste this robust chili and you'll agree that three beans are better than one. Each type has a distinctive flavor and texture, making every spoonful of this meatless meal in a bowl an adventure.

Bean Medley Chili

MAKES 8 SERVINGS

Prep: 25 minutes
Cook: Low 8 to 10 hours,
High 4 to 5 hours

1	15-ounce can black beans, rinsed and drained
1	15-ounce can dark red kidney beans, rinsed and drained
1	15-ounce can garbanzo beans (chickpeas), rinsed and drained
2	large onions, chopped (2 cups)
1	large red sweet pepper, chopped (1 cup)
1	large green sweet pepper, chopped (1 cup)
3	tablespoons chili powder
1	canned chipotle pepper in adobo sauce, finely chopped (see tip, page 10)
1	teaspoon ground cumin
¼	teaspoon salt
12	cloves garlic, minced
2	14.5-ounce cans diced tomatoes, undrained
1	14-ounce can chicken broth
¼	cup snipped fresh cilantro
	Hot cooked white or brown rice (optional)

1. In a 4- to 5-quart slow cooker combine drained black beans, drained kidney beans, drained garbanzo beans, onion, sweet peppers, chili powder, chipotle pepper, cumin, salt, and garlic. Pour undrained tomatoes and broth over mixture in cooker.

2. Cover and cook on low-heat setting for 8 to 10 hours or on high-heat setting for 4 to 5 hours.

3. Before serving, stir in cilantro. If desired, serve chili with hot cooked rice.

Nutrition Facts per serving: 226 cal., 2 g total fat (0 g sat. fat), 1 mg chol., 1,081 mg sodium, 46 g carbo., 12 g fiber, 12 g pro.

So simple, so good. If you think an all-vegetable chili tends to be bland, try this easy recipe. Canned tomatoes with green chile peppers punch up the flavor.

Two-Bean Chili

MAKES 8 SERVINGS

Prep: 15 minutes
Cook: Low 9 to 10 hours,
High 4½ to 5 hours

2   15-ounce cans garbanzo beans (chickpeas), rinsed and drained

2   15-ounce cans red kidney beans, rinsed and drained

2   14-ounce cans beef broth

2   11-ounce cans whole kernel corn with sweet peppers, drained

1   10-ounce can diced tomatoes and green chile peppers, undrained

1   large onion, chopped (1 cup)

4   teaspoons chili powder

¼   teaspoon black pepper

¼   teaspoon crushed red pepper (optional)

2   cloves garlic, minced

Dairy sour cream (optional)

Corn chips (optional)

1. In a 4- or 4½-quart slow cooker combine drained garbanzo beans, drained kidney beans, broth, drained corn, undrained tomatoes and chile peppers, onion, chili powder, black pepper, crushed red pepper (if desired), and garlic.

2. Cover and cook on low-heat setting for 9 to 10 hours or on high-heat setting for 4½ to 5 hours.

3. If desired, top individual servings with sour cream and serve with corn chips.

Nutrition Facts per serving: 267 cal., 2 g total fat (0 g sat. fat), 1 mg chol., 1,294 mg sodium, 53 g carbo., 14 g fiber, 16 g pro.

Cabbage holds up very well in the slow cooker. Stir a bit of homegrown cabbage from your garden or local farmers' market into this flavorful beef soup.

Chunky Vegetable Beef Soup

MAKES 8 SERVINGS

Prep: 20 minutes
Cook: Low 8 to 10 hours,
High 4 to 5 hours

2 cups coarsely chopped cabbage

2 medium carrots, bias-sliced (1 cup)

2 stalks celery, sliced (1 cup)

1 large red potato, peeled and cubed

1 medium onion, chopped (½ cup)

1 tablespoon Worcestershire sauce

1 teaspoon chili powder

2 bay leaves

2 pounds beef shank cross cuts

2 14-ounce cans beef broth

2 cups tomato juice

1. In a 4- to 5-quart slow cooker combine cabbage, carrot, celery, potato, onion, Worcestershire sauce, chili powder, and bay leaves. Add meat. Pour broth and tomato juice over mixture in cooker.

2. Cover and cook on low-heat setting for 8 to 10 hours or on high-heat setting for 4 to 5 hours.

3. Transfer meat to a cutting board. When cool enough to handle, remove meat from bones; discard bones. Chop meat. Return meat to cooker; stir to combine. Remove bay leaves.

Nutrition Facts per serving: 138 cal., 2 g total fat (1 g sat. fat), 26 mg chol., 440 mg sodium, 12 g carbo., 2 g fiber, 17 g pro.

This easy soup full of beef and beans is sure to become a popular choice at your dinner table, especially if you top each serving with sour cream and a few tortilla chips.

Beefy Taco Soup

MAKES 8 SERVINGS

Prep: 15 minutes
Cook: Low 6 to 8 hours,
High 3 to 4 hours

1	pound lean ground beef
1	15-ounce can black-eyed peas, undrained
1	15-ounce can black beans, undrained
1	15-ounce can chili beans in chili gravy, undrained
1	15-ounce can garbanzo beans (chickpeas), undrained
1	14.5-ounce can Mexican-style stewed tomatoes, undrained
1	11-ounce can whole kernel corn with sweet peppers, undrained
1	1.25-ounce envelope taco seasoning mix
	Dairy sour cream (optional)
	Tortilla chips (optional)

1. In a large skillet cook ground beef until brown. Drain off fat. Transfer meat to a 3½- to 6-quart slow cooker.

2. Stir in undrained black-eyed peas, undrained black beans, undrained chili beans in chili gravy, undrained garbanzo beans, undrained tomatoes, undrained corn, and taco seasoning mix.

3. Cover and cook on low-heat setting for 6 to 8 hours or on high-heat setting for 3 to 4 hours.

4. If desired, top individual servings with sour cream and tortilla chips.

Nutrition Facts per serving: 392 cal., 13 g total fat (4 g sat. fat), 41 mg chol., 1,294 mg sodium, 49 g carbo., 12 g fiber, 24 g pro.

If easy is your motto, this is for you. Canned beets, canned tomatoes, and convenient coleslaw mix make this full-bodied soup a simple meal.

Beef and Beet Soup

MAKES 8 TO 10 SERVINGS

Prep: 20 minutes
Cook: Low 9 to 11 hours,
High 4½ to 5½ hours,
plus 30 minutes (high)

2½	pounds beef stew meat
2	14.5-ounce cans cut beets, undrained
2	14-ounce cans beef broth
1	14.5-ounce can diced tomatoes, undrained
1½	cups water
3	medium onions, chopped (1½ cups)
½	teaspoon dried dill
¼	teaspoon black pepper
4	cups packaged shredded cabbage with carrot (coleslaw mix)
½	cup dairy sour cream

1. Trim fat from meat. Cut meat into ¾- to 1-inch pieces. Transfer meat to a 5- to 6-quart slow cooker. Stir in undrained beets, broth, undrained tomatoes, water, onion, dill, and pepper.

2. Cover and cook on low-heat setting for 9 to 11 hours or on high-heat setting for 4½ to 5½ hours.

3. If using low-heat setting, turn to high-heat setting. Stir in coleslaw mix. Cover and cook for 30 minutes more. Top individual servings with sour cream.

Nutrition Facts per serving: 270 cal., 8 g total fat (3 g sat. fat), 89 mg chol., 806 mg sodium, 15 g carbo., 3 g fiber, 33 g pro.

This hearty recipe comes from a region of Switzerland near the border of Italy. There polenta is used in a variety of ways, including as a topper for stews. You may make instant polenta just before serving instead of using this classic version.

Polenta Beef Stew

MAKES 8 SERVINGS

Prep: 30 minutes
Cook: Low 8 to 10 hours,
High 4 to 5 hours

2½	pounds boneless beef chuck roast or lamb stew meat
¼	cup all-purpose flour
1	teaspoon dried thyme, crushed
1	teaspoon dried basil, crushed
½	teaspoon salt
½	teaspoon black pepper
8	ounces frozen small whole onions
4	medium carrots, cut into 1-inch pieces
1	teaspoon snipped fresh rosemary or ¼ teaspoon dried rosemary, crushed
6	cloves garlic, minced
1	14-ounce can lower-sodium beef broth
1	cup water
½	cup dry red wine
1	recipe Polenta
½	cup snipped fresh Italian (flat-leaf) parsley
¼	cup tomato paste

1. Trim fat from meat. Cut meat into 1-inch pieces. In a large plastic bag combine flour, thyme, basil, salt, and pepper. Add meat, several pieces at a time, shaking to coat. Place meat in a 3½- or 4-quart slow cooker.

2. Add frozen onions, carrot, dried rosemary (if using), and garlic. Stir in broth, water, and wine.

3. Cover and cook on low-heat setting for 8 to 10 hours or on high-heat setting for 4 to 5 hours.

4. Meanwhile, prepare Polenta. Before serving, stir fresh rosemary (if using), parsley, and tomato paste into stew. Serve with Polenta.

Polenta: In a large saucepan bring 3½ cups milk just to simmering. Meanwhile, in a small bowl combine 1 cup cornmeal, 1 cup cold water, and ½ teaspoon salt. Slowly stir cornmeal mixture into hot milk. Bring to boiling, stirring frequently; reduce heat to low. Cook for 10 to 15 minutes or until mixture is thick, stirring occasionally.

Nutrition Facts per serving: 357 cal., 8 g total fat (3 g sat. fat), 92 mg chol., 560 mg sodium, 30 g carbo., 3 g fiber, 37 g pro.

Such an impressive main course calls for a simple finish—
a refreshing sorbet and sugar cookies are perfect.

Beef-Vegetable Ragoût

MAKES 8 SERVINGS

Prep: 25 minutes
Cook: Low 8 to 10 hours,
High 4 to 5 hours,
plus 5 minutes (high)

1½	pounds boneless beef chuck roast
	Nonstick cooking spray
3	cups sliced fresh cremini or button mushrooms (8 ounces)
1	large onion, chopped (1 cup)
½	teaspoon salt
½	teaspoon black pepper
4	cloves garlic, minced
¼	cup quick-cooking tapioca, crushed
2	14-ounce cans lower-sodium beef broth
½	cup port or dry sherry (optional)
4	cups sugar snap peas
2	cups cherry tomatoes, halved
	Hot cooked noodles (optional)

1. Trim fat from meat. Cut meat into ¾-inch pieces. Lightly coat a large skillet with nonstick cooking spray; heat skillet over medium-high heat. Brown meat, half at a time, in hot skillet. Drain off fat. Set meat aside.

2. In a 3½- or 4-quart slow cooker combine mushrooms, onion, salt, pepper, and garlic. Sprinkle with tapioca. Add meat. Pour broth and, if desired, port over mixture in cooker.

3. Cover and cook on low-heat setting for 8 to 10 hours or on high-heat setting for 4 to 5 hours.

4. If using low-heat setting, turn to high-heat setting. Stir in sugar snap peas. Cover and cook about 5 minutes more or until snap peas are tender. Stir in tomato.

5. If desired, serve meat mixture over hot cooked noodles.

Nutrition Facts per serving: 208 cal., 4 g total fat (1 g sat. fat), 50 mg chol., 401 mg sodium, 19 g carbo., 4 g fiber, 24 g pro.

Test Kitchen Tip: When a slow-cooker recipe calls for quick-cooking tapioca, you can give the food a smoother consistency if you crush the tapioca before adding it to the cooker. Use a mortar and pestle or grind the tapioca using a spice or coffee grinder.

Mexican-style stewed tomatoes, green salsa, and flour tortillas accent this beef stew. Complete the meal with a festive salad of romaine, orange sections, and avocado slices.

Salsa Verde Beef Stew

MAKES 8 SERVINGS

Prep: 25 minutes
Cook: Low 8 to 9 hours,
High 5 to 6 hours

1½	pounds boneless beef chuck roast
1	tablespoon cooking oil
4	medium round white potatoes (1⅓ pounds), cut into 1-inch pieces
1	15-ounce can pinto beans, rinsed and drained
1	large onion, coarsely chopped (1 cup)
1	medium green sweet pepper, chopped (¾ cup)
1	teaspoon ground cumin
2	cloves garlic, minced
1	14.5-ounce can Mexican-style stewed tomatoes, undrained
1	cup bottled mild or medium green salsa
8	7- to 8-inch flour tortillas, warmed (optional) (see tip, page 118)

1. Trim fat from meat. Cut meat into 1-inch pieces. In a large skillet brown meat, half at a time, in hot oil over medium-high heat. Drain off fat. Transfer meat to a 4½- to 6-quart slow cooker.

2. Stir in potato, drained beans, onion, sweet pepper, cumin, and garlic. Pour undrained tomatoes and salsa over mixture in cooker.

3. Cover and cook on low-heat setting for 8 to 9 hours or on high-heat setting for 5 to 6 hours. If desired, serve stew with tortillas.

Nutrition Facts per serving: 249 cal., 5 g total fat (1 g sat. fat), 50 mg chol., 576 mg sodium, 27 g carbo., 5 g fiber, 24 g pro.

Pork and apples are perfect complements in this fix-and-forget dish that you'll want to enjoy time and again. The deep, nutty kick comes from a sprinkling of caraway seeds. Apple cider gives the stew a captivating sweetness.

Cider Pork Stew

MAKES 8 SERVINGS

Prep: 20 minutes
Cook: Low 10 to 12 hours,
High 5 to 6 hours

2	pounds boneless pork shoulder roast
3	medium red potatoes (1 pound), cubed
3	medium carrots, cut into ½-inch pieces
2	medium onions, sliced
1	medium apple, cored and coarsely chopped (⅔ cup)
1	stalk celery, coarsely chopped (½ cup)
2	cups apple cider or apple juice
3	tablespoons quick-cooking tapioca
1	teaspoon salt
1	teaspoon caraway seeds
¼	teaspoon black pepper

1. Trim fat from meat. Cut meat into 1-inch pieces. Transfer meat to a 3½- to 5½-quart slow cooker. Stir in potato, carrot, onion, apple, and celery.

2. In medium bowl combine apple cider, tapioca, salt, caraway seeds, and pepper. Pour over mixture in cooker.

3. Cover and cook on low-heat setting for 10 to 12 hours or on high-heat setting for 5 to 6 hours.

Nutrition Facts per serving: 272 cal., 7 g total fat (2 g sat. fat), 73 mg chol., 405 mg sodium, 27 g carbo., 3 g fiber, 24 g pro.

Spicy and earthy, this pork stew takes on an autumnal orange from the big chunks of sweet potatoes. It celebrates the fall season with a selection of root vegetables, apples, and roma tomatoes simmered with melt-in-your-mouth pork roast.

Pork, Beer, and Sweet Potato Stew

MAKES 8 SERVINGS

Prep: 25 minutes
Cook: Low 7 to 8 hours,
High 3½ to 4 hours

1	pound boneless pork shoulder roast
	Nonstick cooking spray
2	large sweet potatoes (1 to 1¼ pounds), peeled and cut into 1-inch pieces
3	medium parsnips, peeled and cut into ¾-inch pieces
2	small green apples, cored and cut into wedges
1	medium onion, cut into thin wedges
3	cups vegetable broth or chicken broth
1	tablespoon packed brown sugar
1	tablespoon Dijon-style mustard
1½	teaspoons dried thyme, crushed
½	teaspoon crushed red pepper
2	cloves garlic, minced
1	12-ounce can beer or 1½ cups vegetable broth or chicken broth
4	large roma tomatoes, coarsely chopped

1. Trim fat from meat. Cut meat into ¾-inch pieces. Lightly coat a large skillet with nonstick cooking spray; heat skillet over medium-high heat. Brown meat in hot skillet. Drain off fat. Set aside.

2. In a 5- to 6-quart slow cooker combine sweet potato, parsnip, apple, and onion. Add meat. In a medium bowl combine broth, brown sugar, mustard, thyme, crushed red pepper, and garlic. Pour broth mixture and beer over mixture in cooker.

3. Cover and cook on low-heat setting for 7 to 8 hours or on high-heat setting for 3½ to 4 hours. Stir in tomato.

Nutrition Facts per serving: 209 cal., 4 g total fat (1 g sat. fat), 37 mg chol., 471 mg sodium, 27 g carbo., 5 g fiber, 14 g pro.

Cream of chicken soup, cooked chicken, and chicken broth triple the flavor in this no-fuss soup.

Wild Rice and Chicken Soup

MAKES 8 TO 10 SERVINGS

Prep: 15 minutes
Cook: Low 6 to 8 hours,
High 3 to 4 hours

2½	cups chopped cooked chicken
2	cups sliced fresh mushrooms
1	10.75-ounce can condensed cream of chicken or cream of mushroom soup
2	medium carrots, coarsely shredded (1 cup)
2	stalks celery, sliced (1 cup)
1	6-ounce package long grain and wild rice mix
5	cups chicken broth
5	cups water

1. In a 5- to 6-quart slow cooker combine cooked chicken, mushrooms, soup, carrot, celery, uncooked rice from mix, and the contents of the rice seasoning packet. Stir in broth and water.

2. Cover and cook on low-heat setting for 6 to 8 hours or on high-heat setting for 3 to 4 hours.

Nutrition Facts per serving: 221 cal., 7 g total fat (2 g sat. fat), 44 mg chol., 1,251 mg sodium, 23 g carbo., 2 g fiber, 18 g pro.

Test Kitchen Tip: If you don't have leftover cooked chicken, buy deli-roasted chicken or cooked chicken in the grocer's refrigerator or freezer case. Or do it yourself. Place 1 pound of skinless, boneless chicken breasts in a large skillet with 1½ cups water. Bring to boiling; reduce heat. Cover and simmer for 12 to 14 minutes or until chicken is no longer pink. Drain and chop chicken.

This zesty stick-to-the-ribs soup is loaded with vegetables, ricelike orzo pasta, and browned Italian sausage that punches up the flavor. Vary the spiciness by choosing sweet or hot sausage.

"It's Italian" Sausage Soup

MAKES 8 SERVINGS

Prep: 20 minutes
Cook: Low 8 to 10 hours, High 4 to 5 hours, plus 20 minutes (high)

1	pound bulk Italian sausage
1	large onion, chopped (1 cup)
1	clove garlic, minced
2	medium carrots, chopped (1 cup)
1	stalk celery, chopped (½ cup)
1	14.5-ounce can diced tomatoes, undrained
1	8-ounce can tomato sauce
1	teaspoon dried oregano, crushed
½	teaspoon dried rosemary, crushed
½	teaspoon dried basil, crushed
¼	teaspoon dried thyme, crushed
¼	teaspoon fennel seeds, crushed
1	bay leaf
3	14-ounce cans reduced-sodium chicken broth
½	cup dried orzo pasta or finely broken cappellini pasta

1. In a large skillet cook Italian sausage, onion, and garlic until sausage is brown. Drain off fat. Set aside.

2. In a 4½- to 6-quart slow cooker combine carrot and celery. Add sausage mixture. In a medium bowl combine undrained tomatoes, tomato sauce, oregano, rosemary, basil, thyme, fennel seeds, and bay leaf. Pour tomato mixture and broth over mixture in cooker.

3. Cover and cook on low-heat setting for 8 to 10 hours or on high-heat setting for 4 to 5 hours.

4. If using low-heat setting, turn to high-heat setting. Stir in pasta. Cover and cook for 20 minutes more. Remove bay leaf.

Nutrition Facts per serving: 250 cal., 13 g total fat (5 g sat. fat), 38 mg chol., 923 mg sodium, 17 g carbo., 2 g fiber, 12 g pro.

Parmesan cheese tastes best when freshly grated, so keep a hunk on hand in the refrigerator (because it's a hard cheese, it keeps well). Use a vegetable peeler to cut wide shavings from a wedge of cheese right over each serving.

Turkey Sausage and Tortellini Stew

MAKES 10 TO 12 SERVINGS

Prep: 10 minutes
Cook: Low 8 to 10 hours,
High 4 to 5 hours,
plus 15 minutes (high)

2   14.5-ounce cans Italian-style stewed tomatoes, undrained

3   cups water

2   cups frozen cut regular or Italian green beans

1   10.5-ounce can condensed French onion soup

8   ounces cooked smoked turkey sausage, halved lengthwise and cut into ½-inch pieces

2   cups packaged shredded cabbage with carrot (coleslaw mix)

1   9-ounce package refrigerated cheese-filled tortellini

Shaved or shredded Parmesan cheese (optional)

1. In a 4- to 5-quart slow cooker combine undrained tomatoes, water, frozen green beans, soup, and turkey sausage.

2. Cover and cook on low-heat setting for 8 to 10 hours or on high-heat setting for 4 to 5 hours.

3. If using low-heat setting, turn to high-heat setting. Stir in coleslaw mix and tortellini. Cover and cook for 15 minutes more.

4. If desired, sprinkle individual servings with Parmesan cheese.

Nutrition Facts per serving: 176 cal., 5 g total fat (1 g sat. fat), 28 mg chol., 717 mg sodium, 23 g carbo., 2 g fiber, 9 g pro.

A takeoff on the French classic, cassoulet, this stew features a
trio of beans simmered with leeks, carrots, celery, and turnips.
(Photo on page 129.)

Vegetable Stew with Parmesan Toast

❧

MAKES 8 SERVINGS

Prep: 30 minutes
Cook: Low 10 to 11 hours,
High 5 to 5½ hours

3	15-ounce cans navy and/or cannellini (white kidney) beans, rinsed and drained
2	14-ounce cans vegetable broth
2	medium turnips, peeled and chopped
4	medium carrots, peeled and cut into ½-inch pieces
4	stalks celery, sliced (2 cups)
4	medium leeks, sliced
2	teaspoons dried Italian seasoning, crushed
½	to 1 teaspoon cracked black pepper
¼	teaspoon salt
4	cloves garlic, minced
2	bay leaves
16	slices baguette-style French bread
1	tablespoon olive oil
½	cup finely shredded Parmesan cheese
1	14.5-ounce can fire-roasted or regular diced tomatoes, drained
	Cracked black pepper (optional)

1. In a 5- to 6-quart slow cooker stir together drained beans, broth, turnip, carrot, celery, leek, Italian seasoning, the ½ to 1 teaspoon cracked black pepper, salt, garlic, and bay leaves.

2. Cover and cook on low-heat setting for 10 to 11 hours or on high-heat setting for 5 to 5½ hours.

3. Meanwhile, for Parmesan toast, preheat oven to 400°F. Brush baguette slices with oil; sprinkle with Parmesan cheese. Place on a baking sheet. Bake about 7 minutes or until bread is lightly toasted and cheese is melted.

4. Remove bay leaves from stew. Stir in drained tomatoes. If desired, sprinkle with additional cracked black pepper. Serve stew with Parmesan toast.

Nutrition Facts per serving: 288 cal., 4 g total fat (1 g sat. fat), 4 mg chol., 1,409 mg sodium, 50 g carbo., 10 g fiber, 15 g pro.

Stir a couple of tablespoons of red wine into the beef mixture just before serving to add an even greater depth of flavor to this dish.

Round Steak with Mushroom and Onion Sauce

❧

MAKES 8 SERVINGS

Prep: 20 minutes
Cook: Low 8 to 10 hours, High 4 to 5 hours

2	pounds boneless beef round steak, cut ¾ inch thick
1	tablespoon cooking oil
2	medium onions, sliced (1 cup)
3	cups sliced fresh mushrooms (8 ounces)
1	12-ounce jar beef gravy
1	1.1-ounce envelope mushroom gravy mix
	Hot mashed potatoes (optional)

1. Trim fat from meat. Cut meat into 8 serving-size pieces. In a large skillet brown meat, half at a time, on both sides in hot oil over medium heat. Drain off fat. Set aside.

2. Place onion in a 3½- or 4-quart slow cooker. Add meat and mushrooms. In a small bowl combine beef gravy and mushroom gravy mix; pour over mixture in cooker.

3. Cover and cook on low-heat setting for 8 to 10 hours or on high-heat setting for 4 to 5 hours. If desired, serve meat and mushroom mixture with hot mashed potatoes.

Nutrition Facts per serving: 194 cal., 7 g total fat (2 g sat. fat), 57 mg chol., 479 mg sodium, 7 g carbo., 1 g fiber, 24 g pro.

Beef brisket makes magnificent barbecue sandwiches.
The sweet mango slices add a fresh note and cool texture to
the smoky beef accented with beer.

Tangy Barbecue Beef Sandwiches

MAKES 8 SANDWICHES

Prep: 25 minutes
Cook: Low 10 to 12 hours,
High 5 to 6 hours
Stand: 15 minutes

3	pounds fresh beef brisket
2	tablespoons chili powder
1	teaspoon celery seeds
½	teaspoon salt
½	teaspoon black pepper
2	medium onions, thinly sliced
1	cup bottled smoke-flavored barbecue sauce
½	cup beer or ginger ale
8	large sandwich buns or Portuguese rolls, split and toasted
	Bottled hot pepper sauce (optional)
	Mango slices

1. Trim fat from meat. In a small bowl combine chili powder, celery seeds, salt, and pepper. Sprinkle mixture evenly over meat; rub in with your fingers. If necessary, cut meat to fit into a 3½- to 6-quart slow cooker. Set aside.

2. Place half of the onion in cooker. Add meat. Top with the remaining onion. In a small bowl combine barbecue sauce and beer. Pour over mixture in cooker.

3. Cover and cook on low-heat setting for 10 to 12 hours or on high-heat setting for 5 to 6 hours.

4. Transfer meat to a cutting board. Shred meat by pulling two forks through it in opposite directions. Return meat to cooker; stir to combine with cooking liquid.

5. Using a slotted spoon, spoon meat mixture into buns. If desired, season to taste with hot pepper sauce. Add mango.

Nutrition Facts per serving: 442 cal., 11 g total fat (3 g sat. fat), 98 mg chol., 971 mg sodium, 41 g carbo., 3 g fiber, 41 g pro.

Cajun seasoning and tomatoes give this spunky Louisiana-style pot roast lots of lively flavor. Hot mashed potatoes or noodles make a tasty serve-along.

Cajun Pot Roast with Sweet Peppers

MAKES 8 SERVINGS

Prep: 20 minutes
Cook: Low 8 to 10 hours,
High 4 to 5 hours

1   2- to 2½-pound boneless beef chuck pot roast
1   tablespoon Cajun seasoning
½   teaspoon bottled hot pepper sauce
⅛   teaspoon black pepper
1   14.5-ounce can diced tomatoes, undrained
1   medium green sweet pepper, cut into strips
1   medium red sweet pepper, cut into strips
1   medium yellow sweet pepper, cut into strips
     Cracked black pepper (optional)

1. Trim fat from meat. Sprinkle Cajun seasoning evenly over meat; rub in with your fingers. If necessary, cut meat to fit into a 3½- or 4-quart slow cooker. Place meat in cooker. Add hot pepper sauce and the ⅛ teaspoon black pepper. Pour undrained tomatoes over meat in cooker.

2. Cover and cook on low-heat setting for 8 to 10 hours or on high-heat setting for 4 to 5 hours, adding sweet peppers during the last 30 minutes of cooking.

3. Transfer meat to a cutting board. Slice meat; transfer to a serving platter. Drain vegetables, discarding cooking liquid. Serve meat with vegetables. If desired, sprinkle with cracked black pepper.

Nutrition Facts per serving: 169 cal., 4 g total fat (1 g sat. fat), 67 mg chol., 233 mg sodium, 6 g carbo., 1 g fiber, 25 g pro.

*Don't skimp on the standing time. It allows the cheese to melt
and the pie to cool just enough to be ready to eat.*

Tamale Pie

MAKES 8 SERVINGS

Prep: 25 minutes
Cook: Low 6 to 8 hours,
High 3 to 4 hours,
plus 50 minutes (high)
Stand: 20 minutes

2   pounds lean ground beef
1   large onion, chopped
    (1 cup)
2   cloves garlic, minced
2   10-ounce cans enchilada
    sauce
1   11-ounce can whole kernel
    corn with sweet peppers,
    drained
1   4-ounce can diced green
    chile peppers, undrained
1   8.5-ounce package corn
    muffin mix
1   cup shredded cheddar
    cheese
⅓   cup milk
1   egg, slightly beaten
1   fresh jalapeño chile pepper,
    seeded and finely chopped
    (optional) (see tip, page 10)

1. In a very large skillet cook ground beef, onion, and garlic until meat is brown and onion is tender. Drain off fat. Transfer meat mixture to a 3½- or 4-quart slow cooker. Stir in enchilada sauce, drained corn, and undrained chile peppers.

2. Cover and cook on low-heat setting for 6 to 8 hours or on high-heat setting for 3 to 4 hours.

3. For dumplings, in a medium bowl combine corn muffin mix, ½ cup of the cheese, the milk, egg, and, if desired, jalapeño pepper; stir just until combined.

4. If using low-heat setting, turn to high-heat setting. Stir meat mixture. Drop batter by tablespoons onto hot meat mixture to make 8 dumplings. Cover and cook for 50 minutes more (do not lift cover).

5. Sprinkle the remaining ½ cup cheese over dumplings. Remove liner from cooker, if possible, or turn off cooker. Let stand, uncovered, about 20 minutes to cool slightly before serving.

Nutrition Facts per serving: 474 cal., 24 g total fat (9 g sat. fat), 113 mg chol., 805 mg sodium, 35 g carbo., 1 g fiber, 30 g pro.

The leftover pork roast and chilled sauce is
delicious made into sandwiches. (Photo on page 259.)

Cranberry Pork Roast

MAKES 8 TO 10 SERVINGS

Prep: 25 minutes
Cook: Low 6 to 7 hours,
High 3 to 3½ hours

1	3-pound boneless pork top loin roast (double loin, tied)
1	tablespoon cooking oil
¼	teaspoon salt
¼	teaspoon black pepper
1	16-ounce can whole cranberry sauce
½	cup cranberry juice
¼	cup sugar
1	teaspoon dry mustard
¼	teaspoon ground cloves
2	tablespoons cornstarch
2	tablespoons cold water
	Hot cooked noodles, rice pilaf, or rice (optional)
	Snipped fresh herb (optional)

1. Trim fat from meat. In a large skillet brown meat on all sides in hot oil over medium heat. Drain off fat. Transfer meat to a 4- to 5-quart slow cooker. Sprinkle meat with salt and pepper. In a medium bowl combine cranberry sauce, cranberry juice, sugar, dry mustard, and cloves. Pour over meat in cooker.

2. Cover and cook on low-heat setting for 6 to 7 hours or on high-heat setting for 3 to 3½ hours.

3. Transfer meat to a serving platter, reserving cooking liquid. Cover meat with foil to keep warm.

4. For sauce, pour cooking liquid into a glass measuring cup; skim off fat. Measure 2 cups liquid. In a medium saucepan combine cornstarch and water; stir in the 2 cups liquid. Cook and stir over medium heat until thickened and bubbly. Cook and stir for 2 minutes more.

5. Serve meat with sauce and, if desired, hot cooked noodles sprinkled with a snipped fresh herb.

Nutrition Facts per serving: 381 cal., 11 g total fat (3 g sat. fat), 100 mg chol., 161 mg sodium, 32 g carbo., 1 g fiber, 37 g pro.

Mmmm! Stuffing studded with apples and topped with a peach-glazed roast—now that's a meal to savor! Add a salad and your favorite vegetables, and you have a perfect Sunday dinner.

Peach-Glazed Pork Roast with Stuffing

❊

MAKES 8 SERVINGS

Prep: 20 minutes
Cook: Low 5½ to 6 hours,
High 2½ to 3 hours

	Nonstick cooking spray
1	2- to 2½-pound boneless pork top loin roast (single loin)
¼	teaspoon salt
¼	teaspoon black pepper
1	tablespoon cooking oil
4	cups corn bread stuffing mix
1	medium cooking apple, cored and chopped (⅔ cup)
¼	cup chopped onion
1	cup reduced-sodium chicken broth
½	cup peach or apricot spreadable fruit
1	teaspoon finely shredded lemon peel
¼	teaspoon ground cinnamon

1. Lightly coat the inside of a 3½- or 4-quart slow cooker with nonstick cooking spray; set aside. Trim fat from meat. If necessary, cut meat to fit into the cooker. Sprinkle meat with salt and pepper. In a large skillet brown meat on all sides in hot oil over medium-high heat. Drain off fat. Set aside.

2. In a large bowl combine stuffing mix, apple, and onion. Drizzle with broth, tossing gently to combine. Spoon stuffing mixture into the prepared cooker. Add meat. In a small bowl stir together spreadable fruit, lemon peel, and cinnamon. Spread over meat in cooker.

3. Cover and cook on low-heat setting for 5½ to 6 hours or on high-heat setting for 2½ to 3 hours.

4. Transfer meat to a cutting board. Slice meat. Gently stir stuffing; serve with meat.

Nutrition Facts per serving: 390 cal., 9 g total fat (2 g sat. fat), 71 mg chol., 663 mg sodium, 48 g carbo., 0 g fiber, 30 g pro.

Root beer in barbecue sauce? Why not? It adds a sweet, caramel note to these hearty pork sandwiches. Look for root beer concentrate in the spice section of your supermarket.

Pulled Pork with Root Beer Barbecue Sauce

MAKES 8 TO 10 SANDWICHES

Prep: 25 minutes
Cook: Low 8 to 10 hours,
High 4 to 5 hours

2½	to 3 pounds boneless pork sirloin roast
½	teaspoon salt
½	teaspoon black pepper
1	tablespoon cooking oil
2	medium onions, cut into thin wedges
1	cup root beer*
6	cloves garlic, minced
3	cups root beer* (two 12-ounce cans)
1	cup bottled chili sauce
¼	teaspoon root beer concentrate (optional)
	Several dashes bottled hot pepper sauce
8	to 10 hamburger buns, split and toasted
	Lettuce leaves (optional)
	Tomato slices (optional)

1. Trim fat from meat. If necessary, cut meat to fit into a 3½- to 5-quart slow cooker. Sprinkle meat with salt and pepper. In a large skillet brown meat on all sides in hot oil over medium heat. Drain off fat. Transfer meat to cooker. Add onion, the 1 cup root beer, and the garlic.

2. Cover and cook on low-heat setting for 8 to 10 hours or on high-heat setting for 4 to 5 hours.

3. Meanwhile, for sauce, in a medium saucepan combine the 3 cups root beer and the chili sauce. Bring to boiling; reduce heat. Boil gently, uncovered, about 30 minutes or until mixture is reduced to 2 cups, stirring occasionally. Stir in root beer concentrate (if desired) and hot pepper sauce.

4. Using a slotted spoon, remove meat and onion from cooker; discard cooking liquid. Shred meat by pulling two forks through it in opposite directions.

5. If desired, line bottoms of buns with lettuce and tomato. Top with meat, onion, and sauce. Add tops of buns.

Nutrition Facts per serving: 356 cal., 10 g total fat (3 g sat. fat), 59 mg chol., 786 mg sodium, 44 g carbo., 1 g fiber, 22 g pro.

*Note: Do not use diet root beer.

Shredded tender pork and onion stuff these Caribbean-flavored tortilla wraps. For even more tropical taste, spoon on fruit salsa and avocado dip.

Citrus-Marinated Pork Wraps

MAKES 12 SERVINGS

Prep: 25 minutes
Marinate: 6 to 24 hours
Cook: Low 10 to 12 hours, High 5 to 6 hours

3	pounds boneless pork shoulder roast
½	cup lime juice
¼	cup grapefruit juice
¼	cup water
1	teaspoon dried oregano, crushed
½	teaspoon salt
½	teaspoon ground cumin
¼	teaspoon black pepper
3	cloves garlic, minced
2	bay leaves
1	large onion, sliced (1 cup)
12	flour tortillas, warmed (see tip, page 118)
	Lettuce leaves (optional)
	Chopped tomato (optional)

1. Trim fat from meat. If necessary, cut meat to fit into a 3½- to 5-quart slow cooker. Pierce meat in several places with a large fork. Place meat in a resealable plastic bag set in a shallow dish.

2. For marinade, in a small bowl combine lime juice, grapefruit juice, water, oregano, salt, cumin, pepper, garlic, and bay leaves. Pour marinade over meat. Seal bag; turn to coat meat. Marinate in the refrigerator for 6 to 24 hours, turning bag occasionally.

3. Place onion in the cooker. Add the meat and marinade. Cover and cook on low-heat setting for 10 to 12 hours or on high-heat setting for 5 to 6 hours.

4. Using a slotted spoon, remove meat and onion from cooker, reserving cooking liquid. Skim fat from liquid; remove bay leaves. Cover cooking liquid to keep hot. Shred meat by pulling two forks through it in opposite directions.

5. If desired, line warm tortillas with lettuce. Top with meat, onion, and, if desired, tomato; roll up tortillas. Serve with the hot cooking liquid for dipping.

Nutrition Facts per serving: 265 cal., 13 g total fat (4 g sat. fat), 60 mg chol., 280 mg sodium, 18 g carbo., 1 g fiber, 19 g pro.

Shredded pork sandwiches take on a delicious new attitude with a savory kick provided by chile peppers and hot paprika. For a milder sandwich, use regular paprika instead of the hot version.

Peppery Pork Sandwiches

MAKES 8 OR 9 SANDWICHES

Prep: 25 minutes
Cook: Low 10 to 12 hours,
High 5 to 6 hours

2	to 2½ pounds boneless pork shoulder roast
1	tablespoon hot paprika
1	large onion
2	14.5-ounce cans diced tomatoes, undrained
1	4-ounce can diced green chile peppers, undrained
2	teaspoons dried oregano, crushed
½	to 1 teaspoon black pepper
¼	teaspoon salt
8	or 9 French-style rolls, split and toasted

1. Trim fat from meat. If necessary, cut meat to fit into a 4- to 5-quart slow cooker. Sprinkle meat with paprika; set aside.

2. Cut onion lengthwise into quarters; thinly slice quarters. Place onion in the cooker. Add meat. In a medium bowl combine undrained tomatoes, undrained chile peppers, oregano, black pepper, and salt. Pour over mixture in cooker.

3. Cover and cook on low-heat setting for 10 to 12 hours or on high-heat setting for 5 to 6 hours.

4. Transfer meat to a cutting board. Shred meat by pulling two forks through it in opposite directions. Transfer meat to a large bowl. Using a slotted spoon, remove tomato and onion from cooking liquid; toss with meat. Drizzle meat mixture with enough of the cooking liquid to moisten. Spoon meat mixture into rolls.

Nutrition Facts per serving: 512 cal., 12 g total fat (3 g sat. fat), 73 mg chol., 1,066 mg sodium, 65 g carbo., 5 g fiber, 33 g pro.

The sass in these tender chops comes from the perfect blend of orange juice and chipotle pepper—it really adds a spunky flavor! Note: Freeze leftover chipotle peppers, covered in some of the adobo sauce, in a tightly sealed freezer container.

Sassy Pork Chops

MAKES 8 SERVINGS

Prep: 25 minutes
Cook: Low 6 to 7 hours,
High 3 to 3½ hours

8	pork loin chops (with bone), cut ¾ to 1 inch thick
½	teaspoon garlic salt
¼	teaspoon black pepper
2	tablespoons cooking oil
2	medium red, green, and/or yellow sweet peppers, cut into strips
2	stalks celery, thinly sliced (1 cup)
1	medum onion, chopped (½ cup)
¼	cup reduced-sodium chicken broth
¼	cup orange juice
1	tablespoon chopped canned chipotle pepper in adobo sauce (see tip, page 10)
½	teaspoon dried oregano, crushed

1. Trim fat from chops. Sprinkle chops with garlic salt and black pepper. In a 12-inch skillet brown chops, half at a time, on both sides in hot oil over medium heat. Drain off fat. Set aside.

2. In a 4- to 5-quart slow cooker combine sweet pepper, celery, and onion. Add chops. In a small bowl stir together broth, orange juice, chipotle pepper, and oregano. Pour over mixture in cooker.

3. Cover and cook on low-heat setting for 6 to 7 hours or on high-heat setting for 3 to 3½ hours.

4. Using a slotted spoon, transfer chops and vegetables to a serving platter; discard cooking liquid.

Nutrition Facts per serving: 215 cal., 7 g total fat (1 g sat. fat), 78 mg chol., 363 mg sodium, 4 g carbo., 1 g fiber, 33 g pro.

Americans have recently discovered the creamy richness white kidney beans bring to cooking, but Italians have been savoring the legumes for ages. Give them a go in this hearty and satisfying dish. Serve in shallow bowls.

Italian Chicken with White Beans

❧

MAKES 8 SERVINGS

Prep: 20 minutes
Cook: Low 7 to 8 hours, High 3½ to 4 hours

1	15- or 19-ounce can cannellini beans (white kidney beans), rinsed and drained
1	large onion, chopped (1 cup)
2	medium carrots, thinly sliced (1 cup)
1	stalk celery, thinly sliced (½ cup)
3	cloves garlic, minced
2	pounds skinless, boneless chicken thighs
¼	teaspoon salt
⅛	teaspoon black pepper
1	14.5-ounce can diced tomatoes, undrained
½	cup dry white wine or chicken broth
1½	teaspoons dried Italian seasoning, crushed
¼	cup finely shredded Parmesan cheese (optional)

1. In a 3½- or 4-quart slow cooker combine drained beans, onion, carrot, celery, and garlic. Add chicken. Sprinkle chicken with salt and pepper. In a medium bowl combine undrained tomatoes, wine, and Italian seasoning. Pour over mixture in cooker.

2. Cover and cook on low-heat setting for 7 to 8 hours or on high-heat setting for 3½ to 4 hours.

3. Using a slotted spoon, transfer chicken, beans, and vegetables to a serving bowl, reserving cooking liquid. Skim fat from liquid. Drizzle chicken, beans, and vegetables with enough of the liquid to moisten. If desired, sprinkle individual servings with cheese.

Nutrition Facts per serving: 207 cal., 5 g total fat (1 g sat. fat), 94 mg chol., 354 mg sodium, 14 g carbo., 4 g fiber, 26 g pro.

If you're going to take a dish to a gathering with people you don't know, don't worry. Chicken and stuffing always satisfies! (Photo on page 257.)

Chicken and Stuffing Casserole

MAKES 16 TO 20 SERVINGS

Prep: 25 minutes
Cook: Low 4½ to 5 hours

½	cup butter or margarine
2	stalks celery, thinly sliced (1 cup)
2	small onions, chopped (¾ cup)
	Nonstick cooking spray
1	6-ounce package long grain and wild rice mix
1	14-ounce package herb-seasoned stuffing croutons
4	cups cubed cooked chicken
1	4.5-ounce jar (drained weight) sliced mushrooms, drained
¼	cup snipped fresh parsley
1½	teaspoons poultry seasoning
¼	teaspoon black pepper
2	eggs, slightly beaten
2	14-ounce cans reduced-sodium chicken broth
1	10.75-ounce can reduced-fat and reduced-sodium condensed cream of chicken or cream of mushroom soup

1. In a large skillet heat butter over medium heat. Add celery and onion; cook about 5 minutes or until vegetables are tender. Set aside.

2. Lightly coat the inside of a 5½- or 6-quart slow cooker with nonstick cooking spray. Add uncooked rice from mix (reserve seasoning packet until needed). Using a slotted spoon, transfer celery and onion to cooker, reserving butter. Stir to combine.

3. Place croutons in a very large bowl. Stir in the reserved butter, the chicken, drained mushrooms, parsley, poultry seasoning, pepper, and the contents of the seasoning packet from rice mix.

4. In a medium bowl combine eggs, broth, and soup. Pour over crouton mixture, tossing gently to combine. Transfer mixture to cooker.

5. Cover and cook on low-heat setting (do not use high-heat setting) for 4½ to 5 hours. Stir gently before serving.

Nutrition Facts per serving: 287 cal., 11 g total fat (5 g sat. fat), 76 mg chol., 903 mg sodium, 31 g carbo., 3 g fiber, 16 g pro.

This Tex-Mex take on a one-dish meal has everything—bread, chicken, beans, and salad—stacked on one plate. Customize it with your favorite version of salsa. (Photo on page 131.)

Chicken Tostadas

MAKES 10 SERVINGS

Prep: 30 minutes
Cook: Low 5 to 6 hours,
High 2½ to 3 hours

3	tablespoons chili powder
3	tablespoons lime juice
2	fresh jalapeño chile peppers, seeded and finely chopped (see tip, page 10)
¼	teaspoon bottled hot pepper sauce
8	cloves garlic, minced
1	medium onion, sliced and separated into rings
2	pounds skinless, boneless chicken thighs
1	16-ounce can refried beans
10	tostada shells
1½	cups shredded cheddar cheese
2	cups shredded lettuce
1¼	cups bottled salsa
¾	cup dairy sour cream
¾	cup sliced pitted ripe olives (optional)

1. In a 3½- to 5-quart slow cooker combine chili powder, lime juice, jalapeño pepper, hot pepper sauce, and garlic. Add onion; place chicken on top of mixture in cooker.

2. Cover and cook on low-heat setting for 5 to 6 hours or on high-heat setting for 2½ to 3 hours.

3. Using a slotted spoon, remove chicken and onion from cooker; reserve ½ cup of the cooking liquid. Shred chicken by pulling two forks through it in opposite directions. In a medium bowl combine chicken, onion, and the reserved ½ cup cooking liquid.

4. Spread refried beans on tostada shells. Top with chicken mixture and cheese. Serve with lettuce, salsa, sour cream, and, if desired, olives.

Nutrition Facts per serving: 333 cal., 16 g total fat (7 g sat. fat), 100 mg chol., 574 mg sodium, 21 g carbo., 5 g fiber, 27 g pro.

Whether you like 'em hot and spicy or smoky sweet, everyone will grab for a sample of this barbecue favorite. Just make sure to have plenty of napkins on hand!

Chicken Drumsticks with Barbecue Sauce

MAKES 8 SERVINGS

Prep: 25 minutes
Cook: Low 3 to 4 hours, High 1½ to 2 hours

3	pounds chicken drumsticks
1½	cups bottled barbecue sauce
¼	cup honey
2	teaspoons yellow mustard
1½	teaspoons Worcestershire sauce

1. Preheat broiler. Place chicken on the unheated rack of a broiler pan. Broil 4 to 5 inches from the heat for 15 to 20 minutes or until light brown, turning once halfway through broiling. Transfer chicken to a 3½- or 4-quart slow cooker.

2. Meanwhile, in a medium bowl combine barbecue sauce, honey, mustard, and Worcestershire sauce. Pour over chicken in cooker.

3. Cover and cook on low-heat setting for 3 to 4 hours or on high-heat setting for 1½ to 2 hours.

Nutrition Facts per serving: 83 cal., 4 g total fat (1 g sat. fat), 20 mg chol., 197 mg sodium, 6 g carbo., 0 g fiber, 5 g pro.

Sometimes called Oriental sesame oil, toasted sesame oil is processed from toasted sesame seeds. Its rich, concentrated flavor complements the soy and ginger flavors here. Be sure to refrigerate the oil to delay rancidity.

Sesame Turkey

MAKES 8 SERVINGS

Prep: 20 minutes
Cook: Low 5 to 6 hours,
High 2½ to 3 hours

3	pounds turkey breast tenderloin
¼	teaspoon black pepper
⅛	teaspoon cayenne pepper
¼	cup reduced-sodium chicken broth
¼	cup soy sauce
4	teaspoons grated fresh ginger
1	tablespoon lemon juice
1	tablespoon toasted sesame oil
2	cloves garlic, minced
2	tablespoons cornstarch
2	tablespoons cold water
2	tablespoons sliced green onion (1)
1	tablespoon sesame seeds, toasted (see tip, page 29)

1. Place turkey in a 3½- or 4-quart slow cooker. Sprinkle turkey with black pepper and cayenne pepper. In a small bowl combine broth, soy sauce, ginger, lemon juice, sesame oil, and garlic. Pour over turkey in cooker.

2. Cover and cook on low-heat setting for 5 to 6 hours or on high-heat setting for 2½ to 3 hours.

3. Using a slotted spoon, transfer turkey to a serving platter, reserving cooking liquid. Cover turkey with foil to keep warm.

4. For sauce, strain cooking liquid into a small saucepan. In a small bowl combine cornstarch and water; stir into cooking liquid. Cook and stir over medium heat until thickened and bubbly. Cook and stir for 2 minutes more.

5. If desired, slice turkey. Spoon sauce over turkey. Sprinkle with green onion and sesame seeds.

Nutrition Facts per serving: 222 cal., 3 g total fat (1 g sat. fat), 112 mg chol., 373 mg sodium, 3 g carbo., 0 g fiber, 42 g pro.

Stopping at your favorite Greek restaurant is wonderful, but why not enjoy Mediterranean flavors at home? This recipe makes enough to share with friends. (Photo on page 136.)

Greek Sandwich Wraps

MAKES 8 SERVINGS

Prep: 30 minutes
Cook: Low 8 to 10 hours, High 4 to 5 hours

2	to 2½ pounds boneless lamb shoulder roast
4	teaspoons Greek seasoning
1	medium onion, thinly sliced (½ cup)
¼	cup lemon juice
¾	cup mayonnaise or salad dressing
2	tablespoons Dijon-style mustard
3	cloves garlic, minced
8	8- to 10-inch flour tortillas
½	cup crumbled feta cheese
2	cups shredded fresh spinach
1	medium cucumber, chopped (1½ cups)
1	medium tomato, chopped (½ cup) (optional)

1. Trim fat from meat. Sprinkle Greek seasoning evenly over meat; rub in with your fingers. If necessary, cut meat to fit into a 3½- or 4-quart slow cooker. Set aside.

2. Place onion in the cooker. Add meat; sprinkle with lemon juice. Cover and cook on low-heat setting for 8 to 10 hours or on high-heat setting for 4 to 5 hours.

3. Meanwhile, in a small bowl stir together mayonnaise, mustard, and garlic. Cover and chill until needed.

4. Transfer meat to a cutting board, reserving cooking liquid. Shred meat by pulling two forks through it in opposite directions. If necessary, skim fat from liquid. Return meat to cooker; stir to combine with cooking liquid.

5. Spread one side of each tortilla with mayonnaise mixture. Using a slotted spoon, spoon meat mixture onto tortillas. Sprinkle with feta cheese. Top with spinach, cucumber, and, if desired, tomato; roll up tortillas.

Nutrition Facts per serving: 539 cal., 39 g total fat (12 g sat. fat), 91 mg chol., 607 mg sodium, 21 g carbo., 2 g fiber, 24 g pro.

Place the ingredients for the chunky sauce in your slow cooker and forget it while it cooks to the perfect consistency for coating pasta.

Spaghetti with Marinara Sauce

❦

MAKES 8 SERVINGS

Prep: 20 minutes
Cook: Low 8 to 10 hours,
High 4 to 5 hours

1	28-ounce can whole Italian-style tomatoes, undrained and cut up
2	large carrots, coarsely chopped
3	stalks celery, sliced (1½ cups)
1	large green sweet pepper, chopped (1 cup)
1	large onion, chopped (1 cup)
1	6-ounce can tomato paste
½	cup water
2	teaspoons sugar
2	teaspoons dried Italian seasoning, crushed
1	teaspoon salt
¼	teaspoon black pepper
3	cloves garlic, minced
1	bay leaf
16	ounces dried spaghetti or other pasta
	Finely shredded Parmesan cheese (optional)

1. For sauce, in a 3½- or 4-quart slow cooker combine undrained tomatoes, carrot, celery, sweet pepper, onion, tomato paste, water, sugar, Italian seasoning, salt, black pepper, garlic, and bay leaf.

2. Cover and cook on low-heat setting for 8 to 10 hours or on high-heat setting for 4 to 5 hours. Remove bay leaf.

3. Before serving, cook spaghetti according to package directions; drain. Return spaghetti to pan. Pour sauce over spaghetti; toss gently to coat. If desired, sprinkle individual servings with Parmesan cheese.

Nutrition Facts per serving: 272 cal., 1 g total fat (0 g sat. fat), 0 mg chol., 611 mg sodium, 57 g carbo., 5 g fiber, 10 g pro.

Instead of making sandwiches, serve the vegetable mixture on tostada shells with shredded lettuce, chopped tomato, and shredded cheese for a taco-style salad.

Sloppy Veggie Sandwiches

MAKES 8 SANDWICHES

Prep: 15 minutes
Cook: High 3 to 3½ hours,
plus 30 minutes (high)

2	medium carrots, chopped (1 cup)
2	stalks celery, chopped (1 cup)
⅔	cup brown lentils, rinsed and drained
⅔	cup uncooked regular brown rice
1	medium onion, chopped (½ cup)
2	tablespoons packed brown sugar
2	tablespoons yellow mustard
½	teaspoon salt
⅛	to ¼ teaspoon cayenne pepper
1	clove garlic, minced
2	14-ounce cans vegetable broth or chicken broth
1	15-ounce can tomato sauce
2	tablespoons cider vinegar
8	whole wheat hamburger buns or French-style rolls, split and toasted

1. In a 3½- or 4-quart slow cooker combine carrot, celery, lentils, brown rice, onion, brown sugar, mustard, salt, cayenne pepper, and garlic. Stir in broth.

2. Cover and cook on high-heat setting (do not use low-heat setting) for 3 to 3½ hours. Stir in tomato sauce and vinegar. Cover and cook for 30 minutes more.

3. Serve lentil mixture in buns.

Nutrition Facts per serving: 261 cal., 4 g total fat (1 g sat. fat), 0 mg chol., 1,036 mg sodium, 50 g carbo., 8 g fiber, 11 g pro.

Having a barbecue? Serve this cheesy medley of beans and corn in small bowls with grilled burgers and brats.

Saucy Succotash

MAKES 12 SERVINGS

Prep: 15 minutes
Cook: Low 5 to 6 hours,
High 2½ to 3 hours
Stand: 10 minutes

1	16-ounce package frozen whole kernel corn, thawed
1	16-ounce package frozen lima beans, thawed
1	14.75-ounce can cream-style corn, undrained
1	large red sweet pepper, chopped (1 cup)
1	cup shredded smoked Gouda cheese
1	medium onion, chopped (½ cup)
2	teaspoons cumin seeds
¼	cup water
1	8-ounce carton light dairy sour cream

1. In a 3½- or 4-quart slow cooker combine whole kernel corn, lima beans, undrained cream-style corn, sweet pepper, cheese, onion, and cumin seeds. Pour water over mixture in cooker.

2. Cover and cook on low-heat setting for 5 to 6 hours or on high-heat setting for 2½ to 3 hours.

3. Gently stir in sour cream. Let stand, covered, for 10 minutes before serving.

Nutrition Facts per serving: 158 cal., 4 g total fat (3 g sat. fat), 14 mg chol., 282 mg sodium, 25 g carbo., 4 g fiber, 7 g pro.

Test Kitchen Tip: The easiest way to keep your slow cooker clean is to use the disposable liners you can find at the supermarket. However, if you don't use a disposable liner, cleaning the stoneware liner of a slow cooker is easy. Just cool it completely so it doesn't crack when water touches it. Then, if the stoneware liner is removable, simply put it in the dishwasher. If not, clean the liner with a soft cloth and warm, soapy water. Don't use abrasive cleaners or pads—they can damage the liner. If food sticks badly, fill the liner with warm water and let it stand before cleaning.

Every great summer gathering needs a delicious batch of baked beans. Pineapple tidbits afford these lively and saucy baked beans a hint of sweetness.

Hawaiian Pineapple Baked Beans

MAKES 16 SERVINGS

Prep: 15 minutes
Cook: Low 7 to 9 hours,
High 3½ to 4½ hours

8   ounces lean ground beef
1   large onion, chopped
     (1 cup)
2   15-ounce cans pork and
     beans in tomato sauce,
     undrained
2   15-ounce cans chili beans
     in chili gravy, undrained
1   20-ounce can pineapple
     tidbits (juice pack), drained
1   cup ketchup
1   cup bottled hot-style
     barbecue sauce

1. In a large skillet cook ground beef and onion until meat is brown and onion is tender. Drain off fat. Transfer meat mixture to a 5- to 6-quart slow cooker.

2. Stir in undrained pork and beans, undrained chili beans in chili gravy, drained pineapple, ketchup, and barbecue sauce.

3. Cover and cook on low-heat setting for 7 to 9 hours or on high-heat setting for 3½ to 4½ hours.

Nutrition Facts per serving: 189 cal., 3 g total fat (1 g sat. fat), 13 mg chol., 762 mg sodium, 35 g carbo., 6 g fiber, 9 g pro.

These creamy potatoes are a delicious partner for roast beef, pork, or chicken.

Lemon Pesto New Potatoes

MAKES 10 TO 12 SERVINGS

Prep: 15 minutes
Cook: Low 5 to 6 hours

30 to 36 tiny new potatoes (3 pounds), halved or quartered

1 16-ounce jar Alfredo pasta sauce

⅓ cup refrigerated basil pesto

1 tablespoon finely shredded lemon peel

¼ to ½ teaspoon coarsely ground black pepper

Finely shredded Parmesan cheese

1. Place potato in a 4- to 5-quart slow cooker. Stir in pasta sauce, pesto, lemon peel, and pepper.

2. Cover and cook on low-heat setting (do not use high-heat setting) for 5 to 6 hours.

3. Using a slotted spoon, transfer potato to a serving dish. Whisk pesto mixture in cooker; pour over potato. Sprinkle with Parmesan cheese.

Nutrition Facts per serving: 252 cal., 14 g total fat (4 g sat. fat), 29 mg chol., 431 mg sodium, 26 g carbo., 2 g fiber, 7 g pro.

When baked ham or roast pork are on the menu, cook a batch of these fruity, maple-glazed sweet potatoes to spoon alongside.

Maple-Ginger Sweet Potatoes

❧

MAKES 8 SERVINGS

Prep: 15 minutes
Cook: Low 5 to 6 hours,
High 2½ to 3 hours

3	to 4 medium sweet potatoes (1½ pounds), peeled and cut into bite-size pieces (about 5 cups)
2	medium tart cooking apples (such as Granny Smith), peeled, cored, and coarsely chopped (1⅓ cups)
2	tablespoons dried cranberries, snipped
1½	teaspoons grated fresh ginger
½	teaspoon salt
½	teaspoon ground cinnamon
¼	teaspoon ground nutmeg
⅛	teaspoon black pepper
½	cup water
¼	cup maple syrup

1. In a 3½- or 4-quart slow cooker combine sweet potato, apple, dried cranberries, ginger, salt, cinnamon, nutmeg, and pepper. Pour water and maple syrup over mixture in cooker.

2. Cover and cook on low-heat setting for 5 to 6 hours or on high-heat setting for 2½ to 3 hours.

Nutrition Facts per serving: 104 cal., 0 g total fat (0 g sat. fat), 0 mg chol., 181 mg sodium, 26 g carbo., 3 g fiber, 2 g pro.

Paired with roasted chicken or broiled salmon and steamed broccoli, this earthy herbed pilaf makes a great side dish for an easy and colorful meal.

Creamy Wild Rice Pilaf

MAKES 12 SERVINGS

Prep: 20 minutes
Cook: Low 8 to 9 hours,
High 4 to 4½ hours

	Nonstick cooking spray
1	10.75-ounce can condensed cream of mushroom with roasted garlic or golden mushroom soup
1	cup uncooked wild rice, rinsed and drained
1	cup uncooked regular brown rice
1	cup sliced fresh mushrooms
1	cup packaged julienned or coarsely shredded carrot
1	stalk celery, sliced (½ cup)
1	small onion, chopped (⅓ cup)
1½	teaspoons poultry seasoning
1¼	teaspoons salt
¾	teaspoon black pepper
6	cups water
½	cup dairy sour cream

1. Lightly coat the inside of a 3½- or 4-quart slow cooker with nonstick cooking spray; set aside. In the prepared cooker combine soup, wild rice, brown rice, mushrooms, carrot, celery, onion, poultry seasoning, salt, and pepper. Stir in water.

2. Cover and cook on low-heat setting for 8 to 9 hours or on high-heat setting for 4 to 4½ hours.

3. Before serving, stir in sour cream.

Nutrition Facts per serving: 146 cal., 3 g total fat (1 g sat. fat), 5 mg chol., 430 mg sodium, 27 g carbo., 2 g fiber, 4 g pro.

When cooking for a crowd, chances are your oven will be full. Put a slow cooker on stuffing duty. This savory herb-onion version gets a sweet nod from the raisins.

Raisin-Herb-Seasoned Stuffing

MAKES 8 TO 10 SERVINGS

Prep: 20 minutes
Cook: Low 5 to 6 hours,
High 2½ to 3 hours

Nonstick cooking spray
1 16-ounce package herb-seasoned stuffing mix
1 cup golden and/or dark raisins
1 medium onion, chopped (½ cup)
1½ cups water
1 10.75-ounce can condensed golden mushroom soup
1 8-ounce carton dairy sour cream

1. Lightly coat the inside of a 3½- or 4-quart slow cooker with nonstick cooking spray. In the prepared cooker combine stuffing mix, raisins, and onion.

2. In a medium bowl combine water, soup, and sour cream. Pour over mixture in cooker; stir gently to combine.

3. Cover and cook on low-heat setting for 5 to 6 hours or on high-heat setting for 2½ to 3 hours.

Nutrition Facts per serving: 377 cal., 9 g total fat (4 g sat. fat), 14 mg chol., 1,105 mg sodium, 65 g carbo., 6 g fiber, 9 g pro.

Tart apples simmered with sugar and spices transform into flavorful apple butter. Normally during cooking you don't uncover a slow cooker, but in this recipe you want the liquid to evaporate as it cooks.

Slow-Cooker Apple Butter

MAKES 4 HALF-PINTS

Prep: 40 minutes
Cook: High 6 to 6½ hours
Stand: 1 hour

12	cooking apples, peeled, cored, and sliced (14 cups)
2	cups sugar
1½	teaspoons ground cinnamon
½	teaspoon ground cloves
½	teaspoon ground allspice

1. Place apple slices in a 5- to 6-quart slow cooker. Stir in sugar, cinnamon, cloves, and allspice.

2. Cover and cook on high-heat setting (do not use low-heat setting) for 4 hours. Stir. Cook, uncovered, for 2 to 2½ hours more or until apple is very tender and most of the liquid has evaporated. Let stand, uncovered, for at least 1 hour to cool. Or cover and chill overnight.

3. Process apple mixture with an immersion blender or run mixture through a food mill.*

4. Ladle apple butter into half-pint freezer containers, leaving a ½-inch head space. Seal and label. Store in the refrigerator for up to 3 weeks or in the freezer for up to 1 year.

Nutrition Facts per 2 tablespoons: 70 cal., 0 g total fat (0 g sat. fat), 0 mg chol., 0 mg sodium, 18 g carbo., 1 g fiber, 0 g pro.

*Note: You also may process the mixture, half at a time, in a blender or food processor. When processed this way, the mixture will be slightly lighter in color and thinner in consistency.

Next time you're serving pound cake, toast it!
Toasting adds interesting texture and gives a sugary,
crunchy base to soak up the warm cherry mixture.

Mock Cherries Jubilee

MAKES 8 SERVINGS

Prep: 15 minutes
Cook: High 4 to 5 hours

2   16-ounce packages frozen
      unsweetened pitted tart
      red cherries

½   cup packed brown sugar

½   cup cherry cider, apple
      cider, or apple juice

2   tablespoons quick-cooking
      tapioca, crushed

1   vanilla bean, split
      lengthwise, or 2 teaspoons
      vanilla extract

2   to 3 tablespoons cherry or
      almond liqueur or cherry
      cider

      Pound cake slices, angel
      food cake slices, or vanilla
      ice cream

      Whipped cream (optional)

1. In a 3½- or 4-quart slow cooker combine frozen cherries, brown sugar, cider, tapioca, and, if using, vanilla bean.

2. Cover and cook on high-heat setting (do not use low-heat setting) for 4 to 5 hours. Remove vanilla bean, if using, or stir in vanilla extract. Stir in liqueur.

3. To serve, place cake slices in dessert dishes. Spoon warm cherry mixture over cake. If desired, top with whipped cream.

Nutrition Facts per serving: 428 cal., 15 g total fat (9 g sat. fat), 166 mg chol., 307 mg sodium, 68 g carbo., 2 g fiber, 5 g pro.

Jewel-hued peaches and blueberries cook with peach juice and vanilla to make a luscious fruit meld to serve with French toast sticks and whipped topping. Beautiful to serve, even better to eat.

Peach and Blueberry Dessert

MAKES 8 SERVINGS

Prep: 25 minutes
Cook: Low 4 to 5 hours,
High 2 to 2½ hours
Stand: 1 hour

6 cups sliced, peeled fresh peaches (6 medium) or frozen unsweetened peach slices

1 3-ounce package (⅔ cup) dried blueberries

½ cup peach juice blend or white grape juice

¼ cup sugar

1 tablespoon quick-cooking tapioca, crushed

1 teaspoon vanilla

1 18.8-ounce package (24) frozen French toast sticks

   Frozen whipped dessert topping, thawed (optional)

1. In a 3½- or 4-quart slow cooker combine fresh or frozen peach slices, dried blueberries, juice, sugar, and tapioca.

2. Cover and cook on low-heat setting for 4 to 5 hours or on high-heat setting for 2 to 2½ hours.

3. Remove liner from cooker, if possible, or turn off cooker. Stir in vanilla. Let stand, uncovered, about 1 hour to cool slightly before serving.

4. Prepare frozen French toast sticks according to package directions and separate into sticks. (Discard maple syrup cups or save for another use.)

5. To serve, divide French toast sticks among dessert dishes. Spoon warm peach mixture over toast sticks. If desired, top with whipped topping.

Nutrition Facts per serving: 307 cal., 4 g total fat (1 g sat. fat), 3 mg chol., 236 mg sodium, 66 g carbo., 3 g fiber, 3 g pro.

How easy it is to serve a warm and comforting dessert for a winter meal—especially when it bakes by itself in the slow cooker all afternoon? Muffin mix, frozen berries, and blueberry pie filling make this dessert a snap.

Mixed Berry Cobbler

MAKES 8 TO 10 SERVINGS

Prep: 15 minutes
Cook: Low 3 hours,
plus 1 hour (high)
Stand: 30 minutes

Nonstick cooking spray
1 12- to 14-ounce package
   frozen mixed berries
1 21-ounce can blueberry pie
   filling
¼ cup sugar
1 6.5-ounce package
   blueberry or triple-berry
   muffin mix
⅓ cup water
2 tablespoons cooking oil
   Frozen whipped dessert
   topping, thawed, or vanilla
   ice cream (optional)

1. Lightly coat the inside of a 3½- or 4-quart slow cooker with nonstick cooking spray. In the prepared cooker combine frozen mixed berries, pie filling, and sugar.

2. Cover and cook on low-heat setting (do not use high-heat setting) for 3 hours.

3. Turn to high-heat setting. In a medium bowl combine muffin mix, water, and oil; stir just until combined. Spoon muffin mixture over berry mixture. Cover and cook about 1 hour more or until a toothpick inserted into center of muffin mixture comes out clean.

4. Remove liner from cooker, if possible, or turn off cooker. Let stand, uncovered, for 30 to 45 minutes to cool slightly before serving.

5. To serve, spoon warm cobbler into dessert dishes. If desired, top with dessert topping.

Nutrition Facts per serving: 257 cal., 7 g total fat (1 g sat. fat), 1 mg chol., 155 mg sodium, 50 g carbo., 4 g fiber, 1 g pro.

Brown sugar brings depth to the sweetness in this fruity compote. Serve it topped with vanilla ice cream for an irresistible hot-cold effect. (Photo on page 141.)

Fruit Compote with Ginger

MAKES 10 TO 12 SERVINGS

Prep: 15 minutes
Cook: Low 6 to 8 hours,
High 3 to 4 hours

3   medium pears, peeled if desired, cored, and cubed

1   15.5-ounce can pineapple chunks, undrained

1   cup dried apricots, quartered

3   tablespoons frozen orange juice concentrate

2   tablespoons packed brown sugar

1   tablespoon quick-cooking tapioca

1   teaspoon grated fresh ginger or ½ teaspoon ground ginger

2   cups frozen unsweetened pitted dark sweet cherries, thawed

Flaked coconut, toasted (see tip, page 29) (optional)

Macadamia nuts or pecans, chopped and toasted (see tip, page 29) (optional)

1. In a 3½- or 4-quart slow cooker combine pear, undrained pineapple, dried apricots, orange juice concentrate, brown sugar, tapioca, and ginger.

2. Cover and cook on low-heat setting for 6 to 8 hours or on high-heat setting for 3 to 4 hours. Stir in cherries at the end.

3. To serve, spoon warm compote into dessert dishes. If desired, top with coconut and nuts.

Nutrition Facts per serving: 128 cal., 0 g total fat (0 g sat. fat), 0 mg chol., 3 mg sodium, 33 g carbo., 4 g fiber, 1 g pro.

Studded with plump raisins, dried cranberries, and/or dried cherries, the homey dessert gets a new look to go with its comforting flavor.

Old-Fashioned Rice Pudding

MAKES 12 TO 14 SERVINGS

Prep: 10 minutes
Cook: Low 2 to 3 hours

	Nonstick cooking spray
4	cups cooked rice
1	12-ounce can evaporated milk
1	cup milk
⅓	cup sugar
¼	cup water
1	cup raisins, dried cranberries, and/or dried cherries
3	tablespoons butter or margarine, softened
1	tablespoon vanilla
1	teaspoon ground cinnamon

1. Lightly coat the inside of a 3½- or 4-quart slow cooker with nonstick cooking spray; set aside.

2. In a large bowl combine cooked rice, evaporated milk, milk, sugar, and water. Stir in raisins, dried cranberries, and/or dried cherries; butter; vanilla; and cinnamon. Transfer mixture to the prepared cooker.

3. Cover and cook on low-heat setting (do not use high-heat setting) for 2 to 3 hours. Before serving, gently stir mixture.

Nutrition Facts per serving: 204 cal., 6 g total fat (3 g sat. fat), 18 mg chol., 73 mg sodium, 34 g carbo., 1 g fiber, 4 g pro.

A small slow cooker doubles as a fondue and warming pot for this irresistible chocolate sauce that starts by melting candy bars. Although leftovers are highly unlikely, reheat them and serve over ice cream. Include the dippers!

Candy Bar Fondue

MAKES 12 SERVINGS

Prep: 15 minutes
Cook: Low 2 to 2½ hours

4   1.76-ounce bars chocolate-coated nougat bars with almonds, chopped

1   7-ounce bar milk chocolate, chopped

1   7-ounce jar marshmallow creme

¾   cup whipping cream, half-and-half, or light cream

¼   cup finely chopped almonds, toasted (see tip, page 29)

2   to 3 tablespoons almond, hazelnut, or raspberry liqueur

     Dippers (such as filled sugar wafers, pound cake cubes, strawberries, sweet cherries, and/or pineapple pieces)

     Coconut, toasted (see tip, page 29); toffee pieces; and/or finely chopped almonds, toasted (see tip, page 29) (optional)

1. In a 3½-quart slow cooker combine nougat bar, milk chocolate bar, marshmallow creme, and whipping cream.

2. Cover and cook on low-heat setting (do not use high-heat setting) for 2 to 2½ hours. Stir until smooth. Stir in the ¼ cup almonds and the liqueur.

3. To serve, if desired, transfer chocolate mixture to a 1½-quart slow cooker. Keep warm, covered, on warm setting or low-heat setting for up to 1 hour. Stir occasionally.

4. Spear dippers with fondue forks. Dip into chocolate mixture, swirling as you dip. If desired, dip into coconut, toffee pieces, and/or additional almonds to coat.

Nutrition Facts per serving fondue: 294 cal., 16 g total fat (8 g sat. fat), 25 mg chol., 55 mg sodium, 34 g carbo., 1 g fiber, 3 g pro.

Double-Duty Dinners

Curry lovers as well as newcomers to the flavor will want to try this recipe. Honey and mustard add a pleasing dimension to the dish.

Honey Curry Chicken

❖

MAKES 6 SERVINGS + RESERVES

Prep: 20 minutes
Cook: Low 5 to 6 hours, High 2½ to 3 hours

1	large onion, halved lengthwise and sliced
8	chicken breast halves (with bone) (about 4½ pounds total), skinned
½	teaspoon salt
¼	teaspoon black pepper
¼	cup honey
¼	cup Dijon-style mustard
2	tablespoons butter or margarine, melted
1	tablespoon curry powder
2	large red sweet peppers, cut into bite-size strips
3	cups hot cooked white or brown rice

1. Place onion in a 5- to 6-quart slow cooker. Add chicken. Sprinkle chicken with salt and black pepper. In a small bowl stir together honey, mustard, butter, and curry powder; pour over mixture in cooker. Add sweet pepper.

2. Cover and cook on low-heat setting for 5 to 6 hours or on high-heat setting for 2½ to 3 hours.

3. Remove chicken and vegetables from cooker, reserving cooking liquid. Strain liquid. Reserve 2 chicken breast halves, 1 cup vegetables, and ½ cup cooking liquid; store as directed below.

4. Serve the remaining chicken and vegetables with hot cooked rice. Spoon enough of the remaining cooking liquid over chicken and vegetables to moisten.

Nutrition Facts per serving: 367 cal., 5 g total fat (2 g sat. fat), 104 mg chol., 435 mg sodium, 36 g carbo., 1 g fiber, 43 g pro.

To Store Reserves: Place chicken, vegetables, and cooking liquid in separate airtight containers. Seal and chill for up to 3 days. Use in Asian Chicken Salad, page 327.

Napa cabbage—sometimes called Chinese cabbage—is worth seeking out. Its crinkly texture and delicate flavor bring a unique twist to chicken salad.

Asian Chicken Salad

MAKES 4 SERVINGS

Start to Finish: 20 minutes

Reserved Honey Curry Chicken* (see recipe, page 326)

½ cup mayonnaise or salad dressing

3 cups shredded napa cabbage or iceberg lettuce

1 medium carrot, chopped (½ cup)

½ cup chopped peeled jicama or carrot

½ cup fresh snow pea pods, thinly sliced lengthwise

½ cup chow mein noodles

1. In a small bowl whisk together the reserved cooking liquid and the mayonnaise until smooth; set aside. Remove meat from reserved chicken breast halves; discard bones. Chop chicken and reserved vegetables.

2. In a large bowl combine the reserved chicken, the reserved vegetables, the cabbage, carrot, jicama, and pea pods. Stir mayonnaise mixture, then add to chicken mixture; toss gently to coat. Sprinkle individual servings with chow mein noodles.

Nutrition Facts per serving: 406 cal., 27 g total fat (6 g sat. fat), 62 mg chol., 439 mg sodium, 19 g carbo., 3 g fiber, 22 g pro.

*Note: There should be 2 reserved chicken breast halves, 1 cup reserved vegetables, and ½ cup reserved cooking liquid.

Sweet, salty, spicy, and sour—like so many Thai-inspired dishes, this tasty recipe pushes all kinds of flavor buttons! (Photo on page 268.)

Thai Chicken over Rice Noodles

❖

MAKES 4 SERVINGS + RESERVES

Prep: 25 minutes
Cook: Low 6 to 7 hours,
High 3 to 3½ hours,
plus 30 minutes (high)

8	skinless, boneless chicken breast halves (about 2½ pounds total)
1	15-ounce can whole straw mushrooms, drained
1	14-ounce can chicken broth
1	large red sweet pepper, cut into 1-inch pieces
8	green onions, cut into ½-inch pieces
¼	cup fish sauce
1	to 2 fresh serrano chile peppers, seeded and finely chopped (see tip, page 10)
1	tablespoon ground ginger
6	cloves garlic, minced
1	14-ounce can unsweetened coconut milk
1½	cups bean sprouts
1	8-ounce package dried flat rice noodles
2	tablespoons cornstarch
¼	cup chopped peanuts
	Fresh cilantro sprig (optional)

1. In a 4- to 5-quart slow cooker combine chicken, drained mushrooms, broth, sweet pepper, green onion, fish sauce, chile pepper, ginger, and garlic.

2. Cover and cook on low-heat setting for 6 to 7 hours or high-heat setting for 3 to 3½ hours. If using low-heat setting, turn to high-heat setting. Add coconut milk and bean sprouts. Cover and cook for 30 minutes more.

3. Before serving, cook noodles in a large amount of boiling salted water for 5 to 7 minutes or until tender but still firm; drain. Return to saucepan; cover to keep warm.

4. Remove chicken from cooker; cover and set aside. Strain cooking liquid, reserving vegetables. Reserve 4 chicken breast halves, 1½ cups vegetables, 2¼ cups cooking liquid, and 1 cup cooked noodles; store as directed below.

5. For sauce, in a medium saucepan stir together cornstarch and 2 tablespoons cold water; stir in the remaining cooking liquid. Cook and stir over medium heat until thickened and bubbly. Cook and stir for 2 minutes more. Toss the remaining vegetables and the remaining noodles with some of the sauce; transfer to a serving platter. Top with the remaining chicken; spoon the remaining sauce over chicken. Sprinkle with peanuts. If desired, garnish with a fresh cilantro sprig.

Nutrition Facts per serving: 577 cal., 34 g total fat (26 g sat. fat), 83 mg chol., 1,471 mg sodium, 29 g carbo., 3 g fiber, 40 g pro.

To Store Reserves: Chop chicken (about 3¼ cups). Place chicken, vegetables, and cooking liquid in an airtight container. Snip noodles; place in a separate airtight container. Seal and chill for up to 3 days. Use in Thai Chicken and Coconut-Red Curry Soup, page 329.

If you've ever enjoyed Tom Ka Kai, a specialty soup from Thailand, you'll know exactly where the inspiration for this fascinating bowl came from! (Photo on page 268.)

Thai Chicken and Coconut-Red Curry Soup

❖

MAKES 4 SERVINGS

Start to Finish: 25 minutes

1½ cups sliced baby bok choy or bok choy

2 medium carrots, bias-sliced (1 cup)

2 tablespoons cooking oil

Reserved Thai Chicken over Rice Noodles* (see recipe, page 328)

1 14-ounce can unsweetened coconut milk

¾ cup chicken broth

1 tablespoon lime juice

2 teaspoons red curry paste

¼ cup small fresh basil leaves

1. In a large saucepan cook bok choy and carrot in hot oil over medium heat until crisp-tender.

2. Add the reserved chicken mixture, the reserved cooked noodles, the coconut milk, broth, lime juice, and curry paste; heat through. Before serving, top with basil leaves.

Nutrition Facts per serving: 510 cal., 17 g total fat (10 g sat. fat), 83 mg chol., 1,153 mg sodium, 50 g carbo., 3 g fiber, 40 g pro.

*Note: There should be about 3¼ cups reserved chopped chicken and 1½ cups reserved vegetables mixed with 2¼ cups reserved cooking liquid as well as 1 cup reserved cooked noodles.

Andouille (an-DOO-ee) is a smoky, spicy sausage that's often used in Cajun specialties. Combine it with a jar of picante sauce and you can expect bold results.

Stewed Chicken and Andouille

**MAKES 4 SERVINGS +
RESERVES**

Prep: 25 minutes
Cook: Low 6 to 7 hours,
High 3 to 3½ hours

1	pound andouille sausage, cut in ¾-inch-thick slices
8	chicken thighs (2½ to 3 pounds total), skinned
1	medium onion, cut into thin wedges
1	16-ounce jar picante sauce
⅓	cup water
2	tablespoons quick-cooking tapioca
2	teaspoons Worcestershire sauce
1	teaspoon dried thyme, crushed
2	cups frozen cut okra
6	ounces dried egg noodles

1. In a large skillet cook sausage over medium heat until brown. Drain off fat. Set aside.

2. In a 4- to 5-quart slow cooker combine chicken and onion. Add sausage, picante sauce, water, tapioca, Worcestershire sauce, and thyme. Top with frozen okra.

3. Cover and cook on low-heat setting for 6 to 7 hours or on high-heat setting 3 to 3½ hours.

4. Before serving, cook egg noodles according to package directions; drain.

5. Reserve 4 chicken thighs and 1 cup sausage; store as directed below. Serve the remaining chicken-sausage mixture over hot cooked noodles.

Nutrition Facts per serving: 419 cal., 8 g total fat (2 g sat. fat), 154 mg chol., 1,481 mg sodium, 50 g carbo., 3 g fiber, 36 g pro.

To Store Reserves: Place chicken and sausage in an airtight container. Seal and chill for up to 3 days. (Or freeze for up to 3 months. Thaw in the refrigerator overnight before using.) Use in Bayou Shrimp and Rice, page 331.

It's so easy—cook rice revved up with picante sauce and
stir in shrimp plus leftover Stewed Chicken and Andouille.
Presto! A former Cajun dish becomes a Creole dish
reminiscent of jambalaya.

Bayou Shrimp and Rice

❖

MAKES 4 SERVINGS

Start to Finish: 40 minutes

12	ounces fresh or frozen medium shrimp in shells
	Reserved chicken and sausage from Stewed Chicken and Andouille* (see recipe, page 330)
2¼	cups water
1¼	cups bottled picante sauce
2	teaspoons Worcestershire sauce
1	cup uncooked long grain rice
	Salt (optional)
	Black pepper (optional)
	Bottled hot pepper sauce (optional)

1. Thaw shrimp, if frozen. Peel and devein shrimp. Rinse shrimp; pat dry with paper towels. Set aside. Remove meat from the reserved chicken thighs; discard bones. Chop chicken; set aside.

2. In a large skillet stir together water, picante sauce, and Worcestershire sauce. Bring to boiling; stir in rice. Return to boiling; reduce heat. Cover and simmer for 15 minutes.

3. Stir in shrimp, chicken, and the reserved sausage. Return to boiling; reduce heat. Cover and simmer about 5 minutes or until shrimp is opaque and rice is tender.

4. Remove from heat. Season to taste with salt and black pepper. If desired, serve with hot pepper sauce.

Nutrition Facts per serving: 437 cal., 7 g total fat (2 g sat. fat), 211 mg chol., 1,261 mg sodium, 45 g carbo., 1 g fiber, 44 g pro.

*Note: There should be 4 reserved chicken thighs and 1 cup reserved sausage.

Succotash is a mix of lima beans and corn. Why such an exotic word for such a simple blend? It was derived from a term for boiled corn that was used by the Narragansett Native Americans. Here the duo adds color and heartiness to a creamy soup.

Chicken and Succotash Stew

MAKES 4 TO 6 SERVINGS + RESERVES

Prep: 20 minutes
Cook: Low 8 to 9 hours,
High 4 to 4½ hours

2½	pounds skinless, boneless chicken thighs, cut into 1-inch pieces
1	16-ounce package frozen baby lima beans, thawed
1	16-ounce package frozen whole kernel corn, thawed
2	10.75-ounce cans condensed cream of chicken soup
1	14-ounce can chicken broth or vegetable broth
4	medium carrots, thinly sliced (2 cups)
1	large onion, chopped (1 cup)
1	teaspoon dried sage, crushed
¼	teaspoon black pepper

1. In a 5- to 6-quart slow cooker combine chicken, lima beans, corn, soup, broth, carrot, onion, sage, and pepper.

2. Cover and cook on low-heat setting for 8 to 9 hours or on high-heat setting for 4 to 4½ hours.

3. Reserve 6½ cups (about half) of the stew; store as directed below. Serve the remaining stew immediately.

Nutrition Facts per serving: 402 cal., 11 g total fat (3 g sat. fat), 120 mg chol., 900 mg sodium, 38 g carbo., 7 g fiber, 37 g pro.

To Store Reserves: Place stew in an airtight container. Seal and chill for up to 3 days. Use in Quick Chicken Pot Pie, page 333.

Your grandmother or great-grandmother may have made a dish similar to this one. During the Great Depression succotash was served in a casserole and topped with a piecrust. The comforting, homey stew is due for a revival.

Quick Chicken Pot Pie

❖

MAKES 6 SERVINGS

Prep: 20 minutes
Bake: 12 minutes
Oven: 400°F

Reserved Chicken and Succotash Stew* (see recipe, page 332)

1   cup shredded cheddar cheese
2   tablespoons cornstarch
1   7.5-ounce package (10) refrigerated biscuits

1. Preheat oven to 400°F. In a large saucepan stir together the reserved stew, ¾ cup of the cheese, and the cornstarch. Cook and stir over medium heat just until mixture comes to boiling. Simmer, uncovered, for 2 minutes.

2. Transfer mixture to a 3-quart rectangular baking dish. Cut each biscuit into quarters. Arrange biscuit quarters on top of hot mixture. Sprinkle with the remaining ¼ cup cheese.

3. Bake about 12 minutes or until biscuits are golden.

Nutrition Facts per serving: 467 cal., 19 g total fat (7 g sat. fat), 100 mg chol., 1,110 mg sodium, 44 g carbo., 5 g fiber, 32 g pro.

*Note: There should be 6½ cups reserved stew.

At first glance, some Indian-inspired recipes look long. But take another look—many of the ingredients are spices, which take very little time to measure and add so much pleasure.

Indian-Spiced Chicken Thighs

❖

MAKES 6 SERVINGS + RESERVES

Prep: 20 minutes
Cook: Low 7 to 8 hours,
High 3½ to 4 hours

2	cups thinly sliced onion (4 medium)
¼	cup quick-cooking tapioca
8	cloves garlic, minced
4	to 4½ pounds skinless, boneless chicken thighs (24 to 30)
1	tablespoon ground cumin
2	teaspoons salt
2	teaspoons curry powder
1½	teaspoons ground coriander
½	teaspoon ground cinnamon
¼	teaspoon ground cloves
¼	teaspoon cayenne pepper
¼	teaspoon black pepper
1	14-ounce can chicken broth
1	6-ounce carton plain yogurt
3	cups hot cooked basmati rice
	Snipped fresh mint (optional)
	Finely shredded lemon peel (optional)
	Slivered almonds, toasted (optional) (see tip, page 29)

1. Place onion in a 5- to 7-quart slow cooker; sprinkle with tapioca and garlic. Add chicken. Sprinkle chicken with cumin, salt, curry powder, coriander, cinnamon, cloves, cayenne pepper, and black pepper. Pour broth over mixture in cooker.

2. Cover and cook on low-heat setting for 7 to 8 hours or on high-heat setting for 3½ to 4 hours.

3. Reserve half of the chicken thighs (12 to 15). Transfer the remaining chicken to a serving platter; cover with foil to keep warm. Using a slotted spoon, remove half of the onion (about 1 cup) from cooking liquid. Store the reserved chicken and onion as directed below.

4. For sauce, whisk yogurt into the remaining cooking liquid. Serve chicken and sauce with hot cooked basmati rice. If desired, sprinkle with mint, lemon peel, and almonds.

Nutrition Facts per serving: 347 cal., 7 g total fat (2 g sat. fat), 123 mg chol., 645 mg sodium, 33 g carbo., 1 g fiber, 35 g pro.

To Store Reserves: Cut chicken into ¾-inch pieces. Place chicken and onion in an airtight container. Seal and chill for up to 3 days. Use in Coconut Chicken and Couscous, page 335.

If you enjoyed the Indian-Spiced Chicken Thighs, you're in for a treat. Simply add some nutty-good coconut milk and a little extra spice, and you'll have tonight's equally intriguing meal ready in minutes.

Coconut Chicken and Couscous

MAKES 6 SERVINGS

Start to Finish: 20 minutes

Reserved chicken-onion mixture from Indian-Spiced Chicken Thighs* (see recipe, page 334)

1	14-ounce can unsweetened coconut milk
4	teaspoons cornstarch
½	teaspoon curry powder
¼	cup raisins
3	cups hot cooked couscous
	Shredded coconut, toasted (optional) (see tip, page 29)

1. In a large saucepan heat the reserved chicken-onion mixture over medium heat until heated through. In a medium bowl stir together coconut milk, cornstarch, and curry powder; stir into chicken-onion mixture. Stir in raisins.

2. Cook and stir until mixture is thickened and bubbly. Cook and stir for 2 minutes more. Serve with hot cooked couscous. If desired, sprinkle with toasted coconut.

Nutrition Facts per serving: 466 cal., 19 g total fat (12 g sat. fat), 121 mg chol., 647 mg sodium, 37 g carbo., 2 g fiber, 36 g pro.

*Note: There should be about 5½ cups reserved chicken-onion mixture.

White wine, lemon peel, and mushrooms are a winning trio to flavor chicken. And you can't go wrong adding a little cream cheese to the mix. The result is a lusciously sauced dish.

Lemon-Herb Chicken Thighs

MAKES 4 SERVINGS + RESERVES

Prep: 15 minutes
Cook: Low 7 to 8 hours, High 3½ to 4 hours

16 skinless, boneless chicken thighs (about 2¼ pounds total)

2 10.75-ounce cans condensed golden mushroom soup

½ of an 8-ounce tub cream cheese spread with chive and onion

½ cup dry white wine

1 tablespoon finely shredded lemon peel

2 teaspoons dried thyme, crushed

2 cups hot cooked pasta

1. Place chicken in a 5- to 6-quart slow cooker. For sauce, in a medium bowl whisk together soup, cream cheese spread, wine, lemon peel, and thyme. Pour over chicken in cooker.

2. Cover and cook on low-heat setting for 7 to 8 hours or on high-heat setting for 3½ to 4 hours. Skim off fat.

3. Reserve 8 chicken thighs and half of the sauce (about 2 cups); store as directed below. Serve the remaining chicken and sauce over hot cooked pasta.

Nutrition Facts per serving: 371 cal., 13 g total fat (5 g sat. fat), 119 mg chol., 697 mg sodium, 27 g carbo., 2 g fiber, 31 g pro.

To Store Reserves: Place chicken and sauce in an airtight container. Seal and chill for up to 3 days. Do not freeze. Use in Chicken with Spinach Sauce, page 337.

This recipe is a nod to a good old-fashioned dish, Chicken à la King—chicken in a cream sauce served over rice or toast. Here it is updated with fresh spinach and the spark of lemon and wine from the reserved recipe ingredients.

5 Ingredient Recipe

Chicken with Spinach Sauce

✦

MAKES 4 SERVINGS

Start to Finish: 15 minutes

Reserved Lemon-Herb Chicken Thighs* (see recipe, page 336)

1   4.5-ounce jar (drained weight) sliced mushrooms, drained

3   cups shredded fresh spinach

4   English muffins, split, toasted, and cut into quarters

¼   cup finely shredded Parmesan cheese

1. In a large saucepan or Dutch oven combine the reserved chicken-sauce mixture and the drained mushrooms. Bring to boiling over medium heat, stirring occasionally. Stir in spinach. Cover and cook over medium-low heat for 1 to 2 minutes or just until spinach is wilted.

2. Serve chicken-sauce mixture over English muffin quarters and sprinkle with cheese.

Nutrition Facts per serving: 433 cal., 15 g total fat (6 g sat. fat), 122 mg chol., 1,171 mg sodium, 35 g carbo., 3 g fiber, 35 g pro.

*Note: There should be 8 reserved chicken thighs mixed with about 2 cups reserved sauce.

*Leeks are related to onions and garlic, but their flavor
is more mellow, making them merge well with the other flavors
in this dish. Hint: Look for leeks with clean white ends
and fresh, green tops.*

Garlic and Lemon Chicken with Leeks

**MAKES 4 SERVINGS +
RESERVES**

Prep: 30 minutes
Cook: Low 4 to 4½ hours,
High 2 to 2½ hours

⅓	cup all-purpose flour
½	teaspoon salt
½	teaspoon black pepper
6	skinless, boneless chicken breast halves (2¼ to 2½ pounds total)
3	tablespoons butter or margarine
6	medium leeks, thinly sliced (2 cups)
10	cloves garlic, thinly sliced
2	tablespoons quick-cooking tapioca, crushed
¼	teaspoon salt
1	lemon
1½	cups chicken broth
2	cups hot mashed potatoes
	Snipped fresh Italian (flat-leaf) parsley

1. In a shallow dish combine flour, the ½ teaspoon salt, and the pepper. Dip chicken in flour mixture, turning to coat. In a large skillet melt butter over medium heat. Cook chicken, half at a time, on both sides in hot butter until brown. Drain off fat.

2. Meanwhile, in a 4- to 5-quart slow cooker combine leek and garlic. Sprinkle with tapioca and the ¼ teaspoon salt. Add chicken. Finely shred enough lemon peel to make ½ teaspoon; store as directed below. Peel the lemon, removing all of the white pith; discard peel. Thinly slice the lemon; remove seeds. Place lemon slices on chicken. Pour broth over mixture in cooker.

3. Cover and cook on low-heat setting for 4 to 4½ hours or on high-heat setting for 2 to 2½ hours.

4. Reserve 2 chicken breast halves; store as directed below. Transfer the remaining chicken to dinner plates. Using a slotted spoon, remove leek from cooker, reserving cooking liquid. Spoon leek over chicken. Serve with hot mashed potatoes. If desired, spoon some of the cooking liquid over each serving; discard remaining liquid. Sprinkle with parsley.

Nutrition Facts per serving: 454 cal., 13 g total fat (6 g sat. fat), 126 mg chol., 1,172 mg sodium, 38 g carbo., 3 g fiber, 44 g pro.

To Store Reserves: Place lemon peel in a small airtight container. Chop chicken (2½ cups). Place chicken in a second airtight container. Seal and chill for up to 3 days. Use in Chicken and Mushroom Risotto, page 339.

Treating your family to a rich, creamy, and moist main-dish risotto is much easier than you think—especially when you start with leftovers. You'll enjoy the way the lemon perks up the earthy mushroom flavors.

Chicken and Mushroom Risotto

❋

MAKES 4 SERVINGS

Prep: 20 minutes
Cook: 45 minutes

2	cups sliced fresh mushrooms
1	medium onion, chopped (½ cup)
3	tablespoons olive oil
1¼	cups uncooked Arborio rice
2	14-ounce cans chicken broth
½	cup dry white wine
	Reserved chicken and lemon peel from Garlic and Lemon Chicken with Leeks* (see recipe, page 338)
½	cup finely shredded Parmesan cheese
¼	teaspoon black pepper
	Finely shredded Parmesan cheese (optional)
	Freshly ground or cracked black pepper (optional)

1. In a large saucepan cook mushrooms and onion in hot oil over medium heat about 8 minutes or until onion is tender, stirring occasionally. Add rice; cook and stir until rice starts to brown. (Rice may stick to bottom of pan but will release when wine is added.)

2. Meanwhile, in another large saucepan bring broth to boiling. Cover and reduce heat to low.

3. Add wine to rice mixture, stirring to loosen rice from bottom of pan. Cook, uncovered, about 2 minutes or until wine is absorbed, stirring frequently. Add 1 cup of the broth. Continue to cook over medium heat until liquid is absorbed, stirring frequently. Add another ½ cup of the broth. Cook until liquid is nearly absorbed, stirring frequently. Continue adding broth, ½ cup at a time, and cooking after each addition until broth is nearly absorbed, stirring frequently. When the last of the broth has been added, cook until mixture is creamy. (Total cooking time should take 25 to 30 minutes after the wine is absorbed.)

4. Stir in the reserved chopped chicken, the reserved lemon peel, the ½ cup Parmesan cheese, and the ¼ teaspoon pepper. Cook until heated through but still creamy, stirring frequently. If desired, sprinkle individual servings with additional Parmesan cheese and additional pepper.

Nutrition Facts per serving: 460 cal., 18 g total fat (5 g sat. fat), 66 mg chol., 1,128 mg sodium, 40 g carbo., 1 g fiber, 29 g pro.

*Note: There should be 2½ cups reserved chopped chicken and ½ teaspoon reserved lemon peel.

This dish is for times when you're looking for a simple,
yet refined meal that will ease you into a relaxed evening
at the end of a hectic day.

Chicken with Fennel Braised in White Wine

❖

**MAKES 4 SERVINGS +
RESERVES**

Prep: 20 minutes
Cook: Low 9 to 10 hours,
High 4½ to 5 hours

2	large fennel bulbs, trimmed and sliced (3 cups)
4	medium carrots, coarsely shredded (2 cups)
¾	cup sliced celery
3½	to 4 pounds skinless, boneless chicken thighs (18 to 24)
3	tablespoons quick-cooking tapioca, crushed
2	teaspoons dried thyme, crushed
1	teaspoon salt
¼	teaspoon black pepper
⅔	cup dry white wine
⅔	cup chicken broth
2	cups hot cooked pasta or rice
	Grated Parmesan cheese (optional)
	Snipped fresh fennel tops (optional)

1. In a 5- to 7-quart slow cooker combine sliced fennel, carrot, and celery. Sprinkle chicken with tapioca. Add chicken. Sprinkle with thyme, salt, and pepper. Pour wine and broth over mixture in cooker.

2. Cover and cook on low-heat setting for 9 to 10 hours or on high-heat setting for 4½ to 5 hours.

3. Reserve half of the chicken thighs (9 to 12) and 1½ cups of the vegetable mixture; store as directed below. Serve the remaining chicken and vegetable mixture over hot cooked pasta. If desired, sprinkle with cheese and fennel tops.

Nutrition Facts per serving: 417 cal., 9 g total fat (2 g sat. fat), 158 mg chol., 606 mg sodium, 33 g carbo., 4 g fiber, 45 g pro.

To Store Reserves: Coarsely chop chicken (2½ cups). Place chicken and vegetable mixture in an airtight container. Seal and chill for up to 3 days. Use in Quick Chicken and Dumplings, page 341.

Who says comfort food has to be tame? Here garlic, fennel, and rosemary charge a classic dish with loads of flavor.

Quick Chicken and Dumplings

❖

MAKES 4 SERVINGS

Prep: 20 minutes
Bake: 20 minutes
Stand: 10 minutes
Oven: 375°F

Reserved Chicken with Fennel Braised in White Wine* (see recipe, page 340)

1 15.25-ounce can whole kernel corn, drained

1 10.75-ounce can condensed cream of chicken or cream of mushroom soup

½ cup shredded cheddar cheese

½ teaspoon dried rosemary, crushed

4 cloves garlic, minced

1 7.5-ounce package (10) refrigerated buttermilk biscuits

1. Preheat oven to 375°F. In a large saucepan stir together the reserved chicken-vegetable mixture, the drained corn, soup, cheese, rosemary, and garlic. Cook over medium heat until cheese is melted and mixture is bubbly. Transfer to a greased 2-quart square baking dish.

2. For dumplings, cut each biscuit into quarters. Arrange biscuit pieces on top of hot chicken-vegetable mixture.

3. Bake for 20 to 25 minutes or until mixture is bubbly and biscuits are lightly browned. Let stand for 10 minutes before serving.

Nutrition Facts per serving: 499 cal., 19 g total fat (7 g sat. fat), 180 mg chol., 1,380 mg sodium, 31 g carbo., 4 g fiber, 48 g pro.

*Note: There should be 2½ cups reserved chopped chicken mixed with 1½ cups reserved vegetable mixture.

Toasted sesame oil is made from toasted sesame seeds; rich brown in color, with a concentrated flavor, a little goes a long way to add nutty intrigue to dishes. Refrigerate the oil to delay rancidity.

Sesame Chicken

MAKES 4 SERVINGS + RESERVES

Prep: 25 minutes
Cook: Low 6 to 7 hours,
High 3 to 3½ hours
Stand: 5 minutes

3	to 3½ pounds skinless, boneless chicken thighs or chicken breast halves
1	8-ounce can sliced water chestnuts, drained
1	4.5-ounce jar (drained weight) sliced mushrooms, drained
3	tablespoons quick-cooking tapioca, crushed
3	tablespoons honey
3	tablespoons rice vinegar
2	tablespoons frozen orange juice concentrate, thawed
4	teaspoons toasted sesame oil
¾	teaspoon salt
6	cloves garlic, minced
1	large red or green sweet pepper, cut into strips
1	6-ounce package frozen snow pea pods, thawed
5	cups hot cooked rice
2	tablespoons sesame seeds, toasted (see tip, page 29)

1. Place chicken in a 4- to 5-quart slow cooker. In a medium bowl stir together drained water chestnuts, drained mushrooms, tapioca, honey, vinegar, orange juice concentrate, sesame oil, salt, and garlic. Pour over chicken in cooker. Add sweet pepper.

2. Cover and cook on low-heat setting for 6 to 7 hours or on high-heat setting for 3 to 3½ hours. Turn off cooker. Stir in pea pods. Let stand, covered, for 5 minutes.

3. Reserve half of the chicken and half of the cooked rice; store as directed below. Serve the remaining chicken and the vegetable mixture over the remaining hot cooked rice. Sprinkle with sesame seeds.

Nutrition Facts per serving: 516 cal., 10 g total fat (1 g sat. fat), 98 mg chol., 576 mg sodium, 59 g carbo., 4 g fiber, 46 g pro.

To Store Reserves: Coarsely chop chicken (2¾ cups). Place chicken and rice in separate airtight containers. Seal and chill for up to 3 days. (Or freeze for up to 3 months. Thaw in refrigerator overnight before using.) Use in Spicy Chicken Fried Rice, page 343.

You'll want to make this often: Combine extra rice and leftover Chinese fare with a few ingredients for a whole new recipe. Attention experimental cooks: Use this basic concept to inspire your own fried rice creations!

Spicy Chicken Fried Rice

MAKES 4 SERVINGS

Start to Finish: 25 minutes

2	tablespoons cooking oil
2	eggs, slightly beaten
1	large onion, chopped (1 cup)
1	cup chopped fresh mushrooms
	Reserved chicken and rice from Sesame Chicken* (see recipe, page 342)
⅓	cup reduced-sodium soy sauce
2	tablespoons water
½	teaspoon ground ginger
¼	teaspoon cayenne pepper
	Thinly sliced green onion
	Reduced-sodium soy sauce

1. In a large skillet heat 1 tablespoon of the oil over medium heat. Add eggs; lift and tilt the skillet to form a thin layer of egg. Cook for 1 to 2 minutes or until egg is set. Invert skillet over a baking sheet to remove cooked egg; cut into short, narrow strips and set aside.

2. In the same skillet cook and stir onion and mushrooms in the remaining 1 tablespoon oil just until onion is tender. Add the reserved chopped chicken; cook until chicken is heated through.

3. Stir in the ⅓ cup soy sauce, the water, ginger, and cayenne pepper. Add the reserved cooked rice. Cook and stir for 3 to 4 minutes or until heated through. Stir in the egg strips. Sprinkle with green onion. Serve with additional soy sauce.

Nutrition Facts per serving: 528 cal., 15 g total fat (3 g sat. fat), 204 mg chol., 1,109 mg sodium, 47 g carbo., 1 g fiber, 48 g pro.

*Note: There should be 2¾ cups reserved chopped chicken and 2½ cups reserved cooked rice.

Drumsticks and thighs star in this hearty dish. The dark meat imparts lots of flavor as it slowly cooks, and the chicken stays pleasingly moist and retains its texture. With just one bite, you'll declare dark meat to be the best part of the chicken.

Chipotle Stewed Chicken

MAKES 4 SERVINGS + RESERVES

Prep: 20 minutes
Cook: Low 8 to 9 hours,
High 4 to 4½ hours

- 2 medium red sweet peppers, cut into 1-inch pieces
- 1 medium onion, cut into thin wedges
- 2 tablespoons quick-cooking tapioca
- 8 chicken drumsticks, skinned
- 8 chicken thighs, skinned
- 1 14.5-ounce can diced tomatoes, undrained
- 1 6-ounce can tomato paste
- 2 to 3 tablespoons finely chopped canned chipotle pepper in adobo sauce (see tip, page 10)
- 2 teaspoons sugar
- 1 teaspoon salt
- 2 16-ounce packages refrigerated mashed potatoes

1. In a 5- to 6-quart slow cooker combine sweet pepper and onion. Sprinkle with tapioca. Add chicken drumsticks and thighs.

2. In a medium bowl combine undrained tomatoes, tomato paste, chipotle pepper, sugar, and salt. Pour over mixture in cooker.

3. Cover and cook on low-heat setting for 8 to 9 hours or on high-heat setting for 4 to 4½ hours.

4. Reserve 4 drumsticks, 4 thighs, and 1 cup sauce; store as directed below. Heat mashed potatoes according to package directions. Serve the remaining chicken and sauce with hot mashed potatoes.

Nutrition Facts per serving: 477 cal., 9 g total fat (2 g sat. fat), 136 mg chol., 1,110 mg sodium, 52 g carbo., 4 g fiber, 43 g pro.

To Store Reserves: Place chicken and sauce in separate airtight containers. Seal and chill for up to 3 days. Use in Wraps with Lime Cream, page 345.

Lime juice paired with cilantro ranks right up there as one of the best ways to add spark to leftovers. Taste the delicious combo in this sprightly dish.

Wraps with Lime Cream

MAKES 4 SERVINGS

Start to Finish: 20 minutes

Reserved Chipotle Stewed Chicken* (see recipe, page 344)
¼ cup mayonnaise or salad dressing
¼ cup dairy sour cream
1 tablespoon lime juice
¼ teaspoon salt
4 10-inch flour tortillas, warmed (see tip, page 118)
4 lettuce leaves
2 tablespoons snipped fresh cilantro (optional)
Lime wedges

1. Remove meat from the reserved chicken; discard bones. Shred chicken by pulling two forks through it in opposite directions. In a large skillet heat chicken and the reserved sauce over medium heat until heated through.

2. Meanwhile, in a small bowl stir together mayonnaise, sour cream, lime juice, and salt.

3. To assemble wraps, line warm tortillas with lettuce leaves. Using a slotted spoon, spoon chicken mixture onto tortillas just below centers. Top with sour cream mixture and, if desired, cilantro. Fold bottom edge of each tortilla up and over filling. Fold one side in slightly, then roll up from the bottom. Serve wraps with lime wedges.

Nutrition Facts per serving: 486 cal., 23 g total fat (6 g sat. fat), 146 mg chol., 688 mg sodium, 28 g carbo., 2 g fiber, 39 g pro.

*Note: There should be 4 reserved chicken drumsticks, 4 reserved chicken thighs, and 1 cup reserved sauce.

If you've been getting sweet-and-sour sauce from a jar, take just a few minutes more and make it from scratch. It's not difficult, and the little extra effort adds a lot of great taste to this dish.

Sweet-and-Sour Turkey Thighs

MAKES 4 TO 6 SERVINGS + RESERVES

Prep: 20 minutes
Cook: Low 6 to 7 hours, High 3 to 3½ hours

1	large onion, cut into thin wedges
2	tablespoons quick-cooking tapioca
6	turkey thighs (6 pounds), skinned
1	teaspoon garlic powder
1	teaspoon lemon-pepper seasoning
½	teaspoon ground ginger
½	cup frozen pineapple juice concentrate, thawed
¼	cup red wine vinegar
¼	cup soy sauce
2	cups hot cooked rice

1. Place onion in a 5- to 6-quart slow cooker. Sprinkle with tapioca. Add turkey. Sprinkle turkey with garlic powder, lemon-pepper seasoning, and ginger. In a small bowl stir together pineapple juice concentrate, vinegar, and soy sauce; pour over mixture in cooker.

2. Cover and cook on low-heat setting for 6 to 7 hours or on high-heat setting for 3 to 3½ hours.

3. Remove turkey from cooker; strain ⅔ cup of the cooking liquid. Reserve 2 turkey thighs and the strained cooking liquid; store as directed below. Serve the remaining turkey and unstrained cooking liquid with hot cooked rice.

Nutrition Facts per serving: 510 cal., 8 g total fat (3 g sat. fat), 231 mg chol., 994 mg sodium, 43 g carbo., 1 g fiber, 63 g pro.

To Store Reserves: Place turkey and cooking liquid in separate airtight containers. Seal and chill for up to 3 days. (Or freeze for up to 3 months. Thaw in refrigerator overnight before using.) Use in Turkey Cabbage Slaw, page 347.

Transform last night's dinner into a bright, crunchy salad for a lunch you'll look forward to all morning. To tote it to the office, pack the salad and the dressing separately and combine them when you're ready to eat.

Turkey Cabbage Slaw

❖

MAKES 4 SERVINGS

Start to Finish: 25 minutes

Reserved turkey and cooking liquid from Sweet-and-Sour Turkey Thighs* (see recipe, page 346)

⅓ cup salad oil

2 tablespoons rice vinegar

¼ teaspoon salt

⅛ teaspoon black pepper

1 3-ounce package ramen noodles

6 cups packaged shredded cabbage with carrot (coleslaw mix)

½ cup sliced green onion (4)

½ cup chopped walnuts or almonds, toasted (see tip, page 29)

1. Remove meat from the reserved turkey thighs; discard bones. Chop turkey; set aside. Remove any fat from the reserved cooking liquid. For dressing, in a small bowl whisk together cooking liquid, oil, vinegar, salt, and pepper.

2. In a very large bowl break up ramen noodles (discard seasoning packet or reserve for another use). Add turkey, coleslaw mix, and green onion. Drizzle with dressing; toss gently to coat. Cover and chill for up to 1 hour.

3. Before serving, sprinkle with nuts.

Nutrition Facts per serving: 594 cal., 36 g total fat (5 g sat. fat), 116 mg chol., 670 mg sodium, 31 g carbo., 4 g fiber, 36 g pro.

*Note: There should be 2 reserved turkey thighs and ⅔ cup reserved cooking liquid.

Small amounts of herbs and spices add up to big flavors in this bold and satisfying dish. You'll appreciate the way the turkey thighs cook up nicely tender after the long, slow simmer.

Southwest-Style BBQ Turkey Thighs

❖

MAKES 6 SERVINGS + RESERVES

Prep: 25 minutes
Cook: Low 10 to 12 hours, High 5 to 6 hours

1	14.5-ounce can diced tomatoes, undrained
1	10-ounce can enchilada sauce
1	large red or green sweet pepper, chopped (1 cup)
¼	cup red wine vinegar
3	tablespoons quick-cooking tapioca, crushed
1	to 2 tablespoons finely chopped canned chipotle pepper in adobo sauce (see tip, page 10)
2	teaspoons dried oregano, crushed
1	teaspoon ground cumin
¾	teaspoon salt
¼	to ½ teaspoon cayenne pepper (optional)
¼	teaspoon ground cinnamon
6	cloves garlic, minced
5	turkey thighs (5 pounds), skinned
3	cups hot cooked rice
	Dairy sour cream (optional)

1. For sauce, in a 5- to 7-quart slow cooker stir together undrained tomatoes, enchilada sauce, sweet pepper, vinegar, tapioca, chipotle pepper, oregano, cumin, salt, cayenne pepper (if desired), cinnamon, and garlic. Add turkey, turning to coat with tomato mixture.

2. Cover and cook on low-heat setting for 10 to 12 hours or on high-heat setting for 5 to 6 hours.

3. Remove turkey from cooker. Skim fat from sauce. Reserve 2 turkey thighs and 1 cup sauce; store as directed below. Cut the remaining turkey thighs in half; remove and discard bones. Serve turkey and sauce over hot cooked rice. If desired, top with sour cream.

Nutrition Facts per serving: 406 cal., 7 g total fat (2 g sat. fat), 184 mg chol., 600 mg sodium, 33 g carbo., 1 g fiber, 49 g pro.

To Store Reserves: Place turkey and sauce in separate airtight containers. Seal and chill for up to 3 days. (Or freeze for up to 3 months. Thaw in refrigerator overnight before using.) Use in Turkey and Shrimp Tortilla Soup, page 349.

The tortilla chips, green onion, cilantro, cheese, and lime are all optional—but they make this dish so festive and fun. And because kids love choices, the more garnish options you bring to the table, the more likely you'll entice picky eaters to dig in.

Turkey and Shrimp Tortilla Soup

❖

MAKES 6 SERVINGS

Start to Finish: 30 minutes

8   ounces peeled and deveined fresh or frozen medium shrimp

    Reserved Southwest-Style BBQ Turkey Thighs* (see recipe, page 348)

2   14-ounce cans chicken broth or vegetable broth

1   15-ounce can tomato sauce

1   14.5-ounce can Mexican-style stewed tomatoes, undrained and cut up

¼   cup lime juice

1   to 2 fresh jalapeño or serrano chile peppers, seeded and finely chopped (see tip, page 10)

    Crushed lime tortilla chips (optional)

    Thinly sliced green onion (optional)

    Snipped fresh cilantro (optional)

    Shredded Monterey Jack cheese (optional)

    Lime wedges (optional)

1. Thaw shrimp, if frozen. Rinse shrimp; pat dry with paper towels. Cut shrimp in half lengthwise; set aside. Remove meat from the reserved turkey thighs; discard bones. Chop turkey.

2. In a large saucepan stir together turkey, the reserved sauce, the broth, tomato sauce, undrained tomatoes, lime juice, and chile pepper. Bring to boiling; reduce heat. Cover and simmer for 10 minutes. Stir in shrimp. Simmer, uncovered, for 3 to 5 minutes more or until shrimp are opaque.

3. If desired, top individual servings with tortilla chips, green onion, cilantro, and cheese. If desired, serve with lime wedges.

Nutrition Facts per serving: 265 cal., 5 g total fat (1 g sat. fat), 167 mg chol., 1,383 mg sodium, 13 g carbo., 1 g fiber, 39 g pro.

*Note: There should be 2 reserved turkey thighs and 1 cup reserved sauce.

As you'd expect with two cups of whipping cream, this is an opulent dish! A vinaigrette-tossed salad starring chopped vegetables provides a lively contrast to the entrée.

Creamy Turkey Bow Ties and Cheese

❖

MAKES 6 SERVINGS + RESERVES

Prep: 20 minutes
Cook: Low 3 to 4 hours

4	cups chopped cooked turkey (about 1¼ pounds)
2	large onions, chopped (2 cups)
2	cups whipping cream
8	ounces American cheese, cubed
8	ounces process Swiss cheese slices, torn
1	teaspoon dried sage, crushed
½	teaspoon black pepper
16	ounces dried bow tie pasta

1. In a 4- to 5-quart slow cooker combine turkey, onion, cream, American cheese, Swiss cheese, sage, and pepper.

2. Cover and cook on low-heat setting (do not use high-heat setting) for 3 to 4 hours.

3. Before serving, cook pasta according to package directions; drain. Stir cheese mixture in cooker. Stir in cooked pasta.

4. Reserve 2½ cups of the pasta mixture; store as directed below. Serve the remaining pasta mixture immediately.

Nutrition Facts per serving: 755 cal., 43 g total fat (25 g sat. fat), 186 mg chol., 886 mg sodium, 49 g carbo., 2 g fiber, 43 g pro.

To Store Reserves: Place pasta mixture in an airtight container. Seal and chill for up to 3 days. Use in Turkey and Asparagus Strata, page 351.

This clever rendition of the classic brunch dish is made extra hearty with pasta. A melon-and-apple salad would provide a nice, bright accompaniment.

Turkey and Asparagus Strata

❖

MAKES 6 SERVINGS

Prep: 15 minutes
Chill: 2 to 24 hours
Bake: 1 hour
Stand: 10 minutes
Oven: 325°F

1½ cups seasoned croutons
Reserved Creamy Turkey
Bow Ties and Cheese*
(see recipe, page 350)
1 10-ounce package frozen
cut asparagus, thawed and
well drained
4 eggs, slightly beaten
1¼ cups milk
1 tablespoon dry mustard
½ teaspoon onion powder
⅛ teaspoon ground nutmeg

1. Spread croutons in a greased 2-quart square baking dish. In a medium bowl combine the reserved pasta mixture and the asparagus. Spoon pasta mixture evenly over croutons.

2. In the same bowl whisk together eggs, milk, dry mustard, onion powder, and nutmeg. Pour evenly over pasta mixture in baking dish. Cover and chill for 2 to 24 hours.

3. Preheat oven to 325°F. Cover and bake for 30 minutes. Bake, uncovered, for 30 to 45 minutes more or until the internal temperature registers 170°F on an instant-read thermometer. Let stand for 10 minutes before serving.

Nutrition Facts per serving: 389 cal., 21 g total fat (11 g sat. fat), 208 mg chol., 490 mg sodium, 28 g carbo., 2 g fiber, 23 g pro.

*Note: There should be 2½ cups reserved pasta mixture.

Here's pot roast the way you love it, with tender meat that falls apart with the nudge of a fork and a richly flavored sauce laced with mushrooms.

Mushroom and Onion Pot Roast

MAKES 4 SERVINGS + RESERVES

Prep: 30 minutes
Cook: Low 10 to 12 hours, High 5 to 6 hours

1 3-pound boneless beef chuck pot roast
½ teaspoon salt
¼ teaspoon black pepper
2 tablespoons cooking oil
3 cups small fresh button mushrooms, sliced
2 large onions, halved lengthwise and sliced ¼ inch thick
1 10.5-ounce can condensed beef broth
½ cup dry red wine
1 teaspoon dried thyme, crushed
4 cloves garlic, minced
2 tablespoons cornstarch
2 tablespoons cold water
2 cups hot mashed potatoes

1. Trim fat from meat. If necessary, cut meat to fit into a 5- to 6-quart slow cooker. Sprinkle meat with salt and pepper. In a very large skillet brown meat on all sides in hot oil over medium heat. Drain off fat. In the cooker combine mushrooms and onion. Add meat. In a medium bowl stir together broth, wine, thyme, and garlic. Pour over mixture in cooker.

2. Cover and cook on low-heat setting for 10 to 12 hours or high-heat setting for 5 to 6 hours.

3. Reserve one-third of the meat (about 9 ounces). Transfer the remaining meat to a serving platter; cover with foil to keep warm. Using a slotted spoon, remove 1 cup of the vegetables from cooking liquid. Reserve the vegetables and 1½ cups of the cooking liquid. Store the reserved meat, vegetables, and cooking liquid as directed below.

4. For sauce, in a medium saucepan combine cornstarch and water; stir in the remaining cooking liquid. Cook and stir over medium heat until thickened and bubbly. Cook and stir for 2 minutes more. Serve meat and sauce over hot mashed potatoes.

Nutrition Facts per serving: 523 cal., 18 g total fat (5 g sat. fat), 135 mg chol., 958 mg sodium, 30 g carbo., 3 g fiber, 55 g pro.

To Store Reserves: Shred meat by pulling two forks through it in opposite directions (1½ cups). Place meat, vegetables, and cooking liquid in separate airtight containers. Seal and chill for up to 3 days. Use in French Dip Sandwiches with Red Wine au Jus, page 353.

When it comes to French dip sandwiches, the moister the better!
This version gets extra ooziness from reserved mushrooms and
onions and slices of provolone cheese.

5
Ingredient
Recipe

French Dip Sandwiches with Red Wine au Jus

❖

MAKES 4 SANDWICHES

Start to Finish: 20 minutes

4   French-style rolls or hoagie
     buns, split
     Reserved Mushroom and
     Onion Pot Roast* (see
     recipe, page 352)
8   ¾-ounce slices provolone
     cheese

1. Preheat broiler. Hollow out bottoms of rolls. Divide the reserved shredded meat, the reserved vegetables, and the cheese among roll bottoms.

2. Broil 3 to 4 inches from the heat for 3 to 4 minutes or until cheese is melted and sandwiches are heated through. Add tops of rolls.

3. Meanwhile, in a small microwave-safe bowl microwave the reserved cooking liquid on 100 percent power (high) about 1 minute or until heated through. Serve sandwiches with the hot cooking liquid for dipping.

Nutrition Facts per serving: 718 cal., 24 g total fat (10 g sat. fat), 96 mg chol., 1,500 mg sodium, 73 g carbo., 5 g fiber, 49 g pro.

*Note: There should be about 1½ cups reserved shredded meat, 1 cup reserved vegetables, and 1½ cups reserved cooking liquid.

Hoisin sauce—a reddish-brown bean sauce flavored with soy, vinegar, garlic, chiles, and sesame—easily adds flavor without extra ingredients. The hint of orange contributes a little something extra too.

Asian Flank Steak

MAKES 4 SERVINGS + RESERVES

Prep: 35 minutes
Cook: Low 8 to 9 hours,
High 4 to 4½ hours,
plus 30 minutes (high)

3	pounds beef flank steak
¾	cup bottled hoisin sauce
¾	cup orange juice
¾	cup beef broth
¼	cup dry sherry or orange juice
1	teaspoon ground ginger
12	cloves garlic, minced
2	tablespoons quick-cooking tapioca
3	medium carrots, bias-sliced (1½ cups)
1	large onion, thinly sliced
2	medium red sweet peppers, cut into strips
1½	cups fresh snow pea pods, trimmed
2	cups hot cooked white or brown rice

1. Trim fat from meat. Cut meat to fit into a 4- to 5-quart slow cooker. Set aside. In the cooker combine hoisin sauce, orange juice, broth, sherry, ginger, and garlic. Sprinkle with tapioca. Stir in carrot and onion. Add meat to cooker.

2. Cover and cook on low-heat setting for 8 to 9 hours or on high-heat setting for 4 to 4½ hours.

3. If using low-heat setting, turn to high-heat setting. Add sweet pepper and pea pods. Cover and cook for 30 minutes more.

4. Transfer meat to a cutting board. Thinly slice meat across the grain. Reserve one-third of the meat (about 12 ounces). Using a slotted spoon, remove vegetables from cooker; reserve ¾ cup vegetables. Reserve 1¾ cups of the cooking liquid. Store the reserved meat, vegetables, and cooking liquid as directed below.

5. Serve the remaining meat, vegetables, and cooking liquid over hot cooked rice.

Nutrition Facts per serving: 568 cal., 16 g total fat (6 g sat. fat), 85 mg chol., 647 mg sodium, 48 g carbo., 3 g fiber, 52 g pro.

To Store Reserves: Place meat, vegetables, and cooking liquid in an airtight container. Seal and chill for up to 3 days. Use in Warm Soba Salad, page 355.

Soba are Japanese noodles made of buckwheat flour and wheat flour. Look for them in the ethnic or pasta section of your supermarket or natural food store. Hint: For added flair, top the prepared salad with a splash of soy sauce.

Warm Soba Salad

❊

MAKES 4 SERVINGS

Start to Finish: 30 minutes

8	ounces dried soba
1	cup frozen shelled sweet soybeans (edamame)
	Reserved meat mixture from Asian Flank Steak* (see recipe, page 354)
2	medium yellow sweet peppers, chopped (1½ cups)
1	8-ounce can sliced water chestnuts, drained
¼	cup sliced green onion (2)
¼	cup chopped cashews
	Soy sauce (optional)

1. In a Dutch oven cook soba in boiling salted water for 5 minutes. Add soybeans; return to boiling. Cook for 3 to 5 minutes more or until soba are tender; drain.

2. Meanwhile, in a very large skillet heat the reserved meat mixture over medium heat until heated through, stirring occasionally. Stir in soba mixture, sweet pepper, and drained water chestnuts; heat through. Sprinkle with green onion and cashews. If desired, serve with soy sauce.

Nutrition Facts per serving: 716 cal., 21 g total fat (5 g sat. fat), 51 mg chol., 640 mg sodium, 90 g carbo., 8 g fiber, 50 g pro.

*Note: There should be 12 ounces reserved meat and ¾ cup reserved vegetables mixed with 1¾ cups reserved cooking liquid.

Do you have the weeknight "what's for dinner" blues? You'll sing another tune when you come home to a tender brisket with a wine-enhanced sauce. Serve with mashed potatoes for comfort food at its finest. (Photo on page 260.)

Wine-Braised Beef Brisket

MAKES 6 SERVINGS + RESERVES

Prep: 30 minutes
Cook: Low 10 to 12 hours, High 5 to 6 hours

1	4-pound fresh beef brisket
4	medium carrots,thinly sliced (2 cups)
1	large onion, finely chopped (1 cup)
1	cup dry red wine
½	of a 6-ounce can (⅓ cup) tomato paste
2	tablespoons quick-cooking tapioca
1	tablespoon Worcestershire sauce
2	teaspoons garlic salt
2	teaspoons liquid smoke
1½	teaspoons chili powder
3	cups hot mashed potatoes

1. Trim fat from meat. If necessary, cut meat to fit into a 4- to 5-quart slow cooker. In the cooker combine carrot and onion. Add meat. In a medium bowl stir together wine, tomato paste, tapioca, Worcestershire sauce, garlic salt, liquid smoke, and chili powder. Pour over mixture in cooker.

2. Cover and cook on low-heat setting for 10 to 12 hours or on high-heat setting for 5 to 6 hours.

3. Remove meat from cooker. Using a slotted spoon, remove vegetables from cooker, reserving cooking liquid. Reserve half of the meat (about 1 pound), 1 cup vegetables, and 1 cup cooking liquid; store as directed below.

4. Slice the remaining meat. Serve the meat, the remaining vegetables, and the remaining cooking liquid with hot mashed potatoes.

Nutrition Facts per serving: 355 cal., 11 g total fat (4 g sat. fat), 96 mg chol., 641 mg sodium, 25 g carbo., 3 g fiber, 33 g pro.

To Store Reserves: Chop meat (about 4 cups). Place meat in an airtight container. Place vegetables and cooking liquid in a second airtight container. Seal and chill for up to 3 days. Use in Brisket Pie, page 357.

Stay on the comfort-food bus! Transform leftover home-cooked brisket into a delightfully hearty and moist casserole of chopped beef and veggies topped with biscuits. (Photo on page 260.)

Brisket Pie

❖

MAKES 6 SERVINGS

Prep: 25 minutes
Bake: 30 minutes
Stand: 10 minutes
Oven: 350°F

	Reserved Wine-Braised Beef Brisket* (see recipe, page 356)
1	cup frozen whole kernel corn
1	cup shredded cheddar cheese
1	small green sweet pepper, chopped (½ cup)
2	eggs, slightly beaten
1	cup milk
2	cups packaged biscuit mix
¼	teaspoon onion salt

1. Preheat oven to 350°F. In a large saucepan combine the reserved chopped meat, the reserved vegetable mixture, the frozen corn, ¾ cup of the cheese, and the sweet pepper. Bring to boiling, stirring occasionally. Transfer to a 2-quart rectangular baking dish.

2. In a small bowl combine eggs and milk. In a medium bowl stir together biscuit mix and onion salt. Add egg mixture to biscuit mixture; stir just until moistened. Pour batter over hot meat mixture in baking dish.

3. Bake about 30 minutes or until top is lightly browned. Sprinkle with the remaining ¼ cup cheese. Let stand for 10 minutes before serving.

Nutrition Facts per serving: 577 cal., 25 g total fat (10 g sat. fat), 188 mg chol., 1,046 mg sodium, 42 g carbo., 2 g fiber, 43 g pro.

*Note: There should be about 4 cups reserved chopped meat and 1 cup reserved vegetables mixed with 1 cup reserved cooking liquid.

Forget takeout! The flavors that draw you to your favorite Asian restaurant can be waiting at home with the right mix of ingredients and your slow cooker.

Five-Spice Beef Short Ribs

❖

MAKES 4 SERVINGS + RESERVES

Prep: 25 minutes
Cook: Low 11 to 12 hours, High 5½ to 6 hours

6	pounds beef short ribs
1	large red onion, cut into thin wedges
2	tablespoons quick-cooking tapioca
⅔	cup beef broth
¼	cup soy sauce
¼	cup rice vinegar
2	tablespoons honey
1	tablespoon five-spice powder
1	teaspoon ground ginger
4	cloves garlic, minced
2	cups hot cooked rice

1. Trim fat from ribs; set ribs aside. Place onion in a 5- to 6-quart slow cooker. Sprinkle with tapioca. Add ribs. In a medium bowl combine broth, soy sauce, vinegar, honey, five-spice powder, ginger, and garlic. Pour over mixture in cooker.

2. Cover and cook on low-heat setting for 11 to 12 hours or on high-heat setting for 5½ to 6 hours.

3. Using a slotted spoon, remove ribs and onion from cooker, reserving cooking liquid. Set ribs and onion aside. Pour cooking liquid into a glass measuring cup; skim off fat. Reserve half of the ribs, half of the onion, and half of the cooking liquid; store as directed below.

4. Serve the remaining ribs, onion, and cooking liquid over hot cooked rice.

Nutrition Facts per serving: 369 cal., 12 g total fat (5 g sat. fat), 79 mg chol., 628 mg sodium, 33 g carbo., 1 g fiber, 30 g pro.

To Store Reserves: Place ribs in an airtight container. Place onion and cooking liquid in a second airtight container. Seal and chill for up to 3 days. (Or freeze for up to 3 months. Thaw in refrigerator overnight before using.) Use in Asian Beef Stew, page 359.

*Parlay the intriguing flavors and tender, rich beef of
Five-Spice Beef Short Ribs into a seriously good stew filled
with colorful vegetables.*

Asian Beef Stew

MAKES 4 TO 6 SERVINGS

Start to Finish: 25 minutes

1	14-ounce can beef broth
½	of a 16-ounce package frozen (yellow, green, and red) pepper and onion stir-fry vegetables
5	to 6 tiny new potatoes (8 ounces), sliced ¼ inch thick
2	medium carrots, thinly sliced (1 cup)
	Reserved Five-Spice Beef Short Ribs* (see recipe, page 358)
4	green onions, bias-sliced into 1-inch pieces

1. In a large saucepan or Dutch oven bring broth to boiling. Stir in frozen stir-fry vegetables, potato, and carrot. Return to boiling; reduce heat. Cover and simmer for 10 minutes.

2. Meanwhile, remove meat from the reserved ribs; discard bones. Chop meat. Remove any fat from the reserved cooking liquid-onion mixture. Add meat, cooking liquid-onion mixture, and green onion to vegetables in saucepan. Return to boiling; reduce heat. Cover and simmer about 5 minutes more or until vegetables are tender.

Nutrition Facts per serving: 349 cal., 12 g total fat (5 g sat. fat), 79 mg chol., 1,026 mg sodium, 27 g carbo., 3 g fiber, 32 g pro.

*Note: There should be about 4 reserved ribs and about 1 cup reserved cooking liquid mixed with ½ cup reserved onion.

This is slow cooking at its best! Everything—main dish and side—cooks in one pot for a meal you'll look forward to coming home to all day. Be sure to use light beer because regular beer can make the dish taste a little bitter.

Braised Corned Beef Dinner

MAKES 4 SERVINGS + RESERVES

Prep: 20 minutes
Cook: Low 10 to 11 hours, High 5 to 5½ hours

1	3-pound corned beef brisket with juices and spice packet
4	medium red potatoes, quartered
4	carrots, cut into 1½-inch pieces
2	medium onions, cut into thin wedges
2	teaspoons dried thyme, crushed
1	bay leaf
1	12-ounce bottle light beer

1. Trim fat from meat, reserving juices and spices from packet. If necessary, cut meat to fit into a 5- to 6-quart slow cooker. Set aside.

2. In the cooker combine potato, carrot, onion, thyme, and bay leaf. Add meat. Pour the meat juices and the spices from the packet over meat. Pour beer over mixture in cooker.

3. Cover and cook on low-heat setting for 10 to 11 hours or on high-heat setting for 5 to 5½ hours. Remove bay leaf.

4. Transfer meat to a cutting board. Thinly slice meat across the grain. Reserve half of the sliced meat (about 1 pound); store as directed below.

5. Using a slotted spoon, remove vegetables from cooker, reserving cooking liquid. Serve the remaining meat with the vegetables. Drizzle with some of the cooking liquid; pass the remaining liquid.

Nutrition Facts per serving: 478 cal., 21 g total fat (6 g sat. fat), 86 mg chol., 1,195 mg sodium, 37 g carbo., 5 g fiber, 29 g pro.

To Store Reserves: Place meat in an airtight container. Seal and chill for up to 2 days. Use in Reuben Panini, page 361.

Reuben sandwiches are a classic and beloved way to use leftover corned beef. The beverage of choice is also a no-brainer: A beer is perfect! Round out the meal with a good deli potato salad.

5
Ingredient
Recipe

Reuben Panini

MAKES 4 SERVINGS

Prep: 10 minutes
Grill: 5 minutes

¼   cup bottled Thousand Island salad dressing
8   slices rye bread
    Reserved meat from Braised Corned Beef Dinner* (see recipe, page 360)
1   cup canned sauerkraut, rinsed and drained
4   ¾- to 1-ounce slices Swiss cheese

1. Spread salad dressing on 4 of the bread slices. Top with the reserved meat, the sauerkraut, cheese, and the remaining bread slices.

2. Lightly grease the rack of a covered indoor electric grill. Preheat grill to medium heat. Place sandwiches on grill rack; close the lid. Grill for 5 to 10 minutes or until bread is toasted and cheese is melted. (Or lightly grease a large heavy skillet; heat skillet over medium heat. Place sandwiches, half at a time if necessary, in hot skillet; top with a heavy cast-iron skillet. Cook for 5 to 10 minutes or until bread is toasted and cheese is melted, turning once halfway through cooking.)

Nutrition Facts per serving: 594 cal., 34 g total fat (10 g sat. fat), 110 mg chol., 3,176 mg sodium, 35 g carbo., 8 g fiber, 36 g pro.

*Note: There should be about 1 pound reserved sliced meat.

Here it is—the meat loaf topped with ketchup and brown sugar, beloved by generations. Go ahead and serve it with mashed potatoes, gravy, and canned green beans for a tasty trip down memory lane. Note that you'll need a large oval slow cooker.

Classic Meat Loaf

MAKES 6 SERVINGS + RESERVES

Prep: 30 minutes
Cook: Low 7 to 8 hours,
High 3½ to 4 hours

3	eggs, slightly beaten
¾	cup milk
2	cups soft bread crumbs
1	large onion, finely chopped (1 cup)
2	teaspoons salt
½	teaspoon black pepper
1½	pounds lean ground beef
1½	pounds ground pork
¼	cup ketchup
2	tablespoons packed brown sugar
1	teaspoon dry mustard

1. In a large bowl combine eggs and milk. Stir in bread crumbs, onion, salt, and pepper. Add ground beef and pork; mix well. Shape meat mixture into two 5-inch round loaves.

2. Tear off two 18-inch square pieces of heavy foil; cut each into thirds. Fold each piece of foil in half lengthwise to make strips. Crisscross three of the strips and place one meat loaf in the center of the foil crisscross. Bringing up the foil strips, lift the ends of the strips to transfer meat loaf to a 6- to 7-quart oval slow cooker. Leave foil strips under loaf. Repeat with the remaining foil strips and meat loaf.

3. Cover and cook on low-heat setting for 7 to 8 hours or on high-heat setting for 3½ to 4 hours.

4. Using the foil strips, carefully lift one meat loaf out of cooker; discard foil strips. Store meat loaf as directed below. Transfer second meat loaf to a serving platter; discard foil strips. In a small bowl combine ketchup, brown sugar, and dry mustard; spread over meat loaf on platter.

Nutrition Facts per serving: 239 cal., 11 g total fat (4 g sat. fat), 116 mg chol., 617 mg sodium, 13 g carbo., 0 g fiber, 20 g pro.

To Store Reserves: Place meat loaf in an airtight container. Seal and chill for up to 3 days. (Or freeze for up to 3 months. Thaw in refrigerator overnight before using.)
Use in Meat Loaf Parmesan, page 363.

If you enjoy chicken Parmesan and eggplant Parmesan, why not give the same treatment to meat loaf? The side dish accompaniment could go either way: Italian with pasta or American with mashed potatoes.

Meat Loaf Parmesan

MAKES 6 SERVINGS

Prep: 15 minutes
Bake: 35 minutes
Oven: 350°F

Reserved Classic Meat Loaf* (see recipe, page 362)

2   eggs, slightly beaten

¼   cup milk

½   cup seasoned fine dry bread crumbs

¼   cup grated Parmesan cheese

1   26- to 28-ounce jar spaghetti or pasta sauce

1   cup shredded mozzarella cheese

1. Preheat oven to 350°F. Cut the reserved meat loaf into 6 slices; set aside. In a shallow bowl stir together eggs and milk. In another shallow bowl stir together bread crumbs and Parmesan cheese.

2. Dip meat loaf slices, one at a time, into egg mixture, then dip into bread crumb mixture to coat. Place slices in a single layer in a 3-quart rectangular baking dish.

3. Bake for 20 minutes. Pour spaghetti sauce evenly over meat loaf; sprinkle with mozzarella cheese. Bake about 15 minutes more or until sauce is heated through and cheese is melted.

Nutrition Facts per serving: 469 cal., 22 g total fat (9 g sat. fat), 205 mg chol., 1,542 mg sodium, 33 g carbo., 4 g fiber, 31 g pro.

*Note: There should be one reserved meat loaf.

Succulent pork shoulder simmers for hours in a tomato-based sauce spiked with deeply flavored balsamic vinegar in this easy dish. The results are satisfyingly down-home and a little gourmet.

Balsamic-Sauced Pork Roast

MAKES 6 SERVINGS + RESERVES

Prep: 25 minutes
Cook: Low 12 to 14 hours, High 6 to 7 hours

1	4-pound boneless pork shoulder roast
2	teaspoons dried Italian seasoning, crushed
1	teaspoon seasoned salt
¼	teaspoon black pepper
2	large onions, halved lengthwise and thinly sliced
4	cloves garlic, minced
¼	cup quick-cooking tapioca
2	14.5-ounce cans Italian-style stewed tomatoes, undrained
¼	cup balsamic vinegar
3	cups hot cooked noodles

1. Trim fat from meat. If necessary, cut meat to fit into a 5- to 6-quart slow cooker. Sprinkle meat with Italian seasoning, salt, and pepper. In the cooker combine onion and garlic; sprinkle with tapioca. Add meat. In a medium bowl combine undrained tomatoes and balsamic vinegar. Pour over mixture in cooker.

2. Cover and cook on low-heat setting for 12 to 14 hours or on high-heat setting for 6 to 7 hours.

3. Remove meat from cooker, reserving cooking liquid. Reserve one-third of the meat (about 14 ounces). Skim fat from cooking liquid; reserve 1½ cups liquid. Store the reserved meat and cooking liquid as directed below.

4. Cut the remaining meat into 6 slices. Serve meat and the remaining cooking liquid over hot cooked noodles.

Nutrition Facts per serving: 455 cal., 13 g total fat (4 g sat. fat), 157 mg chol., 662 mg sodium, 37 g carbo., 1 g fiber, 45 g pro.

To Store Reserves: Place meat and cooking liquid in separate airtight containers. Seal and chill for up to 3 days. (Or freeze for up to 3 months. Thaw in refrigerator overnight before using.) Use in Pork and Noodles, page 365.

Beef and noodles rank right up there as a favorite comfort food. Now shake things up a bit with pork for a dinner that's family friendly but also pleasantly unexpected.

5 Ingredient Recipe

Pork and Noodles

❋

MAKES 6 SERVINGS

Start to Finish: 25 minutes

Reserved meat and liquid from Balsamic-Sauced Pork Roast* (see recipe, page 364)

3 cups hot cooked noodles

1 16-ounce package frozen cut green beans, thawed

1 12-ounce jar mushroom gravy

1. Cube the reserved meat. In a large saucepan combine meat, the reserved cooking liquid, the hot cooked noodles, green beans, and gravy.

2. Bring mixture just to boiling, stirring occasionally. Cover and cook for 3 to 5 minutes or until beans are crisp-tender.

Nutrition Facts per serving: 331 cal., 8 g total fat (2 g sat. fat), 92 mg chol., 674 mg sodium, 37 g carbo., 3 g fiber, 27 g pro.

*Note: There should be about 14 ounces reserved meat and 1½ cups reserved cooking liquid.

*What makes this dish special is its sauce—just before
serving, the richly flavored cooking liquid gets an added flavor
boost with two simple stir-ins: Dijon-style
mustard and caraway seeds. (Photo on page 265.)*

Sage-Scented Pork Chops

**MAKES 6 SERVINGS +
RESERVES**

Prep: 30 minutes
Cook: Low 4 to 5 hours,
High 2 to 2½ hours

10   boneless pork loin chops,
      cut ¾ inch thick

2   teaspoons dried sage,
      crushed

1   teaspoon black pepper

½   teaspoon salt

2   tablespoons cooking oil

1   medium onion, thinly sliced

½   cup chicken broth

⅓   cup dry white wine or
      apple juice

3   tablespoons quick-cooking
      tapioca, crushed

½   of a medium head green
      cabbage, cut into ½-inch-
      wide strips

1   tablespoon Dijon-style
      mustard

1   teaspoon caraway seeds

1. Trim fat from chops. In a small bowl stir together sage, pepper, and salt. Sprinkle mixture evenly over one side of chops; rub in with your fingers. In a very large skillet brown chops, half at a time, on both sides in hot oil over medium heat. Drain off fat. Set aside.

2. In a 6- to 7-quart slow cooker combine onion, broth, wine, and tapioca. Add chops. Place cabbage on mixture in cooker.

3. Cover and cook on low-heat setting for 4 to 5 hours or on high-heat setting for 2 to 2½ hours.

4. Reserve 4 chops; store as directed below. Transfer the remaining chops to a serving platter; cover with foil to keep warm. Using a slotted spoon, transfer cabbage and onion to a serving bowl, reserving cooking liquid. Stir mustard and caraway seeds into the cooking liquid. Serve chops, cabbage, and onion with the reserved liquid.

Nutrition Facts per serving: 300 cal., 12 g total fat (4 g sat. fat), 87 mg chol., 351 mg sodium, 9 g carbo., 1 g fiber, 37 g pro.

To Store Reserves: Chop pork chops (3 cups). Place meat in an airtight container. Seal and chill for up to 3 days. (Or freeze for up to 3 months. Thaw in refrigerator overnight before using.) Use in Pork and Potato Gratin with Gruyère Cheese, page 367.

Give this variation a try if you like scalloped ham and potatoes. Rich bits of cooked pork loin chops give the classic a nice change of taste. (Photo on page 265.)

Pork and Potato Gratin with Gruyère Cheese

❖

MAKES 6 SERVINGS

Prep: 25 minutes
Bake: 45 minutes
Stand: 10 minutes
Oven: 375°F

1	medium onion, chopped (½ cup)
3	tablespoons butter or margarine
3	tablespoons all-purpose flour
¾	teaspoon salt
½	teaspoon black pepper
¼	teaspoon ground nutmeg
1¾	cups milk
1¼	cups shredded Gruyère cheese
6	medium red or round white potatoes (2 pounds), peeled and thinly sliced
	Reserved meat from Sage-Scented Pork Chops* (see recipe, page 366)

1. Preheat oven to 375°F. For sauce, in a medium saucepan cook onion in hot butter over medium heat until tender. Stir in flour, salt, pepper, and nutmeg. Cook and stir for 1 minute. Slowly stir in milk. Cook and stir until thickened and bubbly. Add cheese; cook and stir until melted.

2. In a greased 2½- to 3-quart rectangular baking dish or au gratin dish spread half of the potato. Top with the reserved chopped meat; cover with half of the sauce. Repeat potato and sauce layers.

3. Cover and bake about 45 minutes or until potato is tender. Let stand for 10 minutes before serving.

Nutrition Facts per serving: 488 cal., 24 g total fat (12 g sat. fat), 109 mg chol., 618 mg sodium, 29 g carbo., 2 g fiber, 37 g pro.

*Note: There should be about 3 cups reserved chopped meat.

A winning combination of just the right seasonings—orange marmalade, honey, lime, garlic, and chipotle pepper—help your slow cooker get its mojo working, transforming a pork roast into something magically yummy!

Mojo Pork Roast

❖

MAKES 6 SERVINGS + RESERVES

Prep: 25 minutes
Cook: Low 5 to 5½ hours, High 2½ to 3 hours

Nonstick cooking spray
1   3½- to 4-pound boneless pork top loin roast (single loin)
1   12-ounce jar orange marmalade
1   medium onion, finely chopped (½ cup)
1   tablespoon honey
½   teaspoon finely shredded lime peel
1   tablespoon lime juice
1   canned chipotle pepper in adobo sauce, finely chopped (see tip, page 10)
1   teaspoon ground cumin
½   teaspoon salt
½   teaspoon dried oregano, crushed
¼   teaspoon black pepper
2   cloves garlic, minced
½   cup chicken broth

1. Lightly coat the inside of a 4- to 5-quart slow cooker with nonstick cooking spray. Trim fat from meat. If necessary, cut meat to fit into cooker. Place meat in the prepared cooker.

2. In a medium bowl stir together marmalade, onion, honey, lime peel, lime juice, chipotle pepper, cumin, salt, oregano, black pepper, and garlic. Spread mixture over meat in cooker. Pour broth around meat.

3. Cover and cook on low-heat setting for 5 to 5½ hours or on high-heat setting for 2½ to 3 hours.

4. Remove meat from cooker, reserving cooking liquid. Reserve 12 ounces of the meat; store as directed below. Slice the remaining meat. If desired, strain cooking liquid. Drizzle meat with some of the cooking liquid; discard the remaining liquid.

Nutrition Facts per serving: 354 cal., 9 g total fat (3 g sat. fat), 97 mg chol., 292 mg sodium, 29 g carbo., 1 g fiber, 39 g pro.

To Store Reserves: Place meat in an airtight container. Seal and chill for up to 3 days. (Or freeze for up to 3 months. Thaw in refrigerator overnight before using.) Use in Cuban Pork Sandwiches, page 369.

Warm, oozy, and full of lively ingredients, Cuban pork sandwiches have become a hit throughout the country. This recipe shows how easy it is to make the popular delight.

Cuban Pork Sandwiches

MAKES 6 SANDWICHES

Start to Finish: 25 minutes

⅓	cup mayonnaise or salad dressing
½	of a canned chipotle pepper in adobo sauce, finely chopped (see tip, page 10)
	Reserved meat from Mojo Pork Roast* (see recipe, page 368)
12	½-inch-thick slices crusty country bread or 12 slices white or whole wheat bread
12	1-ounce slices Monterey Jack cheese
6	thin lengthwise slices dill pickle
6	thin slices red onion (optional)
3	tablespoons butter or margarine, softened

1. Preheat broiler. In a small bowl stir together mayonnaise and chipotle pepper; set aside. Cut the reserved meat into 6 slices; place slices in a 1½-quart microwave-safe casserole. Cover and microwave on 100 percent power (high) for 2 to 3 minutes or until heated through, rearranging slices once halfway through cooking.

2. Spread mayonnaise mixture evenly on 6 of the bread slices. Top each with a slice of cheese, a slice of meat, a pickle slice, a red onion slice (if desired), and another slice of cheese. Top with the remaining 6 slices of bread. Spread tops of sandwiches with half of the butter.

3. Place 3 of the sandwiches, buttered sides down, on the unheated rack of a broiler pan. Spread the remaining butter on sandwiches. Broil 4 to 5 inches from the heat for 4 to 5 minutes or until bread is toasted and cheese is melted, turning sandwiches once halfway through broiling. Remove sandwiches from pan. Repeat with the remaining sandwiches.

4. To serve, cut sandwiches in half.

Nutrition Facts per serving: 691 cal., 39 g total fat (18 g sat. fat), 118 mg chol., 974 mg sodium, 45 g carbo., 2 g fiber, 39 g pro.

*Note: There should be 12 ounces reserved meat.

When cans of fire-roasted diced tomatoes hit grocery store shelves, clever cooks immediately started using them to rev up their recipes. They add something extra to this classic Italian sandwich. (Photo on page 270.)

Fire-Roasted Tomato and Italian Sausage Grinders

MAKES 6 SANDWICHES + RESERVES

Prep: 20 minutes
Cook: Low 6 to 8 hours, High 3 to 4 hours

10   uncooked hot or sweet Italian sausage links (about 2½ pounds total)

2   14.5-ounce cans fire-roasted diced tomatoes, undrained

1   28-ounce can crushed tomatoes

1   tablespoon balsamic vinegar

2   teaspoons dried basil, crushed

1   teaspoon dried oregano, crushed

½   teaspoon salt

½   teaspoon crushed red pepper

¼   teaspoon black pepper

6   cloves garlic, minced

6   French-style rolls or hoagie buns, split

6   slices provolone cheese, halved

¾   cup bottled roasted red sweet peppers, drained and cut into thin strips

1. Place sausage links in a 5- to 6-quart slow cooker. For sauce, stir in undrained diced tomatoes, crushed tomatoes, balsamic vinegar, basil, oregano, salt, crushed red pepper, black pepper, and garlic.

2. Cover and cook on low-heat setting for 6 to 8 hours or on high-heat setting for 3 to 4 hours.

3. Preheat broiler. Reserve 4 sausage links and 3 cups sauce; store as directed below.

4. Place the remaining sausage links on bottoms of rolls; spoon on some of the sauce. Place a half-slice of cheese on top of sausage mixture on each roll bottom and a half-slice of cheese on the cut side of each roll top. Broil 4 to 5 inches from the heat for 2 to 3 minutes or until cheese is melted and bubbly. Replace tops of rolls. Serve with roasted red pepper and the remaining sauce for dipping.

Nutrition Facts per serving: 859 cal., 39 g total fat (17 g sat. fat), 96 mg chol., 2,305 mg sodium, 81 g carbo., 6 g fiber, 37 g pro.

To Store Reserves: Place sausages and sauce in separate airtight containers. Seal and chill for up to 3 days. Use in Sausage-Stuffed Manicotti, page 371.

Looking for a wine to serve with this delightfully tangy and creamy dish? Try a Chianti from Italy. Many good ones are available at everyday prices. (Photo on page 271.)

Sausage-Stuffed Manicotti

❖

MAKES 6 SERVINGS

Prep: 20 minutes
Bake: 30 minutes
Oven: 350°F

12	dried manicotti pasta
	Reserved sausages and sauce from Fire-Roasted Tomato and Italian Sausage Grinders* (see recipe, page 370)
1	15-ounce carton ricotta cheese
1	cup finely shredded Parmesan cheese
2	teaspoons dried basil, crushed
1½	cups shredded smoked mozzarella cheese
	Snipped fresh basil or parsley (optional)

1. Preheat oven to 350°F. Cook manicotti according to package directions; drain. Cool manicotti in a single layer on a piece of greased foil.

2. Chop the reserved sausages. In a medium bowl combine the sausage, ricotta cheese, Parmesan cheese, and the dried basil. Using a small spoon, fill manicotti with sausage mixture. Arrange filled manicotti in a 3-quart rectangular baking dish. Pour the reserved sauce over filled manicotti. Sprinkle with mozzarella cheese.

3. Cover and bake for 20 minutes. Bake, uncovered, about 10 minutes more or until cheese is melted and bubbly. If desired, sprinkle with fresh basil or parsley.

Nutrition Facts per serving: 764 cal., 46 g total fat (22 g sat. fat), 145 mg chol., 1,696 mg sodium, 39 g carbo., 3 g fiber, 42 g pro.

*Note: There should be 4 reserved sausages and 3 cups reserved sauce.

A nice peppery bite contrasts with the distinct sweetness of pineapple, maple, and earthy spices for a kicky take on ham steak.

Peppered Sweet Ham Steak

❖

MAKES 6 SERVINGS + RESERVES

Prep: 15 minutes
Cook: Low 8 to 9 hours, High 4 to 4½ hours

1	16-ounce package peeled baby carrots
3	pounds cooked center-cut ham steak
1	15.25-ounce can pineapple chunks (juice pack), undrained
⅓	cup apple juice
⅓	cup maple syrup
⅓	cup raisins
¼	cup packed brown sugar
1	teaspoon coarsely ground black pepper
¼	teaspoon cayenne pepper
¼	teaspoon ground cloves
¼	teaspoon ground ginger

1. Place carrots in a 5- to 6-quart slow cooker. Add ham. In a medium bowl stir together undrained pineapple, apple juice, maple syrup, raisins, brown sugar, black pepper, cayenne pepper, cloves, and ginger. Pour over mixture in cooker.

2. Cover and cook on low-heat setting for 8 to 9 hours or on high-heat setting for 4 to 4½ hours.

3. Reserve 12 ounces of the ham; store as directed below. Using a slotted spoon, remove carrots and pineapple, reserving cooking liquid. Serve the remaining ham with the carrots and pineapple. Drizzle with some of the cooking liquid; discard the remaining liquid.

Nutrition Facts per serving: 136 cal., 13 g total fat (4 g sat. fat), 86 mg chol., 2,032 mg sodium, 54 g carbo., 5 g fiber, 26 g pro.

To Store Reserves: Finely chop ham (2 cups). Place ham in an airtight container. Seal and chill for up to 3 days. (Or freeze for up to 3 months. Thaw in refrigerator overnight before using.) Use in Ham Salad Sandwiches, page 373.

Serve the tangy ham salad and creamy Brie on croissants or bread for lunch. The sandwiches go well with steaming bowls of potato soup. For easy entertaining fill tea rolls or mini breads of your choice with the ham-and-cheese duo.

Ham Salad Sandwiches

MAKES 6 SANDWICHES

Start to Finish: 20 minutes

	Reserved ham from Peppered Sweet Ham Steak* (see recipe, page 372)
1	stalk celery, finely chopped (½ cup)
½	cup mayonnaise or salad dressing
¼	cup thinly sliced green onion (2)
1	tablespoon Dijon-style mustard
1	teaspoon snipped fresh chives, basil, or tarragon or ¼ teaspoon dried basil or tarragon, crushed
6	croissants, split, or 12 slices bread
1	4-ounce round Brie or Camembert cheese, sliced

1. In a medium bowl stir together the reserved finely chopped ham, the celery, mayonnaise, green onion, mustard, and chives.

2. Place a scant ½ cup ham mixture on each croissant bottom or on each of 6 bread slices. Top with cheese and the croissant tops or remaining bread slices.

Nutrition Facts per serving: 526 cal., 37 g total fat (14 g sat. fat), 96 mg chol., 1,451 mg sodium, 29 g carbo., 2 g fiber, 19 g pro.

*Note: There should be 2 cups reserved finely chopped ham.

A tagine is a clay pot often used in Moroccan cooking. Dishes made in a tagine are usually cooked at low temperatures for a long time, making them easily adaptable for the slow cooker.

Tagine-Style Lamb Stew

❈

MAKES 4 SERVINGS + RESERVES

Prep: 30 minutes
Cook: Low 11 to 12 hours, High 5½ to 6 hours

3	medium carrots, sliced (1½ cups)
2	medium onions, cut into thin wedges
2	stalks celery, sliced (1 cup)
6	cloves garlic, thinly sliced
⅓	cup quick-cooking tapioca, crushed
3	pounds lean boneless lamb
2	tablespoons cooking oil
2	14.5-ounce cans stewed tomatoes, undrained and cut up
2	14-ounce cans beef broth
1	15-ounce can garbanzo beans (chickpeas), rinsed and drained
½	cup dry red wine (optional)
1	teaspoon dried thyme, crushed
½	teaspoon black pepper
¼	to ½ teaspoon cayenne pepper

1. In a 5- to 7-quart slow cooker combine carrot, onion, celery, and garlic. Sprinkle with tapioca.

2. Trim fat from meat. Cut meat into ¾-inch pieces. In a very large skillet brown meat, half at a time, in hot oil over medium heat. Drain off fat.

3. Transfer meat to cooker. Stir in undrained tomatoes, broth, drained beans, wine (if desired), thyme, black pepper, and cayenne pepper.

4. Cover and cook on low-heat setting for 11 to 12 hours or on high-heat setting for 5½ to 6 hours.

5. Reserve 6 cups of the stew; store as directed below. Serve the remaining stew immediately.

Nutrition Facts per serving: 413 cal., 13 g total fat (3 g sat. fat), 119 mg chol., 947 mg sodium, 29 g carbo., 4 g fiber, 43 g pro.

To Store Reserves: Place stew in an airtight container. Seal and chill for up to 3 days. Use in Cheesy Shepherd's Pie, page 375.

With this clever leftover, you get to do a little continent hopping. Here the specialty of Morocco is transformed into a British favorite for results that are the best of both worlds.

Cheesy Shepherd's Pie

MAKES 4 SERVINGS

Prep: 15 minutes
Bake: 25 minutes
Oven: 375°F

Reserved Tagine-Style Lamb Stew* (see recipe, page 374)
2 tablespoons all-purpose flour
1 24-ounce package refrigerated mashed potatoes
½ cup shredded cheddar cheese

1. Preheat oven to 375°F. In a large saucepan stir together the reserved stew and the flour. Cook and stir over medium-high heat until bubbly.

2. Transfer mixture to an ungreased 2½- to 3-quart casserole. Place large spoonfuls of mashed potatoes on hot mixture.

3. Bake about 20 minutes or until mashed potatoes are heated through. Sprinkle with cheese. Bake about 5 minutes more or until cheese is melted.

Nutrition Facts per serving: 558 cal., 18 g total fat (5 g sat. fat), 117 mg chol., 1,155 mg sodium, 51 g carbo., 5 g fiber, 44 g pro.

*Note: There should be 6 cups reserved stew.

Stop—don't turn the page because you see a lot of ingredients!
Many of these are seasonings that take just seconds to stir
together and taste wonderful after melding in the slow cooker.

Slow-Cooked Lamb

**MAKES 4 SERVINGS +
RESERVES**

Prep: 25 minutes
Cook: Low 8 to 10 hours,
High 4 to 5 hours

1	tablespoon garam masala
2	teaspoons ground cumin
1	teaspoon salt
½	teaspoon ground cinnamon
½	teaspoon black pepper
¼	teaspoon ground cardamom
6	cloves garlic, minced
2½	pounds lean boneless lamb
8	medium carrots, sliced (4 cups)
3	large onions, halved lengthwise and sliced
4	stalks celery, sliced (2 cups)
1	14-ounce can beef broth
½	cup water
½	cup raisins
3	tablespoons quick-cooking tapioca
2	cups hot cooked couscous

1. In a large bowl stir together garam masala, cumin, salt, cinnamon, pepper, cardamom, and garlic. Trim fat from meat. Cut meat into ¾-inch pieces. Add meat to spice mixture; toss to coat. Set aside.

2. In a 5- to 6-quart slow cooker combine carrot, onion, celery, broth, water, and raisins. Sprinkle with tapioca. Add meat to vegetable mixture in cooker.

3. Cover and cook on low-heat setting for 8 to 10 hours or high-heat setting for 4 to 5 hours.

4. Reserve half of the meat-vegetable mixture (about 4 cups); store as directed below. Serve the remaining meat-vegetable mixture over hot cooked couscous.

Nutrition Facts per serving: 310 cal., 4 g total fat (1 g sat. fat), 62 mg chol., 602 mg sodium, 43 g carbo., 5 g fiber, 26 g pro.

To Store Reserves: Place meat-vegetable mixture in an airtight container. Seal and chill for up to 3 days. Use in Lamb and Polenta Casserole, page 377.

If you love Shepherd's Pie—meat stew topped with a hearty mashed potato layer—try this recipe. Instead of potatoes it's topped with creamy polenta and a sprinkling of cheese.

Lamb and Polenta Casserole

MAKES 4 SERVINGS

Prep: 25 minutes
Bake: 55 minutes
Oven: 350°F

2¾	cups water
1	cup cornmeal
1	cup cold water
½	teaspoon salt
	Reserved Slow-Cooked Lamb* (see recipe, page 376)
1	14.5-ounce can diced tomatoes, undrained
½	cup shredded Colby Jack cheese

1. Preheat oven to 350°F. In a medium saucepan bring the 2¾ cups water to boiling. Meanwhile, in a small bowl stir together cornmeal, the 1 cup cold water, and the salt. Slowly add cornmeal mixture to boiling water, stirring constantly. Cook and stir until mixture returns to boiling; reduce heat. Simmer about 10 minutes or until mixture is very thick, stirring occasionally. Set aside.

2. In a large bowl stir together the reserved meat-vegetable mixture and the undrained tomatoes. Transfer mixture to a 2-quart square baking dish. Spoon cornmeal mixture over mixture in baking dish, spreading evenly.

3. Cover and bake for 45 minutes. Sprinkle with cheese. Bake, uncovered, about 10 minutes more or until heated through.

Nutrition Facts per serving: 429 cal., 9 g total fat (4 g sat. fat), 74 mg chol., 1,158 mg sodium, 57 g carbo., 7 g fiber, 29 g pro.

*Note: There should be 4 cups reserved meat-vegetable mixture.

The slow cooker is most often used for braises and stews, but in this recipe it also works as a roaster. Try it for a Sunday noon meal. Put the cooker on high after breakfast and do your favorite Sunday morning things while it cooks.

Greek Lamb Dinner

MAKES 4 SERVINGS + RESERVES

Prep: 25 minutes
Cook: Low 8 to 10 hours, High 4 to 5 hours

1	tablespoon dried minced onion
1	teaspoon garlic powder
1	teaspoon dried oregano, crushed
1	teaspoon finely shredded lemon peel
½	teaspoon salt
½	teaspoon dried mint, crushed
½	teaspoon dried rosemary, crushed
¼	teaspoon black pepper
2	2- to 2½-pound boneless lamb shoulder roasts
4	medium carrots, halved crosswise
2	medium round white or red potatoes, quartered
1	large onion, cut into wedges
½	cup chicken broth

1. In a small bowl stir together dried onion, garlic powder, oregano, lemon peel, salt, mint, rosemary, and pepper; set aside. Trim fat from meat. Sprinkle onion mixture evenly over meat; rub in with your fingers. Set aside.

2. In a 5- to 6-quart slow cooker combine carrot, potato, and onion. Pour broth over vegetables in cooker. Add meat.

3. Cover and cook on low-heat setting for 8 to 10 hours or on high-heat setting for 4 to 5 hours.

4. Remove meat and vegetables from cooker, reserving cooking liquid. Strain cooking liquid; skim off fat. Reserve one of the roasts (12 to 14 ounces); store as directed below.

5. Slice the remaining roast. Serve meat with vegetables. Spoon some of the cooking liquid over meat and vegetables; discard remaining liquid.

Nutrition Facts per serving: 243 cal., 5 g total fat (2 g sat. fat), 72 mg chol., 392 mg sodium, 24 g carbo., 4 g fiber, 26 g pro.

To Store Reserves: Shred meat by pulling two forks through it in opposite directions (about 3 cups). Place meat in an airtight container. Seal and chill for up to 3 days. (Or freeze for up to 3 months. Thaw in refrigerator overnight before using.) Use in Lamb Gyro Salads, page 379.

The yogurt-based sauce, with its cucumber, mint, and garlic, is based on a Greek sauce called tzatziki. This classic combination is an easy way to add a smooth, refreshing, tangy contrast to rich meats such as lamb.

Lamb Gyro Salads

MAKES 4 SERVINGS

Start to Finish: 20 minutes

1	6-ounce carton plain low-fat yogurt
½	cup chopped seeded cucumber
1	tablespoon snipped fresh mint or ½ teaspoon dried mint, crushed
⅛	teaspoon salt
2	cloves garlic, minced
	Reserved meat from Greek Lamb Dinner* (see recipe, page 378)
2	large pita bread rounds, split in half horizontally
2	cups shredded lettuce
2	medium tomatoes, sliced
½	cup crumbled feta cheese or goat cheese (chèvre)

1. In a small bowl stir together yogurt, cucumber, mint, salt, and garlic; set aside.

2. Place the reserved shredded meat in a microwave-safe 1-quart casserole. Cover and microwave on 100 percent power (high) for 2½ to 3½ minutes or until heated through, stirring once halfway through cooking.

3. Place pita halves on salad plates. Arrange lettuce and tomato on pita halves. Top with meat, yogurt mixture, and cheese.

Nutrition Facts per serving: 321 cal., 10 g total fat (5 g sat. fat), 91 mg chol., 703 mg sodium, 26 g carbo., 2 g fiber, 33 g pro.

*Note: There should be about 3 cups reserved shredded meat.

This dish is inspired by the hearty and satisfying cuisine of Tuscany, Italy which often features the much-loved white bean.

Rustic Italian Stew

MAKES 4 SERVINGS + RESERVES

....

Prep: 20 minutes
Cook: Low 7 to 8 hours, High 3½ to 4 hours

....

	Nonstick cooking spray
8	ounces fresh mushrooms, quartered
2	medium yellow summer squash, halved lengthwise and sliced (2½ cups)
1	15-ounce can navy beans, rinsed and drained
2	medium green sweet peppers, cut into 1-inch pieces
1	medium zucchini, halved lengthwise and sliced (1¼ cups)
1	large onion, cut into thin wedges
1	tablespoon olive oil
1	teaspoon salt
1	teaspoon dried Italian seasoning, crushed
⅛	to ¼ teaspoon crushed red pepper (optional)
2	14.5-ounce cans stewed tomatoes, undrained and cut up
1	cup shredded mozzarella cheese

1. Lightly coat the inside of a 5- to 6-quart slow cooker with nonstick cooking spray. In the prepared cooker stir together mushrooms, yellow squash, drained navy beans, sweet pepper, zucchini, onion, oil, salt, Italian seasoning, and, if desired, crushed red pepper. Pour undrained tomatoes over mixture in cooker.

2. Cover and cook on low-heat setting for 7 to 8 hours or on high-heat setting for 3½ to 4 hours.

3. Using a slotted spoon, remove 2 cups of the vegetables; store as directed below. Spoon the remaining stew into soup bowls. Sprinkle with mozzarella cheese.

Nutrition Facts per serving: 433 cal., 12 g total fat (4 g sat. fat), 22 mg chol., 1,768 mg sodium, 60 g carbo., 13 g fiber, 25 g pro.

....

To Store Reserves: Place vegetables in an airtight container. Seal and chill for up to 3 days. Use in Pasta Bowls, page 381.

....

"A simple dish with great flavors" describes some of the best recipes found in everyday Italian cooking, and it perfectly describes this dish. Serve with whole grain bread and a glass of Merlot.

5
Ingredient
Recipe

Pasta Bowls

MAKES 4 SERVINGS

Start to Finish: 20 minutes

1	26- to 28-ounce jar spaghetti sauce
	Reserved vegetables from Rustic Italian Stew* (see recipe, page 380)
¼	cup snipped fresh basil or 1 teaspoon dried basil, crushed
2	9-ounce packages refrigerated cheese ravioli
	Finely shredded Parmesan or Asiago cheese

1. In a medium saucepan stir together spaghetti sauce, the reserved vegetables, and the dried basil (if using). Bring to boiling over medium heat; remove from heat. Stir in fresh basil (if using).

2. Meanwhile, cook ravioli according to package directions; drain. Divide ravioli among bowls. Spoon the sauce over ravioli. Sprinkle generously with cheese.

Nutrition Facts per serving: 531 cal., 9 g total fat (4 g sat. fat), 55 mg chol., 1,910 mg sodium, 91 g carbo., 11 g fiber, 27 g pro.

*Note: There should be 2 cups reserved vegetables.

*Stir together a little butter, honey, and cinnamon to spread
on a slice of warm corn bread to serve alongside this chili
and you'll be set for a warming and surprisingly "meaty"
meatless dinner.*

Spicy Vegetable Chili

❖

MAKES 6 SERVINGS + RESERVES

Prep: 30 minutes
Cook: Low 9 to 10 hours,
High 4½ to 5 hours

- 2 large onions, chopped (2 cups)
- 2 medium green sweet peppers, chopped (1½ cups)
- 2 stalks celery, chopped (1 cup)
- 8 cloves garlic, minced
- 4 15-ounce cans red kidney and/or pinto beans, rinsed and drained
- 2 28-ounce cans diced tomatoes, undrained
- 1 15.25-ounce can whole kernel corn, drained
- 1 6-ounce can tomato paste
- 2 tablespoons chili powder
- 1 tablespoon Worcestershire sauce
- 1 teaspoon ground cumin
- 1 teaspoon dried oregano, crushed
- 1 teaspoon bottled hot pepper sauce
- ¼ teaspoon cayenne pepper
  Dairy sour cream (optional)

1. In a 6- to 7-quart slow cooker combine onion, sweet pepper, celery, and garlic. Stir in drained kidney and/or pinto beans, undrained tomatoes, drained corn, tomato paste, chili powder, Worcestershire sauce, cumin, oregano, hot pepper sauce, cayenne pepper, and 1 cup water.

2. Cover and cook on low-heat setting for 9 to 10 hours or on high-heat setting for 4½ to 5 hours.

3. Reserve 6 cups of the chili; store as directed below. If desired, serve the remaining chili with sour cream.

Nutrition Facts per serving: 229 cal., 1 g total fat (0 g sat. fat), 0 mg chol., 733 mg sodium, 48 g carbo., 11 g fiber, 12 g pro.

To Store Reserves: Place chili in an airtight container.
Seal and chill for up to 3 days. (Or freeze for up to 3 months.
Thaw in refrigerator overnight before using.)
Use in Cincinnati-Style Chili and Noodles, page 383.

Cincinnati chili is often laced with sweet spices such as nutmeg, cinnamon, and cocoa or chocolate and served over spaghetti. American cheese and chopped onion are classic toppers for this regional dish.

Cincinnati-Style Chili and Noodles

❖

MAKES 6 SERVINGS

Start to Finish: 20 minutes

8   ounces dried spaghetti

·   Reserved Spicy Vegetable Chili* (see recipe, page 382)

½   ounce unsweetened chocolate, chopped

½   teaspoon ground cinnamon

⅛   teaspoon ground allspice

⅛   teaspoon ground cloves

Shredded American cheese

Finely chopped onion

1. Cook spaghetti according to package directions; drain.

2. Meanwhile, in a large saucepan heat the reserved chili over medium heat until bubbly. Stir in chocolate, cinnamon, allspice, and cloves. Cook and stir until chocolate is melted.

3. Serve chili over hot cooked spaghetti. Sprinkle with cheese and onion.

Nutrition Facts per serving: 398 cal., 8 g total fat (4 g sat. fat), 16 mg chol., 813 mg sodium, 67 g carbo., 10 g fiber, 18 g pro.

*Note: There should be 6 cups reserved chili.

The word "ragoût" is derived from a French word that means "to stimulate the appetite." With a toothsome mix of earthy and sweet vegetables, plus a hearty helping of white beans and just the right herbs, this recipe will do just that.

Winter Squash Ragoût

❄

MAKES 4 SERVINGS + RESERVES

Prep: 30 minutes
Cook: Low 7 to 8 hours,
High 3½ to 4 hours

2½	pounds butternut squash, peeled, seeded, and cut into ¾-inch pieces (about 5 cups)
4	medium parsnips, peeled and chopped (3½ cups)
1	large onion, cut into thin wedges
2	14.5-ounce cans fire-roasted diced tomatoes, undrained
1	19-ounce can cannellini beans (white kidney beans), rinsed and drained
1	14-ounce can vegetable broth
1	teaspoon salt
1	teaspoon dried thyme, crushed
½	teaspoon dried sage, crushed
½	teaspoon dried rosemary, crushed
½	teaspoon black pepper
3	cloves garlic, minced
	Packaged shredded Italian-blend cheeses (optional)

1. In a 5- to 6-quart slow cooker combine squash, parsnip, and onion. Stir in undrained tomatoes, drained beans, broth, salt, thyme, sage, rosemary, pepper, and garlic.

2. Cover and cook on low-heat setting for 7 to 8 hours or on high-heat setting for 3½ to 4 hours.

3. Using a slotted spoon, remove 4 cups of the vegetables; store as directed below. Serve the remaining ragoût in soup bowls. If desired, sprinkle with cheese.

Nutrition Facts per serving: 210 cal., 1 g total fat (0 g sat. fat), 0 mg chol., 1,104 mg sodium, 49 g carbo., 10 g fiber, 9 g pro.

To Store Reserves: Place vegetables in an airtight container. Seal and chill for up to 3 days. Use in Winter Squash Pasta Shells Alfredo, page 385.

There's a lot to love about this recipe. Hearty, vegetable-filled shells are enriched with Alfredo sauce and Italian cheeses. The clincher, however, is the crunchy topping of bread crumbs and nuts.

Winter Squash Pasta Shells Alfredo

❋

MAKES 4 SERVINGS

Prep: 30 minutes
Bake: 30 minutes
Oven: 375°F

	Nonstick cooking spray
12	dried jumbo shell macaroni
	Reserved vegetables from Winter Squash Ragoût* (see recipe, page 384)
1	10-ounce container refrigerated Alfredo pasta sauce
⅔	cup shredded Italian-blend cheeses
½	cup panko (Japanese-style) bread crumbs or soft bread crumbs
¼	cup chopped pecans, toasted (see tip, page 29)
2	tablespoons butter or margarine, melted

1. Preheat oven to 375°F. Lightly coat a 2-quart rectangular baking dish with nonstick cooking spray; set aside. Cook shell macaroni according to package directions (cook 2 or 3 extra shells in case any tear while cooking); drain. Spoon the reserved vegetables into cooked macaroni shells.

2. Arrange filled shells in the prepared baking dish. Spoon any remaining vegetables around the shells. Pour Alfredo sauce evenly over shells. Sprinkle with cheese. In a small bowl stir together bread crumbs, pecans, and butter. Sprinkle crumb mixture over tops of shells.

3. Bake about 30 minutes or until heated through.

Nutrition Facts per serving: 616 cal., 38 g total fat (7 g sat. fat), 63 mg chol., 985 mg sodium, 55 g carbo., 7 g fiber, 18 g pro.

*Note: There should be 4 cups reserved vegetables.

This chunky veggie-packed stew was inspired by caponata, an Italian dish that typically stars eggplant, onions, olives, and tomatoes. While the Italian specialty is often served as a side dish, here the concept gets simmered into a stew.

Italian Eggplant Stew

❖

MAKES 4 SERVINGS + RESERVES

....

Prep: 30 minutes
Cook: Low 8 to 10 hours, High 4 to 5 hours

....

1   large eggplant, peeled and cut into 1-inch pieces

1   large red sweet pepper, cut into 1-inch pieces

1   large onion, coarsely chopped (1 cup)

1   4.5-ounce jar (drained weight) sliced mushrooms, drained

⅓   cup pimiento-stuffed green olives, halved

3   tablespoons tomato paste

1   teaspoon dried Italian seasoning, crushed

½   teaspoon salt

2   cloves garlic, minced

2   14-ounce cans vegetable broth

1   14.5-ounce can diced tomatoes, undrained

¼   cup finely shredded Parmesan cheese

1. In a 5- to 6-quart slow cooker stir together eggplant, sweet pepper, onion, drained mushrooms, olives, tomato paste, Italian seasoning, salt, and garlic. Pour broth and undrained tomatoes over mixture in cooker.

2. Cover and cook on low-heat setting for 8 to 10 hours or on high-heat setting for 4 to 5 hours.

3. Using a slotted spoon, remove 2 cups of the vegetables; store as directed below. Divide the remaining mixture among soup bowls. Top with Parmesan cheese.

Nutrition Facts per serving: 124 cal., 3 g total fat (1 g sat. fat), 4 mg chol., 1,310 mg sodium, 20 g carbo., 6 g fiber, 5 g pro.

....

To Store Reserves: Place vegetables in an airtight container. Seal and chill for up to 3 days. Use in Individual Caponata Pizzas, page 387.

....

The terrific combination of vegetables in the Italian Eggplant Stew gets a little extra boost from balsamic vinegar and red pepper sauce for a creative pizza topping. No need to pretoast the pine nuts; they'll toast when they bake.

Individual Caponata Pizzas

❖

MAKES 4 SERVINGS

Prep: 15 minutes
Bake: 12 minutes
Oven: 425°F

	Reserved vegetables from Italian Eggplant Stew* (see recipe, page 386)
⅓	cup bottled Italian salad dressing
1	tablespoon balsamic vinegar
	Few dashes bottled hot pepper sauce
4	8-inch Italian bread shells (such as Boboli brand)
1	cup shredded provolone or mozzarella cheese
¼	cup finely shredded Parmesan cheese
¼	cup pine nuts

1. Preheat oven to 425°F. Lightly mash the reserved vegetables; drain in a colander. In a large bowl stir together vegetables, salad dressing, balsamic vinegar, and hot pepper sauce.

2. Spread vegetable mixture evenly on Italian bread shells; arrange on a large baking sheet. Sprinkle with provolone cheese, Parmesan cheese, and pine nuts.

3. Bake about 12 minutes or until cheese is melted and pizzas are heated through.

Nutrition Facts per serving: 634 cal., 29 g total fat (7 g sat. fat), 29 mg chol., 1,737 mg sodium, 72 g carbo., 4 g fiber, 29 g pro.

*Note: There should be 2 cups reserved vegetables.

Eggplant stars as the robust beefy hero in many a meatless recipe. The brawny veggie certainly adds a nice heft to this chunky sauce.

Zesty Vegetable Pasta Sauce

❖

MAKES 6 SERVINGS + RESERVES

Prep: 25 minutes
Cook: Low 10 to 12 hours, High 5 to 6 hours

2	small eggplants, peeled, if desired, and cut into 1-inch pieces (6 cups)
2	large green or red sweet peppers, chopped (2 cups)
1	large onion, chopped (1 cup)
8	cloves garlic, minced
4	14.5-ounce cans Italian-style stewed tomatoes, undrained and cut up
1	6-ounce can Italian-style tomato paste
2	tablespoons packed brown sugar
2	tablespoons dried Italian seasoning, crushed
¼	to ½ teaspoon crushed red pepper
12	ounces dried fettuccine or linguine
⅓	cup sliced pitted kalamata olives or ripe olives
	Finely shredded or grated Parmesan or Romano cheese (optional)

1. In a 5- to 7-quart slow cooker combine eggplant, sweet pepper, onion, and garlic. Stir in undrained tomatoes, tomato paste, brown sugar, Italian seasoning, and crushed red pepper.

2. Cover and cook on low-heat setting for 10 to 12 hours or on high-heat setting for 5 to 6 hours.

3. Before serving, cook pasta according to package directions; drain. Return to saucepan; cover to keep warm.

4. Reserve 5 cups of the sauce; store as directed below. Stir olives into the remaining sauce. Serve with hot cooked pasta and, if desired, Parmesan cheese.

Nutrition Facts per serving: 339 cal., 4 g total fat (0 g sat. fat), 0 mg chol., 548 mg sodium, 65 g carbo., 5 g fiber, 10 g pro.

To Store Reserves: Place sauce in an airtight container. Seal and chill for up to 3 days. Use in Double-Sauced Vegetable Lasagna, page 389.

Here's an unexpected bonus—this luscious recipe makes twelve servings. Unless you're serving a crowd, that means you'll have yet another night's dinner ready when you are.

Double-Sauced Vegetable Lasagna

❖

MAKES 12 SERVINGS

Prep: 35 minutes
Bake: 50 minutes
Stand: 10 minutes
Oven: 350°F

1   16-ounce jar Alfredo pasta sauce

1   10-ounce package frozen chopped broccoli, thawed and well drained

2   cups shredded mozzarella cheese

¾   cup finely shredded Parmesan cheese

     Reserved Zesty Vegetable Pasta Sauce* (see recipe, page 388)

1   9-ounce package no-boil lasagna noodles

1. Preheat oven to 350°F. In a large bowl stir together Alfredo sauce and broccoli; set aside. In a medium bowl combine mozzarella cheese and Parmesan cheese.

2. Spread 1 cup of the reserved sauce in the bottom of a greased 3-quart rectangular baking dish. Top with 4 lasagna noodles, overlapping and breaking noodles as necessary to fit the dish. Spread half of the broccoli mixture over the noodles. Sprinkle with ½ cup of the cheese mixture.

3. Top with 4 more noodles. Spread 1 cup of the reserved sauce over the noodles. Sprinkle with ½ cup of the cheese mixture. Top with 4 more noodles. Spread the remaining broccoli mixture over the noodles. Sprinkle with ½ cup of the cheese mixture. Top with the remaining lasagna noodles, reserved sauce, and cheese mixture.

4. Cover and bake for 40 minutes. Bake, uncovered, for 10 to 15 minutes more or until lasagna is heated through. Let stand for 10 minutes before serving.

Nutrition Facts per serving: 329 cal., 18 g total fat (3 g sat. fat), 37 mg chol., 341 mg sodium, 28 g carbo., 2 g fiber, 13 g pro.

*Note: There should be 5 cups reserved sauce.

This red sauce, chock-full of veggies, calls for a refreshing accompaniment. How about a crisp green salad tossed with a vinaigrette and sprinkled with Gorgonzola cheese?

Marinara Sauce

MAKES 6 SERVINGS + RESERVES

Prep: 30 minutes
Cook: Low 10 to 12 hours,
High 5 to 6 hours

2	28-ounce cans Italian-style or regular whole peeled tomatoes in puree, cut up
6	medium carrots, shredded* (3 cups)
4	stalks celery, thinly sliced (2 cups)
2	large red and/or green sweet peppers, chopped (2 cups)
3	medium onions, finely chopped (1½ cups)
2	6-ounce cans tomato paste
½	cup water
½	cup dry red wine
5	teaspoons dried Italian seasoning, crushed
1	tablespoon sugar
2	teaspoons salt
¼	to ½ teaspoon black pepper
8	cloves garlic, minced
12	ounces dried penne pasta
⅓	cup grated Parmesan cheese

1. In a 6- to 7-quart slow cooker combine undrained tomatoes, carrot, celery, sweet pepper, onion, tomato paste, water, wine, Italian seasoning, sugar, salt, black pepper, and garlic.

2. Cover and cook on low-heat setting for 10 to 12 hours or on high-heat setting for 5 to 6 hours.

3. Before serving, cook pasta according to package directions; drain. Return to saucepan; cover to keep warm. Reserve 6 cups (about half) of the sauce; store as directed below.

4. Serve the remaining sauce over hot cooked pasta. Sprinkle with Parmesan cheese.

Nutrition Facts per serving: 327 cal., 3 g total fat (1 g sat. fat), 4 mg chol., 844 mg sodium, 62 g carbo., 5 g fiber, 13 g pro.

*Note: For quicker preparation, use purchased coarsely shredded carrot.

To Store Reserves: Place sauce in an airtight container. Seal and chill for up to 3 days. Use in Marinara-Sauced Shells, page 391.

What are you looking for in a baked pasta dish?
Something cheesy, saucy, and zesty, of course.
This recipe is definitely all that.

Marinara-Sauced Shells

❖

MAKES 6 SERVINGS

Prep: 30 minutes
Bake: 65 minutes
Stand: 10 minutes
Oven: 350°F

18	dried jumbo shell macaroni
1	12.3-ounce package firm, silken-style tofu (fresh bean curd)
1	15-ounce carton ricotta cheese
1	egg, slightly beaten
⅓	cup finely shredded Parmesan cheese
1	teaspoon dried basil, crushed
⅛	teaspoon black pepper
	Reserved Marinara Sauce* (see recipe, page 390)
1	cup shredded mozzarella cheese

1. Preheat oven to 350°F. Cook shell macaroni according to package directions (cook 2 or 3 extra shells in case any tear while cooking); drain and set aside.

2. Meanwhile, pat tofu dry with paper towels. In a medium bowl combine tofu and ricotta cheese; mash with a potato masher or fork. Stir in egg, Parmesan cheese, basil, and pepper. Spoon about 3 tablespoons of the tofu mixture into each cooked macaroni shell. Arrange the filled shells in a greased 3-quart rectangular baking dish. Top with the reserved sauce, spreading sauce evenly over the shells.

3. Cover and bake for 30 minutes. Bake, uncovered, for 30 to 35 minutes or until heated through.

4. Sprinkle with mozzarella cheese. Bake, uncovered, about 5 minutes more or until cheese is melted. Let stand for 10 minutes before serving.

Nutrition Facts per serving: 444 cal., 18 g total fat (10 g sat. fat), 89 mg chol., 1,060 mg sodium, 44 g carbo., 4 g fiber, 26 g pro.

*Note: There should be 6 cups reserved sauce.

*A specialty in the South of France, ratatouille is a versatile dish
that can be served warm or at room temperature, as a side (try
it with broiled chicken or beef), or as an appetizer (serve with
bread or crackers for scooping). (Photo on page 262.)*

Ratatouille

MAKES 4 SERVINGS + RESERVES

Prep: 20 minutes
Cook: Low 6 to 7 hours,
High 3 to 3½ hours,
plus 30 minutes (high)

1	small eggplant, peeled and cubed (4 cups)
2	large red and/or yellow sweet peppers, chopped (2 cups)
1	15-ounce can tomato puree
1	14.5-ounce can diced tomatoes with green pepper and onion, undrained
1	teaspoon salt
1	teaspoon dried oregano, crushed
1	teaspoon dried basil, crushed
¼	teaspoon black pepper
5	cloves garlic, minced
2	medium zucchini and/or yellow summer squash, halved lengthwise and sliced (2½ cups)
2	cups hot cooked couscous
¼	cup finely shredded Parmesan cheese

1. In a 4- to 5-quart slow cooker stir together eggplant, sweet pepper, tomato puree, undrained tomatoes, salt, oregano, basil, black pepper, and garlic.

2. Cover and cook on low-heat setting for 6 to 7 hours or on high-heat setting for 3 to 3½ hours.

3. If using low-heat setting, turn to high-heat setting. Add zucchini. Cover and cook about 30 minutes more or until vegetables are tender.

4. Reserve 2 cups ratatouille; store as directed below. Serve the remaining ratatouille over hot cooked couscous. Sprinkle with Parmesan cheese.

Nutrition Facts per serving: 206 cal., 2 g total fat (1 g sat. fat), 4 mg chol., 812 mg sodium, 40 g carbo., 7 g fiber, 8 g pro.

To Store Reserves: Place ratatouille in an airtight container. Seal and chill for up to 3 days. Do not freeze. Use in Southwest Vegetable Empanadas, page 393.

Add a few quintessential Southwestern flavors to the tender ratatouille vegetable mixture, then tuck it inside piecrust easily made from a mix. The result? Something completely out of the ordinary in less than half an hour. (Photo on page 263.)

Southwest Vegetable Empanadas

❈

MAKES 4 SERVINGS

Prep: 25 minutes
Bake: 20 minutes
Oven: 400°F

1	11-ounce package piecrust mix (for 2 crusts)
	Reserved Ratatouille* (see recipe, page 392)
1	cup shredded Monterey Jack cheese with jalapeño chile peppers
1	4-ounce can diced green chile peppers, drained
1	2.25-ounce can sliced ripe olives, drained
½	teaspoon ground cumin
	Milk
¼	to ½ teaspoon Ancho chile powder or chili powder
⅔	cup frozen avocado dip (guacamole), thawed
½	cup bottled salsa
⅓	cup dairy sour cream
	Thinly sliced green onion (optional)

1. Preheat oven to 400°F. Prepare piecrust mix according to package directions for 2 crusts. Divide dough into 4 portions. Set aside.

2. Drain excess liquid from the reserved ratatouille. In a medium bowl stir together ratatouille, cheese, drained chile peppers, drained olives, and cumin; set aside.

3. On a lightly floured surface, roll one portion of dough into a 7-inch round. Spoon one-fourth of the ratatouille mixture into the center of the round. Moisten edge with water. Fold in half; press edge with the tines of a fork to seal. Place empanada on a foil-lined baking sheet; pierce top with fork. Repeat with the remaining dough and ratatouille mixture.

4. Brush tops of empanadas with a little milk and sprinkle with chile powder. Bake for 20 to 25 minutes or until golden.

5. Serve hot empanadas with the avocado dip, salsa, and sour cream. If desired, sprinkle with thinly sliced green onion.

Nutrition Facts per serving: 717 cal., 48 g total fat (16 g sat. fat), 32 mg chol., 1,407 mg sodium, 51 g carbo., 6 g fiber, 15 g pro.

*Note: There should be 2 cups reserved ratatouille.

Beans pack a powerful one-two punch of fiber and protein.
With three kinds of beans and brown rice, this dish makes for a
healthful meatless dinner. Thanks to kicky seasonings,
it's an exciting one too.

Cowboy Rice and Beans

❖

MAKES 4 SERVINGS + RESERVES

Prep: 15 minutes
Cook: Low 5 to 6 hours,
High 2½ to 3 hours,
plus 30 minutes (high)

2   15-ounce cans chili beans in chili gravy, undrained

1   15-ounce can butter beans, rinsed and drained

1   15-ounce can black beans, rinsed and drained

1   large onion, chopped (1 cup)

1   medium green sweet pepper, chopped (¾ cup)

1   medium red sweet pepper, chopped (¾ cup)

1   fresh jalapeño chile pepper, seeded and finely chopped (see tip, page 10)

1   18-ounce bottle barbecue sauce

1   cup vegetable broth

1   cup uncooked instant brown rice

1. In a 5- to 6-quart slow cooker combine undrained chili beans in chili gravy, drained butter beans, drained black beans, onion, sweet peppers, and jalapeño pepper. Pour barbecue sauce and broth over mixture in cooker.

2. Cover and cook on low-heat setting for 5 to 6 hours or on high-heat setting for 2½ to 3 hours.

3. If using low-heat setting, turn to high-heat setting. Stir in rice. Cover and cook about 30 minutes more or until rice is tender.

4. Reserve 3 cups of the bean mixture; store as directed below. Serve the remaining bean mixture while warm.

Nutrition Facts per serving: 365 cal., 3 g total fat (0 g sat. fat), 0 mg chol., 1,676 mg sodium, 68 g carbo., 17 g fiber, 19 g pro.

To Store Reserves: Place bean mixture in an airtight container. Seal and chill for up to 3 days. Use in Baked Cowboy Chimichangas, page 395.

Baking chimichangas is much easier than frying them. Add a spoonful of sour cream and your favorite purchased salsa to this Mexican standby, and you may never again want the traditional fried version.

Baked Cowboy Chimichangas

❖

MAKES 4 SERVINGS

Prep: 15 minutes
Bake: 15 minutes
Oven: 350°F

Reserved Cowboy Rice and Beans* (see recipe, page 394)

8   8-inch flour tortillas

2   cups shredded Mexican-blend cheeses)

Dairy sour cream (optional)

Bottled salsa (optional)

1. Preheat oven to 350°F. Spread about ⅓ cup of the reserved bean mixture down the center of each tortilla. Top each with ¼ cup of the shredded cheese. Fold in sides of each tortilla; roll up tortilla. If necessary, secure with wooden toothpicks. Place chimichangas, seam sides down, on a baking sheet.

2. Bake for 15 to 20 minutes or until crisp and browned. If desired, serve with sour cream and salsa.

Nutrition Facts per serving: 580 cal., 24 g total fat (11 g sat. fat), 50 mg chol., 1,558 mg sodium, 66 g carbo., 9 g fiber, 26 g pro.

*Note: There should be 3 cups reserved bean mixture.

Pour a few items into the slow cooker and let the soup simmer to creamy, veggie-chocked perfection. It's recipes like this that have made the slow cooker a favorite appliance.

Cheesy Cauliflower, Broccoli, and Corn Soup

❖

MAKES 6 SERVINGS + RESERVES

Prep: 20 minutes
Cook: Low 6 to 7 hours,
High 3 to 3½ hours,
plus 30 minutes (high)

- 2 10-ounce packages frozen cauliflower, thawed and well drained
- 2 10-ounce packages frozen cut broccoli, thawed and well drained
- 1 10-ounce package frozen whole kernel corn, thawed and well drained
- 3 14-ounce cans vegetable broth
- 2 teaspoons dried dill
- 16 ounces American cheese, cubed

1. In a 5- to 6-quart slow cooker combine cauliflower, broccoli, and corn. Add broth and dill to mixture in cooker. Cover and cook on low-heat setting for 6 to 7 hours or on high-heat setting for 3 to 3½ hours.

2. If using low-heat setting, turn to high-heat setting. Stir in cheese. Cover and cook about 30 minutes more or until cheese is melted.

3. Using a slotted spoon, remove 4 cups of the vegetables. Remove 1 cup of the cooking liquid. Store the reserved vegetables and cooking liquid as directed below. Serve the remaining soup immediately.

Nutrition Facts per serving: 295 cal., 20 g total fat (12 g sat. fat), 58 mg chol., 1,609 mg sodium, 15 g carbo., 4 g fiber, 17 g pro.

To Store Reserves: Place vegetables and cooking liquid in an airtight container. Seal and chill for up to 3 days. Use in Cheese and Vegetable Rice Casserole, page 397.

A casserole speckled with rice, beans, and vegetables is one of the most satisfying ways to go meatless. Here diced green chile peppers and roasted red sweet peppers help the flavors blast off.

Cheese and Vegetable Rice Casserole

❋

MAKES 6 SERVINGS

Prep: 20 minutes
Bake: 35 minutes
Stand: 10 minutes
Oven: 350°F

Nonstick cooking spray

Reserved vegetable mixture from Cheesy Cauliflower, Broccoli, and Corn Soup* (see recipe, page 396)

4 cups cooked rice

1 15-ounce can black beans, rinsed and drained

1 12-ounce jar roasted red sweet peppers, drained and coarsely chopped

2 4-ounce cans diced green chile peppers, drained

1 cup shredded cheddar cheese

½ cup seasoned fine dry bread crumbs

2 tablespoons butter or margarine, melted

1. Preheat oven to 350°F. Lightly coat a 3-quart rectangular baking dish with nonstick cooking spray; set aside. In a large bowl stir together the reserved vegetable mixture, the cooked rice, drained black beans, roasted red peppers, and drained chile peppers. Spread in the prepared baking dish. Sprinkle with cheddar cheese.

2. In a small bowl stir together bread crumbs and butter. Sprinkle over mixture in baking dish.

3. Bake for 35 to 40 minutes or until heated through and top is golden. Let stand for 10 minutes before serving.

Nutrition Facts per serving: 446 cal., 17 g total fat (10 g sat. fat), 47 mg chol., 1,080 mg sodium, 57 g carbo., 7 g fiber, 21 g pro.

*Note: There should be 4 cups reserved vegetables mixed with 1 cup reserved cooking liquid.

If you love Thai cooking with its spicy, nutty, sweet, and hot flavors, you'll appreciate this fascinating meatless dish.

Asian Vegetable Rice with Coconut Milk

❖

MAKES 4 SERVINGS + RESERVES

Prep: 35 minutes
Cook: Low 6 to 7 hours,
High 3 to 3½ hours,
plus 30 minutes (high)

4	large red and/or green sweet peppers, cut into ¼-inch-thick strips
1	pound carrots, bias-sliced ¼ inch thick
2	medium onions, cut into thin wedges
1	8-ounce can sliced water chestnuts, drained
1	teaspoon salt
1	teaspoon ground ginger
1	teaspoon green curry paste
½	teaspoon garlic powder
¼	teaspoon crushed red pepper
2	tablespoons cornstarch
1	14-ounce can unsweetened coconut milk
12	ounces firm tofu (fresh bean curd), cubed
2	cups hot cooked rice
⅓	cup sliced green onion (3)
¼	cup snipped fresh cilantro
¼	cup chopped peanuts

1. In a 5- to 6-quart slow cooker combine sweet pepper, carrot, onion, drained water chestnuts, salt, ginger, curry paste, garlic powder, crushed red pepper, and ⅓ cup water.

2. Cover and cook on low-heat setting for 6 to 7 hours or on high-heat setting for 3 to 3½ hours.

3. If using low-heat setting, turn to high-heat setting. In a small bowl stir together cornstarch and 2 tablespoons cold water; stir into mixture in cooker. Stir in coconut milk. Cover and cook about 30 minutes more or until thickened.

4. Reserve 3 cups (about half) of the vegetable mixture; store as directed below.

5. Stir tofu into the remaining vegetable mixture in cooker. Serve tofu mixture over hot cooked rice. Top with green onion, cilantro, and peanuts.

Nutrition Facts per serving: 420 cal., 19 g total fat (9 g sat. fat), 0 mg chol., 419 mg sodium, 50 g carbo., 5 g fiber, 15 g pro.

To Store Reserves: Place vegetable mixture in an airtight container. Seal and chill for up to 3 days. Use in Creamy Carrot and White Bean Soup, page 399.

Presto change-o! With the addition of just a few well-chosen ingredients, the Asian Vegetable Rice with Coconut Milk becomes a satisfying soup for lunch or a light supper.

Creamy Carrot and White Bean Soup

❖

MAKES 4 SERVINGS

Start to Finish: 20 minutes

2	15-ounce cans navy beans, rinsed and drained
2	14-ounce cans vegetable broth
	Reserved vegetable mixture from Asian Vegetable Rice with Coconut Milk* (see recipe, page 398)
1½	teaspoons ground cumin
¼	teaspoon salt
⅛	teaspoon cayenne pepper
1	cup half-and-half or light cream

1. In a large saucepan stir together drained beans, broth, the reserved vegetable mixture, the cumin, salt, and cayenne pepper. Bring to boiling over medium-high heat; reduce heat. Cover and simmer for 10 minutes. Remove from heat.

2. Add mixture to a blender or food processor in batches; cover and blend or process until smooth.

3. Return pureed mixture to the saucepan; stir in half-and-half. Heat through but do not boil.

Nutrition Facts per serving: 538 cal., 19 g total fat (13 g sat. fat), 22 mg chol., 2,362 mg sodium, 76 g carbo., 15 g fiber, 22 g pro.

*Note: There should be 3 cups reserved vegetable mixture.

Index